THE
WORK
AND THE
GLORY
So Great a Cause

Splitting Rails at Mount Pisgah

VOLUME 8

THE
WORK
AND THE
GLORY

So Great a Cause

A HISTORICAL NOVEL

Gerald N. Lund

BOOKCRAFT
Salt Lake City, Utah

THE WORK AND THE GLORY

Volume 1: Pillar of Light
Volume 2: Like a Fire Is Burning
Volume 3: Truth Will Prevail
Volume 4: Thy Gold to Refine
Volume 5: A Season of Joy
Volume 6: Praise to the Man
Volume 7: No Unhallowed Hand
Volume 8: So Great a Cause

Visit us at www.deseretbook.com

Library of Congress Catalog Card Number: 97-76972

ISBN 1-57008-358-4
ISBN 1-57345-877-5 (softcover)

Printed in the United States of America   72082-6761

For behold, this is my work and my glory—to bring to pass the immortality and eternal life of man.

—Moses 1:39

To Kim—Kenneth I. Moe—
without whose vision, determination,
and dedication this series would not be.
His friendship and influence shall be sorely missed.

Preface

In *No Unhallowed Hand*, volume 7 of the series *The Work and the Glory*, we saw the Steed family wrenched once again from their homes as hatred and persecution exploded into open conflagration. The Prophet Joseph Smith and his brothers Hyrum and Samuel were dead, victims of the blind rage that swept across Hancock County, Illinois, in 1844. Brigham Young and the Quorum of the Twelve Apostles took the reins of leadership and quickly proved that, as Joseph had prophesied a few years before, no unhallowed hand could stop the work of God from progressing. Work on the Nauvoo Temple, a remarkable and beautiful structure, continued with even greater urgency. Missionary work was expanded and the task of proclaiming the gospel to the world hastened even further. But as thousands continued to join the Church and come to Nauvoo—that beautiful city set on a sweeping bend of the Mississippi—the enemies of the Church were stirred to action once more. Lies and misunderstandings led to accusations and threats. These quickly gave way to violence—burnings, whippings, mobbings, and eventually murder. The leaders of the Church had no choice. They would leave their beloved Nauvoo to their enemies and turn their faces west. They would find that place which God had prepared for them, far away in the West, where none would come to hurt or make afraid. Thus it was that at the end of volume 7, after the tragic loss of Benjamin, the Steeds left Nauvoo, crossed the river for the last time on a bridge of ice, and joined the camp at Sugar Creek in Iowa Territory.

Volume 8, *So Great a Cause*, picks up the story at that point. It is 28 February 1846. Conditions in the camp, just seven or eight miles from Nauvoo, are wretched. It is bitterly cold. Supplies are insufficient. Many Saints have nothing more than a bedroll to shelter them from the cold. But the Steeds have most of their family there, in obedience to the call of their leader. Carl and Melissa Rogers, however, are not with the rest of the family. Still bitter over the practice of plural marriage, even the powerful bonds of love within the family are not enough to change their minds about leaving. Joshua has determined to go west so that he can care for his widowed mother and help the family find their new home, but Caroline and the children are not with him. This is Joshua's choice and not their own.

On March first, Brigham Young decides that they can wait no longer. The others will have to come as they can. He gives the signal and the first wagons begin rolling westward. What should have been the easiest part of their journey to the Rocky Mountains quickly becomes a never-ending nightmare as winter gives way to one of the wettest springs in memory. Roads become mile-long bogs that consume men and animals and leave them broken and exhausted. Sickness sweeps the camps. Women give birth in the most difficult of circumstances. Soon wagons are strung across a hundred miles of prairie. And Death, as it has so many times before, rides along, always seeking company.

Now it becomes evident why Brigham Young and Heber C. Kimball and others were sent on Zion's Camp twelve years before. It was an experience that will now prove to be invaluable. The knowledge that Brigham and Heber gained during the exodus from Far West, while Joseph languished in the horror of Liberty Jail, is also put to the full test. Faced with the almost impossible task of taking fifteen thousand or more exiles into the wilderness and keeping them fed and sheltered, Brigham quickly shows that the prophetic mantle of Joseph Smith has been passed on to him. He will come to be known as the "American Moses," as names like Sugar Creek, Richardson's Point, Garden Grove, Mount Pisgah, and Winter Quarters become part of the Latter-day Saint heritage.

Once again, through the eyes of the Steeds, now more than two dozen in number, we see the historical tapestry unfold. With them we experience the terrible trek across Iowa, slogging onward at an average rate of barely two miles per day. They are moving west toward their destiny; but for a time, at least, it looks as though that destiny approaches at a rate that is frustratingly slow. But on they move, convinced that they are engaged in so great a cause.

It hardly seems possible that it has now been nine full years since this project began. It was the summer of 1988 when I received a letter from a person in North Carolina whom I had never before met. Kenneth I. Moe—"Kim" to his friends and family—caught me completely off guard when he said he wanted to discuss with me the idea of putting the story of The Church of Jesus Christ of Latter-day Saints into the form of a historical novel. He indicated that he had read all of my previous novels and felt that I was the one to author such a project.

It is with considerable chagrin that I have to admit that I did not greet the proposal very warmly. I was flattered, of course, and told him that I had always dreamed about someday doing that very thing. But not now. I was currently in the process of creating another novel that I found intriguing and was having an enjoyable time writing—a story set at the time of the fall of Jerusalem in A.D. 70. I also indicated to Kim that because the project he had in mind was such a huge undertaking, requiring massive amounts of research, travel, purchase of books, etc., etc., I didn't feel that I could pull away from my other writing projects to do this. I had several children in college and needed to keep generating some extra income to handle that drain on my finances.

I barely knew Kim then. Had I known him better, I would have seen that treating such an important idea so lightly was not something that he would easily accept. He asked if he could fly out to Utah with his wife, Jane, and meet with me and my wife. Lynn and I agreed, though again I must confess that I tried to discourage him from coming, telling him that it might prove to be a waste of his time and money. They came anyway, and it was our privilege to meet Kim and Jane Moe. We were warmed and charmed by their grace, their testimony, and their devotion to the Church. I also quickly learned that this was not just a passing idea for Kim. He had deep and powerful feelings about the importance of this work and a driving sense of mission to see that it was accomplished. Only later did I learn that he had had an unusual spiritual experience which filled him with a great sense of urgency to become the catalyst in getting the novel written. As I look back on that now, and the fact that he did not tell me everything on that first visit, I am impressed with his wisdom. He did not try to unduly influence me through claiming a "spiritual directive" in the matter. He saw the importance of letting me come to this on my own without feeling excessive pressure.

He was, however, very persuasive in convincing me that this was more than just a whim. When he and Jane returned to North Carolina a few days later, they had my verbal commitment—not to write the book but to give it serious consideration and to make it a matter of pondering and prayer. The rest of the story can be easily guessed. After several days, including a day alone in the mountains, I called Kim and told him I was convinced that he was right—this was something that needed to be done and other projects would have to wait.

Note that to this point I have referred to the project in the singular—"the novel," "the book." How naive we were back then in the initial stages! We envisioned one long volume of about a thousand pages which would cover the history from 1827 when Joseph received the gold plates up to modern times. When I finally began to write, after several months of research and plotting, it quickly became evident that this story was far too great in scope to be adequately told in one volume. Thus was born *The Work and the Glory* "series," which nine years later is still not completed.

Through all of those years, Kim and Jane were an integral part of the project. Their vision of what it should be never flagged. They were converted to the Church at a later point in their lives, and so they brought not only strong testimonies to the project but also the perspective of the nonmember. Kim pored over the manuscripts and illustrations and made hundreds of suggestions on each volume. He constantly reminded me to avoid LDS cliches and to be sensitive to those who do not know our vocabulary and our way of seeing the world. Retired from active business life by the time all of this began, he devoted almost his full time to the series. His influence, though not specifically marked, is felt throughout each of the various volumes. Without Kim Moe, the series as it has now developed would not be in existence at this time.

It was with shock and sorrow that I learned in the late summer of 1996 that Kim had been diagnosed with lung cancer. Gratefully, he lived long enough to read and critique the complete manuscript of volume 7 and to see it published and on the shelf. How he wanted to see the Saints—and the Steeds—reach the Valley of the Great Salt Lake! But it was not to be. He passed away in October 1996. His presence and influence will be sorely missed. *The Work and the Glory* continues as a monument to his vision, his determination, and his great desire to be of service in the Lord's kingdom.

GERALD N. LUND

Bountiful, Utah
September 1997

I would like to express my gratitude to the many generous friends who have stepped in to help me carry on my responsibilities in the production of this historical saga, *The Work and the Glory*.

It has been a most fulfilling project for both Kim and me for these many years. Since Kim died in October 1996 I have tried to carry on for both of us. It is a project in which I still find great fulfillment. Since the onset of macular degeneration my vision has been reduced to "legal blindness," so that I now have a select group of friends who read the manuscript to me. It is to them I want to express my deep gratitude. Their names are not in any particular order, but my love and appreciation for each of them is deep and enduring: To Julia and William Ince, Robert and Susannah Winston, Kay Wilson, Dianne and George Elges, Cheri Henderson, and our son, Terry Moe, who makes frequent visits from Florida. Also to Janet Anderson, who not only reads manuscript pages but also has taken over the computer side of this endeavor, and to her wonderfully thoughtful husband and compassionate children. Last but never least, to Sandy and Tim Vos and their three delightful children, who have all been willing—and available—right hands for me.

A special expression of gratitude to Jerry and Lynn Lund for their thoughtful understanding of my situation.

JANE MOE

Highlands, North Carolina
September 1997

Characters of Note in This Book

The Steed Family

Mary Ann Morgan, widow of Benjamin Steed, and mother and grandmother; not quite sixty as the story opens.

Joshua, the oldest son (almost thirty-nine), and his wife, **Caroline Mendenhall** (almost forty).

William ("Will"), from Caroline's first marriage (nearing twenty-two), and his wife, Alice Samuelson (nineteen).

Savannah; almost nine.

Charles Benjamin; six.

Livvy Caroline; not quite two years old as the book opens.

Jessica Roundy Garrett (forty-one), Joshua's first wife, widow of John Griffith, and her husband, **Solomon Garrett** (almost forty-one).

Rachel, from marriage to Joshua; fourteen.

Luke and Mark, sons from John Griffith's first marriage; thirteen and eleven, respectively.

John Benjamin, from marriage to John; about eight.

Miriam Jessica, from marriage to Solomon; two and a half.

Solomon Clinton; eleven months.

Nathan, the second son (almost thirty-seven), and his wife, **Lydia McBride** (about the same age).

Joshua Benjamin ("Josh"); nearing fifteen.

Emily; not quite fourteen.

Elizabeth Mary; not quite eight.

Josiah Nathan; five.

Nathan Joseph (called Joseph); nearly three.

Melissa, the older daughter (thirty-five), and her husband, **Carlton ("Carl") Rogers** (thirty-six).

Carlton Hezekiah; almost fourteen.

David Benjamin; eleven and a half.

Caleb John; not yet ten.

Sarah; seven.

Mary Melissa; a year and a half.

Rebecca, the younger daughter (twenty-eight), and her husband, **Derek Ingalls** (twenty-eight).

Christopher Joseph; almost seven.

Benjamin Derek; almost four.

Leah Rebecca; eleven months.

Matthew, the youngest son (twenty-five), and his wife, **Jennifer Jo McIntire** (twenty-four).

Betsy Jo; not quite four.

Emmeline; eleven months.

Peter Ingalls, Derek's younger brother (almost twenty-two), and his wife, **Kathryn Marie McIntire,** Jennifer Jo's sister (nearly twenty).

Note: Deceased children are not included in the above listing.

The Smiths

* Lucy Mack, the mother.
* Mary Fielding, Hyrum's wife.
* Emma Hale, Joseph Smith's wife.
* William, Joseph's youngest living brother; age thirty-five.

Others

* William Clayton, an English convert; clerk to Brigham Young and an accomplished musician.
* George and Jacob Donner, well-to-do farmers from Springfield, Illinois, who decide to go to California in 1846.

*Designates actual people from history.

* Heber C. Kimball, friend of Brigham Young's and a member of the Quorum of the Twelve Apostles.

* Jesse C. Little, president of the Eastern States Mission and President Young's envoy to President James K. Polk.

* Orson Pratt, member of the Quorum of the Twelve Apostles.

* Parley P. Pratt, member of the Quorum of the Twelve Apostles.

* James Reed, wealthy businessman who heads for California with the Donner brothers and his own family.

* Willard Richards, member of the Quorum of the Twelve Apostles.

* George A. Smith, member of the Quorum of the Twelve Apostles.

* John Taylor, member of the Quorum of the Twelve Apostles.

* Wilford Woodruff, member of the Quorum of the Twelve Apostles.

* Brigham Young, President of the Quorum of the Twelve Apostles and head of the Church; three months short of his forty-fifth birthday as the novel opens.

Though too numerous to list here, there are many other actual people from the pages of history who are mentioned by name in the novel. James and Drusilla Hendricks, Eliza R. Snow, Ezra T. Benson, George Miller, Stephen Markham, Orson and Catharine Spencer, and many others mentioned in the book were real people who lived and participated in the events described in this work.

*Designates actual people from history.

The Benjamin and Mary Ann
Steed Family

Shown below are the various Steed family groups. The chart for Benjamin and Mary Ann is followed by separate charts for their children—actual and "adopted." (These charts do not include those deceased children who play no part in the novel.)

BENJAMIN AND MARY ANN

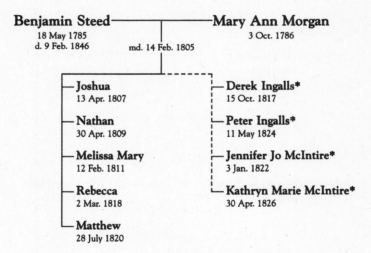

Benjamin Steed
18 May 1785
d. 9 Feb. 1846

md. 14 Feb. 1805

Mary Ann Morgan
3 Oct. 1786

Joshua
13 Apr. 1807

Nathan
30 Apr. 1809

Melissa Mary
12 Feb. 1811

Rebecca
2 Mar. 1818

Matthew
28 July 1820

Derek Ingalls*
15 Oct. 1817

Peter Ingalls*
11 May 1824

Jennifer Jo McIntire*
3 Jan. 1822

Kathryn Marie McIntire*
30 Apr. 1826

JOSHUA AND CAROLINE

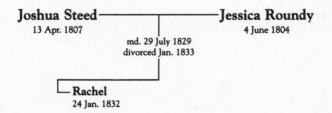

Joshua Steed
13 Apr. 1807

md. 29 July 1829
divorced Jan. 1833

Jessica Roundy
4 June 1804

Rachel
24 Jan. 1832

* Indicates a person who, though never legally adopted, became a part of the Steed family.

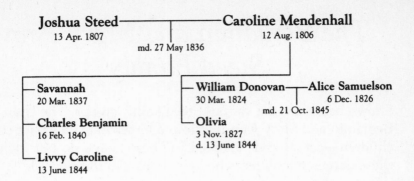

Joshua Steed ——————— Caroline Mendenhall
13 Apr. 1807   12 Aug. 1806

md. 27 May 1836

— Savannah   — William Donovan ——— Alice Samuelson
20 Mar. 1837   30 Mar. 1824   6 Dec. 1826

                                                        md. 21 Oct. 1845

— Charles Benjamin   — Olivia
16 Feb. 1840   3 Nov. 1827
                                       d. 13 June 1844

— Livvy Caroline
13 June 1844

JESSICA

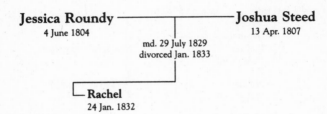

Jessica Roundy ——————— Joshua Steed
4 June 1804   13 Apr. 1807

md. 29 July 1829
divorced Jan. 1833

— Rachel
24 Jan. 1832

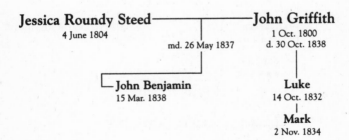

Jessica Roundy Steed ——————— John Griffith
4 June 1804   1 Oct. 1800
                                                    d. 30 Oct. 1838

md. 26 May 1837

— John Benjamin   Luke
15 Mar. 1838   14 Oct. 1832

                                                Mark
                                                2 Nov. 1834

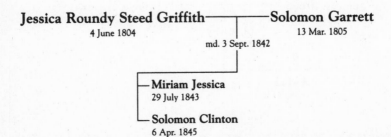

Jessica Roundy Steed Griffith ——————— Solomon Garrett
4 June 1804   13 Mar. 1805

md. 3 Sept. 1842

— Miriam Jessica
29 July 1843

— Solomon Clinton
6 Apr. 1845

NATHAN AND LYDIA

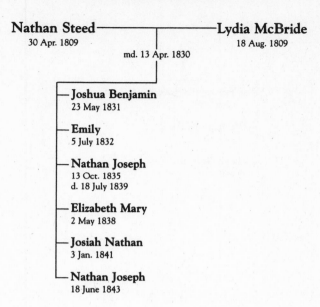

Nathan Steed
30 Apr. 1809

Lydia McBride
18 Aug. 1809

md. 13 Apr. 1830

— **Joshua Benjamin**
23 May 1831

— **Emily**
5 July 1832

— **Nathan Joseph**
13 Oct. 1835
d. 18 July 1839

— **Elizabeth Mary**
2 May 1838

— **Josiah Nathan**
3 Jan. 1841

— **Nathan Joseph**
18 June 1843

MELISSA AND CARL

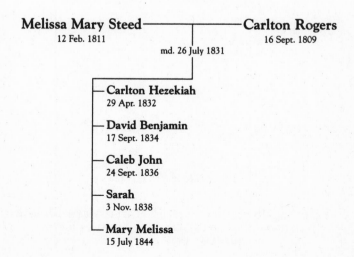

Melissa Mary Steed
12 Feb. 1811

Carlton Rogers
16 Sept. 1809

md. 26 July 1831

— **Carlton Hezekiah**
29 Apr. 1832

— **David Benjamin**
17 Sept. 1834

— **Caleb John**
24 Sept. 1836

— **Sarah**
3 Nov. 1838

— **Mary Melissa**
15 July 1844

REBECCA AND DEREK

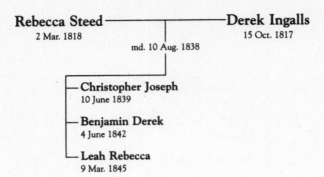

Rebecca Steed ——————— Derek Ingalls
2 Mar. 1818   15 Oct. 1817

md. 10 Aug. 1838

— Christopher Joseph
10 June 1839

— Benjamin Derek
4 June 1842

— Leah Rebecca
9 Mar. 1845

MATTHEW AND JENNY

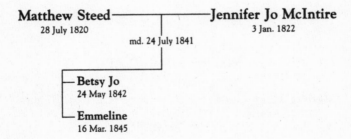

Matthew Steed ——————— Jennifer Jo McIntire
28 July 1820   3 Jan. 1822

md. 24 July 1841

— Betsy Jo
24 May 1842

— Emmeline
16 Mar. 1845

PETER AND KATHRYN

Peter Ingalls ——————— Kathryn Marie McIntire
11 May 1824   30 Apr. 1826

md. 21 Oct. 1845

Key to Abbreviations Used in Chapter Notes

Throughout the chapter notes, abbreviated references are given. The following key gives the full bibliographic data for those references.

CN   *Church News*

Iowa Trail   Susan Easton Black and William G. Hartley, eds., *The Iowa Mormon Trail: Legacy of Faith and Courage* (Orem, Utah: Helix Publishing, 1997.)

LDSBE   Andrew Jenson, comp., *Latter-day Saint Biographical Encyclopedia*, 4 vols. (1901–36; reprint, Salt Lake City: Western Epics, 1971.)

MHBY   Elden J. Watson, ed., *Manuscript History of Brigham Young, 1846–1847* (Salt Lake City: Elden J. Watson, 1971.)

"Voyage"   Lorin K. Hansen, "Voyage of the *Brooklyn*," *Dialogue* 21 (Fall 1988): 47–72.

So Great a Cause

Brethren, shall we not go on in so great a cause? Go forward and not backward. Courage, brethren; and on, on to the victory!

—Joseph Smith, 1842
Doctrine and Covenants 128:22

They were out in the open, gathered around the common fire the men had built within the tight circle of their wagons. Supper was over—plates of beans with slivers of bacon to give them flavor, hard biscuits—and the dishes had been scrubbed out in the frigid waters of Sugar Creek. Now, while the women bedded down the youngest in the tents, the others stood around the fire, talking quietly or just staring into the flickering flames.

The air that had turned cold enough to make an ice bridge across the mighty Mississippi still held them in its grip. Small clouds of mist burst from their mouths, gleamed momentarily gold from the fire, then dissipated into nothingness. Three days ago, when they had arisen and started their preparations to depart, the thermometer on Joshua's barn registered six degrees above zero. The night before that, it had been twelve below. It was a miracle, of that Nathan had no doubt. The miracle was not that the mighty river had frozen solid—it had done that before—but that it had done so this late in the season and at just the right time. Probably two hundred wagons had crossed with them that day, something that would have taken a week or two had they waited for the ferries. Hundreds more had come since then. If the weather continued to hold—unlikely, since this was the last day of February—perhaps everyone who was ready to go could cross. So in that sense the cold was a blessing. But as he pulled his coat around him more tightly, feeling the chill seeping through his clothing, Nathan realized the blessing was not without its drawbacks.

He glanced around, taking note of his family. The children, except for the oldest three—Rachel, Emily, and young Joshua—were in the tents or the wagons. The babies were asleep. Inside Matthew and Jenny's wagon, the other children were playing some game in the dark. There would be an occasional burst of giggles, a soft cry of dismay, some protest over unfairness, followed instantly by the hushing of others lest it bring the parents over to mediate. But for tonight at least, these three who were in their teens were content to be adults rather than children.

There were twenty-five of them here in their little portion of the Sugar Creek Camp now. A frown pulled at the corners of Nathan's mouth. There should have been eleven more. If you counted Carl and Melissa and their five children and Caroline and her three children, there would be eleven more. It saddened him to think of that. Carl and Melissa refusing to come. Caroline aching to but Joshua steadfastly refusing.

His face suddenly twisted. *Not eleven more! Twelve!* It was as if the bitter cold had suddenly coalesced into a single blade and pierced his heart. There should be another Steed at the fire this night. But Benjamin Steed had seen the flash of Savannah's blue dress in the murky waters and dove in without hesitation. Savannah now lived, but Benjamin lay in a frozen grave overlooking a frozen river. That had been almost three weeks ago now. How long before the pain became bearable?

His eyes pulled away from the fire. He glanced at his mother to see if she was thinking the same dark thoughts that he was, but her head was down, and he looked away again. He couldn't make himself watch her for more than a moment. That was a major source of his hurt—knowing her pain and feeling her loneliness. Benjamin Steed—beloved husband, esteemed father, adored grandfather, patriarch to the Steed clan—should have been sitting right there at the head of the circle beside Mary Ann. But he was not and never would be again—not in this life—and the circle seemed only half of what it should be because of it.

He forced his thoughts away to other things, too tired to hold the pain so close to him. There were now close to three thousand people in the Sugar Creek Camp, but without stars or moon, the blackness hid all but the dull glow of campfires. Around the nearest ones he could see shadowy figures moving about or sitting motionless as he was. *How many fires now?* he thought. *A hundred? No, three hundred, at least. Maybe more.* He shook his head. Just as well he couldn't see more. Morning's light would reveal the ugliness that was Sugar Creek Camp now. The ground would be chocolate brown, churned by thousands of boots and shoes and hooves. Scattered among the wagons, like the aftermath of a children's party, would be the tents and the makeshift shelters and, in too many cases, the bedrolls laid out on the open ground. On the perimeter, the stock—an insane mix of beef and milk cows, oxen, mules, horses—would be seen and heard and smelled. Smoke from the fires would hang in the still, cold air, filling the trees and brush along the creek with its own fog that stung the eyes and irritated the throat.

He felt a touch of guilt. The camp was a muddle of disarray, but for the Steeds this would be only their fourth night here. Some had been here for over three weeks now. *Three weeks!* He could barely imagine that. Had the tragedy with Benjamin not occurred, they would have come here on the ninth and been here ever since. So they had no reason to complain.

Beside him, Lydia straightened and stretched, rubbing her hands as she held them out toward the fire. She took one look at his face and reached up and took his hand. Her hand was cold, but he welcomed it and what it said to him.

Seeing the movement, Mary Ann looked up, clearly brought out of her own reverie. "William Clayton came by a while ago."

Nathan turned to his mother in surprise. "Really?"

"Yes, while you and Joshua were out seeing to the stock."

Lydia, who had gone with them to help milk the cow, was also surprised. "So he's out of Nauvoo?"

"Yes. He arrived yesterday afternoon. He came to pay his respects for Benjamin."

Jessica spoke up. "That's a good sign, don't you think?" She sat alone tonight. Their baby was asleep in the tent and she made Solomon stay with him. Solomon was still recovering from pneumonia resulting from his plunge in the river to help save Savannah.

Derek and Rebecca were seated on a log beside Joshua, Rebecca leaning back against her husband to keep warm. "A very good sign," she agreed.

Joshua looked a little puzzled. "William Clayton? Wasn't he one of Joseph's clerks?"

Mary Ann nodded. "Yes. He is also a clerk for Brother Brigham and the Twelve."

"So why is that a good sign?" Joshua, Nathan's eldest son, spoke up.

Jessica turned to him. "Well, young Joshua, if I am correct, that means—"

Young Joshua's hand came up. Jessica stopped in surprise. "Yes?"

"I'm sorry to interrupt, Aunt Jessica, but may I say something?"

Lydia was a little surprised. It was not like her oldest child to break in like that. He of all her children was always the most polite. "What is it, Joshua?"

"Why does everyone keep calling me 'young Joshua'? I'll be fifteen in May."

Nathan laughed. That seemed like a strange thing, coming out just like that right now. "We do it so we can distinguish between you and your uncle."

"So should we call Uncle Joshua 'old Joshua'?"

Joshua hooted aloud at that one. "I think not."

"Why not just call me Josh? That's what all the younger children call me anyway." Now a little bit embarrassed, he turned back to Jessica. "I'm sorry, I shouldn't have interrupted. But I've been thinking about this a lot."

"I'm glad you said something," Jessica said warmly. "Josh is a good solution, I think."

The other adults were all nodding. "Josh it is," his father said.

"Anyway," Jessica went on, "Solomon heard that one of the things Brother Brigham has been waiting for is for Brother Clayton to bring the Church property across so we can leave."

Derek spoke up now. "Heber C. Kimball brought the first of it across in some of his wagons. We heard that Brother Clayton and others were to make sure the rest was brought out."

Now Rachel was curious. "What kind of Church property, Mama?"

Beside her, Emily giggled. "Who gets to bring the temple?"

That brought a chuckle from around the fire. That was Emily, always looking for a way to bring a smile.

Jessica, still smiling, spoke to both of the girls. "Well, there are lots of things. The sacred manuscripts, records that have been kept, Joseph's history of the Church—"

"The records of the temple ordinances," Derek broke in.

"I thought Emma kept the sacred manuscripts," Rebecca said.

For some reason, they all looked to Lydia at that, knowing of her deep and close friendship with Emma Smith. She nodded slowly, and with just a trace of sadness. "Yes, she did keep some, the ones that she brought out of Missouri when Joseph was in prison. She felt very strongly that they were part of Joseph's possessions and not the Church's. She has the manuscript of the work Joseph did in translating the Bible and—"

Growing impatient now with the detail, Joshua broke in abruptly. "So, you think that Clayton's coming means Brigham will finally move out now?"

"That's what Brother Clayton said," Mary Ann explained. "He thinks we'll leave tomorrow."

Nathan spoke up. "I heard that a few already left today."

Jessica nodded. "That's what Solomon heard too. Brother Shumway's company. Also Daniel Spencer and others. So that could mean we'll leave tomorrow. I don't think President Young would let them go off by themselves."

They were all nodding at that. Now, *that* would be good news.

Matthew stood behind Jenny, holding his coat partially around her but letting her get the benefit of the fire. "Before we left, Brigham told me he plans to have Brother Clayton keep a journal record of the trail."

"He's got fine literary skills," Lydia supplied in agreement.

Derek grinned. "He's English, you know."

That brought a hoot from Rebecca, who poked at her husband. "And that's the reason, you think? Just because he's English?"

Now Jenny spoke up. "Aye," she said, letting her Irish accent roll out broadly. "There's something about the British Isles that gives a person a special gift of wisdom, don't you think, now, Derek?"

"Aye, indeed," Derek agreed. This was followed instantly by a sheepish grin. Here was the man who was a notoriously bad speller and who did just about anything to get his wife to write whatever had to be written. "However, in some cases, the talent may trickle down to the youngest member of the family."

Rebecca laughed lightly. "I'd say that in Peter's case that was sure true."

The mention of Peter's name brought a sobering moment around the circle. No one spoke their names, but all thoughts turned to Peter and Kathryn. After a moment, Rebecca spoke again. "I wonder how they're doing."

"Well," Nathan said, trying to keep his voice cheerful, "sounds to me like traveling with this Reed fellow is going to be a lot more comfortable than traveling with us. That wagon Peter described in his last letter sounds unbelievable."

Emily looked puzzled. "If they go with someone else and go a different way, how will they ever find us?"

Surprisingly it was Joshua who spoke up, wanting to comfort. "They'll be taking the same trail as we are, Emmy," he explained. "They'll go to Independence, Missouri—that's the jumping-off point for the Oregon Trail—and we'll be going across Iowa, but the trails are likely to join somewhere out beyond the Missouri River. We'll find them."

"You really think so?"

"I know so," Nathan said firmly. "They're not going to leave until April, so we'll be ahead of them. But we'll just leave word along the trail so they'll know where we are."

"And while we're speaking of the family who are not with us," Lydia said softly, "where do you suppose Will and Alice are by now? Do you think they've left New York City yet?"

Mary Ann's head came up. "Oh, that's the other thing Brother Clayton said. I'm sorry. I forgot to tell you that. The Twelve got a letter from Samuel Brannan a few days ago. He said that Will and Alice had arrived safely in New York City and were proving themselves to be of great value. He said they planned to set sail on February fourth."

"Really?" Joshua said, completely attentive now. "That means they're well on their way, then. I'll have to write to Caroline."

Mary Ann shook her head. "Brother Clayton stopped and told Caroline before he came across the river. So she knows too."

"That was thoughtful of him," Lydia said.

"Yes, it was," Joshua agreed. "Maybe I'll try and find him tomorrow and thank him."

They fell silent for a moment, and then Mary Ann stood slowly. Her face was lined with weariness, but there was satisfaction in her eyes. "If it is true that we leave tomorrow—and it sounds like it is—then perhaps we had better go to bed."

Joshua stood now too. He was nodding soberly. "I don't know about the rest of you, but I'm ready. I hate this waiting."

"Yes," Nathan agreed. "I think we're all ready."

———◆———

Caroline Steed slipped out the door and onto the front porch, pulling the door shut with great care. Young Livvy, now a robust twenty-month-old toddler, was like a cat when it came to sleeping. Even the faintest noise would bring one eye open, and if she saw anything of the slightest interest, that was it for the remainder of the night or morning, as the case might be. Caroline had left a brief note on the table for Savannah, who at nine years of age would be responsible enough to care for Livvy and her brother until Caroline returned.

She looked around. The sky in the east was light now, though it would be another three-quarters of an hour before sunrise. The sky was clear, the air cold. But even as she felt it touch her cheeks, she knew that the biting, bitterly frigid temperatures of the previous week were gone. Even yesterday it had finally reached near to forty degrees. And today was going to be a beautiful day. Once the sun was up, the temperature would likely move into the forties again and it would start to thaw.

Pulling her heavy woolen shawl more tightly around her, she tiptoed off the porch and walked to the front gate. Once again, she opened it carefully, holding the weight up slightly so that the metal hinges did not screech as they had started to do in the past few days.

"Good morning, Caroline."

Caroline gasped and whirled around. "Oh!" she cried softly.

Melissa Rogers waved her hand sheepishly. "I'm sorry. I thought you saw me here. I didn't mean to startle you."

One hand came up to Caroline's throat. "No, I didn't. I . . . My goodness, what are you doing out here so early?"

Melissa's head dropped slightly. "Same as you, I guess."

Caroline understood immediately. "You heard?"

There was a mute nod. The rumor was all over Nauvoo. Brigham Young was starting west today.

Melissa looked up and smiled wanly. "Were you going down to the river?"

Caroline nodded. "Would you like to come?"

"If you don't mind."

"I would like that, Melissa."

They turned and started south along Granger, walking slowly, glad for each other's company, but not speaking until they turned west on Parley Street and reached the landing that marked the main departure point for crossing the river.

The river was still a solid sheet of ice, but if Caroline's predictions that the warming trend would continue were correct, today might be one of the last days one would dare venture across the river on the ice bridge, especially with loaded wagons. From this point on, those leaving Nauvoo would have to wait for the ice to break up enough for the ferries to start running again.

On the far shore, a quarter of a mile away from them, the light was brighter. The sun was just touching the bluffs as it crept slowly toward them.

"Can you see it?" Melissa asked softly.

Caroline turned. "The camp? No, that's seven or eight miles inland along Sugar Creek."

Melissa was staring westward, her head averted enough that Caroline couldn't see her face. There was a quick shake of her head. "Not the camp."

"Oh." Caroline turned away and peered in the direction Melissa was looking. "It's by a solitary oak tree," she said, her eyes narrowing as she too searched. Then her hand came up. "There! There's the tree. And if you look closely, I think you can even see the headstone."

Melissa leaned forward, going up on the balls of her feet, as if she might break and run for it. "Oh, yes. I see it." Then after a moment, "Yes, I think you're right. That is the headstone." It came out in sorrow and pain.

Melissa turned now to look at Caroline and tears were streaming down her cheeks. "I miss him so much, Caroline."

"We all do," Caroline answered, putting an arm around her. When there was no response, she went on. "I found Savannah crying in her bed the other night. When I asked her what was wrong, she said that she was thinking of Grandpa and just started to cry."

"She and Papa had something very special between them."

"Yes, and . . ." Suddenly it was Caroline's throat that closed off and her eyes that were burning. "And if it weren't for that, Savannah would not be here now." She could not repress a shudder. Even now, after three weeks, whenever she closed her eyes she had to fight back visions of the cold blackness closing in around her daughter.

"I wish Mama had buried him on this side of the river. Then we could visit the grave whenever we want."

"I know. But Mother Steed felt so strongly that he would have wanted to be buried on that side of the river."

There was a sudden edge of bitterness. "Yes, to prove that he was faithful to the end."

Caroline said nothing. This was Melissa's struggle and she would have to work through it herself. It was not a time for pointing that out to her.

"Maybe after the ice clears, we could take the children across and visit the grave."

"We would like that," Caroline answered. "That's a good idea."

"I would give anything to see him again," Melissa whispered in anguish. "There's so much I wanted to say when we were saying good-bye."

"I know."

Her voice dropped even lower. "I want to see Mama again, Caroline."

Turning, Caroline wrapped her arms around her sister-in-law. "Do you want to go across and try and find them before they leave?"

Melissa's eyes were wistful, but her mouth pulled down. "No. Carl would not be pleased. It's . . ." She stopped and then slowly shook her head. "No."

Caroline felt a sharp pang of disappointment. She already missed Joshua with an intensity far greater than she had ever expected. If Carl and Melissa wanted to go across and say good-bye, it would have been all right. But she couldn't go over there alone. It would only make things harder for Joshua.

"No, you're right," she said in a tight whisper. "We've said our good-byes. It's better not to have to do that again."

And with that, Melissa's shoulders began to tremble. She laid her head against Caroline's and began to sob softly.

$\mathbf{B}$righam Young stood alone on a small knoll overlooking the camp on Sugar Creek. From there he had a commanding view of the camp below him. In one way, it was a stirring sight and left him thrilled to the point of being unable to
speak. In another way, it was terribly discouraging and left him
heavy with anxiety. He had not felt well all morning, and what
he saw before him was not helping his sense of well-being.

The bugle had blown at five a.m. It had still been pitch-black
then, and one could know the great camp was coming awake
only by the sounds starting up all around. Mothers called their
children awake. Men stumbled out of tents and wagons to start
chopping wood or start their fires. Others went to the creek to
break through the ice for water. Soon small fires dotted the darkness, reflecting a dull light off mud and snow. Gradually, as dawn
lightened the sky, the activity increased. Breakfasts of johnnycake or porridge were cooked on skillets or boiled in kettles over

the fires; children raced back and forth, squealing and shouting, always quick to find excitement in the simplest things.

At eight a.m. the decision was made. Today was the day. He called for a meeting of the captains at ten o'clock. They would move out at noon. But just as he had so many times before, he learned again that it was one thing to make a pronouncement, and it was something else to have it carried out. Everything moved with such agonizing slowness.

Brigham reached in his vest pocket and withdrew his watch. He lifted the cover, then let out his breath in exasperation. It was ten minutes to noon. Almost four hours now and still there were many who were not ready. From where he was, he could still see men out in the trees trying to find their stock. Directly below him he saw a family squatting around the fire, just finishing a midday meal as though there were not another care in the world. Next to the creek, he could hear a man yelling at his wife as they tried to take down their large tent in an orderly fashion. Almost noon, and they were just trying to strike their tent. He blew out his breath, fighting to keep his irritation in check.

He turned as a horseman approached. It was Heber C. Kimball. His wagons and family were directly behind Brigham's fifteen wagons and the thirty-plus people who would be with him. Heber's group was all hitched up and ready to roll. Brigham sighed. He was ill enough that he had sent to Nauvoo for his carriage so that he could ride and not have to delay his departure further. But the carriage had not arrived yet, and Heber would start out the camp without him. If only there could be a hundred Heber Kimballs, how much simpler life would be!

Heber wheeled his horse around and pulled it up alongside his longtime friend and fellow Apostle. He swept off his hat and wiped at his brow with his sleeve. "How are you feeling, President?"

Brigham just shook his head. "I'm going to have to wait for that carriage. But I don't want you waiting. You lead them out."

Heber nodded. "It's really something, isn't it?" he said, inclining his head in the direction of the scene below them.

"Yes." And it was that. Brigham had to remind himself of that. The scene below was discouraging, especially when he felt as unwell as he did now, but if he turned his head to the left, what he saw there was much better. The line of wagons snaked down from where the two of them sat all the way to the creek and beyond. Here were the ones who *were* ready. In camp it might still be chaotic, but that did not represent everyone. Here there were drivers sitting in their wagon seats or standing by the heads of their oxen, waiting for the signal to move. Wives sat or stood beside them. Young children poked their heads out of the wagon covers, faces shining with anticipation. Older children stood alongside, holding the lead rope on a milk cow or ready to herd the few head of sheep or cattle their families might have.

It was true that more than a third of the wagons were not in line yet. It was true that many would likely have to wait until tomorrow before they started. It was true that many families unable to purchase or procure sufficient draft animals had sent their wagons on ahead to Sugar Creek, then returned with the teams to Nauvoo to get other wagons. It was true that, by Stephen Markham's estimate, there were nearly eight hundred people in camp who had barely enough supplies to last them another week. It was true that way too many had no tents and had insufficient winter clothing and bedding. And all of that truth was like a great burden resting on Brigham's shoulders.

But there were the hundreds—no, thousands—who *had* followed counsel. In line now there must have been nearly three hundred wagons. They had their teams. They had food. They had tools and blankets and clothing. There were the Kimballs and the Stouts, the Whitneys and the Steeds, the Pratts and the Rockwoods, and a hundred other names. They stood ready now, eyes turned to him, hearts prepared to follow wherever they were asked to go. And that was enough to make his heart soar. With these kinds of people, it would be enough. It wouldn't be simple, but it would be enough.

Beside him, Heber seemed to sense his thoughts. "President, I think we're ready. The others will come as they can."

Brigham nodded. "Yes." He smiled broadly at Heber, feeling a sudden burst of exhilaration. "Yes, we are. Give the signal."

Heber went up tall in his stirrups, lifting his hat high above his head. "Attention, Camp of Israel!" he shouted loudly.

All down the line heads lifted and turned towards him. Mouths clamped shut, mothers hushed their children. Men moved closer to their oxen.

He waved his hat in a big circle above his head. "To the west! Roll 'em out!"

When Alice Samuelson Steed woke up, Will was already gone. She lifted her head slightly and looked around the tiny cubicle walled in by canvas dividers. She sank back with a soft moan. The sound was half in protest at knowing that while she slept Will had risen and cleaned their small space so that it would be ready for seven o'clock inspection. It was also half in pleasure knowing that she could now lie here for another ten minutes. That was her Will, she thought with a sleepy smile. Up at the crack of dawn, cheerfully doing her work for her. He was probably up on the prow of the ship now, face in the wind, hair blowing freely, and laughing in sheer joy to be at sea again.

Pulling the blanket up around her chin—not for warmth but for comfort—she turned her attention to the rolling motion of the ship. The deck was moving up and down perhaps as much as two feet, but it was gentle and smooth, signaling that the ship was still moving through the swells of a calm sea. With a start, she realized that once again she had slept clear through the night without waking. She could not even remember hearing reveille blown at six o'clock. She stared up at the bulkhead above her, surprised and pleased. That was four nights in a row now. She was finally getting used to the never-ceasing motion of the floor beneath her feet.

She wiggled her body slowly, feeling the strength that the rest had restored to her, feeling a great sense of gratitude that the weather was still calm. If there were not ever one more moment of the violent pitching and yawing, it would be too soon for her. Within a week of the ship's passing Sandy Hook at the eastern edge of New York harbor and moving out into the Atlantic, the weather had turned violent. For four days and four nights, they had been gripped by the howling gale. It had been the most terrifying experience of her life. The "passenger deck" became like something in a nightmare. Luggage, clothing, pots, pans, boxes, barrels, benches, stools—anything that was not either part of the *Brooklyn* or nailed down firmly to her decks was thrown about as if by some petulant child. People were hurled from their bunks. Terrible seasickness became everyone's lot. The smell within the confined and closed quarters was unbearable, but no one dared open the hatches to the fury of the storm.

Elder Brannan had fought the ensuing terror by admonishing the Saints to sing hymns and call upon the Lord for deliverance. Surprisingly, though more miserable than she could have ever imagined, Alice and the others had not lost their faith. Even Captain Richardson had come down near the end of the fourth day in total despair. They were being blown toward the Cape Verde Islands, which were just four hundred miles off the coast of West Africa, and would be dashed upon the rocks before morning. He came down to tell them to prepare for shipwreck at best and death at the worst. To his utter amazement he found the Saints composed and unwilling to lose hope. And within hours the winds died, the seas calmed, and they were spared.

Gratefully that had been the last of it. The mountainous waves which had threatened to swamp the ship became light chops or gentle swells. The skies cleared, the breezes were stiff but favorable, the temperatures of the northern latitudes gave way to warm and pleasant days. There had been those two dreadful days in the doldrums—those latitudes north of the equator where the winds died and there was not so much as a gentle breeze to fill the sails—but they quickly passed. Now the winds were steady again and favorable, as the sailors called them.

With a groan, she threw back the covers and sat up, her feet dangling over the side board of their bed. It wouldn't do to have the inspectors—perhaps Elder Brannan himself—catch her like this. A set of twenty-one rules had been established by Elder Brannan to govern life on ship. Reveille was at six a.m. At seven, rooms were inspected and opened for airing. No one could leave their "state-rooms" without being fully and properly dressed, including coats for the men. At eight-thirty the children began breakfast, followed by the adults. Dinner was served from three to five o'clock, with a "cold lunch" served at eight in the evening. There were times set aside for group and individual prayer, with the Sabbath days—like today—being devoted to rest and worship. They would have worship services at eleven this morning.

The rules helped to maintain order and cleanliness, and most accepted them cheerfully. Most of what little grumbling there was went toward Samuel Brannan, who seemed to view himself as more like a ruler or governor than simply their priesthood leader. His insistence that they always refer to him as "First Elder," for example, grated on several. He ate with the captain and did not share the simple quarters of the others. After the storm had blown itself out, he had determined that they had to put themselves under covenant to prepare for that time when the voyage was completed and they reached Upper California. He established an order, patterned after the united order set up by Joseph Smith, wherein they all agreed to form a company and put the returns from their labors in a common pot for three years. The fact that it was obviously advantageous to him and that he titled the company "Samuel Brannan and Company" added to the irritation of some, but everyone signed. As usual, Will said little, even to Alice, though she could tell that their leader's high-handed ways disturbed him.

Chiding herself for getting lost in thought again, Alice hopped down onto the deck, feeling the coolness of the wood beneath her bare feet. Absently, her right hand rose to her stomach and rested there for a moment. She knew it was mostly her imagination, but she thought she could feel the first swellings. She smiled in the half darkness. She had thought about telling Will this day, it being the first of March and seemingly a good time. But now she had another thought. When they crossed the equator there would be a party in celebration for King Neptune—a tradition among sailors, according to Will. Whenever the equator was crossed in either direction, King Neptune, god of the sea, was crowned in a celebration by all on board the ship. It would be a jolly and rollicking time—less so for the Mormons than for others perhaps, because the Saints would not toast the occasion with ale or rum; but it would be a genuine party nevertheless. In light of the monotony of shipboard life, this would be something to look forward to indeed.

Her hand moved up and she began to unbutton her nightdress. Yes, that would be the time. Just before the celebration began, she would whisper it in his ear. Then they would have more than King Neptune and the crossing of his great line of demarcation to be glad about.

———•———

She was nearly right in guessing where her husband would be. Will was at the prow of the ship, but he was not just standing there with his face in the wind. He was working with two of the crew, helping them stow the rigging and check on some of the crates that were lashed down to the deck. When he saw her, he immediately left them and came over. "Good morning," he said cheerfully. He leaned down and kissed her. "How are you feeling?"

"Glorious. Thank you for letting me sleep."

"I'm not sure there was much choice. I thought for sure you'd wake up when I dropped that kettle on the floor right next to you."

"You dropped a kettle?" she burst out, and then she saw the laughter in his eyes. "Oh, you," she said, poking at him.

"Well, you were sleeping pretty soundly."

"I know, and it felt so good." She slipped an arm through his and they walked back to about midship. There were several other passengers out and about, and they spoke briefly with them. Then they stopped at the railing where they could be alone.

"Another beautiful day," Will said.

"It is. I'm so glad." She waited a moment. "I'm coming to understand why you so love the sea."

"It is beautiful, isn't it?"

"At times. At other times it can be terrifying."

"I won't argue that point."

And then, since they were talking about the sea, she decided this might be the time to raise a question that had been on her mind of late. "Can I ask you something?"

"Sure."

"You know how we were blown off course during the storm."

"Yes."

"How long do you think that will delay our arrival in California?"

He was a little surprised by her question. "Oh, two or three days, maybe. Why?"

"Two or three days? That's all?"

"Yes, why?"

"Didn't you tell me that the Cape Verde Islands were off the coast of Africa?"

"Yes."

"Africa? Not South America?"

He was clearly puzzled. "That's right. They're about four hundred miles west of the westernmost shoulder of Africa."

"But that's a thousand miles off course, Will. How can you say it will delay us for only two or three days?"

Now he understood. His first impression was to chuckle, but then he caught himself. Why shouldn't she assume that that was what had happened? He had not taken the time to explain things to her.

"Look," he said, holding up his left hand, fingers pointing up and palm facing the two of them. "Picture South America in your mind. The tips of my fingers are the northern coast; the palm is the fat part of the continent. My thumb is the western coast; my little finger and the side of my palm are the eastern coast. My arm is where the continent narrows."

"Okay." It was a crude similarity, but for his purposes it was fine.

"If you can picture it, the continent is long and mostly straight down the west coast. But here"—he tapped the side of his little finger—"there is a great bulge eastward. It is called Brazil. Can you picture what I mean?"

"Yes."

"Good. Now tell me where this eastern tip of Brazil—what they call Cabo de São Roque—is in comparison to New York City."

She looked at him for a moment, then tapped a spot in the air above the tip of his little finger. "About here?"

He smiled. "That's what most people in North America think. They picture South America as being directly south of us. But it's not true. Mexico and Central America have a great eastward curve and South America is offset quite a bit to the east of North America." Now he tapped a spot above the tip of his thumb. "Would you believe New York is about here, directly above the western coast of the continent, and is more than a thousand miles west of Brazil's eastern tip?"

"Really?"

"Yes. The east coast of North America is about even with the west coast of South America."

She looked at him closely to see if he was teasing her. But he was quite serious.

"Okay," he continued, "that's the first problem. If you want to go around Brazil, what direction do you have to sail?"

"Southeast," she said promptly.

"That is correct. And there is the second problem. We've talked about the prevailing winds. You remember that?"

"Yes." Will had been trying to teach her a little about sailing and had spent an hour one day after the storm describing how around the globe various winds blew in predictable, reliable patterns. Because they were so important to sailors and ships, they were called the trade winds.

"Well, if you were to head directly southeast from New York"—with his right forefinger he drew a line from above the tip of his thumb to the right side of his palm—"not only would you not clear South America, but right here at the eastern end of the Caribbean you would run into the northeasterly winds. What is that going to do for us?"

She nodded slowly, understanding starting to come now. The winds were always named for the direction from which they came, not the direction in which they blew. So a northeasterly would blow them southwest. "It would blow us directly toward South America."

He beamed. She was really very quick and it pleased him greatly. Not only that, she really wanted to know. "Okay. Now, when you sail mostly east from New York you hit the westerly trades. They take us out far enough that we clear the land mass of Brazil and miss the northeasterly winds."

"I see that, but do we go all the way to Africa?"

"No, not all the way, but almost. When the storm hit, it drove us farther east than we would normally go. That's when we came dangerously close to the Cape Verde Islands and nearly shipwrecked. But we were not a thousand miles off course. This is the route that all the China traders and the whalers use. It is about a thousand miles longer, but it cuts nearly two weeks off the total journey."

She nodded and turned back to the railing, glad she had asked him. It was a simple answer, and she felt foolish for having harbored the fears for so long.

"Did you know that in about three days we'll have been at sea for one month?" he asked.

She turned her head and nodded. She had already remembered that it was the first day of March. They had sailed from New York on the fourth of February. "It seems longer in a way. It's like we've been on board for a lifetime. And yet in another way, it seems like only a week."

"That's how the sea is," he said. "I have found—"

"Mr. Steed?"

Will turned. The first mate, the ship's second officer, was approaching them. With him was the bosun and several sailors. They were sober faced, but there seemed to be some hidden amusement.

"Yes, Mr. Lombard?"

"I think we've just spotted it." He held out a telescope.

"Really?" Will turned around and peered out to sea.

"Oh, you can't see it without help yet," Lombard said quickly. "You'll need the glass."

"Thank you." Will took the spyglass and held it up to his eye.

"You'll have to look closely," the bosun spoke up. "It's still a long way off."

"What is it, Will?" Alice asked, looking in the direction Will was facing.

He grunted, lifting his other hand to adjust the focus slightly. And then he straightened. "I've got it!"

"What, Will? What is it?"

Still he didn't answer. After a moment he lowered the glass and turned back to the ship's officer. "I guess you're right. I thought we were still too far away."

Seeing what was going on, other sailors and some of the passengers began to gather around them. Alice noted that one or two of the sailors were grinning and chuckling to themselves. Whatever it was, it must be something exciting. She turned back to Will. "What is it? What are you looking at?"

He turned solemnly. "It's the equator."

"What?"

The other passengers moved to the rail, peering out across the vast expanse of water. "Where?" one of the men asked.

"Oh, you can't see it with the naked eye," Will explained. "It's still too far away." He handed the telescope to Alice. "Here. You have to look really close. You can barely see it."

Eagerly she took the glass and turned to brace herself on the railing. "Where is it?"

"Almost straight ahead. You have to keep your other eye closed tightly."

She did so, searching through the lens, trying to see anything but the blue water.

"Do you see it?" Will asked.

"No. What am I looking for?"

"It's a long black line right on the surface of the water."

"Really?" She leaned forward.

Behind her she could hear the people chuckling softly now. She was so intent on her search that she gave it no thought. Then suddenly she stiffened. "There it is! I see it! I see it!"

Will was standing right beside her now. "You do? What does it look like?"

"It's really fuzzy, but it's there. A long dark line in the water."

"That's it," he exclaimed. "That's the equator."

It was the laughter that made her pull away from the telescope. Several of the women were tittering. There were some loud snickers. A couple of the sailors—the same ones who had been grinning before—were laughing uproariously, slapping their legs or doubled over. Mr. Lombard was trying to repress a broad smile.

And then she understood. Her face flamed brilliant red. Will had reached out with both hands and was holding a piece of black yarn in front of the lens of the telescope. That was the "equator" she had seen.

Seeing her face and her expression, the whole company erupted with a roar. Will was grinning as if he had just found a pot of gold.

"You—," she started, still blushing furiously.

"I'm sorry, honey." This was a joke played on just about every sailing ship taking passengers across the equator, but it was always great fun when there was one so innocent and so trusting. And to have her own husband in on the sham delighted the crew. "If it makes you feel any better, I fell for the same trick the first time I approached the equator."

"And you think that makes it all right?" she said archly.

The crew exploded again. They liked Will a lot, and from what they had seen of his wife, they liked her as well. That she would not take this lying down was all the more delightful. She looked around at the crew. "Gentlemen, I put you on notice that I shall have my day as well. I don't know when. I don't know how. But I *shall* get even."

"Yes!" one of the men chortled.

"We'll help, Miz Steed," another sang out.

Will was laughing now too. "Doesn't the Bible talk about turning the other cheek?"

"It does," she said sweetly, "but unfortunately that page has been torn out of my Bible."

Chapter Notes

On the first day of March, 1846, almost one full month after the first wagons left Nauvoo and crossed the Mississippi River, Brigham Young decided to wait no longer. Though he was feeling somewhat ill and would not leave the camp until evening when a carriage came to convey him, he did not have the others wait. Moving out from Sugar Creek about noon, with not all the wagons leaving, the Saints started west. They moved about five miles that first day. Brigham caught up with them later that evening. (See *MHBY*, pp. 57–58; *CN*, 9 March 1996, p. 12.)

Information about life on the ship *Brooklyn*, including the great storm that blew them so far off course, comes from reports of those who participated in the journey (see Paul Bailey, *Sam Brannan and the California Mormons* [Los Angeles: Westernlore Press, 1943], pp. 31–35; *Church History in the Fulness of Times* [Salt Lake City: The Church of Jesus Christ of Latter-day Saints, 1989], pp. 327–28).

Whand Caroline returned home from a brief trip to her store, wheeling Livvy in the baby carriage, the house was empty. Surprised, she took off her coat, got the baby out of hers, all the while calling out for Charles and Savannah. She sat Livvy up to the table with a piece of bread and butter and a cup of milk, then went methodically through the house, looking in every room. They were not there. Neither were they out in the backyard or in the barn.

Feeling the first touch of anxiety, she picked Livvy up, then went next door to Melissa and Carl's house. "Yes," Melissa said when she asked about Savannah, "I saw her about half an hour ago."

"Where?"

"Pulling a wagonload of stuff out the gate of your house."

"A wagonload of stuff?"

"Yes. You know, the little wagon Joshua gave her for Christmas a year or so ago."

"Oh." There were too many wagons and teams in Nauvoo right now and Caroline's first thought had been of a full-sized wagon, which made no sense at all. "What kind of stuff?"

Melissa shrugged. "I couldn't really tell. It looked like there were some clothes and some of her toys. I saw that big doll she loves so much."

Caroline considered that. It still made no sense. Where would she be going with those kinds of things? "And she had Charles with her?"

"Yep. He was pushing the wagon." She smiled. "I called out and asked them where they were going. She said they were going to the store. But then she turned south and not north."

"She didn't come to the store."

"Maybe she meant the Red Brick Store. That would be the right direction."

Caroline started a little at that. "Why would she be going there?" And then, realizing that Melissa wouldn't know, she made up her mind. "Can I leave Livvy here while I go look for them?"

"Of course."

———— ·•· ————

Emma Smith glanced out the window; then, surprised, she walked over to it and looked more closely. Two children were just pulling a small wagon filled with an assortment of things up to the store. They were bundled up in their winter clothing, and for a moment she couldn't tell who they were. Then the larger of the two turned and looked up at the store. There was no mistaking that face and the tufts of red hair poking out from beneath the woolen cap.

Smiling, she moved to the door and got her coat, then stepped outside.

Savannah looked up. "Oh, hello, Sister Emma."

"Good afternoon, Savannah. How are you today?"

"Fine, thank you."

"And good afternoon to you too, Charles."

He had a scarf wrapped around the lower part of his face and looked like a bear cub with nothing but eyes peering out at her. "Afternoon, Sister Emma," came the muffled reply.

"What brings you out on a cold, wintry afternoon?"

Savannah stepped forward. "Trading."

"Trading?" Emma asked in surprise. "Trading for what?"

"For supplies to go west."

Emma's eyebrows lifted and she nearly smiled, but Savannah was very serious and Emma decided she had better be too. "I see. And who are these supplies for, may I ask?"

"For us," Charles said proudly.

"And you are going west?" Emma asked. "I thought your family had decided they weren't going to go west. At least not yet."

Savannah's wide green eyes shadowed momentarily. "That's what Pa said, but me and Charles are praying every day that he will change his mind."

"You want to go west."

"Oh, yes. Very much."

"Maybe it's better if you wait until you're sure you are going before you start trading. What do you think?"

There was an emphatic shake of her head. "No. If Heavenly Father answers our prayers, we have to be ready, don't we, Charles?"

There was a nod of deepest gravity. "Yep."

Emma was fighting now not to smile or laugh aloud. "All right, and what do you have to trade?"

Savannah turned to the wagon and pulled a dress off the pile of clothing at the back. "This," she said, not without some sadness.

"But isn't that the dress your father bought you in St. Louis for Will's wedding?"

"Yes. It's my best one. He paid fifty dollars for it."

"Fifty dollars!" Emma looked suitably impressed. "I don't think I could give you fifty dollars for it."

"How about some sugar and salt?"

"For the dress?"

There came that emphatic nod again. "Won't be much use for a dress like this out on the trail," she said soberly.

"I see."

Savannah turned now and went through the rest of her merchandise, holding it up and briefly describing it and its value, as though she were an old mountain man bringing in his load of furs for the buyers to evaluate.

The last thing she held up was a large doll with porcelain head, arms, and feet. She held it longingly for a moment, then handed it to Emma. "This is Betsy."

"And you want to trade Betsy away?"

"I have to," came the short reply.

Now Emma wanted to cry. "You're absolutely sure?"

Savannah looked away. "We can't expect Heavenly Father to bless us if we are not willing to give some things up."

Caroline saw them while still half a block away, two small figures putting things in a child's wagon in front of the Red Brick Store. She also saw a woman standing with them. She broke into a half run. "Savannah!"

Savannah turned in surprise, then waved cheerfully. "Hi, Mama!"

She came up to them, feeling a great relief and a growing anger. "Savannah Steed, where in the world have you been?"

Savannah looked surprised. "Here." Her cheeks were red from the cold and emphasized the innocence in the wide green eyes that looked up at her mother.

Charles said nothing, and Caroline was sure that in this case, as in so many others, he was the follower. He had just turned six two weeks before, and though he had an independent streak of his own, he adored Savannah and seemed to enjoy being led into her various exploits, even though it frequently got them both into trouble.

Caroline bent down, taking Savannah by the shoulders.

"Why didn't you tell me where you were going? I've been worried sick, Savannah. I've been looking all over for you."

"But Mama, I left you a note."

That stopped Caroline. "You did? Where?"

"I wrote it on the kitchen table, and—" There was a sudden widening of the eyes, and then a sheepish look. "Oh!" She fished in her coat pocket and a moment later withdrew a crumpled note. "Sorry, Mama."

Caroline straightened and blew out her breath and looked at Emma. "Hello, Emma. Have my children been bothering you?"

"Oh, not at all. I wondered if you knew where they were." There was a faint smile. "We've been doing some trading."

"*What?*"

Emma laughed softly. "Your daughter and I have been doing some trading. I think you and I had better talk."

"You've been trading?" Caroline asked Savannah, still not quite comprehending.

"Yes, Mama, for when we go west."

"Savannah, we're not going west. Not for a long time."

"Don't say that, Mama. I've been praying and—"

Caroline threw up her hands, looking heavenward. "Savannah!"

"Well, we have," she said, not flinching at all from her mother's anger.

Caroline stood there, looking down at her daughter, this redheaded, stubborn imp that was so full of tease, so in love with life, and so much like Joshua sometimes that it frightened her. "You and Charles go on home now," she finally said. "I'll be along in a minute."

"Yes, Mama." Savannah reached down and got the handle to the wagon.

"No, leave the wagon."

"Mama! You're not going to trade back, are you?"

"Just leave the wagon."

Her grip on it only tightened. "No, Mama, you can't. I don't want my doll back."

Emma stepped closer to Caroline. "It's all right," she said softly. "We can work out something later if you wish."

Caroline blew out her breath. "All right, but you go right home, young lady, and don't you leave until I get there."

"Yes, Mama," Savannah said dejectedly. Charles nodded gravely and fell in behind the wagon to help her by pushing.

As they walked away, Caroline shook her head. "I don't know what I'm going to do with that girl."

"Give her a hug and a kiss," Emma smiled. "I think she's the most endearing child I've ever met. No wonder she had Benjamin wrapped around her little finger."

"And her father too." She turned away from the children. "So what all did she bring in?"

"Several dresses—probably her nicest, I would guess—a few toys, and that beautiful doll. She also had three dollars and fifty cents cash."

Caroline was astonished.

"She drives a mean bargain too," Emma said ruefully. "I can tell she's worked a lot with you in the store."

"So what do I do with her, Emma?"

She was thoughtful for a moment. "Well, you know how I feel about going west, but as I listened to her, Caroline, she is absolutely convinced that her father is going to change his mind and take you with him because she prays about it every day. She wants to do her part to be ready when that happens."

"I know. I've told her and told her that she can't get her hopes too high. Joshua is pretty set on this. But it doesn't make any difference to her."

"So I wouldn't do anything."

"You wouldn't?"

"No. If it means that much to her, I'd let her make the trade. It will break her heart if you bring it back."

Caroline thought about that, then finally nodded. "I suppose that may be best, at least for now."

Emma was smiling again, watching as the two figures trudged up the street. "You can't help but love her, can you?"

"No," Caroline said wistfully. "There's no helping that."

———————

Nathan let the flap of the tent close and moved over to the fire. His mother was sitting on a log there. Now that supper was done, the fire was dying down and was mostly a bed of hot coals. He sat down beside her. Behind them, the sun was low in the sky. It would be dark in less than an hour. The air had cooled noticeably since the sun had set, but it was still not unpleasant.

"How's Lydia?"

"Very tired."

"She has a right to be. Today was enough to tire a normal person out, let alone a woman who is less than two months from delivering a child."

Nathan nodded wearily. He couldn't imagine how Lydia had done it. Young Joshua—Josh, he corrected himself—and Emily had taken the responsibility for watching the three younger children. Yesterday they had come about five miles from Sugar Creek. The weather had been beautiful and much warmer. Today had been the same. That was a blessing in one way, a challenge in another. By midday the temperature reached the midforties, Nathan guessed. That made for pleasant walking, with light coats or sweaters on. On the other hand, under the bright sun the ground quickly thawed, and the soil that had been rock solid for the past two weeks turned soft and muddy. The Steeds were back about a third of the way in the great line of wagons. Between the warming air and the weight of the wagons in front of them, the road quickly became a morass. He couldn't imagine what it must be like for those at the back of the last company.

They had reached the east bank of the Des Moines River and would follow its path now. This would keep them close to water and timber, but it also made the terrain a series of one gently rolling hill after another. Normally, one would not have given these hillocks a second thought. They barely caught the attention of the eye from a distance. But start up each one when the wagon wheels were six inches deep in mud, when the hooves of the oxen or the horses found little solid grip, when your own boots were like great clogs of lead and every step was labor, then those seemingly gentle inclines became dreaded obstacles.

At Nathan's insistence, Lydia had started out in the wagon yesterday, but that lasted less than a quarter of an hour. The wagon had springs, but even then the jolting, pounding, hammering ride was too much for her and she had elected to walk. The image of Joseph and Mary came into Nathan's mind. How was it Luke had described Mary's condition? She was *great* with child. How far was it from Nazareth to Bethlehem? A hundred miles? More? Maybe less? Well, Lydia was also great with child, and they had perhaps a thousand miles ahead of them. Joseph had been fortunate to find a stable when there had been no room at the inn. Where Nathan was taking Lydia, there were no inns and there would be no stables.

She was doing well in her coming motherhood and made light of his growing anxiety, but that didn't make it go away. It said much that she had accepted his suggestion after supper that she should lie down for a while. Normally, she would not tolerate any attempt on his part to coddle her.

He sighed now and decided to change the subject. "I'm sure you're tired too, aren't you, Mother?"

"Oh yes," she answered easily. "But it feels so good to have started at last." There was a quick smile. "I'm not very patient at waiting."

"It does feel good, doesn't it?"

"It's only the second day of many, but at least we're counting now."

He looked around. Joshua was over helping Solomon Garrett and Jessica secure their tent ropes. Next to them, Matthew and

Jenny were outside their tent, Matthew scraping off the thick
goo from his boots. Jenny held little Emmeline in her lap with a
blanket over her, and Nathan suspected she was nursing her.
Across the fire from where they sat, he could see the shadows of
Derek and Rebecca on the walls of their tent. There was a burst
of giggles and Nathan smiled. Derek was probably telling his
three children a story. That would account for the laughter. He
would begin straight-faced, using his finest English accent,
telling one of the fairy tales as originally written. Then, without
warning, he would give it an unexpected twist. Papa Bear would
come home and instead of going to the house he went out to the
barn. "Someone's been driving my wagon," he would thunder.
The children would squeal in delighted protest, pounding him
on the arm to get it right. Back he would come to the original,
but only for a few minutes. They loved it and sat on the edge of
their seats waiting for the next digression.

"Nathan?"

"Yes, Mama?"

"Did your father ever tell you about my dream?"

He turned. "What dream?"

There was a long, slow release of breath, as though she had
been holding something in for a long time. "About the plain?"

He shook his head. "I guess not. That doesn't sound familiar."

"Oh."

She was staring into the fire now, her eyes hooded and distant.

"Tell me, Mother."

She looked up, a little surprised. "Tell you what?"

"About the dream."

"Oh. Yes, of course." She straightened, folding her hands in
her lap. "The dream."

Nathan waited, watching her face with concern, but he
could see that she was not necessarily saddened. It was more like
she was thoughtful, bemused rather than sorrowful.

"It first came while we were still in Far West. It came once, and then I had it again several times over a matter of weeks."

"And you told Pa about it?"

"Yes. It really bothered him, though I did not find it disturbing in any way."

"Bothered him? How?"

"Well, actually, he never said anything at first, until that July."

That July? And then as his mind went back, Nathan understood. "The time when Papa was so sick?"

"Yes. Along with everyone else."

He nodded. In the summer of 1839, the ague had swept through the new settlement on the Mississippi River that would come to be called Nauvoo. Hundreds were desperately ill. Many died, including his own son. His father had contracted the sickness and hovered near death. He had nearly lost Lydia as well.

Now Mary Ann was staring down at her hands, which lay open on her lap, as though she were surprised to find them there. "He was sure he was going to die."

"So were we," Nathan said softly. "Remember how he called us around to give us his last blessing and counsel?"

"Yes, I remember it perfectly." She looked up. "Well, one night, when he was at his sickest, he asked me to tell him about the dream again. I was surprised, because it hadn't happened for several months and I had all but forgotten it. At first I wasn't sure why he had remembered it."

"What was the dream?"

She closed her eyes. It was over seven years ago now. After that initial period when it came several times, the dream had never been repeated, but it was still vivid and clear in her mind. She let the images sweep over her and felt the joy all over again. It had been a wonderful thing, and it had come at the most desolate time in Far West.

She began speaking softly, more to herself than to her son.

The dream had begun on a vast, open plain. She was the only one there at first. She was walking steadily forward. There was not a tree anywhere to break the vastness of the landscape, but neither was it desolate or barren. There were flowers everywhere, butterflies, birds—the beauty of it all filled her with a great sense of joy and wonder. Only after a time had she realized that she was moving towards a glittering point in the distance, a source of light so brilliant that it seemed to be the source of the radiant daylight rather than a sun overhead.

She turned to Nathan. "I was surprised to see you there suddenly. You were the first. Suddenly you were just there, coming toward me. You called and waved, and ran to join me. I was so happy to see you. I remember that you took my hand."

Nathan watched her closely, saying nothing, amazed to see the joy that infused her face.

"A moment later, Melissa appeared. It was in the same way. Suddenly she was just there and running toward us, laughing and calling. Then it was Matthew."

She half closed her eyes, seeing it all again. Her family began appearing rapidly now, each one raising a hand in greeting and coming to join them. There was no particular order. They just came, first one by one, then in pairs and small groups. There was Lydia, Derek and Rebecca, Jessica and Rachel and the two Griffith boys that Jessica had adopted as her own when she married John Griffith.

"Was John there?" Nathan asked, cutting into her thoughts.

She considered that for a moment, then nodded. "Yes, he was."

"Even though . . . ?"

"Yes, even though he had been killed at Haun's Mill a few weeks before. He was there, but not necessarily with Jessica and the children. He was just there and it felt all right." She smiled softly now. "At first it was just the adults, but then the grandchildren joined us too. I remember that young Joshua—or Josh—and Emily were there too. Only they were older, more like they are now. I can remember how proud I was of them. Soon we were all there, moving together across the plain toward the great light. We were laughing and singing and pointing toward our destination, which we could now tell was a glorious city, lying on the horizon, shimmering with light, beckoning us onward."

As she fell back into her own thoughts, Nathan was puzzled. "And that bothered Papa?"

She nodded gravely. "Terribly so."

"But why? It sounds wonderful."

"Because he was not there."

Nathan's head rose slowly. "He wasn't?"

"No, he was the only one. All the rest of us were there."

"But . . ."

She nodded. "He was sure that was a sign that he was going to die that night. That's why he called you all to his bedside."

Nathan remembered that night very clearly. Then the next morning had been what came to be known as the day of power. Joseph Smith had risen from his own sickbed and started among the Saints. It was as if an angel were passing through the ranks of the sick and the dying. Everywhere he went, the sick were spared, the stricken were healed. And Benjamin was one of those.

Mary Ann was still talking. "I was cross with him. I told him to stop talking like that."

"You didn't think that his not being in the dream meant he would die?"

"No. I don't know why, but I knew he wasn't going to die." There was a long pause; then her eyes were suddenly shining in the firelight. "Not then."

"But why wasn't he in the dream? I would probably have thought the same thing."

"Because somehow in the dream I knew that your father was already in the city. I knew he was waiting for us to join him. There was no sadness in me at all."

"I see." It came out as a husky whisper, for Nathan now found his own chest constricting as he thought of a headstone on the western banks of the Mississippi River.

For several moments there was no sound except for the crackling of the fire and the soft laughter coming from Derek's tent.

His mother reached out a hand and laid it over Nathan's. "The fact that I miss him—sometimes so fiercely that I think I will surely be unable to bear it—doesn't mean that I am despairing, Nathan. I grieve, but I do not despair. I know he's there in that glorious city. I know he's waiting for me and for the rest of us."

He nodded mutely, taking her hand in his. He slid closer to her and put an arm around her shoulder. "Thank you, Mama. Thank you for telling me."

A movement off to their left caught Mary Ann's eye. Joshua called out to Solomon as they secured the last of the tent ropes and pegs.

Suddenly Mary Ann's voice was urgent. "Nathan, in my dream, no one was missing except your father."

He wasn't sure what that meant. "What are you saying?" he asked tentatively.

"Caroline was there. Melissa and Carl were there." She looked over to where Joshua and Solomon were finishing tightening the guy ropes on Solomon's tent. "Joshua was there."

"He was?"

"Yes. Everyone! It's not right that they are not here, Nathan. Caroline especially. She needs to be here with Joshua."

"I know, Mama, but . . ."

She shook her head quickly. Joshua was finished and was starting toward them. "I don't know how you will do it, but you must get them here with us, Nathan."

And then, as Joshua came up to them, she looked up and smiled. "Come sit down, son. Nathan and I are just visiting."

———◦———

There were several more around the fire now—Jessica and Solomon, Derek and Rebecca, Jenny. Jenny was alone, however, as Matthew had guard duty tonight and had gone to take his station. Rachel, Josh, and Emily were with them, feeling more comfortable here than playing games with the children. After lying down for half an hour, Lydia had come out again and sat beside Nathan. It was full dark now and getting chilly again. They sat in a tight circle talking quietly. The subject of Caroline and Melissa and Carl did not come up again.

Then suddenly a noise was heard that brought up every head. Off somewhere in front of them, someone had started to play a trumpet. It was not playing anything in particular, just running up and down scales, as though the player were warming up his horn. In a moment, another trumpet started, and then a trombone.

Behind them, the wagon flap on Matthew's wagon flew open and Christopher came bursting out, followed by the other children. "It's the band, Papa. They're gonna play. Can we go!" Christopher was seven now and proving to be as husky as his father. His eyes were wide and his face infused with excitement. "Please, Papa."

Emily and Rachel had jumped to their feet and were staring off in the direction of the sounds, which were swelling in volume now with every moment. "Is there going to be a dance?" Emily said, her eyes shining.

Lydia groaned in mock horror. "You can think about dancing after today?"

"Oh, yes, Mama!" came the instant reply.

In the distance, the trumpeter started the first line of "Now Let Us Rejoice," then let it disintegrate into a series of trills and runs.

People were coming to their feet, and tent doors and wagon flaps were being opened all across the camp now. People were pointing and calling out to one another. Just then a man came riding toward them on a horse. He was hollering something as he passed. They turned to listen. "Concert at the main campfire in five minutes. Brother Pitt has his band together. Concert in five minutes."

Nathan turned to his mother and smiled. "What do you say, Grandma? Shall we go and hear Brother Pitt tonight?"

Mary Ann started to shake her head, then immediately changed her mind. If she begged off, claiming she was tired—which she truly was—she knew what would happen. Nathan would volunteer to stay with her. Lydia would then insist on staying with him. Then Joshua and the others would decide maybe it wasn't such a good idea after all, and none of them would end up going. She turned and looked into her grandchildren's eyes. They were shining brightly in the firelight, and they were filled with pleading. She couldn't help it. There was a soft laugh and she got slowly to her feet. "But of course we're going."

As the children whooped and threw their arms around her, Jenny stood and spoke up quickly. "I'll stay with the babies. You all go on."

She waved her hand as the other mothers started to protest. "No, really. Another night, when I have Matthew with me, then one of you can stay and we'll go."

That settled it. As one they moved off, Joshua taking one of his mother's arms, Emily taking the other. The whole camp was stirring now as people came out of their tents or climbed down from the wagons and streamed toward the central part of camp where the Twelve had their wagons. And Joshua, watching the other families moving together, talking excitedly, felt a great longing for Caroline and the children. It was hard enough being gone from them, without times like this. And yet, at the same time, he also felt a grudging admiration for Brigham Young's wisdom.

Brigham hadn't missed much. He had organized a pioneer company under the direction of Stephen Markham, the members of which would go ahead of the main camp, breaking trail, building bridges, securing work and food, preparing ferries for the wider rivers. Bishop George Miller, leading a dozen or so wagons and three or four dozen men, had moved out a few days before, the surest sign that Brigham was serious about starting west. Brigham had asked Hosea Stout, the chief of police in

"The Upper California—Oh, That's the Land for Me!"

Nauvoo, to create a "police" company. These men, most of whom owned rifles, served as guards, provided protection for the camp, and dealt with those few disagreements that could not be settled by the captains of tens or captains of fifties. The creation of a police company was sobering evidence that Brigham Young was still worried about the threat from their enemies. There were also commissaries appointed to secure food, treasurers to handle the finances, wagon masters, blacksmiths, carpenters, and a dozen other positions required to keep a large body of people moving.

And there was William Pitt and his brass band. And who would have guessed that that would be part of the organization? In Nauvoo, Pitt and his band, while perhaps not the finest in the land, had been immensely popular. When Pitt, a British convert, came to America, he brought with him a large collection of music for brass bands and found many opportunities to use it. The Nauvoo Brass Band, as it was called, played grand marches, quicksteps, and gallops, as well as the hymns. They played for dances and gave concerts at the Masonic Hall, which served as the city's cultural center. When it came time for the exodus, Pitt had specifically been asked by Brigham Young to keep his musicians together in one company so that the band could continue to function on the trail. Joshua had spent years hauling freight across the back roads of western America. He knew how lonely the trail could be and how important morale was. The decision to keep the Nauvoo Brass Band together and functioning was already proving to be a brilliant move.

And then, even as they approached the central campfire, the band began to play a song that in the last few months had become one of the most popular among the Saints. They heard the distant sounds of applause and cheers. Holding on to Joshua's arm tightly as they moved across the frozen ground of the camp, Mary Ann tipped her head back and began to sing. Momentarily startled, Lydia laughed, then joined in. Then it was Emily and Rachel and others around them. In moments, the whole stream of people moving toward the fire were singing lustily.

The Upper California—Oh, that's the land for me!
It lies between the mountains and the great Pacific sea;
The Saints can be supported there,
And taste the sweets of liberty.
In Upper California—Oh, that's the land for me!

———•———

Kathryn Marie McIntire Ingalls was worried, and Peter could see it in her eyes, though her head was high and her chin firm with determination. As he pushed her along the boarded walk toward the home of James Reed, he sought for the words that might make her less anxious, but he sensed that unless his attempt was positively brilliant, it would do more harm than good, so he said nothing.

As they approached the large brick home in one of the finer neighborhoods of Springfield, Illinois, he saw her shoulders come back and she drew a deep breath. They were not yet to the corner of the Reed property, with its wrought-iron fence and its beautiful flower gardens. She turned her head. "All right, Peter. I'd like to walk from here."

He frowned, but immediately nodded. "All right." He stopped the wheelchair and untied the crutches from the back of it. Stepping around to face her, he held out his hands.

There was a sudden shake of her head—quick, emphatic, stubborn. "Don't help me, Peter, someone may be watching."

He took a breath, letting it out slowly, and handed her the crutches. Then he stepped back to brace the chair so it wouldn't roll. It was not as if he hadn't seen this stubborn streak in her before they were married. It fact, he had nearly lost her when she thought he might be marrying her out of pity. But in the four and a half months since then, he had come to understand just how fiercely it burned within her. And while sometimes it exasperated him beyond measure, he understood its source and loved her all the more for her determination to make the best of her handicap.

And she was getting very strong. He watched as she put one crutch under her arm and then hoisted her body up, steadying herself on the arm of her wheelchair. With a little flip of her upper torso, the second crutch was in place and she moved away from the chair. "All right."

Looking around, Peter found a place beside some bushes and pushed the chair into them, well off the walk so it would not be in anyone's way. When he turned back, she was already moving forward with smooth, even motions. He walked forward to her side. "You really are getting very good, Kathryn."

"Thank you, dear." She smiled one of her prettiest smiles at him, but it darkened almost instantly. "I just don't want the Donners to think Mrs. Reed made a mistake when she hired me."

"They won't. And even if they did, Mrs. Reed and the children think you're wonderful. She won't change her mind."

"I know," Kathryn said, her jaw thrust out, "but I want them all to know that I am not going to be a burden to anyone."

He grinned at her. "Are all the Irish like this?"

She flashed him a smile back. "All right, Peter. I'll behave myself."

They had reached the gate that opened onto the walk that led to the front door of the home of James Reed. Peter moved forward, opened the gate, and stepped back, holding it open for Kathryn. She gave him an impish look, that look that reflected so well her temperament. "Well," she said with mock primness, "I don't give a fig what anyone else thinks. We have been hired by the Reeds to help them out, and all we need to do is please *them*."

"Which you have," Peter said firmly, ignoring the fact that she was lying shamelessly to herself.

As they reached the ornately carved wooden door, she hesitated, and he could tell that her bright courage was wavering just a tiny little bit. Peter touched her elbow. "It will be all right, Kathryn. You'll win them over, just as you won over Mrs. Reed."

She bit on her lower lip for a moment, then again brought forth her best smile. "But of course, Mr. Ingalls. What else would you expect from the woman you married?"

———•———

There were about twenty people squeezed into the large and sumptuously furnished parlor of the Reed home. Originally, this whole thing had started in a reading society. During the fall and winter of 1845–46, westward fever began to sweep the country. Newspapers wrote articles about that great unknown that lay west of the Mississippi River. Books were published and became immensely popular. A few months earlier, Mrs. George Donner had persuaded her reading society group to turn their focus to readings about the West. Very quickly the fever had infected most of the group.

But it was no longer just a reading society. The decision had been made. Now it was planning time. Most present came from three families. The rest, like Peter and Kathryn, were the few "bullwhackers" and assistants who had been hired so far. There were even some of the older children present, wide-eyed and a little breathless to think that this was really going to happen. But it was the Donners and the Reeds who were behind it all. George and Jacob Donner were brothers. Jacob, the older of the two, and his wife, Elizabeth, had seven children who would be accompanying them (two of these being Elizabeth's by a previous marriage). George had lost his first two wives and married again to the present Mrs. Donner. He had eleven children in all, but many were married. Only five would be going west. James Reed and his wife, Margret, had four children and Mrs. Keyes, the aged and infirm mother of Mrs. Reed.

As Peter looked around the room, there was no question but what the Donner brothers and James F. Reed were well-to-do men. The Donners were both older men, probably in their sixties, Peter guessed, and had made good as farmers in western Illinois. Reed, considerably younger at forty-five, was probably the richest of the three, having had success in such enterprises as furniture manufacturing and railroad contracting. Even now it staggered Peter to think that these men were not selling all their property to finance their trip. George Donner had been trying to sell one of his farms, but even if that fell through, it wouldn't stop him from going. So if the promise of California proved to be ephemeral, they would still have something to which they could return. That left Peter a little bit dizzy. He had seen the outfits these three families were putting together. Brand-new wagons. The finest of Durham steers, already well proven as draft animals. They would have new tools, ample supplies of food, riding horses, milk cows, beef cows. An average wagon and team, with supplies enough to take one west, cost about seven hundred dollars. But each of these families was taking not one wagon but three, which meant they were easily spending twice or three times that amount; and the fact that they did not need to sell off land in order to do so took Peter's breath away.

This was the first meeting to which Peter and Kathryn had been invited, and they sat quietly in the corner, listening to the discussion, both of them a little cowed by their surroundings and their company. George Donner stood before them, waving a book in the air as though it were a flag and he was using it to call them to battle.

"Listen to this," he cried loudly. "Just listen to this." He opened the book and started thumbing for the place he wanted.

"Tell them what book it is, Mr. Donner," Tamsen Donner told her husband, with a tolerant smile toward the others. "That's important."

He shoved it toward them, spine first, as if they could read the small print from that distance when it was bobbing and dancing like a living thing. "It's called *The Emigrants' Guide to Oregon and California*. The author is Lansford Hastings, one of the few men who have been west and learned the country."

Now, compliance to his wife's request done with, he opened

the book, thumbed a few more pages, then found his place. "He says here that the climate of western California 'is that of perpetual spring.' And over here"—George turned the page over— "he says that since there aren't any marshy regions in California, 'the noxious miasmatic effluvia, so common in such regions, is here, nowhere found.'"

He looked up in triumph, daring anyone to fully comprehend the wonder of that statement.

"Noxious mia what?" Kathryn whispered out of the side of her mouth.

Peter suppressed a grin. "Bad smells that make you sick," he whispered back, nudging her.

She did not answer but seemed suitably impressed.

Donner lowered the book again, too excited to simply read the words. "He says that oats grow to be eight feet tall and that you can get seventy bushels of wheat per acre, a hundred and twenty in some of the richer spots."

One of the drivers let out a low whistle. While the bull-whackers and the other hired help traveling in this company would earn little more than room and board while going west, such people usually had dreams, as this man did, of picking up three or four hundred acres of the free land that was waiting in California. While Peter was no farmer and had other reasons for wanting to go with this party, reasons that would likely be incomprehensible to this group, he did not find it hard to understand the look of astonishment he saw on the faces around him.

"Tell them the part about the fires," Jacob Donner urged his brother.

"Oh, yeah. I read you the part about it being eternally spring there. Well, Hastings says that the only time you ever have to build a fire is when you want to cook your food."

Margret Reed leaned forward. "And he's been there, this Mr. Hastings? That sounds a bit like a fairy tale."

George Donner didn't like that. "Been there? He's lived

there. He's got land there. He's one of the few men who know what California's really like." Again he held up the book as proof positive. Everyone nodded and the doubts were dispelled.

Peter smiled inwardly. As a newspaperman, he well knew the power of words. He also knew that the printed word could carry the testimony of charlatans as easily as it could carry the testimony of saints. Not that he was about to say anything. He was certainly no expert on California.

James Reed now stood up beside Donner. "Thank you, George. You have whetted our appetites and fired our vision. I'm ready to start in the morning whether the wagons are ready or not."

There was a burst of laughter from the group as George Donner sat down. Reed let it die, then plunged in immediately. "Today is the third day of March. Our plan is to leave Springfield about mid-April, just over a month from now. So far, we are the only three families leaving from here. Others may join us on the way."

He let that register and waited for the whispers to end again. "As you know, Independence, Missouri, is the start of the Oregon Trail. That's about three hundred miles from here. That will toughen us and our teams up. At Independence we'll resupply and then, hopefully, join a larger train and accompany them."

"Will there be danger from the Indians?" asked Solomon Elijah, Jacob Donner's teenaged stepson.

Jacob, turning to look at his stepson, spoke up. "Not when we're in a train of fifty to a hundred wagons. None of those savages would dare try to attack us. However"—he looked at Reed—"may I address the group for just a moment?"

"Certainly," said Reed.

Jacob reached under his chair and pulled out a small box, then stood and faced the group. Opening the box, he brought out a strange-looking pistol and held it up, turning it back and forth for all of them to see. "Just in case, I'd recommend you all do what I've done. This is one of them brand-new Sam Colt six-shot revolvers. I think it will come in mighty handy on the trail, for Indians, snakes, or whatever else we may encounter."

Kathryn saw Mrs. Reed shudder and wasn't sure whether it was the mention of the Indians or the snakes or the sight of the pistol that caused it. In her own case, there was no question. Even the very word *snake* made her skin crawl.

"How much?" someone called out.

"Fifty dollars."

Peter shook his head. He had never owned a gun and didn't particularly like them, but he and James Reed had already talked about the need for weapons on the trip. Reed had said he would take care of it. At fifty dollars for a pistol, there was no way Peter would be doing it.

A mood of jubilation filled the room. From her seat beside him, Kathryn looked up at Peter. She had a strange expression on her face.

"What?" he asked softly.

"We really are going to do it, aren't we?"

He laughed softly. "Yes," he answered. "I think we are."

Chapter Notes

William Pitt and his brass band would become a significant part of the trek west. Brigham's wisdom and foresight were such that he knew that keeping up morale on the plains would be very important. Pitt was an English convert, as were most of the band members. William Clayton was a member of the band. It was recorded that on the second night after the Saints' departure from Sugar Creek, 2 March 1846, after they made camp, the band began to play. The Saints enjoyed the music so much that in spite of their weariness after a difficult day, "they lit huge bonfires and sang and danced throughout the whole evening" (*CN*, 9 March 1996, p. 12).

The vast unsettled territories of the western part of the North American continent were much on the minds of Americans by 1846. The Louisiana Purchase of 1803 and its exploration by Lewis and Clark had started this interest. Then, as mountain men and trappers and explorers like John C. Frémont brought back descriptions of rich valleys and vast wilderness, the idea of free land became a powerful draw. In 1845 a New York publisher coined the phrase "manifest destiny." It captured the belief held by most Americans that it was part of the will of Divine Providence that the United States of America should fill the entire continent. In that climate it was no surprise that Lansford Hastings's book *The Emigrants' Guide to Oregon and California,* published in 1845, quickly became a best-selling book across America. The fact that Hastings owned land in California and was a shameless promoter may partly account for the "glowing" description of California. (See Timothy Foote, "1846: The Way We Were—and the Way We Went," *Smithsonian,* April 1996, pp. 45–46.)

Samuel Colt first patented the revolving six-shooter in 1835. Over the years he greatly improved the design. When the federal government ordered thousands of the weapons for their soldiers during the Mexican War of 1846, the Colt would take its place as a significant influence in the opening of the West. (See James Trager, *The People's Chronology: A Year-by-Year Record of Human Events from Prehistory to the Present,* rev. ed. [New York: Henry Holt and Co., 1992], pp. 419, 441.)

It was worse than mud. It was worse even than wet clay. It was more like a blend of clay and bookbinder glue mixed with cement. It stuck to the wheels, buried now almost to their hubs, as though it had been smeared on with a brick mason's trowel. It clung to the feet of the animals in huge globs that left them panting just to walk. For Joshua, it was like one of those nightmares where some horrible danger is bearing down on you and your feet will not respond. His upper thighs were on fire. His knees ached as though they were rheumatic. His ankles were getting mushy. His lungs felt like great bellows that couldn't suck in enough air to feed the fire within. Around him, he could hear the others gasping for air as he was.

"Hit it again," Solomon yelled. "Ready?"

They took their positions again. Joshua and Nathan were at the back wheels. Matthew and Derek were at the front ones. The teenaged children—Josh, Emily, Rachel, Luke and Mark Griffith—ringed the wagon box, getting what grip they could on it.

"Go!" Solomon shouted at the oxen and cracked the long bullwhip over their heads. All nine of them threw their weight against the wagon. Joshua clawed at the spokes, grunting and muttering under his breath. The veins on his forehead stood out like great knots, and he could feel the blood rush to his face. Ahead of him, he could see the two off oxen pawing to get a grip in the miry clay, and he could hear their own grunts as they fought for some kind of movement. The wagon rocked forward maybe five or six inches, the wheels making a great sucking sound, then stopped again.

Joshua's feet suddenly gave way in the slippery mud. With a cry, he went down. His shoulder slammed against the wagon wheel, and his head cracked sharply against the steel-rimmed tire. "Ow!" he yelped, grabbing for his forehead. When he pulled his hand away, the muddy glove had a smear of red on it. He dropped his head, down on all fours now, chest heaving, staring down at the hated mud, and began to swear, softly and steadily.

"Uncle Joshua!" Emily gasped.

Pulled back into awareness, he saw Emily and Rachel, not two feet away, gaping at him in utter disbelief. The two Griffith boys were likewise in shock. It took him a second or two before it registered that they were not looking at his bleeding forehead. They were staring at him, eyes wide, faces flaming.

"Well," he snapped, lifting his arm and pressing the sleeve of his shirt against the wound. "Just close your ears. That hurt."

Nathan stepped around the children, panting as heavily as Joshua. "You all right?"

He wanted to swear again, but bit it off this time. "Oh, yeah," he said sarcastically. "Never been better. And the blood makes a nice contrast to the mud, don't you think?"

Mark Griffith giggled, then went stone sober as Joshua glared at him.

But Nathan was smiling too. "The blood and the mud. Sounds like a title for a good ghost story." That set all of the kids to snickering.

Joshua hauled himself to his feet, brushed at the mud caked on his trouser legs, then stopped when he saw he was only smearing it around. He glowered at his brother. "I'm glad someone is finding some amusement in all this."

Lydia, who had been following behind the wagons, helping her two youngest, came forward enough that she was parallel to Joshua. She took a rag from her apron pocket. "Come over here and let me have a look at you."

He shook his head. Now the whole family was coming up to see what had happened. "It's nothing. I'll be fine."

She put one hand on her hip. "Are you going to make me wade into the mud or are you going to come over here."

He mumbled something, shot Nathan, who was trying to hold back a grin, a dirty look, then hauled himself out of the slough and up to where she waited. She pulled his head down and began to dab at the cut, carefully wiping away the mud Joshua's glove had left there. "You'll have a goose egg, sure enough, but the cut doesn't look too deep." She pressed the rag against it, making him wince. "Here, hold this in place for a minute. My insensitive husband may like the idea of mud and blood, but I don't." She shot Nathan a look, but it was more a look of warning than of condemnation. Couldn't he see when Joshua was in no mood to be funned with?

But if Nathan saw the look, he didn't pay her any mind. He came up and peered at his older brother. "Did it help?"

"What?"

"Swearing."

"Nathan," Joshua growled, his eyebrows narrowing, giving a warning of their own. "I don't need a sermon right now."

"No, no sermon," Nathan said innocently. "I was just wondering. If it did any good, I might be persuaded to become a cussing man."

He said it with such longing and such feeling that it broke the tension. Even Joshua had to laugh. Nathan a cussing man? Now, that would be something. Joshua turned to the older children who had been pushing on the wagon box. "Sorry, kids. I kind of forgot that I'm not out on the trail with a bunch of cigar-smoking teamsters."

"It's all right, Uncle Joshua," Rachel said, recovered now. "Does your head hurt?"

Joshua was strangely hit by a sudden pang of sorrow. Rachel had called him Uncle Joshua as naturally as Emily did. And yet she was his daughter. They—he and Jessica—had long ago determined that that was best, but every now and then it hit him, and it always left him wincing with guilt. Why the thought hit him now he wasn't sure.

He managed a wobbly grin back at her. "My head's fine, but someone better check the wagon wheel."

"I'll say," Derek quipped. "It sounded like steel ringing on steel to me. I heard it from where I was."

Now the whole family laughed merrily. Joshua pulled a face and looked at Lydia. "Why is it that everyone feels like my tragedy gives them the right to make jokes?"

"I don't know," she answered solemnly. She looked at her British brother-in-law. "Derek, I think you need to apologize to Joshua." Then her eyes twinkled. "Right after you check the wheel to see if it is broken."

"See?" Joshua said, looking hurt.

His mother joined them now, coming from the other wagons which were hanging back until Solomon's wagon was through this muddy part of the road. "Are you all right?"

"I'm fine. The bigger question is, how are we going to get this through?"

Solomon grunted. Of the men, he was the only one not still wheezing from their exertions, but only because he had been driving and not pushing. "Maybe we're going to have to unhitch the other teams and bring them up here. It's a sure thing we're not moving it much this way."

Matthew was squatting down, peering under the wagon, sizing up the depths and thickness of the mud. "I say we find us a pole and try to lift it up a little, then try again. Those wheels are what are giving us the problem. They're in too deep."

Nathan straightened, all seriousness again. "Good idea." He half turned. They had crossed a creek a quarter of a mile back. A scattered stand of trees lined its banks. "Solomon. Derek. Get some axes. Let's go cut us a lever."

Forty-five minutes later, they were ready. They were using a two-foot length of old log they had found as the fulcrum and a ten-foot, six-inch-thick length of elm as the lever. Joshua, being the tallest—cut head and aching shoulder now forgotten— grasped the end of the pole. Matthew, Nathan, Derek, and Josh lined up in front of him. Once again the others—women now as well as the older children—waded into the mud and found a place to push. Solomon was once more at the head of his oxen.

Joshua called forward. "Solomon. We'll try to lift it first, then holler at you." Then to those at the wagon, "Don't push until you feel the wagon come up."

Everyone nodded and took their places. Those on the log pole raised their hands, getting a solid grip.

"All right," Joshua said. "Ready? Go!"

As one they yanked down on the log, letting their feet come off the ground to put their full weight into it. For a moment nothing happened; then there was a creak, followed by a deep sucking sound, and the wheels started to rise.

"Go, Solomon!" Nathan and Joshua shouted it together.

Again the whip cracked sharply. "Giddap! Go, boys! Go!"

The animals lunged forward, hitting the yokes hard. Hooves dug in and clawed. On the wagon, the human beasts of burden heaved forward as well, gasping and grunting, feet fighting for a grip.

"Higher!" Nathan bellowed. "It's working."

And it was. Getting the rear wheels four or five inches out of the mud seemed to be the key. The wagon lurched forward. But as it did so, the axle slid off the pole and sunk down again.

"Quick," Joshua yelled. "Get it under there!"

They shoved the log fulcrum forward, reset the pole, then yanked down hard again. There was a loud ripping sound, then a sharp snap. The pole jerked violently downward, throwing all four men off their balance. For one instant, Joshua thought the pole had snapped, but as he caught himself, he saw the back wheels splay outward and the wagon box drop sharply.

Gasping, he went down on one knee, and then groaned at what he saw. It wasn't the pole, it was the rear axle. The thick wooden shaft had cracked like an egg.

As the others bent down to look, Nathan sank down beside him, panting heavily. Joshua looked at him. "Now might be a good time to consider becoming a cussing man," he said softly.

Mary Ann looked around the circle of faces, seeing the firelight flickering in their eyes and across the tightness of their faces. *It's another Steed family council*, she thought, only one unlike anything they had ever held before. This was no comfortable parlor filled with soft lamplight. They sat on logs and stumps or on blankets folded on the ground. And when it was done, there would be no apple pie and cold milk from the icehouse. There would be no sitting on the porch and talking lazily as the children played night games around them. In fact, there were no children present. The babies were asleep. The younger children were getting a bedtime story or saying their prayers. The older ones were serving as parents while the adults met together and tried to determine how to deal with their crisis.

She could not remember a family council where the problem before them had left the family more grim than what she could see now. They were exhausted. They were terribly discouraged. It was not a good combination. It had been a day where even the strongest had expended the last of their strength and where even the weakest had been required to give all that they had. But there would be no rest until decisions were made. This was not something that could wait until a better day, or be set aside for some future discussion.

After the axle had broken, which was around noon, they had unhitched Nathan's pair of oxen and brought them up to join Solomon's two pair to see if they could drag the crippled vehicle off the road and out of the way of those coming behind. That was not enough either. Finally, two additional yoke were borrowed from a man who came up to see what was happening. He was a brother from Yelrome and recognized Joshua and Nathan as being part of the rescue party that had brought their families to Nauvoo after the burning of the Morley Settlement. Five yoke of oxen—ten animals—and even then they barely managed to get the wagon free.

They unloaded Solomon's wagon and crammed the supplies into the other wagons; then Derek and Matthew took the family on to make camp. The only encouraging thing for the day was that Brigham Young's party had finally caught up with the advance scouting party and the President had called an early halt to the day's march. It had been a punishing day on equipment, animals, and men, and many more besides the Steeds were stranded along the road. That was good news for the Steeds, for the camp was no more than a mile and a half from the broken wagon.

Nathan, Solomon, and Joshua stayed behind and went to work. They removed the rear wheels, put two small logs beneath the back of the wagon to serve as skids, and dragged it back to camp using Solomon's oxen. Once that was done, Derek and Matthew rode back to the stand of timber and hewed down a foot-thick hickory tree. Tomorrow they would spend the day hewing out another axle and shaping it so it could take the wheels. That would, they hoped, solve the immediate problem. But they had a greater problem to solve now. They simply did not have sufficient animal power to pull in this kind of terrain.

Mary Ann tipped her head back, feeling the weariness in her own body, the kind that goes so deep that it feels as if it were something received at birth. Above, the sky was clear. Ah, she thought. Now, there was something to lift the soul. The stars seemed like they were laid on a fabric of black silk that was so close that if she chose to she could reach up and pluck one for each of the children. She smiled sadly to herself at that thought. There probably wasn't much beside that—a star straight from heaven—that could lighten their mood right now.

"We've got to have more oxen," Solomon Garrett declared. "Especially for that big wagon. Two yoke are just not enough to pull that much weight."

There was no response. There was no need for one. Everyone knew what the problem was. Originally there had been three yoke of oxen for Solomon's wagon and two yoke for Nathan's wagon. Then had come that terrible day when the man had spit tobacco juice into the eyes of one of Nathan's animals while they were ferrying across the river. Thankfully, there had not been room enough on the ferry for Nathan to keep his two yoke attached to his wagon. They had sent one across on the other ferry with Solomon's rig. Had it not been so, instead of two oxen going over the side into the river, there would have been four.

Mary Ann shook her head quickly, pushing away the memories. Oxen had not been the only thing lost that day.

Then Joshua said what they all were thinking. "What? Do you think we can walk to the nearest livery stable and pick up an extra span or two?"

No wonder they looked so grim. Solomon was right and Joshua was right, and the two truths were totally incompatible. They desperately needed oxen and there were no oxen to be had. The silence stretched on as they considered how few were their options. Finally, Nathan raised his head. "We've got to trade the horses."

Derek nodded. His wagon, the lightest of the three, was pulled by the draft horses. They were fine animals but no match for the solid pulling power of a pair of oxen. Much more expensive than oxen, they were faster by half again, but they did not adjust well to the dry prairie grass as the oxen did. There would be no new grass for another few weeks, maybe longer, and without that, the horses would languish. Horses also needed grain to keep up their strength. And grain was something in desperately short supply, even for the humans.

"What about the mules?" Matthew asked. His team was a strong set of nearly black mules bought a few months before from a breeder in Missouri. More ill-tempered than the horses, they were nevertheless a better choice. They were better able to adapt to poor water, especially alkali water, and had better endurance. But they still did not have that steady, day-in-and-day-out strength and endurance of the oxen.

Nathan turned to Joshua. He was the expert. He had driven wagons behind about every combination of teams through his freighting years. Joshua looked around the circle, then shook his head. "If we had a choice, yes, no question about it. I'd get two span of oxen for each wagon, three for the big one, four if we could get them. In our wildest dreams, it would be wonderful to have a spare yoke or two. And under normal circumstances, we could make that trade and come out to the good, maybe buy some more wheat or sugar."

They had all become experts in animal power. Before all this started, Mary Ann might not have understood a word of what Joshua was saying. But now they all knew the relative value of various draft animals. A good workhorse could go for as much as two hundred dollars. Mules went for fifty to ninety dollars a head, less than half of what a horse cost. But one could buy a yoke of oxen, meaning a pair that worked together well, for fifty to sixty-five dollars. That lesser cost, plus the fact that oxen were the proven animal for a long haul across the Great Plains, had quickly exhausted the market for them. That's why the Steeds had one team of horses and one team of mules. It was not a matter of choice. And the loss of that yoke at the river had been a serious blow.

"I'm not talking about going back to Nauvoo," Nathan said. "I don't think there's much hope there. I'm talking about maybe going to some of the local settlements."

Joshua gave a low hoot. "You'll pay top dollar, even if you are lucky enough to find oxen out here. These people know how desperate we are."

"We've got a thousand miles of country to cross," Nathan answered quietly. "We've at least got to try."

Joshua shrugged. He wasn't trying to be negative and Nathan was right. But he knew that it was such a long shot that there was not even sense in getting one's hopes up.

Now Derek spoke. "It's more likely some of these farmers out here would have horses. Even if we could find another team of mules, maybe we could make do. We'll—"

Joshua blew out his breath. "Mules hate water. They'll give you fits every time you have to ford a stream deeper than a foot or two. And turn your back on them for one second, they're gone back to Missouri."

Nathan straightened and rubbed his eyes. "We may have to go through some of our stuff, see what we can spare to trade. Probably some of the furniture. That can be pretty scarce out here on the prairie."

Jessica responded immediately. "I've got that drop-leaf table Solomon bought me."

Jenny looked at Matthew, sudden tears in her eyes. "And I've got the cedar chest Matthew made me when Betsy Jo was born. We can put the linens that are in it in a sack."

One by one they enumerated things that could be spared. These were not things that were surplus, Mary Ann noted sadly, or at least they hadn't thought so even as late as this morning. Now . . .

When they were done, Nathan nodded. "That should give us a start. I'd like to suggest that Matthew, Derek, and Solomon stay here and help fix the wagon. That's not going to be an easy job. I'll take one wagon and the animals and see what I can do.

Joshua, what if you took the saddle horse and rode south to see if you might purchase some grain with what little cash we have."

"Fine."

"How far back will you go, Nathan?" Matthew asked.

"Only as far as I have to."

Matthew nodded. "I saw Brigham just before supper. He's going to stay here for another day. Bishop Miller's found some good places to camp, but we weren't the only ones with problems today. There are at least three other broken axles, two broken wagon tongues, several collapsed wheels. He'll take another day to give time to fix the wagons."

"Good," Nathan said, pleased at that news. "That means I won't get too far behind you."

"You're not going as far as to Nauvoo, are you?" Joshua asked.

Nathan had already thought that whole thing through, but he hadn't come to any conclusion. And he wasn't ready to discuss it with Joshua yet. "I hope not," he finally answered. And in one sense that was true. They were now a good two-day trip— four, if you counted both ways—from Nauvoo on these roads. And the family would have to wait for his return because he'd have four of the draft animals with him.

Joshua stared moodily into the fire, thinking of Caroline and the children, debating about whether he might go back too. "Nauvoo's no answer. You know that every family there is scrambling for wagons and teams and supplies. You're better off to try the Iowa settlements—Farmington and the likes. Stay along the Des Moines River. There'll be more people." He thought for a moment. "Or maybe I ought to take the horses and mules south with me."

Now it was Nathan who hooted. "Into Missouri? Wouldn't they love to get their hands on some Mormon horseflesh."

"I'm not a Mormon," Joshua grunted irritably. "I can handle them."

"You're traveling with Mormons," Nathan retorted. "They won't even stop to ask. No, the animals go with me."

Mary Ann stood suddenly. "Then it's settled," she said. There was a moment of silence; then all nodded. Her eyes softened and she smiled at them now. "I would like to have a family prayer. I think we need to ask for the Lord's help."

"Yes, Mama," Rebecca said fervently. "We could certainly use that."

"How are *you* doing, Lydia?"

She was on her side, her swollen stomach cradled by a pillow. With a soft grunt, she rolled partially onto her back and looked at her husband. Not that she could see much. The inside of the tent was nearly pitch-black. "I'm fine."

"Really?"

"Yes, really."

"Maybe it's better if I don't go tomorrow and—"

"Nathan, I'm fine. I'm not just being brave and noble. Sure, I get tired, but I'm feeling good. And the children are wonderful."

"I know. It pleases me to see how Emily watches out for you."

"And Josh too."

"Oh, I know, but he's always been responsible."

"He's learned it from you."

He groped for her hand in the darkness, brought it up to his lips, and kissed it softly. "You're sure?"

"Yes. It's better that you go now than to have you do it later when my time is closer."

He sighed. "You're probably right."

"We'll be fine."

He turned onto his side so he was facing her, still holding her hand against his face. "Lydia?"

"Yes?"

"I think I may go to Nauvoo."

Her head came up slightly. "But you told Joshua that you didn't think you were."

"I know." He began to use her finger to trace patterns on his cheek, barely aware of what he was doing. "The other night, when I was talking to Mother out by the fire, she said something that I can't get out of my mind."

"What?"

Speaking softly so as not to awaken the children, he told her quickly about the dream and his mother's final admonition to him. "She was quite forceful about it, Lydia. She said that we had to get Caroline and the children to join us. She made me promise to do something about it."

For several long seconds his wife said nothing, but he could feel her mind weighing that. "You're not thinking of going to Nauvoo and just bringing her back, are you? Not without telling Joshua."

He frowned into the darkness, not sure what he was thinking.

"Nathan!" Her voice was urgent and low. "He'd be absolutely furious."

"Maybe." That was way too optimistic, he thought, so he amended it a little. "Yeah, he would be. At first. But then, I wonder if he wouldn't be glad. He's worried about them, you can see that. Maybe in the long run he'd thank me."

"Maybe. I watched him tonight when you were talking about it. But . . ." The idea that Nathan had just dropped on her was enormous in its potential hazards.

"Nauvoo is not a safe place, Lydia. We both know that. Oh, I don't think they are in imminent danger, but there's still trouble brewing, and it won't be over until every faithful Latter-day Saint has left."

"Faithful Latter-day Saint?" Lydia repeated softly.

Nathan's frown deepened. "Yes, I know. Mother wants Carl and Melissa to come too, but I don't have much hope there. But Melissa isn't alone with no husband to watch out for her."

"Carl promised to watch out for Caroline and the children. He'll be good in that way."

"Yes, he will. But he's not her husband. And Caroline doesn't want to stay. She wants to be here with Joshua, you know that. So does Savannah." He half chuckled in the darkness. "I'm a little surprised that we haven't found her stowed away in some of the baggage by now."

Again Lydia was silent for a considerable time. Then, "You really are serious about this?"

He blew out his breath in exasperation. "I don't know. I won't be surprised if I have to go all the way back to find something to trade for. And if so, then of course I'll stop by and see her. Carl and Melissa too."

There was no answer. So after a minute, he let go of her hand and went up on one elbow. "You don't think it's a good idea, do you?"

"I . . . I'm not sure, Nathan. You know how happy I'd be to have Caroline here. How happy she would be. But Joshua? It could really be bad. You know that, don't you?"

"I do. But darn it all, why is he being so stubborn? I think he's made up his mind that once we find a place in the West and get settled, he'll bring his family out. So why won't he just give in now?"

He stopped again, coming back to a major reason behind all this. "And I promised Mother I'd do something."

"Have you told her what you're thinking?"

"No." He hadn't dared express his thoughts out loud, even to himself, until now.

He could hear her breathing evenly in the darkness and could feel her mulling it all over in her mind. Finally she turned her head to face him. "You know that I trust your judgment, Nathan." It was a simple statement, not a question.

"Yes. And you know that I trust yours. That's why I wanted to talk to you about it."

"Have you prayed about it?"

"I've been praying about it since Mother told me her dream. Then when everything happened today, I thought, maybe this is the answer."

"And maybe it is."

"But you're not sure?"

"No. And neither are you."

"I know," he answered glumly.

"Why don't you talk to Brother Brigham?" she said on sudden impulse. "You said you wanted to go by anyway and tell him that we would be laying back until we can get the wagon fixed and team situation solved."

There was instant relief at that suggestion. "Yes. That's a good idea. He knows the situation well enough to give good counsel."

"He does."

"Thank you, my love." He felt the tension easing out of him just that quickly. "Maybe now I can get some sleep."

She laid her hand on his chest, smiling softly at him in the darkness. "It's hard being Benjamin, isn't it?"

Chapter Notes

During the first week of March the weather over Iowa mellowed considerably. It was a blessing in one way, but many of the primitive roads the Saints were following quickly turned into a morass of nearly impassable mud. On the afternoon of the third of March, after several wagons were broken, Brigham Young called a halt to the camp for a time of rest and repairs. They laid over for the fourth as well. The first wagons had left the city on the fourth of February. It had been one full month now, and they were still less than thirty miles from Nauvoo. (See *CN*, 9 March 1996, p. 12.)

If this isn't a good time, Brother Brigham," Nathan started, watching the President of the Quorum of the Twelve as he peered into the small mirror hung from a tree branch and finished shaving, "I could—"

"No, no, Nathan." He got the last vestige of shaving soap off, reached for a towel, and scrubbed at his face. "In fact, with us laying over here today, this is a good time. Better than most."

Nathan looked around as the Apostle wiped the straight razor and put it back in its case. Brigham's camp was laid out with his fifteen wagons forming a rough square. In his group alone there were nearly three dozen people, more than the Steeds had with all of their families. Nathan wasn't sure how many wives Brigham had now—he had never felt it proper to ask. Rumor said as many as twelve, some said nine, others many more. Some of those women, such as Lucy Ann Decker, Nathan knew for certain had been taken as a direct result of Joseph's commandment to the Twelve to live the principle of plural marriage. More recently, some had been taken as wives because they were women who had lost their husbands through death or divorce or abandonment and had no way of going west. So Brigham had married them and taken them in, and in some cases their children too, and made them part of his own family.

Though it was a large camp that Brigham kept, it was neat and well organized. Many campsites were strewn with bedding or clothing or other personal belongings. Some cooked a meal and then, too tired to walk to the nearest stream, would pack their pans and kettles back in the wagons with only a cursory scraping. Not Brigham, even though he had a far better excuse for neglecting personal things than most.

As if to verify Nathan's thoughts, Brigham picked up his razor, the razor strap, the towel, and his hairbrush and walked over to the nearest wagon. He slipped them into a box, laying the towel across the top so it could dry out. He said something to someone inside the wagon, then came back over to Nathan. "All right. How about we walk? If we stay here . . ." There was a sudden wry grin. "Let's just say there sure are a lot of people who want Brother Brigham to solve their problems." His voice became mimicking. " 'There's not enough grease in the grease bucket.' 'The bacon is rancid.' 'Brother Brigham, so-and-so borrowed my hammer and now they won't give it back.' " He took Nathan's arm and steered him away from the wagons. "Sometimes I feel more like *Mother* Brigham than Brother Brigham."

Nathan started to chuckle, but then instantly sobered. "And here I am bringing you another problem."

Brigham looked startled for a minute, then laughed heartily. "I wasn't thinking about you, Nathan. And I didn't mean to complain. We've got a lot of good families, like your own, that are taking care of themselves. They're just out there being faithful and dependable. But we've also got a whole lot of people who somehow think that it's the responsibility of the Twelve to lace their boots and sugar their mush and tuck them into bed every night."

Seeing that he wasn't helping Nathan's mood, he clapped him on the shoulder. "Tell you what. If I think you're bothering me with something frivolous, I'll turn right around and send you back to your wagon. Fair enough?"

"Fair enough." Nathan took a breath and plunged in. He didn't have to say much about Joshua because Brigham knew the whole situation well. He had even talked to Joshua personally about going west some months before. It had done no good, but the President had been pretty direct with him. So Nathan mentioned only briefly the circumstances he was facing now, beginning with his mother's dream. From there he moved to his conversation with Lydia the night before.

They were now some three or four hundred yards out away from the wagons on a slight knoll that gave them a clear view of the camp below them. Brigham tested a patch of grass with the toe of his boot to see if it was wet; then, satisfied, he sat down, motioning for Nathan to do the same. Once settled, Brigham folded his arms across his knees and rested his chin upon them.

Brigham Young was nearly forty-five years old now. Unlike some others in the Quorum, Brigham was still clean shaven. That and the fact that he wore his hair to his collar and that it naturally turned under in what women called a bob made him look younger than he was. But Nathan could tell the responsibility of being "Mother Brigham" was wearing on him. As President of the Quorum of the Twelve, he had led the Church for almost two years. Nathan thought he could see some deepening lines that were probably the direct result of that.

Brigham's face had filled out some over the years, and there was the first hint of gray in his reddish brown hair, but the blue-gray eyes were not dimmed in any way. They gazed out now on the sprawling camp before them, alert, thoughtful, perceptive. When Nathan finished and sat back, the Apostle finally turned and looked directly at him. "So you're asking me if I think you ought to fetch Caroline and the children without Joshua knowing beforehand?"

"Yeah, I suppose," Nathan answered, a little lamely. "I'm really torn on this one. I feel so strongly that Caroline and the children need to be out here with us—with him."

"I couldn't agree more on that point."

"We've tried everything to convince Joshua of that, but . . ." He shrugged. "Well, you know Joshua."

"Yes, I do know Joshua. And so do you. And I suspect that's one of the reasons why you're not sure this is a wise thing to do."

Looking away, frustrated and confused, Nathan nodded.

"He might eventually accept it and thank you for it. Or it could do some pretty serious damage."

Nathan nodded glumly. That was what was giving him fits in this whole thing.

Brigham's head came up. "But there's a great principle here, isn't there?"

"Are you talking about agency?"

"Well, yes, that too. A man's family is his own stewardship—" A wry smile flashed suddenly. "And we need to be careful about minding another person's stewardship. But it really wasn't agency I was thinking about. I was thinking more along the lines of faith."

Nathan caught himself. "Faith?"

"Yes, faith. Did you happen to be in the meeting last December where I read to the people a letter from Elder Orson Pratt? It was his farewell letter to the Saints in the East, including those that would be taking sail on the *Brooklyn*."

"I guess not."

"Well, Brother Orson was exhorting them to come west and join with us—or take the ship around the horn of South America. And he said something like this: 'Do not be fainthearted or slothful, but be diligent and courageous. Be prayerful and faithful and you can accomplish almost anything that you undertake. What great and good work can we not do if we have faith and ambition?' "

Brigham's eyes were pensive now as he tried to recall the

exact words. " 'We can do almost anything, for our Father in heaven will strengthen us if we are strong. He will work according to our faith. If we say we cannot go west, God will not help us. But if we say, in the name of the Lord, that we will go, and set ourselves to do it, then we will go and he will help us.' "

Nathan was nodding vigorously. "Exactly. If Joshua had even a touch of faith, there wouldn't be any problem. And that is really troubling to me. He's seen so much. He should be dead, but he was blessed by the priesthood and survived a terrible wound. He was there when Joseph blessed Pa and saved him from dying. On that same day, he went across the river and watched Joseph raise Elijah Fordham from his deathbed."

"I know," Brigham said quietly. "I was there that day too, remember?"

"Yes, that's right. So why can't Joshua believe? He's a good man, President. You know that, but he's just so darn stubborn."

There was an enigmatic smile now on the senior Apostle's face. "Actually, Nathan, when I referred to faith, I wasn't thinking about Joshua's faith—or lack of it."

Nathan blinked in surprise. "Oh?" And then he saw Brigham's expression. Nathan's eyes suddenly widened. "You're talking about *my* faith?"

"Or lack of it," Brigham answered gently.

"But . . ." He sat back, completely astonished.

"Nathan, you said you came to me for counsel."

"Yes, I did. I—"

"Do you remember what Joseph always used to say? When he was asked how he governed his people, he said, 'I teach them correct principles, and they govern themselves.' "

"Yes, I remember that."

The wry smile that made Brigham seem suddenly more like a young boy broke out again. "Actually, I've thought that what Joseph might have said was, 'We teach them correct principles, and we teach them correct principles, and we teach them correct principles, and *then* they govern themselves.' "

Nathan laughed aloud at that. How true that was!

"Be that as it may. Rather than counseling you, Nathan, let me teach you a principle or two, and then you can decide for yourself what is best."

"Yes, sir," he said meekly, still too dumbfounded by Brigham's accusation to do anything but listen.

"I wish I had thought to bring my scriptures," Brigham went on, "but I'll give you one reference as best I can. It comes from the Doctrine and Covenants. It's one that has taken on special meaning for me in these last few weeks."

"All right."

"This was a revelation given back in eighteen thirty-four, I believe. You remember back then, Nathan? We were still building the temple in Kirtland. We had hundreds of people coming to Kirtland with nothing but what they carried. They expected the Church to help them. We had no money. No resources. And yet there we were, building this massive building to our God."

"Yes, I remember it well."

"Well, near the end of this revelation the Lord said a remarkable thing. Joseph and the Church were deeply in debt at that time, so the Lord started out by saying, 'It is my will that you should pay your debts.' When you think about it, that alone is a little strange. This is God, remember, and it was his house that we were building. He could have simply said, 'Don't worry about paying back those worldly men who have given you money. All things are mine anyway, so forget about paying it back.' But he did not. He said that it was his will that Joseph pay off his debts. Then what follows is very profound. I've thought about it over and over."

Nathan, curious now, was trying to remember. He knew the revelation to which Brigham was referring, but he couldn't recall what came next.

"The Lord says, 'It is my will that you humble yourselves, and obtain this blessing'—and by that I assume he means the blessing of getting out of debt—'and obtain this blessing by . . .'"

Brigham stopped and looked directly at Nathan for a moment. "Think about that for a minute. Joseph and the Church are deeply in debt and the Lord says that he can obtain the blessing of being freed from that debt by something. What would you expect to come next?"

Nathan's brow wrinkled. "I'm not sure."

"Well, if you came to me and told me you were in debt, how would you expect that I would counsel you?"

"Well, the usual ways, I suppose. Work harder. Be more frugal."

"That's exactly right. There are only two ways out of debt, or so you would think. One is to increase your income. The other is to reduce your outgo."

"Yes, that's about it."

"But that's the point, Nathan. Those are not the only solutions. Listen. This is what the Lord says. He doesn't tell Joseph to work harder or to be more careful with money. He says, 'It is my will that you humble yourselves, and obtain this blessing by'"—Brigham held up his hand and began to tick the items off on his fingers—"'by your humility and diligence and the prayer of faith.' Note that. Three things. Humility. Diligence. Prayer of faith."

"I understand."

"No, you don't understand, Nathan. And neither did I. The great lesson is in what comes next. 'And inasmuch as you are diligent and humble, and exercise the prayer of faith, I will soften the hearts of those to whom you are in debt, until I shall send means unto you for your deliverance.'"

He stopped, watching Nathan closely to see how the words were registering.

Nathan did not notice his gaze. The words hit him in a way they had never done when he had read those words before. "So there is another way."

"Yes!" Brigham was exuberant now. "And we have to be very careful that we don't assume that our ways are the only ways to solve a problem. What the Lord is suggesting is a whole different dimension, Nathan. In many ways you're like me, Nathan. Independent. Ambitious. Determined not to be a burden on others. So when you face a problem, what do you do?"

"I look for a solution."

"Right. You try everything you know how to do to work it through. And that is good. I believe the Lord expects that of us. I think that's what he means by diligence."

"But—"

"But that's not all. He listed three things, remember. Diligence. Humility. The prayer of faith. So in addition to our diligence, if we turn to the Lord in humility and ask for his help in faith, then we have brought him into the process. We are getting his help in solving the challenge." He waved a hand in frustration. "I wish I had the actual scripture so I could read it to you, but this is how he concludes the passage. 'And if ye are humble and faithful and call upon my name, *I will give you the victory*.'"

Nathan was nodding ever so slowly, his mind racing, beginning to glimpse why his question about Joshua had brought this scripture to Brigham Young's mind. Finally, he turned. "And you think that's my problem?"

"Yes." It was said with great love and tenderness. "You have been diligent, Nathan. But you've forgotten to bring the Lord into this." He held up his hand quickly. "Oh, I know you've been praying, but you've only been praying to know if *your* solution is acceptable to the Lord. Don't seek to counsel God, Nathan. He knows what to do. He knows how to work his work."

"But—" And then he bit it off. There were no buts. That was exactly what he had been doing. He had worked out a solution and now wanted the Lord to ratify it. Or to have Brigham ratify it for the Lord. He felt deep shame wash over him. "I think I understand."

Brigham got to his feet. For a moment, he gazed down on the camp, lost in his own thoughts. Finally, he turned and looked down at Nathan. "It's a lesson I'm learning anew every day,

Nathan. It's so easy to get caught up in the work—His work, mind you!—and yet forget that it is He who best knows how to work that work." He was peering deep into Nathan's eyes now. "And that's true of Joshua too, Nathan. God is pleased that you are so deeply concerned about helping him. But it is the Lord who knows best how to help him. So what you need to do is have more faith in the Lord."

His face softened as he saw the pain on the younger man's face. "You need to know, Nathan, lest you be too hard on yourself, there are not many men I know who are faithful enough to be told that what they lack is faith." He laughed without humor. "Sounds like a contradiction, doesn't it? But you think about it. If you weren't a man filled with faith, I would never have dared tell you that what you need is more faith." He raised an arm in farewell. "Good luck."

———◆———

They were just finishing breakfast when Nathan came back to where his family was camped. Lydia saw him first and straightened slowly, her eyes following him as he approached. He smiled at her but said nothing.

Then Joshua saw that something had caught Lydia's attention and turned. "Well, well, little brother, we about gave you up for lost."

"Sorry. I didn't think it would take me this long."

"Couldn't you find Brother Brigham?" Mary Ann asked.

"Oh no, I found him. I just . . ." He brushed it aside. "It just took longer than I thought."

"There's still some breakfast left," Lydia said, jumping in to help him fend off further questions. "You didn't eat at Brigham's camp, did you?"

"No." He moved over and squatted down by the fire, holding out his hands toward the flames. It was going to be another clear, sunny day, but right now, with the sun not yet up, the air temperature was still near freezing.

Lydia moved to a small kettle nestled in the coals and lifted the lid off with a pair of tongs. As she finished spooning some porridge into a bowl, Rebecca brought a crock of milk, uncorked it, and came over to stand beside Lydia, taking care that her skirts did not swirl too close to the coals. She added it to the bowl, then Lydia spooned in some sugar and handed it to Nathan.

"So," Joshua said after a minute of watching his brother eat, "where are you going to start first?"

The spoon hung in midair for a moment, then Nathan took the bite, barely tasting it. "Well, actually," he finally said, "that's one of the reasons I'm so late. I stopped for a time to think through this whole thing."

Derek moved over to squat down beside Nathan. "What whole thing?"

"Trading the horses and mules. Sending Joshua off for flour."

"Oh?" Joshua said, surprised but a little wary too. He had thought Nathan's early-morning disappearance a little strange. Lydia's explanation that he had gone to tell Brigham of their plans had worked for a time. After all, besides being the chief Apostle and leader of the Church, he was the head of the wagon train. But it didn't take an hour to tell a man that your wagon axle was busted and you were going to have to lay back for a few days.

Now Solomon and Matthew moved closer. All work on cleaning up breakfast stopped as the women turned to listen too.

"First of all," said Nathan, "I'm not sure that we have to make fixing the axle such a high urgency. Until we get back with the oxen, we're not going anywhere, and that could be several days."

"*If* you come back with oxen," Joshua started. Then his head came up. "Wait a minute. You said, until *we* get back with the oxen."

"Yes, I did." He took one last bite of the mush and set the bowl aside. "I think you and Derek and me all ought to go. Matthew and Solomon can stay and work on making us an axle."

That surprised them all. "But what about trying to buy some more flour?" Derek asked.

"We can do that on the way too."

"What brought on this sudden change of plans?" Joshua asked, half-puzzled, half-suspicious.

Nathan took a quick breath, then decided there was no use postponing it. Besides that, there was the issue of faith. "I want to go back to Nauvoo and get Caroline and the children," he said slowly.

Mary Ann gasped. Rebecca's hand flew to her mouth. Jessica, in the act of turning to see what her youngest child was up to, froze and turned back slowly. Lydia's eyes widened, but she was not staring at Nathan, she was staring at Joshua.

The silence stretched on for several seconds. Every eye was on Joshua now. Even the children, playing around the wagons, sensed something significant was happening and stopped to watch.

"Just like that," Joshua said flatly, not making it a question.

"No," Nathan responded, "not just like that. I have thought about it a lot. And not just this morning. A good part of last night." He glanced at Mary Ann. "Mother and I have talked about it." Which was mostly true. His mother had no idea he was going to come back and drop this rock in the middle of the pond, but they had talked about the general subject.

Joshua's head turned very slowly.

"That's true," Mary Ann said firmly. "Caroline needs to be here with you, Joshua. Your children need to be here with you. I told Nathan I wanted him to do everything in his power to make that happen."

"I see." His voice was emotionless, and therefore all the more filled with tension. "And do I get any say in the matter?"

"I'm asking you right now," Nathan answered. "You get all the say in the matter."

"And if I say no?"

Nathan didn't flinch from that one. His eyes caught Joshua's and held them. "Then I want you to go back to Nauvoo and stay with your family. We were wrong to have you leave them. It's not going to be safe in Nauvoo and—"

"They're safe!" Joshua cut in sharply. "Don't be pulling the boogeyman stuff on me, Nathan. I'm not one of your children. Caroline is fine."

"She is now. And maybe she will be until you get back. But what if you're gone a year, Joshua? Are you willing to bet that things will stay calm for a full year?" He didn't wait for him to answer. "If anyone knows what hatred can do, it's you Joshua. It nearly killed Caroline once. It took Olivia. You lost a barn and a stable full of horses. You were financially ruined. You think that's all over now?"

"Now that the Mormons are leaving, yes."

Nathan rubbed his hands on his trouser legs, not sure how blunt he dared to be. "Your wife is a Mormon, Joshua," he finally said in a low voice. "So is Savannah."

Now the quiet was utter and complete. Joshua's eyes were dark and moody, and Nathan could see the first real anger starting to stir in them. He sat back, ready for what was coming.

"So Brother Brigham put you up to this?" Joshua finally sneered. "Is that what you were doing? Out there talking about how to save poor Caroline from her gentile husband?"

"No, actually, I went to tell Brigham that I was going to get your family without your knowing it. I was just going to get them and bring them here, and then let you deal with it."

"*What!*"

Nathan looked up at Lydia. "Is that true?"

She answered to Joshua. "That's what he was talking about doing last night."

"Brigham said he thought it was a mistake. And I knew he was right. So, I'm here asking. Please, Joshua. You know it's right. You said once we get out west, you'd get them and take them there too. So why wait? Let's get them now."

"And if I say no?" Joshua asked again, his voice dangerously low.

Nathan dropped his eyes. "I can't tell you what to do about your family, Joshua, but the family has appointed me captain of our little company. And I'm telling you, it's my decision that you need to be with your family. If they're not with us, then I'm asking you to go back and stay with them."

Joshua looked from one face to another. One by one they each nodded. When he looked at his mother, she was near tears. "Oh, Joshua, I know you are doing this for me, and I love you for it. But Nathan is right. It was a mistake to leave Caroline and the children alone."

His lips tightened into a hard line. "Then maybe I *will* go back."

"We don't want you to go back," Lydia cried. "Don't you understand? We want you here with us. But we want Caroline and Savannah and Charles and little Livvy. They belong here too, Joshua. That's what we're saying."

He stood now, his hands balled tightly. "You don't think I worry about them? You don't think I want to be with them?"

"Of course we do. So let's go get them," Nathan said. "Let's just go get them and bring them back with us."

He whirled, throwing up his hands. "With what, Nathan? You and your grand ideas. Did you ask yourself that question? With what? Just how am I supposed to bring them back here? I don't have a wagon. I don't have any supplies." He waved an arm angrily toward where the stock were grazing. "You don't even have what *you* need for teams. What am I supposed to do? Tie my family on the back of a mule and come on, all full of faith and singing hymns?"

Nathan jerked a little at the reference to faith, then a smile stole slowly across his face. "You sing the hymns, and leave the faith to me."

Joshua muttered something under his breath and started to stalk away. "I don't need your little jokes, Nathan."

"I wasn't joking," Nathan said evenly.

Joshua stopped and after a moment turned back around. "And what's that supposed to mean?"

"Are you saying that's the only reason you won't bring your family out here? that if you had a wagon and oxen and sufficient supplies you'd do it?"

"Well . . ." Joshua was obviously thrown on the defensive with that question.

"Well, nothing. Is that what you're saying or not?"

"That's a concern, of course. Yes, it's the major concern, but—"

Nathan cut him off, knowing he had him now. "Tell you what," he said, feeling his heart suddenly racing at what he was about to propose. "We'll go back—you and me and Derek. We'll take the mules and the horses and see what we can do in trade. If the Lord wants Caroline and your children out here, then he's just going to have to help us. But if he does . . ."

Joshua was shaking his head. Matthew jumped in eagerly. "Last night you said you didn't think we had any hope of trading our mules and Derek's team for any oxen."

"I don't."

"What if you're wrong?"

Joshua's shoulders lifted and fell. He was clearly uncomfortable with the turn the conversation had suddenly taken.

"If you're wrong," Matthew bore in, "will you promise to bring Caroline out and join us?"

Before Joshua could answer that, Nathan moved toward his elder brother. He stopped directly in front of him. "No. No promises, Joshua. You don't have to agree to do anything but come along and see what the Lord does for us. If you do that, I'll not say another word, no matter what you decide. All right?"

"Even if I want to come back here without my family?"

"No conditions. I'll not say anything more."

"Now, that would be a refreshing change," he growled.

"Does that mean you'll go?" Nathan asked, holding his breath for a moment.

Joshua's head lowered for a moment, then he nodded. "All right. We'll go and see what happens."

Mary Ann stood now and moved to her two sons as well. She said nothing, just took both their hands and squeezed them tightly.

Finally Joshua put his arm around his mother, turning away from Nathan. "Mother, did I ever tell you that this boy you raised can be the most irritating, the most exasperating, the most frustrating, knot-headed, mule-stubborn man in all of North America?"

Mary Ann smiled sweetly up at him. "Are you talking about you or Nathan?" Then, before he could answer, she took his hand. "Come on. I'll help you get ready and you can tell me all about it."

The man walked slowly around the two mules, eyeing them up and down carefully, reaching out from time to time to run his hand over their shoulders or down their withers. He stepped back about five feet and looked at them again, chewing thoughtfully on the wad of tobacco he had stuffed in one cheek. He turned and spat a brown stream into the mud of his front yard. "I judge they'd be all right," he said to Nathan.

There was a rush of relief. *Finally!* "Good. Then it's a trade?" Nathan turned toward the corral where four oxen stood munching on a pile of meadow hay, and he felt a little burst of exultation. Now Joshua would have no choice but to see that the Lord was in this. This was only their second stop.

"Yep! My two yoke of oxen for your two mules and your two Belgians."

"What?" Derek yelped. "We're talking only the mules for the oxen. That's—"

Joshua laid a hand on Derek's arm. "Mr. Jackson, one good mule, which these are, sells for more than a yoke of oxen. With two mules for your four oxen, I figure you're coming out about seventy-five dollars to the good."

The man spat again, this time not bothering to turn his head. "Well," he drawled, "me and the missus, we're maybe thinking of going west next season. Hear that land out in California is free for the taking and so rich you can plow it with your bare foot." His eyes narrowed. "Not like this cursed prairie sod. So I wasn't really fixin' to sell my oxen. I'd have to get a real good trade to change my mind."

"But the Belgians alone are worth four hundred dollars," Nathan protested. "I could buy eight span of oxen for that."

"Not out here, you can't." And he spat again.

———— ◆ ————

As they rode away from their sixth homestead three hours later, Nathan kept his eyes down. He didn't want to meet Joshua's arched eyebrows or his I-told-you-so look. They had finally traded off Jenny's oak chest to the wife of the man with a cheek full of tobacco and came away with three sacks of wheat and some cornmeal. Beyond that, there had been nothing. This last one had been a Missourian from Jackson County, come north to Iowa Territory to get his own spread. Though he had a fine pair of oxen, he asked only one question. "You all Mormons?" When they nodded, his face twisted with hate. "Then git off my land."

I wasn't talking about Joshua's faith, or lack of it, Nathan. I was talking about yours. Brigham's words ran through Nathan's mind like a litany. *Diligence. Humility. The prayer of faith.* He shook his head, smiling sardonically. Well, the humility was no problem, anyway. Right now he was feeling about as humble as he could remember ever feeling.

"What?"

That brought his head up and he saw Joshua watching him. Joshua was riding the saddle horse alongside. Nathan was driving the wagon, pulled by the two mules and the two draft horses. Derek had chosen to walk for now. It had rained lightly during the night and the overcast had kept the temperature above freezing, so the roads were a muddy mess and sitting on the wagon seat was a punishing experience. But with a lightly loaded wagon and four animals, the roads were not proving to be a problem.

"What do you mean, what?"

"What are you grinning about to yourself?"

Nathan had not realized his face was reflecting his thoughts. He considered several possible answers, then finally shrugged. "You're going to make me eat my words, aren't you?"

There was a soft hoot as Joshua considered that. "Could be some real pleasure in that, I'll grant you. But if you think I'm hoping we won't be successful so I can say I told you so, you're wrong."

"I know," Nathan said quickly, knowing that Joshua meant it, and appreciating it.

"We've still got ten or fifteen miles before we hit the Mississippi. There'll be more homesteads."

Nathan murmured something in assent and fell back into his own thoughts again. Humility, diligence, and faith. Too bad that two out of three wouldn't do it.

Chapter Notes

The letter from Orson Pratt to the Eastern Saints was written on 8 November 1845 (see Joseph Smith, *History of The Church of Jesus Christ of Latter-day Saints*, ed. B. H. Roberts, 2d ed., rev., 7 vols. [Salt Lake City: The Church of Jesus Christ of Latter-day Saints, 1932–51], 7:516–17). The scripture cited by Brigham here is found today in Doctrine and Covenants 104:78–82.

Caroline set the ledger book on the counter and laid the pen down beside it. She looked around, trying to ward off the discouragement.

"Are we done, Mama?"

She laughed softly, and it was touched with bitter irony. "Yes, we are, Savannah. Balancing the books doesn't take nearly as long as it once did."

Livvy looked up from where she was playing with a box full of spools, arranging them first in one pattern and then another on the small table. She would be two years old in three more months and was very much aware of things going on around her. She had Joshua's large dark eyes, so brown that they were almost black. And though still quite light, just in the past few months her hair had started to darken, and Caroline suspected she would turn out to be a full brunette, also like her father.

"Mama sad?" Livvy said, watching Caroline gravely.

She laughed. How perceptive this one was. "No, Livvy, Mama's not sad. Just tired."

Charles, now a very grown-up six-year-old, raised his head. He was stretched out on the rug, poring over a catalog from an Eastern manufacturer. "Are we done, Mama?"

"Almost, son. Savannah and I will finish up in a minute and then we'll go home."

"Mama sad," Livvy said to her brother in a matter-of-fact voice.

Caroline shook her head, feeling a sudden stab of pain. Little Livvy, as they called her, had been born on the same day that her older sister and namesake had been killed. They hadn't called her Olivia, just Livvy, Olivia's nickname. How different she was going to be! Olivia, born to Caroline and her first husband back in Savannah, Georgia, had been fair skinned and had had her mother's dark auburn hair and striking green eyes. Livvy was going to be all Joshua—the dark, dark eyes, the black hair, the finely cut features. She was going to be a beauty, this one. Olivia had been quiet and more pensive, thoughtful, and gentle. Livvy was already showing more of Savannah's temperament—strong willed, impetuous, full of fun and daring.

Caroline sighed. She would be forty in six months. Livvy was likely her last child. No, she corrected herself, *surely* her last child, what with Joshua being gone now for the next year. And that being the case, how grateful she was for this little imp! She was the joy of Caroline's life, and she knew Livvy was God's way of compensating her for her other loss. And while naming her Livvy had sometimes caused Caroline pain, as it had a moment before, she was still glad she had insisted on doing it. The older Livvy now had a living namesake who would carry on life for her and do so at the fullest.

"Can I add the figures, Mama?" Savannah asked.

Caroline tried not to look too pleased. Savannah would be nine in two more weeks. In school, mathematics had proven to be her favorite subject. She loved going through and totaling up all the sales figures. Caroline hated that part most of all. "Yes, Savannah. Total them up, and then we'll go."

Charles sprang to his feet as the noise of an approaching wagon was heard. He went to the store window and pulled back the curtain. It was just nearing dusk now and most of the traffic on the streets of Nauvoo had ceased. "It's coming this way," Charles sang out.

That was enough for Livvy. She dragged a three-legged stool over beside her brother and climbed up beside him, pressing her nose against the windowpane.

"Who is it, Charles? Anyone we know?" Savannah asked as she picked up the ledger book and opened it.

"I don't know. It's too dark."

Caroline moved across the main room of the Steed Family Dry Goods and General Store and down the hall past the storage rooms. She was checking to make sure the back door was securely locked when she heard Charles scream. Then Livvy's voice joined in.

She whirled and raced back the way she had come, but as she did so it registered that this was not a scream of pain but of joy. As she came back into the main room of the store, she saw Charles tearing at the front door. "It's Papa! It's Papa!" he was shouting. Livvy was off her stool and right behind him, hopping up and down and waving her arms. "Papa! Papa! Papa!"

Caroline was stunned.

The door was open now and Charles shot through it, Livvy hard on his heels. Savannah dropped her book and darted across the room and out the door behind her brother and sister. Caroline couldn't believe they were right, but she moved forward swiftly, feeling a sudden rush of excitement. Could it really be?

As she reached the door, she saw three men by the wagon. But the figure that drew her eye was the one being swarmed by her children. "Joshua?" she gasped.

Nathan looked up at her and grinned. "Hello, Caroline."

———•———

"I can't believe this," Caroline said to Derek. "I just can't believe it."

Joshua sat on one of the chairs by the stove in the corner of the store. Livvy was tucked in under one arm, Charles sat on one leg, and Savannah stood behind her father, her arm across his shoulder. Nathan, Derek, and Caroline stood close together, smiling as they watched the joy of the reunion.

"We thought we might surprise you," Derek said, chuckling. "We went to the house first, but when we didn't find anyone home, Joshua suggested we try here."

"But where is the rest of the family?"

Nathan explained quickly about the broken wagon and the decision to try and trade their stock.

"How is Mother Steed doing, Nathan? And Lydia? How's Lydia?"

"Mother is fine," Nathan answered. "Still grieving, of course, but very strong."

"And Lydia?"

"Well, she is doing remarkably well. She tires easily, but she's holding up."

"Oh, Nathan, I wish I could see them. Will you give everyone a big hug for me when you get back? I miss them so."

Joshua looked up from whispering something in Livvy's ear. "How would you like to do that yourself, Caroline?"

Her head came up slowly. A hint of a smile was playing around the corners of his mouth, and there was some inner amusement dancing in his eyes. Nathan and Derek had spun around, as dumbfounded as she was.

"Do you mean that?" she started, very tentatively. "Don't joke with me, Joshua. Not about this."

Instead of answering, he looked up at Savannah. "You still praying every day that you can go west?"

"Oh, yes, Papa."

He turned back to Caroline and shrugged helplessly. "Now, how can a man fight against that?"

Caroline took three quick steps and dropped to her knees in front of him. "Do you mean it, Joshua? Do you really mean it?"

Joshua nudged Livvy. "Tell Mama our secret, Livvy."

She looked at him, the dark eyes questioning. He nodded his approval and she turned to her mother. "Go see Gramma, Mama."

Savannah whirled away, dancing up and down with raised arms. "I knew it! I knew it!" she cried.

Caroline went utterly still. Nathan's mouth was open and he simply stared. Derek was just starting a huge grin. Joshua set Livvy down and gently pushed Charles to a standing position. Then he stood and came to his wife. He took her into his arms. "Do you want to go, Caroline?"

Her eyes showed her answer. They suddenly filled with tears, and all she could do was nod mutely.

He turned to Nathan. "Maybe you'd better sit down, little brother. You look a little faint."

"But . . ." Nathan stammered. "I thought . . . When? When did you decide this?"

Derek had to know absolutely if he was reading his brother-in-law correctly. "Are you saying that you're taking your family west?" he asked bluntly.

Turning back to Caroline, Joshua reached up and touched her cheek. "I'm saying I want our family together. And since the rest of our family seems intent on going west, I guess that's what we'll be doing too."

"Oh, Joshua!" Caroline threw her arms around him. "I can't believe it!" She kissed him hard. "Thank you."

Charles too now was dancing a little jig on the rug, waving his arms in the air. "We're going west! We're going west!" Savannah hurled herself across the space between her and her parents and threw her arms around her father's back. "Oh, thank you, Papa! Thank you!"

He reached out with one arm and pulled her in to him and Caroline. His voice suddenly went husky. "I wish your grandfather were here so I could tell him too."

Nathan was still dazed. "When, Joshua?" he asked again. "When did you decide to go?"

"When that Missourian told us to get off his land." His eyes darkened with sudden anger as he looked at Caroline. "When I saw his eyes, I suddenly understood. I don't know what's going to happen here, but as long as there are men out there with that kind of hate—blind, irrational, without mercy—I don't want my family here."

Caroline moved in closer against him. "Say it again. My ears hear you, but my heart is still having a hard time catching up."

"We're going, Caroline." He looked suddenly bleak. "Don't ask me how. We've no wagon, no team, no supplies." There was a bitter, derisive hoot. "No money."

"I've been trying to gather some things," Caroline said. "I was hoping I could send it with someone out to the family. Some wheat and rice. A barrel of salted pork. About a hundred pounds of corn."

"And I've been trading stuff too, Papa," Savannah exclaimed. "I knew Heavenly Father would help us. I knew it."

"That's wonderful," he said, and he meant it. That Caroline had found that much was amazing. That his daughter was gathering supplies too was especially touching. But it was a pittance compared to what they would need. And there was still the matter of a wagon and oxen. "Maybe Nathan can come up with one of his miracles for the rest of it."

Nathan laughed softly. "We've already had our miracle for today. Let's not get greedy here."

———◆———

Derek and Nathan were in the parlor of Joshua's home, bedrolls laid out on the rug. Nathan lay on his back, hands under his head, staring in the darkness at the unseen ceiling. The house was quiet now, though an hour before it had been filled with noise. Carl and Melissa and their five children came over. It had been a happy reunion in some ways, a sad one in another. Melissa was close to tears for most of the evening. Now she would be the only one left behind. And yet both she and Carl were adamant. They were not leaving. Joshua's talk of the Missourian and the danger that hung over Nauvoo was brushed aside.

After supper, the two families separated into informal groups. The children went upstairs to help Savannah and Charles and Livvy decide what they would and would not take. There was no mistaking the envy in Melissa's children as those choices were made. Caroline took Melissa aside and told her that she and Joshua and Nathan had made a decision. They would deed the store to Melissa and Carl. She overrode Melissa's protests. In a dying city, a general store was not a sure source of income. The men went into the parlor and talked quietly of what had to be done to get Joshua's family ready. Carl offered them his wagon and team—his last one—but they were unanimous in refusing that. Carl had already seriously cut his capability to haul bricks, and if he did more he wouldn't be able to care for his family. That was assuming that there would be any new construction to keep a brickyard going.

Now, lying there in the dark, Nathan sighed, thinking yet again of Brigham's words and challenge.

"We'll just have to make do until we get across Iowa," Derek said beside him. "Maybe once we reach the Missouri River we can find someone and get what we need."

Turning in surprise—Nathan had assumed Derek was asleep—he came up on one elbow. "You're worrying about it too?" he asked.

"Yeah. But I figure even if worse comes to worst, we've got a wagon, we've got the two mules and my horses. We can get Joshua and his family back to our camp, at least. Then we'll just make do. If we have to let those mules and horses pull us all the way to the Rocky Mountains, we'll make do."

"Yes," Nathan said. He lay back down, smiling in the darkness. "You're right. What matters is that Caroline and the children are coming with us."

"Yes. Can you believe that? I thought we'd have a real battle on our hands with Joshua."

"Seems like there's a lesson in that somewhere," Nathan mused.

"Like what?"

"Like maybe the Lord does know what he's doing in all this."

———— •-• ————

Joshua and Caroline were in the kitchen, separating out the dishes into two stacks—a small one of essentials that would go in the wagon, a much larger one to be given to Carl and Melissa. They would have the option of either keeping them for themselves or trying to sell them at the store. The sorting process was nearly done, and they would next move into the parlor to go through the twin china hutches that were there. Joshua could only guess what this was costing his wife emotionally. In those hutches was the set of porcelain dishes that Will had bought for her in China. There was an expensive set of sterling silver that Joshua had given her as a wedding gift. Three shelves were filled with treasured memorabilia she had collected over the years. And most of it would stay. Perhaps they would take a few of the items, such as the silver—not for sentimental value but as possible items for trade on the trail—but most would stay.

In the light of day and with the sheer foolishness of this undertaking hitting him, Joshua was having second thoughts. It was challenge enough to sort through the accumulation of the years and glean out only enough to go into a single wagon, but that was only half the problem. It was two in the afternoon. Still no sign of Derek and Nathan. Which meant that they were having no success finding a wagon and trading for oxen.

He shook his head. They didn't even have a tent of their own. That meant sleeping out in the open, cramming into the wagons and sleeping on top of the bags and boxes, or sharing one of the tents with family members—an unpleasant prospect for them as well as for Joshua. He glanced at Caroline. If he weren't absolutely sure of what her answer would be, he might have said something to her even now, asked her to reconsider maybe.

And then he had to admit that Caroline wasn't the only thing holding him back from changing his mind. The feelings he had experienced as they drove slowly through the streets of Nauvoo just after dark the previous evening had been very powerful. He was filled with a sense of deep foreboding. It wasn't so much what he saw. There were the boarded-up houses and the deserted businesses, the empty corrals and abandoned barns, but there was still plenty of life in Nauvoo. Carl said that with the people from the outlying settlements coming in for safety, there was still somewhere between ten and twelve thousand Saints in town preparing to move out and follow the path Brigham had set. And yet . . . He had tried to convey what he had felt to Carl. Nauvoo was dying. Carl found the phrase irritating and vehemently disagreed. Joshua let it drop, but his feelings hadn't changed. He didn't want to leave Caroline and his children here alone. He had done that once and it had cost him the life of his daughter.

Just then, somewhere in the house, a piano started to play softly. Someone was playing their scales. Joshua looked toward the door, then back at Caroline.

She smiled sadly. "It's Savannah. She knows this will be her last day to play for a very long time."

"Yes, it will." Even if they had three or four wagons, taking a piano along would not be likely. He thought of the bogs, the broken axles, the teams flecked with mud and sweat as they tried to pull even the lighter wagons through. "A piano is not high on our list of necessities," he noted dryly.

"I know, and she knows it too. But she's always said she would give up the piano if we could go west."

"I know. She told me that too. Too bad the city is emptying

out. In a good market, that piano alone would fetch enough to buy a dozen yoke of oxen."

"Carl will keep trying to find a buyer for it," Caroline suggested quickly, sensing his discouragement. "And if he doesn't, maybe in a few years, when we're settled wherever we're going to be, we can come back and get it."

"Yeah," he grunted, knowing how unlikely that was. The sound of the scales being played continued for another minute. On impulse, he stood up and walked quietly down the hall to the door of the parlor. It was ajar and he pushed it open slightly. Savannah was at the piano, her back to him. Her fingers moved up and down the keyboard, tinkling the keys at random. He thought he could sense what she was thinking, this determined young girl of his. Her loss of the instrument saddened him greatly, and suddenly he realized that she would celebrate her ninth birthday in about two weeks now. There wouldn't be much of a party, not out on the trail. But as quickly as the thought had come, he knew what her answer would be if he said something to her. "But Papa, going west is all I want for my birthday."

Her hands stopped moving and silence fell over the room. She was looking at the keys now, her red hair falling softly around her face as her head was down. Then she straightened and began to play. This time it was neither scales nor random plunking. Joshua stiffened. It took him only an instant to recognize what it was she was playing. It was as if someone had slapped him.

This piano, a Knabe he had brought in from the East at considerable expense, had been a posthumous birthday gift for Olivia. Back in Georgia, before Joshua had ever come to Savannah to buy cotton, Caroline had owned a piano—actually a pianoforte—and played it well. She had started Olivia on piano lessons at the age of six and was pleased to learn that her daughter had a natural affinity for the instrument. Joshua had bought a piano for them both when they moved to Independence. That had been destroyed when Joshua's enemies set fire to their house. Once they were settled in Nauvoo, he had purchased another one. Through it all, Olivia's abilities grew and her talent increased. She proved to be not only an accomplished pianist but a gifted musician as well. She loved to compose little songs or snatches of melody and play them over and over. When Joshua had read about a new piano manufacturer in the East whose pianos were quickly gaining an excellent reputation, Joshua had decided he would get one for Olivia. Then she had been killed.

One of Olivia's songs had been written during those agonizing weeks when Joshua was certain that Joseph Smith was trying to convince Olivia to be one of his plural wives. Even now the memories seared him. He and Olivia had fought bitterly over it. She had been shattered by his refusal to believe her denials. And so, in those terrible few days, she had written a song. The music was hauntingly beautiful; it was simple and yet filled with all the pain, all the sorrow, all the pathos of a young woman whose heart was broken. She had played it over and over, and Caroline had come to call it simply "Olivia's song." After Olivia's death Joshua spoke one day of his previous plans to buy the Knabe. At Caroline's suggestion he had gone ahead, presenting it to Savannah and the other children on what would have been Olivia's seventeenth birthday. He had not regretted that decision, but the piano would ever serve as a painful memorial to Joshua's stupidity.

But now what had jerked him up and twisted him with pain was that Savannah was playing Olivia's song. And she was playing it with all the feeling that her sister had once put into it.

There was a soft sound behind him and he turned to see Caroline coming down the hall to join him. She stopped at the sight of his face. "Joshua! What's wrong?" She spoke in a soft whisper, not wanting to interrupt Savannah's playing.

It was as if he hadn't heard her. He turned back, his eyes, large and dark and burning, fixed on the girl at the piano. It was Savannah he saw, but it was Olivia that he remembered.

And then Caroline understood. "It's Olivia's song," she murmured.

He turned to her slowly. "How does she know it?"

"Savannah has a wonderful ear for music, Joshua. She's playing it from memory."

The song stopped. They both peered through the crack of the door. Savannah sat pensively for a moment, then started again. Once more the haunting music filled the room, this time joined by Savannah's singing along with it, not with words but letting her voice follow the melody line. He reached out and shut the door quietly, then backed away a few steps. "I don't know if I can stand hearing it again, Caroline." His voice was low and strained, and she was amazed at the depth of his emotions.

"I know," she answered, her own voice soft. "The first time Savannah played it, I just wept. And yet . . ." She slid across the floor closer to him. "And yet, it's like having Olivia back again, in a way."

"But she's not back," he said. It came out more sharply than he had intended.

"No, Joshua, she's not."

They listened quietly, touching hands lightly but not speaking. "She is never going to be as technically accomplished as Olivia was," Caroline finally said. "But she has her sister's feel for the music. Can you hear that?"

"It's beautiful. It's—" He looked away. "It's Olivia. That's what hit me so hard. It is just Olivia all over again."

"I know."

For almost a full minute he stared down the hallway as the music softly filled the house. "Caroline?"

"Yes?"

"I'm not going to give the piano to Carl. I'm going to ask him to keep it for us, but once we get settled, I'll come back for it. For Olivia. And for Savannah."

Tears welled up. "I would like that, Joshua."

Then, in one moment, his face twisted and was filled with the most tortured anguish Caroline had ever seen. "If there was any way—any way!—to relive that time, I . . ." His head dropped and he closed his eyes. "I would give my own life to have her back."

They left Nauvoo late that same afternoon. It was Friday, March sixth. By then, Nathan and Derek had returned from scouring the city for oxen and another wagon. There had been a brief but joyous reunion when the two had happened to see Joseph Young up near the temple. Joseph was Brigham's brother and the senior president of the Seventy. Brigham had left him in charge here in Nauvoo to oversee the exodus. Joseph told Nathan and Derek that the instructions from Brother Brigham were to wait until the temple was finished and dedicated— which would take place, it was hoped, by the end of April—and then to lead a second group west to join up with the Camp of Israel. This would be a much larger group, judging by the activity going on in Nauvoo. So while there were hundreds of wagons and teams to be found, no one was looking to sell them or trade oxen for mules and horses. By two o'clock they decided their chances for success were going to be better out among the scattered settlements of Iowa. They returned home, loaded the few belongings Joshua and Caroline had selected onto the wagon, had another tearful farewell with Carl and Melissa and their children, and headed down to the ferry.

That night they camped on the west bank of the Mississippi, at the base of the bluffs. After supper they all trekked up to pay one final visit to the grave site of Benjamin Steed. By unspoken consent, they left Joshua and Savannah there alone for a time so Savannah could say a private good-bye to the man who had saved her life.

Next morning they were on the road west by the time there was sufficient light to see. Over the past two days the weather had stayed mild and pleasant, with very little rain, and the roads had dried considerably. Those roads were still violently rutted and pitted and provided a bruising ride for anyone in the wagon, but with a team of mules and a team of horses pulling the lightly loaded wagon, they made good time. They passed Sugar Creek Camp before noon. Where once there had been several hundred wagons and two or three thousand people, now there was nothing but a few stragglers amid the blackened splotches of dead campfires, churned up soil, and bits and pieces of soggy debris stuck beneath bushes or trampled into the mud.

By late afternoon they reached the Des Moines River and passed the site where they had camped the second night and danced to the music of William Pitt's band. It was a good place to camp, but they pushed on another few miles before stopping for the night.

By midday on Sunday their pace was starting to tell on the teams, but they pressed on anyway. They had broken the axle on Tuesday and started back on Wednesday. Brigham Young had planned to stay encamped that Wednesday and move out on Thursday, which meant that he was now four days ahead of where they had left the family. Three, Nathan corrected himself. He assumed that Brigham would use today, the Sabbath, as a rest day. There had been no question in his mind about whether their own group should do that. The situation was too urgent. They had to get the family on the road again and catch up to the main camp. Now the clear skies were gone. A high overcast could be the first sign of coming rain.

It was shortly after three that afternoon when they crested a low rise and saw the white blotches of two wagons in the distance. Nathan, on the saddle horse, went up high in the stirrups, shading his eyes against the lowering sun. Joshua, who was driving the wagon, reined up. He stood up too. Caroline and Derek, walking alongside with Savannah and Charles, moved forward quickly, peering ahead.

"Is that them?" Savannah asked excitedly.

"No," Nathan said slowly. "That's the slough where we got stuck, but we dragged the wagon on another mile or so into camp."

"Besides," Joshua said, "that's only two wagons down there. We've got three besides this one."

"Looks like someone else found our hole," Derek said. He could see several oxen, but none were yoked to the two wagons, and one of the wagons sat directly in the blackest part of the slough, the very place where they had sunk in so deeply a few days before.

"Well, let's go give them a hand," Joshua said, sitting down again. "They can travel with us if they choose."

What they found in the low spot was two families of brothers. The younger had three children, all under ten. The older had a teenaged boy and girl and three younger than that. Before they ever reached them, they could see what had stopped them here. The lead wagon, the one stuck hub-deep in the drying mud, had a shattered tongue. It had snapped off in a jagged tear just where the long beam had been attached to the forward axle.

The two families saw the wagon coming from the east and gathered in a circle as the Steeds reached them.

"Howdy," Nathan said. He looked at the wagon. "Looks like you got trouble."

"You might say that," the older man drawled. His accent sounded like they might be from Kentucky or Tennessee. Not surprising. Several members from branches of the Church in the southern states had come to Nauvoo over the past two or three years, though none of these people looked familiar to him.

"Know what you mean," Derek said. "This is the exact spot where we lost an axle five days ago. 'Bout busted a blood vessel trying to get it out, too."

Now the younger brother spoke. "That wouldn't be your family waiting on the trail about a mile west of here, would it?"

"The Steeds?"

"That's the ones."

"Are they all right?" Caroline asked.

The younger wife pitched in. "They're all fine. We went looking for help after we got stuck here last night and found them."

The second wife was nodding. "That was a welcome sight, I can tell you. Thought we might have to go fifteen or twenty miles to find someone."

"And they were real good to us too," said the first woman. "Took us in and fed us. Real decent folks."

"We're glad to hear they're all right." Nathan swung down from his horse and stuck out his hand. "Nathan Steed. This is my brother-in-law Derek Ingalls and my brother Joshua."

Joshua hopped down to stand beside Caroline and his two children. "This is my wife, Caroline Steed. This is Savannah and Charles." He motioned toward the wagon. "Got another little one asleep in the wagon."

"Calvin Weller," the older man responded, taking first Nathan's hand, then Joshua's, in a solid grip. "This here's my brother, Jacob."

The Wellers introduced their wives and children. When they were done, Nathan turned back to the slough. It was late in the afternoon and the day wasn't too much longer with them. "Well, let's see if we can give you a hand and get that wagon out of there. We've got some rope. Let's try that. We'll probably have to use your animals and ours."

The five men turned to survey the mud hole as Caroline and the children moved over and began to talk with the Weller women and their children.

"We got stuck last night just as it was coming on sundown," Calvin Weller said in disgust. "This morning we hitched up all seven span of oxen to it. That's when the tongue snapped."

"The mud's hardening some," Joshua observed. "Derek, get the shovels and we'll dig around the wheels while they get the animals harnessed up."

"Once we get you out," Nathan said, "you're welcome to travel on with our family until we catch up with Brother Brigham and the main party."

The older man glanced quickly at his brother. Behind them, the women had heard that too, and went suddenly quiet. After a moment, Jacob Weller cleared his throat. "We're obliged for that, but uh . . . we won't be headed on. We're turnin' around."

"You're going back to Nauvoo?" Derek blurted.

"For a time. Then on to Chattanooga, I think."

No one said anything for a moment, and the older Weller looked down at the ground. "I know everybody's saying that going to the Rocky Mountains is the Lord's will, but figger this— if we're doing the Lord's will, how come my wagon tongue broke in half?"

"You can't blame the Lord for things like that," Nathan answered. "It just happens. Our axle broke when we put too much pressure on it trying to lift it with a pole."

"It's more than that," Jacob Weller said, not meeting Nathan's eyes. "It's everything. Dragging our families out here. Not having a place to go. Knowing there're Indians waiting for us." He shrugged. "We've been having a meeting. It's decided. We don't think the Lord expects that much of us. If he did, why isn't he blessing us? We're going back home."

Out of the corner of his eye, Nathan saw the women nodding emphatically. So it wasn't just the men making this choice. He thought of what he might say that could make a difference, then knew that wasn't his charge. "No one called us to sit in judgment," he said, meaning it. "It's not an easy thing we're asked to do."

Joshua was relieved at Nathan's response. He didn't like the idea of people losing heart so easily—they weren't even fifty miles from Nauvoo yet!—but it wasn't their place to live other people's lives. "You know what those going across the Oregon Trail call the trek?" he asked the two brothers. "They call it 'seeing the elephant.' No one's going to fault you for choosing another way."

"Obliged for that. Wouldn't make much difference if you tried to change our minds."

"Well," Derek said, "let's get you out. You're not going either way as long as you're stuck in there. And we're anxious to get on and catch Brother Brigham."

"Man passed about half an hour ago," Jacob Weller said, "taking a message back to Nauvoo. He said that Brigham Young has stopped at a place called Richardson's Point and is waiting there for a time, giving people a chance to catch up."

The Steeds perked up at that news. "Did he say how far along Richardson's Point is?" Nathan asked.

"Twenty, maybe twenty-five miles is all."

Nathan felt a great relief. That was one very long day, or perhaps a day and a half, but then they would have caught up with the main company again. That was good news. "Thank you. That will help us greatly."

Joshua tossed his head toward the slough. "So let's see if we can't get you your wagon back."

It took three-quarters of an hour. Fortunately, the Wellers had already unloaded everything from the mired wagon except some blankets and a few articles of clothing. They unhitched the mules and the horses from Derek's wagon—they were too tired to do much good here—and put four yoke of oxen on instead. Then they tied two thick ropes from the back of Derek's wagon to the back of the Weller wagon. Joshua and Derek and Jacob Weller waded into the slough and dug a track for the wheels. The mud was still a very thick goo that grabbed at them like a hundred unseen hands, but since Tuesday, it had dried enough that when they dug it away from the wheels, it only oozed back very slowly.

When they were ready, the older Weller stood at the head of the oxen. Nathan, Derek, Joshua, and Jacob Weller took their places at the wagon and leaned into it. "All right," Joshua hollered. "Go!"

Calvin Weller cracked the bullwhip over the heads of the oxen. They lunged against their yokes, bellowing and grunting. The four men threw their weight against the wagon. For a moment nothing happened, and then slowly the wagon started to move.

"Go! Go!" Nathan urged.

And it did. Once they got the momentum, the wagon was pulled backwards up and out of the slough. As it rolled free and the men dropped to their knees, gasping for breath, the children clapped and the women laughed and pointed. Everyone ran forward to gather around. "Much obliged," Calvin Weller said, coming around to join the men who were staggering to their feet. He began to untie the ropes off his wagon.

Derek wiped his hands against his trousers, eyeing the other wagon. "Well, you're out of the mud, but that doesn't solve your other problem. What are you going to do about getting a new wagon tongue?"

The two Weller brothers turned to survey the damaged wagon. Finally, Jacob shrugged. "We've already put most of the stuff in the good wagon. We'll go on back to Nauvoo. If we can get another tongue, we'll come back out and get it. If not . . ." He shrugged.

Nathan's head came up slowly and he stared at the disabled wagon, feeling his pulse suddenly pounding. "I've got another solution for you," he said carefully, his mind racing even as he started to speak.

"What's that?"

"How about trading us your wagon?"

Joshua was bent over, wiping the mud from his hands on the dry prairie grass. His head snapped up. Derek jerked around too.

"You want *that* wagon?" the older Weller brother said in surprise.

Nathan grinned. "Well, we'd love to get your other one too, but I'm assuming you're going to need that to get you back home. So yes, I'm talking this one." He gestured toward the wagon they had just retrieved. The tongue was shattered, that was true, but other than that it was solidly built and looked relatively new. It was bigger than Derek's and more trail worthy. "You probably met my brother Matthew last night. He's a carpenter. He can make us another tongue."

"That's right," Derek said eagerly.

Jacob Weller was nodding thoughtfully. "Yeah, he showed us the axle he made. It was good work."

"And what are you trading?" Calvin asked warily.

Nathan felt as if he were sprinting effortlessly down a path with the wind at his back. The thoughts were coming with perfect clarity. "Actually," Nathan said, choosing his words carefully, "if you're serious about heading back, not going on with Brigham—" He stopped, giving them a chance to reconsider. He didn't want to be the factor that nudged them into making what was in Nathan's mind a terrible mistake.

"We are," Calvin Weller said flatly.

"All right. Then I'd like to make you a better offer." He laughed shortly. "You want to sit down first?"

Joshua was staring at him, starting to see what was happening but saying nothing, letting Nathan run with whatever idea he had.

"We'd like to buy you out completely."

"What?" The two brothers said it almost as one.

"We're looking for an outfit for Joshua and his family, so here's what I'd suggest. You take our wagon and the mules and the horses. You take whatever you need to get you back to Nauvoo and leave everything else here."

The Wellers were dumbfounded and gaped at him. "You mean everything?" asked Calvin.

"I mean everything," Nathan said, trying to hold down his exultation. "Food, wagons, oxen. I assume you have a tent."

"Two of them," Jacob Weller said, still not believing what he was hearing.

"We'd take the better of the two." Nathan glanced quickly at

Joshua, who had stood up and was looking as astonished as the two Wellers. Caroline had come forward now and was watching Nathan with wide eyes.

"But . . . ," Jacob started, with a splutter. "Are you crazy? That's everything we have."

"You're right. It doesn't seem like much of a trade, does it?" He stopped, letting it all sink in for a moment, then went on eagerly. "But remember, it's only two days back to Nauvoo. Do you have a place to stay there?"

"No," Calvin answered. "We never had enough money to do anything but rent a small cabin for the two of us."

"Well," Nathan said slowly, letting the final piece drop into place, "what if we gave you a house in trade for the tent?"

There was a collective gasp but Nathan ignored it. He turned to Joshua and Caroline. "That is," he said quietly, "assuming the owners of the house are willing to consider that."

"You mean that—" Joshua stopped, first staring at his brother, then at his wife. His mind was whirling. The sheer audacity of it was stunning. And yet it was so simple. This would solve his concerns. Two wagons. Plenty of oxen. A tent. Food. In a word, a complete outfit. It was enough. *No, not enough. More than enough. Enough and to spare.* It was incredible.

"What do you think?" he said to Caroline, already knowing the answer.

She smiled, gave one brief nod, then turned to the Wellers. "It's our home. It's on Granger Street, between Mulholland and Ripley Streets."

Both shook their heads. "We've only been in Nauvoo since November," Calvin explained. It was clear that both he and his brother were dazed by what was happening.

"It's a beautiful home," Caroline rushed on, turning to the two women. "It's two stories, all brick. There's a large barn. Most of the furnishings are still there." She described the inside of the house quickly.

The Wellers listened to her, then on signal from Calvin

stepped back and went into a quick huddle, whispering urgently amongst themselves. As they did so, the Steeds went into a huddle of their own. Nathan looked at Joshua. "I should have asked you first," he whispered. "But it came in such a rush. I would have offered our home, but we deeded it to the Church trustees in Nauvoo."

"And I deeded mine to Carl and Melissa," Derek added.

Joshua was shaking his head. "It's enough, Nathan."

Nathan misunderstood. "I'm sorry, Joshua. I didn't mean to—"

Joshua reached out and took him by the shoulders and stopped him. "It's enough. We'll probably never sell the house anyway. Carl will be lucky to get ten cents on the dollar for it."

"Less, maybe," Derek said. "John D. Lee told me that the Church trustees got twelve dollars and fifty cents for his house and farm, and he estimates they're worth about eight thousand dollars."

Joshua shrugged. "The house isn't going to do us any good where we're going."

"Then it's all right?" Nathan asked slowly, hardly daring to believe it was this easy.

"All right?" Joshua cried. "It's wonderful!"

"Oh, yes, Nathan," Caroline exclaimed. "This is the answer to our prayers."

"Yes," Nathan said in wonder, "it is, isn't it?"

Before she could respond to that, the Wellers broke up and the two brothers came back over, followed by the women and children now, who were clearly excited. But Calvin was still troubled. "Look," he began, "your offer is more than fair, but we're not sure we need a house. We've got to get back to Tennessee. We can't do that with one wagon and a couple of mules."

"And the horses," Joshua pointed out. "You know that the horses alone will bring more than enough to replace your oxen."

"If they're available," Jacob spoke up. "You know what it's like in Nauvoo right now."

"But that's just it," Nathan burst out. "We have no choice. But you do. You can stay in Nauvoo for a time. By summer, our people will be gone. Then there won't be the shortages anymore."

Joshua jumped in. "You could even stay in the house until next spring if you had to. The house alone is worth four or five thousand dollars."

Calvin looked at Jacob. Clearly they were torn, but they were not yet convinced. Suddenly, to everyone's surprise, Savannah spoke up. "Mr. Weller?"

Calvin turned. "Yes?"

"There's a beautiful piano in the house."

Caroline and Joshua both whirled.

Calvin's wife stepped forward. "And that would be included?"

Joshua went to his daughter. "Savannah, are you sure? I told you I would come back for it."

"I know, Papa. But it's more important that we go west."

Joshua straightened slowly and looked at Caroline, who nodded.

Then, again catching everyone by surprise, Savannah looked at Calvin Weller. "It's a Knabe piano. The best they make. We'd have to have the second tent too if we give you the piano."

Caroline's mouth opened, then shut again. Nathan choked a little. Derek tried to suppress a grin.

"But what will we—"

Calvin Weller's wife came forward and grabbed his arm. "We can sleep on the ground for one night if we have to," she said urgently. "It's a piano, Calvin. For Sarah. A piano!"

The teenaged girl came up beside her mother. "Please, Papa."

The two brothers stepped back again, whispering urgently with one another. Finally, the older one turned back to face Joshua and Nathan. "Tell me again exactly what you are offering."

Nathan spoke slowly and distinctly. "You get our wagon, the two mules, the two horses, and a deed to the house in Nauvoo with all its furniture—" He looked at Savannah. "Including the piano. For that, you take what is necessary to see you back to Nauvoo and we take the rest."

"Including both tents," Savannah reminded him.

Nathan grinned. "Including both tents."

One more time Calvin Weller turned and looked at his family. They were all nodding, including Jacob. He swung back around, extending his hand. "I guess you've got a deal."

On Saturday, March seventh, Brigham Young called a halt to the westward march and made camp at a place known as Richardson's Point. The muddy roads had cost them dearly. Wagons were in need of repair, teams were exhausted, and many of the Saints were strung out for miles behind the main company. A rest was badly needed. He would stop for two days before pushing on, he decided.

The next day being the Sabbath, no work was done. The Twelve called for a combined worship service, the first such joint meeting held since they had crossed the Mississippi River more than a month before. The rest of the day was spent quietly visiting with friends, neighbors, and family, reading the scriptures, and cooking simple meals. But come Monday morning, the day of rest was over and everyone pitched in so that they could depart the following day. Throughout the day, other families continued to straggle into the camp. Though they would have little rest, they were grateful that they had caught up with the main company.

Brigham wished there was time to let the stragglers lay over and rest as well, but he was growing increasingly anxious. They had been on the road for over a month now and were still only fifty-five miles from Nauvoo. That was not acceptable. Winter came early in the Rocky Mountains, and they had to find a home in time to plant crops and get food enough to see them through until spring. At suppertime he sent out the word. They would move out in the morning.

But nature has a way of reminding men that they are only intruders in her domain and that while on her terrain they must dance to her music. That same Monday evening, shortly after dark, it began to rain. It came softly at first, almost more a mist than actual raindrops. Those wise to Mother Nature's capricious moods understood the gentle warning for what it was. They immediately saw to their tents and wagons. They lashed down the wagon covers, trenched around the tents, checked to make sure everything was covered or put away. Within an hour the mist had turned to a steady drizzle. By the time the trumpeter sounded lights out at nine o'clock, the rain had become torrential and the camp was quickly becoming a quagmire.

In his tent, Brigham stopped for a moment and listened to the drumming of the rain on the canvas above him. Finally, with a weary sigh, he leaned over and blew out the lamp. There would be little sleep tonight, he thought. Not that it would make a lot of difference. No one would be going anywhere in the morning.

The Steeds had not caught up with the main company by Tuesday as hoped. First of all, after Nathan's group had rejoined the rest of the family—who were elated that Joshua had brought with him Caroline and the children—it had taken almost a full day to fix the wagon tongue on their newly acquired wagon. They started off late Monday afternoon, but made only three miles before the rain commenced and they had to stop. The next morning, rain or no rain, they pushed on, slogging onward at a snail's pace in the miserable conditions. By Tuesday night, when

Nathan had hoped to be back with the main camp, they were still eleven miles from Richardson's Point. Once again they made camp in a pouring rain.

"Mama!"

Lydia turned her head toward her youngest son. In the blackness of the tent she could see nothing, not even the shapes in the bedrolls that filled the tent. She went up on one elbow. "What is it, Joseph?"

"A leak, Mama."

"Another one?" Nathan said with a groan.

"Yes, Papa. This one hit me in the face."

"We only have one more pan, Papa," Emily said from another corner.

"I'll get it," Josh said. Nathan heard the bedclothes rustle as his son got himself out from beneath the covers.

"It's in the corner by your feet," Lydia said, lying back down again, grateful that she did not have to try to get up herself.

"Hurry, Josh," Joseph wailed, "it's coming faster."

"Coming," Josh soothed. He brushed past his father, got the small cooking pot, and made his way carefully between Josiah and Elizabeth Mary. There was silence for a moment, then a new plinking sound as Josh located the drip and put the pan under it. It added to the tiny symphony of sounds as water dripped into the various pots and pans scattered around the tent.

The other children were silent for the moment, but Lydia knew they weren't asleep. No one in the Nathan Steed tent was asleep, even though they had been in bed for over an hour. Thus far they had six pots, two pans, and three serving bowls scattered around the tent, catching the water that was oozing through the saturated canvas in one place after another. And with the rain still roaring like water over a millrace, she knew it was not going to get any better. So much for the promises of the merchant who sold them the canvas and assured them that it would shed rain like the back of a goose. Instantly she was repentant. The man had been honest. He had just never envisioned anything like what was pouring down upon them now.

"We're going to have to move your bed, Joseph," Josh was saying.

"Where?" Emily muttered. "There're no more empty places that are still dry."

"Yeah," Elizabeth Mary joined in. "My quilt is wet around my feet."

"And I've got a rock where I'm sleeping," Josiah mourned. "Right where my bottom wants to be."

"Children," Lydia called out. "What am I hearing right now?"

There was a deep silence except for the dripping water; then, meekly, Joseph answered. "Murmuring?"

"Yes. Remember when we talked about this? What was it that caused the children of Israel to lose the Lord's blessings? And what did Laman and Lemuel in the Book of Mormon keep doing that got them in trouble?"

The tent went silent and Nathan smiled to himself. They had read some of those passages just the night before.

"Why is it called murmuring?" Lydia asked.

There was an instant response from all five children. "Mur-mur-mur-mur-mur," they sang out in low, melodious, singsong voices.

Now Nathan chuckled aloud. Lydia had given the family a lesson before they ever left Nauvoo, and as part of that lesson she taught them a great big word she had learned as a schoolgirl back in Palmyra, New York. The word was *onomatopoeia*. She had described how proud she had been when she had learned to pronounce that huge word without hesitation, and soon had all the family repeating after her, "O-na-ma-ta-*pee*-a, o-na-ma-ta-*pee*-a." Then she explained that onomatopoeia referred to using words that sounded like what they described, such as *gurgle* or *cuckoo*. To that point, Nathan had been perplexed, not sure why his wife had felt compelled to gather them around to teach them this one unusual word. Then she made her point. Taking them into the Old Testament and the Book of Mormon, they read together several verses that talked about the people murmuring. "Why do you suppose they call it murmuring?" she asked. They shook their heads. "Because this is what it sounds like. *Mur-mur-mur-mur-mur*. It isn't raising your voice and making your complaint known. It's muttering under your breath, whispering behind someone's back, lowering your voice and barely getting the sounds out."

She then made them mimic the sound, which had brought peals of giggling. Now each time one of them started to complain, or heard someone in the camp start to complain, Lydia would cock her head, put her hand to her ear, and whisper, "What was that I just heard?" Back would come the chorus, "Mur-mur-mur-mur-mur," and in a moment the complaining would be gone and they would all be laughing.

"Come, Joseph," Lydia called out. "There's room for you between Papa and me. You'll be warm here."

Nathan got to his knees and began making room on the canvas floor beside his bed. In the darkness a hand touched his. "You didn't really think you were going to sleep, did you?"

"I had hopes," he said forlornly, squeezing Lydia's hand back. And then Joseph was there, crawling awkwardly around his mother. Nathan laid a hand on his head and guided him so that he wouldn't knee Lydia's stomach as he made his way to his new place. "But if I'm not going to get any sleep," he mourned, "is it too much to ask that we at least be dry?"

"What was that I just heard, children?" Lydia sang out clearly.

Back came the response, the children delighted that it was Papa who had just been caught. "Mur-mur-mur-mur-mur."

By the afternoon of March eleventh, after two days of relentless rain, Richardson's Point was a sea of mud. Nearby Chequest Creek had gone from a narrow stream of clear water to a roaring, angry, muddy torrent, too dangerous for fording in a wagon. It came as a surprise to no one when Brigham Young declared that they would not move on until the weather cleared. What they had thought would be a two-day rest stop was now becoming a full week, and no end in sight. Richardson's Point had become the next Sugar Creek, a rest camp where the Saints could regroup and marshal their strength before moving on. With that in mind, Brigham ordered what work was possible on the sprawling camp-site to make it more suitable for those who would follow, but there was not much that could be done in the continuing downpour.

"Utter misery" was the phrase that best described conditions during those two days. Families stayed mostly in their tents—crowded, wet, irritable, trying to catch the water seeping through the canvas as best they could, working desperately to keep children who were confined to a space no larger than ten feet by ten feet occupied and happy. Those who did venture out not only were quickly soaked through but also brought globs of mud back in with them and fouled the tents and bedding at every turn. Bedding was damp at best, soaked in many cases. Starting a fire was virtually impossible. Food consisted of what-ever could be had cold—mostly biscuits and a thin gruel of flour and water—which did little to eliminate the growing frustration and shortening tempers.

Sometime well after dark on the night of the eleventh, the Steeds and their five wagons finally reached Richardson's Point. They were drenched, filthy, exhausted, and utterly miserable. But they had Caroline and the family with them and the wagons and teams to carry them. As if in celebration, sometime during the night the skies began to clear.

In the morning, when the first heads began popping out of tents and wagons after the bugle sounded, there were cries of relief. The morning star shone brightly in a lightening sky that was perfectly clear. It was going to be a glorious day.

"They'll be black in ten minutes."

Caroline lifted her eyes and let them sweep across the end-less mud that was the campground. Joshua was right. The rain had stopped and the sun was shining brightly. The black prairie soil was already starting to send up wisps of steam as the sun's rays bored into it, and she could smell the rich aroma of the earth. But it would take a lot more than that before the mud dried sufficiently to make the camp livable again.

"They can't get any worse than what they've been for the last two days," she answered, "but I think I'd rather cope with that than try to keep them inside when it's such a beautiful day."

Joshua looked down at the faces of his two youngest children. They were standing before him and Caroline outside the entrance to their tent. Their eyes were wide and pleading, their faces twisted with anticipation. He turned and looked to where Lydia was standing at the door of her tent.

"What do you think?" he called.

"I say let them go," Lydia answered. To her, as with Caroline, the thought of another day of mud-covered children was less horrifying than trying to keep them confined to the tents.

One campsite farther on, the flap to Derek's tent opened and Derek stepped out. He was followed by Christopher, who was almost seven, and little Benjamin, who was nearly four. Both had their coats on and their heavy shoes, still caked with mud. Derek was grinning. "You all can do what you want, but I'm not holding these two in for one more moment." He swatted at Benjamin's backside. "Get out of here," he growled menacingly.

With a whoop of pure joy, the two boys plunged away, instantly sinking into the deep goo.

"Can I go, Papa?" Charles cried, tugging at his father's coat.

Joshua glanced at Caroline, who nodded.

"Go," he said, "but you hold onto Livvy's hand. You watch her, all right?"

"Yes, Papa."

"And don't go near the creek!" Caroline called after them as they took off after their cousins.

In a moment Lydia's three were darting away and the five of them fell into line with Derek's two. They trooped off first to

Jessica and Solomon's tent to collect their children, and then to Matthew and Jenny's to make the gathering of cousins complete. Cajoling and pleading, they talked their grandmother into joining up with them and headed for a small copse of trees for a game of hide-and-seek.

The other parents stood beside their tents, watching them go, relieved beyond measure. Finally, Matthew walked over to Nathan. "I thought I'd go out and check on the stock. Want to go?"

"Well," Nathan said, glancing sideways at Lydia, "we need to do that, but I've got to get the bedding out and hung up to dry. I don't want Lydia doing that."

"I can manage just fine," she retorted, but she was pleased that he had considered her before answering.

"I need to find Heber Kimball too," Nathan said to Matthew. "He said he's got something to soften that leather pouch I've been making."

"You just go," Lydia said. "I'll be fine."

Beside Joshua, Caroline spoke up. "I can help Lydia, Nathan," she called. "We've got to get our bedding out as well."

"Look," Joshua said on an impulse, "it will do you and Lydia good to get away from here for a time too. You've been talking about visiting some of the ladies. Just go, and I'll do the bedding for both tents."

Caroline looked at him in surprise, then smiled. "Do you mean it?"

"I do."

"Did you hear that, Lydia?"

Lydia was nodding. "I did."

All the Steeds were out of their tents now, and in the tight half circle of their campsite all could easily follow the conversation.

"I'll just do the bedding before we go check on the stock," Nathan said, feeling guilty that Joshua was volunteering to do his work.

"Just get out of here," Joshua snapped back at him in mock severity. "I'm capable of handling the bedding. All the bedding! So take Solomon and Derek and Josh with you. Those oxen could be scattered anywhere by now."

Caroline hesitated for only a moment before turning. "Jessica. Rebecca. Jenny. Get your babies. Lydia, get your shawl. Mud or no mud, let's go visiting."

Getting the bedding outside and hung up in the sun was not as simple a job as Joshua had imagined. First of all, he had to remove his boots each time he went into a tent so that he didn't drag in mud behind him. Then to free up the bedding he had to move around the chests and small items each family kept in the tent. The wet bedding itself was heavy and bulky. He would wad it up and move it over to the tent door. Slipping his boots on again, he would then take it outside. Then came the problem of where to hang it once he had it outside. The tents and wagon covers needed to dry as badly as did the quilts and blankets, so he couldn't just hang the bedding there. The tent ropes were too steep to hold anything that wasn't fastened down, and so he finally rummaged through various boxes until he found some hand-carved clothespins. Even then, one blanket took a full length of rope, and so they were quickly used up. Next he went to the wagons, using the tongues for the smaller blankets, careful not to let them drag in the mud, and the wagon boxes for the larger ones. From there he went to small bushes, tree limbs, barrels, boxes, and every other square inch of space that could hold something up to the air. All over the camp, he could see that he was not the only one struggling with the problem.

He decided to leave his own tent until last. He started on Matthew's first, wanting to be sure that his mother's place of sleeping would be thoroughly dry. Then he did Solomon and Jessica's tent. That was the largest challenge because they had eight in their family. Derek and Rebecca's went swiftly, and finally he moved to Nathan's tent. By now, the inside of the tents were like the inside of a steam bath. That was good in a way, for it was proof that the sun was doing its work. But it left Joshua pouring sweat.

As he was gathering up the few items in Nathan's tent and stacking them on Lydia's small oak chest, Joshua stopped. Beside one of the pillows, in the very corner of the tent, a leather-bound book lay face down on the canvas. Curious, he picked it up and turned it over. When he saw the title on the spine, it came as no surprise. It was a Book of Mormon. Lydia's Book of Mormon, he corrected himself, as he noted the dark stain on the back cover.

The stain identified its owner. The whole family knew the story of that book and how it had become scarred with coffee stains. Sent by Nathan in brown paper to Lydia's store, it was Nathan's last desperate attempt to help Lydia understand what the Mormons believed so that Joseph Smith would not stand as a great barrier between them. But when Melissa made the delivery, Lydia was not there, and her father, a bitter opponent of "Joe Smith" and his new church, threw the book in the trash barrel. When Lydia finally found it, coffee grounds had been dumped into the barrel and covered one corner of the leather cover. Furious at her father for interfering, still angry at Nathan for trying to convert her, she had taken the book and finally read it. The rest was history. Lydia was a Mormon now, she and Nathan had married, and . . .

He opened the book, curious as he saw a red ribbon serving as a bookmark. It marked a place about halfway through the book. At the top of the pages he saw the words "Book of Alma." That meant little to him other than he had heard his family refer to Alma as one of the writers of the book. One part, beginning at the bottom of the left-hand page and going over to the right, was neatly bracketed with black ink. Curious as to what had struck Lydia's interest, he held the book up closer, the light of the sun through the canvas turning the pages a yellowish white.

And now, my brethren, I would that after ye have received so many witnesses, seeing that the Holy Scriptures testify of these things, come forth and bring fruit unto repentance; yea, I would that ye would come forth and harden not your hearts any longer; for behold, now is the time, and the day of your salvation; and therefore, if ye will repent and harden not your hearts, immediately shall the great plan of redemption be brought about unto you.

He stopped, cocking one ear. He had heard some voices outside and now listened intently, poised to close the book and put it away if it was anyone in the family. But then he could tell that whoever it was they were not coming this way. His eyes dropped again. This time his lips began to move as he read silently to himself.

For behold, this life is the time for men to prepare to meet God; yea, behold, the day of this life is the day for men to perform their labors. And now as I said unto you before, as ye have had so many witnesses, therefore I beseech of you, that ye do not procrastinate the day of your repentance until the end; for after this day of life, which is given us to prepare for eternity, behold, if we do not improve our time while in this life, then cometh the night of darkness, wherein there can be no labor performed.

This time when he lowered the book he was irritated. A sudden thought leaped into his mind. Had Lydia somehow known he would find her book and marked a place in hopes that he would read it? He pushed that thought aside immediately. He had been standing there when she ducked back into the tent to get her shawl. She had reappeared almost instantly. There was no way she could have . . .

He started a little, realizing what the implications of his thoughts were. The scripture was too perfect. It was exactly the kind of thing his family would do, to plant some subtle message that he would stumble upon and then to look innocent if he questioned them. And yet he knew there was no way they could have done so. It was purely coincidence.

He shut the book quickly, as though he might squelch the message emanating from its pages. Angrily he tossed it atop Lydia's chest and started wadding up the wet bedding. Once he was done, he pushed the pile to the tent's entrance and reached for his boots. His head turned. The book lay there like a gold coin in the sunshine. He opened the tent flap and looked out, making sure no one was coming back. Then he crawled back over to the chest. He opened the book to the same place.

He read it once, then again, more slowly now, trying to understand exactly what the words meant. He saw something he had missed before. One phrase was used twice. The writer talked about having "so many witnesses." He read the first use, and then dropped down and found the second. The message was almost identical: "Since you have had so many witnesses, you ought to repent." That was basically it.

For the second time he closed the book and put it on the chest, but his mind was working, chewing on the question that had been presented to it. A witness was someone who testified to the truthfulness of what he knew, generally in court. *So many witnesses*. He pulled a face. If that was what was meant, heaven knew he had plenty of those. Caroline, Will, Alice, Savannah, his mother, Nathan, Lydia—the whole family were witnesses in that sense, trying to tell him what they believed to be true.

Ah! That was a key word. What they *believed* to be true. In a court of law, one could not be convicted by what someone else believed to be true, only by what they knew for themselves. Strangely, that brought a great relief to him. There was no question about how strongly his family believed it, but they—

And then four words popped into his mind. *What about the Wellers?*

He was stunned. After that remarkable trade— No. He was

too honest to simply call it remarkable. What had happened was absolutely incredible. One moment he had no hope of getting an outfit for his family; the next he had found all that he could have hoped for and more. It had been so simple, so natural. He grunted. "And so incredible," he muttered to himself.

And this was not something someone else believed was true. He knew it for himself. Nathan had not said a word about it, had not crowed about God's intervention, as Joshua had expected. Neither had Derek. But he knew what they believed. They believed it was an answer to prayer. In their minds it was a miracle. It was miraculous, there was no disputing that. But *miraculous* was a more comfortable word than *miracle*. It was something anyone might say.

His mind turned back to the idea of witnesses. If one could think of events as witnesses, then Joshua had an infallible one. This was not something someone believed. It was not what someone had told him. This one he knew for himself. The memory of his shock and wonder as Nathan suddenly began to bargain with the Wellers was fresh and powerful.

Finally, totally frustrated with himself, he started back for the tent door. He sat down and pulled on his boots, careful not to knock any mud off them. And then, once they were on, instead of crawling back outside again, he stayed where he was, his eyes fixed on the book with the brown cover that sat on the small wooden chest.

The ladies found it best to stick to areas where the wagon wheels or the hooves of several hundred oxen and horses had not chewed up the ground and opened it up to the rain. It meant going quite a bit farther out of their way in many cases, but avoiding the miry mud was well worth the effort. Even with that, the bottoms of their skirts were soaked from the wet grass and black from those places where they could not avoid the open ground.

They started with that area of the camp that comprised the members of the trailing company. These were at the northeastern edge of the large camp. This company was different from the others in that it contained many of the newcomers to the Camp of Israel. They weren't just the stragglers who had fallen behind but those who had left Nauvoo after the main groups had departed and who had caught up with them. The Steed women thought it worth a visit to see if anyone they knew might be among this group. To their pleasant surprise, almost immediately they found Abigail Pottsworth, her daughter Jenny—now Jenny Stokes—and Jenny's two children, a boy three and an infant daughter.

It was a warm and happy reunion. The Pottsworths had been next-door neighbors to Derek and Peter Ingalls in Preston, England, and were converted to the Church at the same time. When mother and daughter came to Nauvoo, they happened to be on the same ship as Will Steed, who was returning to his family after an absence of nearly two years. Will had been smitten by the flaxen-haired beauty and was shattered when she decided she wanted a member of the Church and married Andrew Stokes. Andrew was not there, but they promised to bring him over in the near future because Sister Pottsworth wanted to see Derek again.

After the Pottsworths, they moved on again, stopping here and there to visit with former neighbors or longtime customers of the Steed dry goods store. About eleven o'clock they decided they had better start back. They were feeling guilty about being gone so long, and yet, at the same time, they were so buoyed up by the blue skies and the warm sunshine and the chance to be away from the demands of their children for a time, they could not resist postponing their return for just a little longer.

"Isn't that the Markhams' wagon?" Lydia asked. She was feeling the weight of the baby inside her and needed a place to sit down for a few minutes. They were still a quarter of a mile from their campsite.

"Yes, yes," Rebecca said eagerly, "there's Eliza Snow."

"So it is," Caroline said, laughing easily. "What say we, ladies? Are we up to one more visit before we return?"

"Yes!" Jenny, Jessica, Rebecca, and Lydia said it in perfect unison, which brought a peal of laughter from them all.

As they moved closer to the two wagons, picking their way carefully, Caroline, who was in the lead, suddenly stopped, holding up her hand. "What is that?" She lifted her head and sniffed the air.

The others followed suit. Rebecca's eyes widened. "Can it be?"

"Fresh bread," moaned Jenny in agonized pleasure. "It smells like fresh baked bread."

"It can't be!" Jessica breathed. "Not out here. How did they even find dry firewood?"

There was no answer to that question, but there was no mistaking the fact that Sister Markham was bent over a fire. She stood and turned at the sound of their voices, then waved. Eliza Snow, kneeling beside a kettle, also straightened, then waved happily.

As the five women joined the two at the fire, there were quick hugs and kisses on the cheeks, then a rapid series of questions about the state of their health, how they were doing without Brother Markham's presence—he was leading the advance scouting party and was often away from his family—and how things were going in general.

Then Rebecca could stand it no longer. She looked around. "We had the strangest experience just a moment ago. As we started toward your camp, we thought we smelled fresh bread."

Hannah Markham laughed merrily and turned and pointed to the wagon. There, lined up along the wagon seat, were three pans. The brown rounded tops of loaves of bread could be seen in all of them. "They're just cooling now," she explained. "I think they may be a little burned on the bottom—a Dutch oven is not as dependable as my brick one at home. But Sister Eliza and I were about to break out a bottle of raspberry preserves and see how we did. Would you like to join us?"

"I can't believe it," Jessica said, staring at the bread in astonishment. "You actually baked bread today?"

Eliza walked to the wagon, looking back over her shoulder. "Isn't she a wonder?" She gingerly lifted one of the bread pans, turned it upside down, and let the loaf drop into her apron. "Yes," she called back to Hannah, "it is burned a little, but only the crust."

Jenny McIntire Steed leaned back against the small length of log she was using for a backrest. "What do we call this place?" she asked of no one in particular.

"What place?" Eliza Snow answered.

"Here. Where we're camped."

"Richardson's Point," Caroline volunteered.

"I say we change the name," Jenny, who knew the name as well as anyone, said with a smile. "I say from now on we call it Bread Loaf Point."

That won her a laugh. "No, no!" Rebecca spoke up. "I have one better. How about—" Her eyes half closed. "How about, Paradise Creek?"

"Or Dutch Oven Heaven," Lydia laughed, getting caught up in the game.

Hannah Markham was embarrassed. "Oh, you," she said, waving her hand at them. "It's not *that* good."

"It's absolutely wonderful," Jessica answered back. "And out here? It's a miracle."

Still blushing slightly, Sister Markham explained. "When I got up this morning and saw that it had stopped raining and that it was going to be a clear day, I said to myself, 'I feel like baking bread today.' So I did."

"Well, it was delicious, and we are very glad that we stopped by at just the right time," Caroline said. Then she turned to Eliza Snow. "Have you been writing any poetry lately, Sister Eliza?"

Eliza Snow was about forty now, Lydia guessed. A small woman with piercing dark eyes and fine features, she was beloved of all who knew her. And she was a gifted poet and writer. Now it was her turn to blush. "No, not much lately."

"You wrote those verses at Sugar Creek Camp," Hannah Markham corrected her.

"Well, yes, but that was two or three weeks ago."

Caroline laughed and spoke to the others. "Only Eliza Snow would think one poem in two or three weeks wasn't much." Then she turned to Eliza. "Would you read it for us?"

Eliza's color deepened. "It was just something I wrote in my journal," she demurred.

"I'll get it for you," Hannah said, starting to rise.

Eliza pulled her back down again. "You know I always carry my journal with me." She patted the pocket of her apron.

"Then read it for us," Rebecca cried. "Please, Sister Eliza. I love your poetry."

"Yes," Jenny pleaded. "Really. We do all want to hear what you wrote."

Eliza looked around at the eager faces, then finally nodded. "All right." She brought out the leather-backed notebook and opened it, leafing back a few pages. "As Hannah said, I wrote this while we were still languishing at Sugar Creek."

She opened the book wider, then looked around at their faces once more. "I think I'll call it, 'The Camp of Israel.'" Then she began to read.

Altho' in woods and tents we dwell,
Shout, shout, O Camp of Israel;
No Christian mobs on earth can bind
Our thoughts, or steal our peace of mind.

Tho' we fly from vile aggression,
We'll maintain our pure profession—

Seek a peaceable possession
Far from Gentiles and oppression.

Eliza looked up from her journal for a moment. "That last stanza is a chorus that comes after each verse," she explained, "but I'll just read the rest of the verses now." She looked back down and continued.

We better live in tents and smoke
Than wear the cursed gentile yoke—
We better from our country fly
Than by mobocracy to die.

We've left the City of Nauvoo
And our beloved Temple too,
And to the wilderness we'll go
Amid the winter frosts and snow.

Our homes were dear—we lov'd them well,
Beneath our roofs we hop'd to dwell,
And honor the great God's commands
By mutual rights of Christian lands.

Our persecutors will not cease
Their murd'rous spoiling of our peace,
And have decreed that we must go
To wilds where reeds and rushes grow.

The Camp—the Camp—its numbers swell,
Shout, shout, O Camp of Israel!
The King, the Lord of Hosts, is near,
His armies guard our front and rear.

She closed the book and lowered it slowly. There was silence around the circle. Then Lydia said what they all were feeling. "Thank you, Eliza. Thank you for reminding us of who we are, why we are here, and who it is that leads us on."

Chapter Notes

The scripture which Joshua reads in the Book of Mormon is now Alma 34:30–33.

In her journal entry for 11 March 1846, Eliza R. Snow, who was traveling with Stephen and Hannah Markham, recorded, "My good friend Sis. M[arkham] brought me a slice of beautiful, white light bread and butter, that would have done honor to a more convenient bakery, than an out-of-door fire in the wilderness." Assuming the bread was baked that same day, that seems a little odd, since the eleventh supposedly had heavy rain. One possibility is that, since Hannah Markham apparently baked eleven loaves of bread on the ninth of March, on the eleventh she may have given Eliza a slice from one of those. (See Maureen Ursenbach Beecher, ed., *The Personal Writings of Eliza Roxcy Snow* [Salt Lake City: University of Utah Press, 1995], pp. 118–19.) In any case, for the purposes of the novel this incident has been placed on the following day, 12 March, once the weather had cleared.

Eliza R. Snow was sealed to Joseph Smith as a plural wife in 1842. Sometime after the Prophet's death, she was married to Brigham Young for time so that he could care for her. However, Brigham had taken several other women to care for them and had a large company traveling west with him. He asked Stephen Markham, a trusted friend of Joseph's, to take Eliza with his family and care for her. The poem cited here was written in her journal under date of 19 February 1846 (see Beecher, ed., *Personal Writings of Eliza Roxcy Snow*, pp. 113–14).

By the time Mary Ann returned to the wagons, Joshua had all the bedding out to dry and was sorting through the boxes and bags and barrels in his wagon—something he had not yet had a chance to do since making the trade for the wagon and all that was in it. He looked up and smiled. "They do you in?"

She sat down on a log beside the cold campfire, shaking her head. "If I had even half that much energy, I could pull the wagons to the Rocky Mountains all by myself."

"Are they all right?"

"Yes, Josh is with them. And Rachel and Emily. They're fine. It feels so good to them to be outside and running again. I'm not even sure they know I'm gone." She patted the log beside her. "So come and sit for a while. It looks like you've been busy. Did everyone run off and leave all this for you?"

He replaced the lid on a barrel of beans and tapped it into place with the heel of his hand, then looked around. Their camp looked like a strong wind had hit in the middle of laundry day at the river. "No, actually it was my idea. The men went to see to the stock, you had the children, so the women decided to go visiting."

Her face fell slightly. "Oh, I would have loved to be with them."

Finished, he moved over to sit beside her. "Maybe you can go out this afternoon."

"It does feel good to have sun again, doesn't it?" she murmured, tipping back her head so the sunlight fell full upon it.

"It feels great. And if the weather holds, I think we'll be able to roll out of here by tomorrow afternoon."

"I hope so. I hate the waiting. Don't you want to be up and going, getting on with it?"

He nodded. "But in a way this has been good. We would never have caught them by now if they had kept moving."

She smiled at him. "I am so glad you went back, Joshua. It feels so right to have Caroline and the children here with you."

"Yes. It does, doesn't it? I'm still not sure it's wise to pack them up and move them out to nowhere, but I didn't feel good about leaving them in Nauvoo."

She clucked reprovingly at him. "Nowhere? Just because we don't yet know where the Lord has in mind doesn't mean that we're going nowhere, Joshua."

He laughed easily. "Oh, Mother. Sometimes I envy you your simple faith."

"Faith *is* simple," she retorted. "You just believe."

"Right," he said, a little wistfully.

She leaned away from him enough that she could look directly at him. "Well, it is simple. Look what happened to you. You had the faith to decide to bring Caroline back with you and—"

He shook his head. "That wasn't faith, Mother. I was just worried about them."

"Faith is nothing more than taking action when you don't have any evidence that something is true or that it is the best thing to do. Why did you choose to come out here? If it was just worry for your family's safety, why not take them to Chicago or back to Georgia?"

"Because we wanted to be with the family."

"That's part of it, no question about it. But if you thought you were taking your family into great danger, you wouldn't have done it, family or not."

"Probably not."

"So, you had faith that coming with us was the best thing, even though you had no proof of it."

He laughed. "I can think of a lot of people who would hoot right out loud to hear you use *faith* in the same sentence with Joshua Steed."

"Let them hoot," she said easily. "It's true. And look what happened as a result of your faith. You were able to make a wonderful trade and get the things you needed. That's pretty simple, I would say."

"And you think the two are related?" He was openly skeptical.

"Of course." She leaned forward, very earnest now. "Joshua, what happened to you out there was remarkable."

He remembered his choice of words earlier. "No, it was incredible."

"Then what greater witness do you need?"

He stiffened a little. "What did you say?"

"I said, what greater proof can you have than what happened to you with those two families? It is a marvelous—"

"No. You didn't say 'proof.'"

Puzzled by his sudden intensity, she thought back. "I said, what greater witness can you have? Why?"

He was staring at her, remembering the words that had jumped out at him this morning. Again his first thoughts were of some benign conspiracy. Had his mother somehow known he would see the Book of Mormon? Had she and Lydia—? Again he had to reject it. There was no possible way. Finally, he leaned back, visibly relaxing. "Nothing. I . . . I just thought it was an odd choice of words."

"Well, odd or not, that's faith. And it *is* simple. When you believe enough to act in certain ways, then wonderful things happen. Take this thing with your family. Doesn't it feel good to be together again, to have Caroline right here beside you?"

"You know it does."

"Then just extend that to the next life. Think how sad you'd be if you were to be separated from her again, only this time forever. You don't want that, do you?"

"Well, I—"

"Do you?" she persisted.

He finally shook his head. "You know that my family is the most important thing in the world to me now, Mama. Losing everything in these past few months—my businesses, the stables, all my money—has just made that all the clearer."

"So you *hope* that this idea of an eternal marriage is true. You have no proof that it is, but you want it to be. So all faith is, is a willingness to act on that hope, to do things which will move you toward that goal. That's what the Apostle Paul meant when he said, 'Faith is the substance of things hoped for, the evidence of things not seen.'"

He shook his head. "That sounds pretty lofty to me."

"No, Joshua. Listen. When you decided to bring your family back with you, you hoped that you would be able to find a way to care for them, but you had no evidence that you could. In fact, you had every reason to think you couldn't find the supplies you needed. But you went ahead and acted. On what basis? Knowledge? No, faith. In other words, faith was the substance, or the assurance, of what you hoped for. It was out of faith that you acted."

"All right, I see what you're saying. I'm not sure I would use those words, but go ahead."

"So what else did Paul say? He said faith is the evidence of things not seen. What happened next? You acted out of faith and *then* you got your evidence. You ended up stumbling onto this miraculous opportunity to trade for what you needed. That was the proof, or the evidence, of what you could not see before."

He was nodding slowly, not convinced but intrigued by her logic, which was simple and clear.

"Moroni, in the Book of Mormon, used almost the same words. He said, 'Faith is things that are hoped for and not seen.'" She reached out and took his hand. "Now, here is the point, Joshua. Here's what I wish I could make you see. Moroni then said, 'Dispute not because you see not, because you receive no witness until after the trial of your faith.'"

Again he was startled. "And what's that supposed to mean?" he asked, half to cover himself, again thrown off guard by her second use of the word *witness*.

"It means simply this. Suppose you had said to Nathan back in Nauvoo, 'Give me some evidence that everything is going to be all right first. Help me find a trade for our horses and mules, and *then* I'll agree to take Caroline west.' What would have happened?"

He frowned, suddenly seeing where she was taking him. "Nothing. There were no trades to be made in Nauvoo."

"Exactly. So what Moroni calls the trial of faith had to come first. Would you act without knowing for sure it would work out? You did, and then—and only then—you got the proof that your faith worked. Then—*after* the trial of your faith—you received the witness."

He rose, his mind churning. It was simple. At least in explanation. But . . . There were so many other questions. Maybe it was all just a wonderful coincidence. If it had even happened to Nathan, he might be more inclined to talk about divine favor. But who was he to ask a blessing from God? After all he had done with his life, why would God—if there was such a personal being as his mother envisioned—why would he ever choose to respond to Joshua Steed?

"Do you remember how the Savior warned the people about sign seeking?" his mother went on, sensing that she had struck some kind of chord within him. "It's the same principle. A sign seeker says, 'Show me first, give me the proof, and then I will believe.' The Lord asks just the opposite. 'Believe first. Act on that belief. And then I'll give you the confirmation.'"

He didn't answer. He wasn't sure what to say. There was no anger in him, only a sudden hollowness, a sadness that it would never be that clear for him, that uncomplicated. He bent down and kissed her cheek. "Thank you, Mama. Thanks for trying, but I'm afraid I'm hopeless."

Her eyes narrowed. "Hopeless? That means you're without hope. If you were hopeless, you wouldn't be here, and neither would your wife and children. So let's have no more of that talk, you hear me?"

He laughed and took her in his arms. "Oh, Mother. You are wonderful."

She punched him lightly in the stomach. "Don't you patronize me, young man."

"Yes, Mother," he said meekly, holding her close and hoping that she could feel just how much he loved and admired and respected her.

Half an hour later the women returned. They were laughing merrily and talking all at once as they approached. Mary Ann came out of her tent at the sound of their voices and stood beside Joshua, who was building a fire for the midday meal. "You'd think they had just come from a party."

He nodded. When Lydia looked up and saw the two of them, she raised a hand and began to wave it back and forth. She held something small and white. "Mother Steed," she called. "A messenger has arrived from Nauvoo. We have a letter from Melissa and Carl."

They sat around the fire after supper was done. As usual, the adults gathered to talk. The children were nearby, scattered about in the tents and wagons or just lying on blankets on the grass, reading books or playing quiet games together. And this felt almost as good as the warm day had. Between the men's trip to Nauvoo and the rush for the family to catch up with the camp, the last two days and nights of which were in incessant rain, there had been little opportunity for a family gathering. Lydia hadn't realized until this moment how important times like this were to them all—and especially now to have Caroline and the children in the circle too.

She was brought out of her thoughts as she realized that Emily had spoken to her. "What did you say, Emmy?"

"Do you think Brother Pitt's band will play tonight, Mama?"

Nathan spoke up, answering for his wife. "I don't think so. They probably need a break after being so busy the past while."

There was a murmur of disappointment at that from several around the fire. A night of music and dancing would have been a perfect end to the day.

Seeing their faces, Matthew explained. "The concerts they've been doing for the locals are proving to be of great benefit. Brother Clayton told me that two nights ago at Keosauqua, the people paid the band twenty-five dollars in cash."

"Really?" Jenny exclaimed. "Twenty-five dollars?"

"Yes," Matthew answered. "And they received such a welcome that they went back last night and earned another twenty dollars."

"They were out in that terrible weather last night?" Mary Ann asked in surprise.

Derek had been with Matthew cutting willows for the oxen when William Clayton had passed by. Since Derek and Clayton were both Englishmen, it was natural for the band member to stop and talk. Derek broke in now. "In fact, they didn't get back until three this morning. It's about ten miles. But think of it. Forty-five dollars in cash. Think how much corn and wheat Brigham can buy with that."

"But where did they play?" Rachel asked. "Did they play outside in the rain?"

Derek shook his head. "No, the two concerts they got paid

cash for were held during the evening inside the courthouse. But Brother Clayton was saying that the first afternoon they went there they were also asked to go through town and play at various places, including some stores."

"Which reminds me," Matthew said eagerly, "Brother Clayton said that at one store the storekeeper was so pleased, he told each band member to take anything they wanted. So they each took a little. Before they could leave, the next storekeeper sent someone to get them. When they went there the same thing happened. They were highly popular."

"That is wonderful," Jenny said. "Surely the hand of Providence is in all of that."

"What is wonderful?" Rebecca said. She had been in the tent nursing little Leah, who had turned one year old three days previously. Now she came out to join them.

Jenny told her quickly about the band and its success. Then the conversation turned to Melissa's letter.

Rebecca turned to Lydia. "Read me again what Melissa said about Mary Fielding Smith."

Nodding, Lydia reached into the pocket of her apron and withdrew the letter. In the spring of 1836, Nathan had accompanied Parley P. Pratt to Upper Canada on a mission. There they met and converted a British family, John and Leonora Taylor. The Taylors introduced them to another family from England, Joseph Fielding and his two sisters, Mercy and Mary, and they too were baptized. The following year, the two families came to Kirtland and met the rest of the Steeds. Though there was seventeen years' difference in their ages, Mary Fielding and Rebecca Steed hit it off immediately and became fast friends.

Lydia found the place in the letter and read in a clear voice so that all could hear. "'Carl and I saw Mary Fielding Smith day before yesterday. She was coming out of the Webbs' blacksmith shop as we passed by. We had a wonderful visit, and she inquired after each of you. She especially wished me to convey her greetings to Rebecca.'"

Lydia looked at her sister-in-law and smiled. "That's just like Mary, isn't it?"

"Yes. Even with all she has to worry about, she remembers to think of us."

Lydia continued reading. "'She and Mercy, and their brother Joseph Fielding, are having difficulty preparing to leave. As you know, Hyrum Smith had considerable property both in and near Nauvoo. He had some fifteen building lots in the city and about two hundred and fifty acres on his farm east of here. Mary has been trying to sell that off to raise sufficient funds to purchase teams, wagons, and supplies. She also needs funds to leave something with Hyrum's oldest daughter, Lovina, who is now married and will not be going yet either. Mary feels Hyrum would want Lovina to have part of his inheritance. Thus far, however, she has had no success in finding a buyer who will pay even half of what the property is worth. Knowing Mary, this next will not surprise you. She seemed not at all discouraged and is sure the Lord will bless them.

"'Carl—much to my surprise, I might add—inquired of Mary about the rest of the Smith family. He had heard that they were putting much pressure on Mary to change her mind about leaving. At that inquiry, her mood did darken somewhat. She told us that Emma and the others have been pleading with her not to leave. William Smith, the Prophet's hotheaded brother, who has now turned very bitter against the Church since the Twelve excommunicated him, came to Mary's home a short time ago. Evidently young John Smith, Hyrum's oldest son and Mary's stepson, quietly left with Heber Kimball's party and is going west with all of you. This infuriated William and he showed up at Mary's home in a fit of temper. He accused her of letting the Church leaders "spirit away" Hyrum's son and demanded that she bring him back. As you know, William has a violent temper, and when she refused, for a time Mary was in fear that he might strike her. But she stood her ground and eventually he went away again.

" 'Young Joseph F., who is the pride of his mother's eye, was with her when we met her. Bless his heart, he told us that he was upstairs at the time, but could hear everything his uncle was saying through the stovepipe in his room. He said if only he were bigger—what is he, eight years old perhaps?—he would have run down and given his uncle a thrashing for being so harsh with his mother. Anyway, that saddened us somewhat. We have always had warm feelings for the Fieldings and will be sad to see them leave.' "

There was silence around the fire as Lydia refolded the letter and returned it to her pocket. Then Matthew spoke. "Could you ever believe that two brothers could be so different? What a contrast! Joseph, always so kind and cheerful. And William. Now, there's a real pickle sucker if you ever saw one."

"Matthew!" Jenny said, surprised at the vehemence in his voice.

"Well, he is," Matthew said, only partially sorry. "He's got a hot temper and cares only for himself. And he's as sour as a potful of brine."

Joshua had been sitting quietly by, saying little but following the conversation. Now he broke his silence. "I can think of a couple of brothers who were pretty different," he said quietly.

For a moment no one was quite sure what to say. They knew exactly what he meant. The differences between Nathan and Joshua had run so deep that it had eventually led to a confrontation that left Nathan's back and chest scarred in a dozen places or more.

Then Mary Ann smiled. "I knew two boys like that once too, but the one died a long time ago and a new one took his place."

"And the other one finally grew up," Nathan said, just as quietly.

Nathan lay on his back, staring up at the canvas above him, listening dejectedly to the pounding of the rain. So much for their beautiful day. Barely one day and then the rain was back. They had one kerosene lantern lit, with the wick turned down about halfway. Elizabeth Mary, Josiah, and little Joseph were all asleep now. Emily and Josh were lying side by side on Emily's bed, reading from the Bible, which was pushed up close to the lamp so they both could see. Lydia was in the opposite corner, rummaging through her chest.

Nathan was barely aware of them as he scanned the heavy fabric above him. He and Josh had moved the tent about an hour ago, as they realized that they were in for another night of it. They found a place with a bit more slope to it so that the water would carry on past it. They had been especially careful to make sure the canvas was stretched as tight as possible so that the water would not puddle on it. It was raining as hard as it had before, and it had been doing so for over an hour now, and so far the changes they had made seemed to be working.

"Nathan?"

He turned his head. "Hmm?"

"Have you seen my Book of Mormon?"

Emily rose up. "It was over in the corner, Mama, beneath your pillow."

Lydia frowned, straightening and sitting back on her heels. "That's what I thought too, but it's not there."

Nathan rolled over. He had seen her put the book away this morning before they had gone out to start the fire and begin breakfast. He lifted the pillow, pulled back the bedding, then patted his hand up and down along the edge that was nearest the tent. Nothing. He sat up, remembering. "I'll bet Joshua put it away when he was getting the bedding out to dry."

"That's what I thought too," she said, turning back to the chest and a few other small boxes that held their belongings, "but I've gone through everything and I cannot find it."

"You're sure?"

"I've looked everywhere."

He shrugged. "Maybe he took it out with the bedding and put it in the wagon or something. I'll ask him in the morning."

Lydia nodded, turned, and shut the chest again, then crawled over to join Nathan. "Come, children. It's time for lights out. Let's say our prayers."

Maybe it was the sound of the rain drumming on the canvas above her. Perhaps it was being upset about not being able to find her Book of Mormon. More likely it was because she was so tired that sleep was driven away, as sometimes happened. Whatever it was, Lydia lay there awake in the darkness, lying on one side, with a pillow cushioning the weight of her stomach, eyes wide open, staring at nothing. And finally she was honest enough with herself to face what it really was that kept sleep at bay.

That afternoon word had spread around the camp that Catharine Spencer, wife of Orson Spencer, was dying. The Spencers were about ten miles behind the main camp now, back near Indian Creek. Already weak from an illness she had had before leaving Nauvoo, Catharine Spencer suffered from a serious cold as she and her family made their way west, and her condition just got worse and worse. Finally, this beautiful, graceful, cultured woman could no longer endure the cold and the wet, the interminable mud, and the thin shelter of a tent soaked with water. The night before, so the report went, she had gathered her husband and children around her and told them that they had to let her go. She felt that it was only their prayers that held her back, and she pleaded with them to let her go. Devastated, Orson had finally found a nearby farmer who was willing to take them in so that she could at least have a dry place to die.

Lydia grunted softly, feeling the hard ground through the thin straw mattress, trying to find a comfortable position. Two days ago, when the Steeds were still trying to catch up to the main company, they had been near the Spencers' camp, and now

Lydia was feeling guilty that she had let the rain keep her from going out to see Catharine. Lydia and Nathan had not known the Orson Spencer family very well before leaving Nauvoo, the two families having lived in different parts of the city. But when the Steeds crossed the river for the second time and camped at Sugar Creek, Nathan and Lydia ended up only a few tents away from the Spencers and quickly became "neighbors." It was a friendship that came easily. The Spencers were about the same age as Nathan and Lydia, with six children. They learned that Orson had been a popular Baptist minister back in the East. Catharine was the youngest—and, according to Spencer, the favorite—child of a very well-to-do family. That was not hard to believe. Highly educated, deeply refined, thoroughly cultured, Catharine was a woman of intelligence, grace, and charm. The family was understandably pleased when their youngest chose to marry the popular young cleric and their lives prospered.

Then came the day when the Mormon missionaries came to town. When they heard the message of the Restoration, both Orson and Catharine knew it was true and determined to be baptized. Their decision was met with bitter opposition from both families, and threats of rejection and banishment were used to try to dissuade them. But they had received their confirmation and nothing could sway them from it. With that simple decision they lost their popularity, their employment, their friends, their home, and their families. Eventually they came to Nauvoo to be with the Saints, undeterred by what they had sacrificed when they chose to follow their Savior.

And now she was dying.

Just a little over a week ago, when Lydia and Mary Ann went to visit the Spencers, Orson had told them a story that had nearly broken Lydia's heart. Once the decision was made to go west, Orson said he wrote to Catharine's parents. Because her health was so poor, he asked if they would take Catharine into their home until the Saints could find a place to abide, and then he would send for her. The answer came back. It was short. It was blunt. "Let her renounce her degrading faith and she can come back, but never on any other condition."

That had struck Lydia hard. And what followed struck her harder, for it brought back a flood of memories. When Orson had read the letter to Catharine, he asked if she wanted to consider her parents' request. She asked him to get the Bible and turn to the book of Ruth. And then she had asked him to read the very words that Lydia had had Nathan read some sixteen years before. "And Ruth said, Intreat me not to leave thee, or to return from following after thee: for whither thou goest, I will go; and where thou lodgest, I will lodge: thy people shall be my people, and thy God my God. Where thou diest, will I die, and there will I be buried: the Lord do so to me, and more also, if ought but death part thee and me."

Where thou diest, will I die.

Lydia closed her eyes, trying to shut out the drumming rattle of the rain. This was not weather for dying. It needed to be bright and clear, perhaps with a night sky spangled with stars. She sighed. It was not weather for birth either, but that hadn't stopped that from happening any more than it postponed death. A few days before, a hut had been hastily thrown together with walls formed from blankets hung from poles and a crude bark roof overhead. Here a woman gave birth as friends and sister Saints stood around holding dishes and pans to keep the rain from showering the mother and her newborn.

Was that what awaited her? Lydia wondered. Or would she have to find some willows or a clump of brush along a creek somewhere? If she had calculated correctly, the baby was still two or three weeks away, but the farther west they went, the fewer would be the signs of civilization. Now at least there were a few villages within riding distance. They saw isolated farms from time to time. But three weeks would take them—what? Another two hundred miles? Then what would there be? A tepee or a wigwam if she was lucky; nothing but a jolting wagon and a thousand square miles of mud if she wasn't.

She sighed. Something in her mind told her to stop this gloomy train of thought. But she brushed it aside. It was a wonderful night for despair, what with the rain pounding down and the creeks on the rise again and a friend trying to find a dry place to die. And in a way, it was a luxury to feel sorry for oneself. Tomorrow that luxury would be gone. Tomorrow there would be children to keep occupied and entertained, there would be food to cook, bedding to air out, the relentless grime and mud to combat.

She sighed again and closed her eyes. She began to pray for Catharine Spencer and her husband and children. And then, in the midst of praying, a terrible thought struck her. It chilled her and she shuddered involuntarily.

Nathan turned in the darkness. "Are you still awake?"

"Yes." She reached out, needing to touch him.

"How come?"

"I was thinking about Catharine Spencer."

"Oh." She didn't have to say more. That explained a lot.

"Nathan, if I—"

He saw it coming and cut her off quickly. "Don't!" he whispered, then slid closer and took her into his arms. "You're not going to die, Lydia."

"I know, but what if—"

"No buts. No what ifs. You are going to be fine, Lydia. Remember your patriarchal blessing?"

That caught her by surprise. Her blessing? the one given so many years before by Father Smith back at Kirtland? And then she understood what Nathan meant. It hit her with more of a jolt than had the sudden thought of death. "Yes," she said slowly, feeling immense relief wash over her. Her patriarchal blessing. She closed her eyes. She had read it so many times she knew it by heart. Father Smith had talked about her motherhood, promised her that her children would be blessed by her influence. And then came the promise: "In your old age, your children and their children and their children shall rise up and, with a joyful noise, shout praises unto your name."

In your old age! She would be thirty-seven come August. That was getting older—and she certainly felt every year recently—but did it qualify as old age? She could have shouted. No! Not yet. It was as if a soothing balm had anointed her soul.

Realizing that he had settled her mind, Nathan went on. "You're going to be fine. I've already talked to Patty Sessions. She said to get her any time, day or night. She's only minutes away."

"I know. Thank you, Nathan. I know I shouldn't worry. I really do feel good, better than with the other children." She laughed softly in the darkness. "Maybe this being a pioneer and trudging through the mud every day is good for motherhood."

He reached out and touched her cheek. "It must be. I know this—you are more beautiful than you have ever been."

Startled, sudden tears sprang to her eyes. "Why, thank you, Nathan."

He came up on one elbow and kissed her softly. "And you're going to be the most beautiful grandmother and great-grandmother this world has ever seen."

She didn't trust her voice to answer. She just moved in closer against him, loving the peace and security that being in his arms brought to her.

Chapter Notes

Originally, Brigham Young's plan was to camp for two or three days at Richardson's Point so as to rest and to repair wagons. When a prolonged and heavy rain set in, departure was delayed. Eventually it proved to be almost a full two weeks before they moved west again. (See *CN*, 9 March 1996, p. 12; Wallace Stegner, *The Gathering of Zion: The Story of the Mormon Trail* [New York: McGraw-Hill, 1964], p. 53.)

An unexpected and very welcome source of income for the Saints crossing Iowa came when William Pitt and his brass band went into the surrounding settlements and gave concerts. The response of the locals to this unexpected touch of culture as described here is recorded by William Clayton

144

in his journal. Clayton was a member of the band. (See CN, 16 March 1996, p. 7.)

The confrontation between Mary Fielding Smith and William Smith described here only led to further estrangement between Joseph's branch of the Smith family and Hyrum's. While Mary Fielding Smith and her sister, Mercy, maintained a warm relationship with Mother Smith, Emma and the others in Joseph's family were disappointed that Mary would not reconsider her decision to follow Brigham Young to the West. (See Don Cecil Corbett, *Mary Fielding Smith: Daughter of Britain* [Salt Lake City: Deseret Book Co., 1966], pp. 185–86.)

Catharine Curtis Spencer, wife of Orson Spencer, died on 12 March 1846. The day before, a man who lived near the Indian Creek Camp (which was not far from Keosauqua, Iowa Territory) had allowed Catharine to be brought to his house because of the wet weather. She was nine days short of her thirty-fifth birthday and left six children. (See Susan W. Easton, "Suffering and Death on the Plains of Iowa," *BYU Studies* 21 [Fall 1981]: 435–37.)

Orson Spencer was called to labor in England not long after this event and presided over the British Mission for about two years until 1849. When the University of Deseret was founded in 1850 (later to become the University of Utah), Orson Spencer was appointed as chancellor, a position he held until his death in 1855. (See *LDSBE* 1:337–38.) He died in St. Louis, where he had been called to serve as a stake president. Today there is a building named for Orson Spencer at the University of Utah. One of Catharine's daughters, Aurelia Spencer Rogers, later generated the idea for the Primary organization in Farmington, Utah, in 1878.

Chapter Nine

The rain continued all through the night, and by the following day the creeks were once again running swift, muddy, and frightening. Not that there were plans to move out. With the return of the rain, Brigham Young again postponed the departure, and the Saints settled in to endure the cold, wet misery that had become so much a part of their lives now.

By morning the rain stopped, but it was cold and windy. Some people stayed in their tents and wagons to wait for better weather to return. Jenny was one who did not venture out much that day because baby Emmeline was showing signs of a cold. By afternoon Matthew had finished his chores and joined her. So it was with some surprise that late that afternoon Matthew and Jenny heard footsteps outside that stopped in front of their tent. There was a sharp rap on the main tent pole. "Matthew Steed? Are you in there? Do I have the right tent?"

Matthew, who was reading a story to Betsy Jo, who was not quite four yet, sprang up. "Yes. This is Matthew Steed. Come in." He looked at Jenny in surprise. They both knew that voice and knew it well.

The tent flap pulled back and Brigham Young stepped in beneath it. He dropped the flap immediately but Matthew felt the cold air sweep through the tent.

Jenny was on her feet now too, smoothing her apron and hefting little Emmeline onto her hip. Matthew went over to greet him. "Brother Brigham, this is a surprise."

Brigham removed his hat and smiled. "Thought it might be. Afternoon, Sister Jenny."

"Afternoon, President Young."

Betsy Jo got up and came over behind her mother, shyly peeking out from behind her skirts. "And how are you, little sister?" Brigham said, dropping down to a crouch. "Do you remember me?"

There was a moment's hesitation, then a slow nod.

"Sure you do," Jenny said, reaching down to touch her head. "Papa used to work with President Young."

Brigham hooted softly. "More like your papa used to do President Young's work for him."

"Only because you were running the Church," Matthew said. Then he gestured. "Won't you sit down?"

"No, no," came the quick reply. "Can't stay but for a moment." He frowned. "Actually, I'm sorry to have to come. Wish it could be under better circumstances."

Jenny felt her heart drop a little. Matthew and Brigham Young were good friends, though there was nearly twenty years' difference in their ages. They had run a cabinet shop in Nauvoo for a time until Brigham had taken over the leadership of the Church and simply had no more time for the business. But with the press of leading a company of several thousand Saints into the wilderness, it was not like him to simply drop in for a social call. That meant he had something for Matthew to do.

Seeing her face, Brigham laughed. "Now, Sister Steed, I'm not going to be calling him to go back to England again." He looked suddenly wistful. "Though I might be tempted to do so if we could return there together. Those were simpler times, my friend, weren't they?"

"They were indeed," Matthew replied. "Wonderful times."

"Yes. And there's still a lot of work to do there, but it will have to be attended to by different men than you and me, Matthew. But I do have something else I need of you."

"Just ask it."

His brows lowered and his mouth pulled into a thin line. "Have you seen the creeks today, Matthew?"

"Yes. Solomon, Derek, and I were down earlier trying to get some browse for our oxen." By getting browse he meant pulling branches off the trees or cutting willows and letting the animals glean off whatever buds and leaves there were on them. With nothing but last season's dry grass, the animals were not doing well. "We had expected the water to be some higher, but it must be up four or five feet. It is high, swift, muddy, and dangerous."

"Exactly. We won't be leaving here soon. Between the weather and the sickness, we're going to have to stay here several more days."

"Sickness?" Jenny asked in concern, looking down at the baby.

"Yes, it's starting to break out everywhere. Fever, coughs, aches, and chills. Little wonder, what with all the wet and cold. We're in no shape to be moving out. Nor are the roads in any shape for travel."

In a way that was a relief, Matthew thought. Trying to move out in this weather would prove to be costly for both man and beast.

Brigham reached inside his coat and withdrew an envelope. "And if we stay here, we have a problem. As you know, we've got several small companies out in front of us. Bishop Miller's is one of those."

Matthew nodded. Miller, one of the general bishops in the Church, had been sent ahead with a pioneering company, supposedly under the direction of Stephen Markham. But rumor had it that Miller, always independent, was often on his own.

"I don't like us getting all scattered out," the chief Apostle went on. "I keep sending word for Bishop Miller to wait for us, but it has made no difference as yet. Sounds like the whole thing is in disarray to me. So I'd like you to take this letter to him for me."

"All right," Matthew said immediately.

"How much farther on is he?" Jenny asked.

"A day, maybe two. They can't be making much time in this weather either." He looked at Matthew. "Leave first thing in the morning. When you find them, learn what you can. Keep your eyes open. Then come back and report, will you?"

"Yes, sir."

"I already talked to Nathan. He said you can take his saddle horse." He turned to Jenny. "I'm sorry to take your man away, Jenny, but this is important."

"You know we're ready to do whatever you need, President."

His face softened and for a moment the lines of worry smoothed. "I know you are. That's why I thought of you. He shouldn't be gone for more than five or six days."

Brigham Young's estimate of how long Matthew would be gone proved to be quite accurate. On horseback it was a fairly easy task to stay off the roads and thus avoid the worst of the mud. Fording the streams proved to be a challenge on two occasions, but he made it. He caught up with Bishop Miller's company about sundown of the second day. Miller was camped at the Chariton River, about forty miles west of Brigham's location, where he was splitting rails for payment in corn. Matthew stayed the night and part of the next day, then headed east again. Returning just before sundown of the fifth day, he took a quick supper with the family and then went off to report to President Young and Heber C. Kimball. The report was not all that encouraging.

Miller had been sustained as a bishop of the Church in 1841 when Bishop Edward Partridge died. Converted personally by Joseph Smith, he was totally devoted to the Prophet and gave considerable service to him and to the Church. But after the Martyrdom, which hit him especially hard, things began to change. He did not have that same unswerving loyalty to Brigham Young, and sometimes the two strong wills clashed. As one of the general bishops of the Church, he had a major role in the exodus to the West. Brigham Young appointed him to be part of a "pioneer company" of about a hundred men who were to move out ahead of the main body of Saints. Supposedly led by Stephen Markham, another trusted friend of the Prophet, they were to find the best routes, smooth out the roads, locate fords for the rivers and streams, bridge them if there was no other choice, secure—through purchase or trade—grain and other needed supplies for the Saints. But Miller quickly struck out on his own, leading his own smaller company their own way.

Often he had not bothered to send word back as to his whereabouts. President Young had sent more than one message asking him to hold up, but thus far the counsel had been ignored.

"He says you're being too cautious, President," Matthew reported. "He read the letter while I was there, and to my surprise he made no bones about the fact that it irritated him. When he learned we are still here at Richardson's Point, he flew off the handle. 'The man is much too cautious,' he said. 'He's moving at a snail's pace. This is no time for wavering. We've got to reach the Rocky Mountains, get crops in and harvested before first frost. At the rate he's moving, we'll be lucky to make the Missouri River by first snow.' Those were just a few of the things he said." Matthew shook his head. "I was surprised at how open he was in front of me. It was like he forgot that it was me who brought your letter to him."

Heber C. Kimball snorted in disgust. "Don't kid yourself. He forgot nothing. He wanted you to bring this report back to the President. What about Elder Pratt?"

Matthew shook his head. He had seen Parley Pratt, but he too had expressed frustration with Bishop Miller's independence. He reported as much. "He was obviously embarrassed by Bishop Miller's tirade. He tried to offer a balancing voice, suggesting that the problems you are facing in stragglers and broken equipment and lack of supplies—to say nothing of the mud—are real problems that can't simply be ignored. I think he was terribly embarrassed by it all."

"Good. And how did Miller respond to that?"

"It only irritated him the more. He said that what we need is decisive leadership, the kind that Joseph Smith had provided. He acknowledged that there were problems, but went right on to say that problems didn't change reality. That didn't delay the frosts or shorten the journey that had to be made."

Matthew was embarrassed to have to report that to the chief Apostle. Miller was a restive man chafing under the restraint of someone else's leadership. That was the real problem, in Matthew's mind. Miller wanted to be the leader. And this was his way of showing that he was the better qualified.

Brigham listened to it all quietly, not seeming the least bit surprised. When Matthew was done, the President thanked him sincerely and dismissed him. And that was that, Matthew thought. He had done as Brigham wanted and now he was back with Jenny and the children.

———◆———

They moved out of Richardson's Point the following morning, Thursday, March nineteenth, 1846. It was a full twelve days after they had stopped there "for a brief rest and respite." They caught up to Orson Pratt's company, another part of the advance group, the following day, and pushed on. The weather was holding warm and dry, but there were still spots in the roads that were huge muddy sloughs. It took hours to get one company through. They made twelve or thirteen miles for each of those first three days. By Saturday, the twenty-first, they camped a few

miles east of the Chariton River. Brigham was fuming, still trying to rein Miller in. The previous day a messenger had brought
a letter from Parley Pratt, who wrote that they were waiting for
the main camp to catch up with them but said that they thought
it best to go several miles farther on to Shoal Creek, where corn
was plentiful. Brigham sent the messenger back with permission
to go that far but no farther.

When the main company reached the Chariton River the
next day, about forty miles west of Richardson's Point, Brigham's
irritation turned to open anger. The river itself was not a challenge. Although it was about four rods across—maybe sixty or
seventy feet—it was only two feet deep and with a good, solid
bottom. The banks, however, were steep and still quite muddy.
They easily found the spot where Miller had crossed a few days
before, but no effort had been made to cut down the banks and
prepare a fording spot for those coming behind. He had several
men. It was for exactly this purpose that they had been sent
ahead.

The plan had been to make the easy four-mile trip to the
Chariton—about an hour and a half's drive—then cross to the
western side and press on the final seven miles to Shoal Creek,
where the advance party would be waiting—or should be!
Instead they spent an exhausting four hours getting the wagons
across. They did not have the manpower to dig down the banks,
so they unhitched all but one yoke of oxen to each wagon, then
roped up the wagons. Men and animals held the wagons back as
they went down the precipitous bank. Once across the river, the
wagons had to be double or triple teamed to get them out.

To their dismay, they went only another mile west before
reaching a steep hill leading up out of the river bottoms. Again
they had to double and triple the teams. Oxen bawled and bellowed as they slipped and clawed their way up the steep slope.
Men burned hands and arms on the rough ropes as they gave
what help they could to the struggling teams. It was tedious,
backbreaking, utterly exhausting work. Once up on the top,

oxen stopped without urging, heads lowered and foam dripping from their mouths.

Brigham was right there with the rest of them, pulling ropes, driving oxen, helping women and children across the shallow river and up the hill. As the last wagons reached the top after sundown, he turned to Heber C. Kimball. "We'll have to stop here and rest the teams, Heber," he said in a low, hard voice. "There's no way we can move out again tomorrow." And then, mouth tight, he added, "When we get to Miller's encampment, we will organize. If Bishop Miller moves again before our arrival he will be disfellowshipped from the camps, unless he repents."

The next morning, Monday, March twenty-third, 1846, a messenger rode into camp from the west. He carried another letter from Elder Parley Pratt to Brigham. The frustrated Apostle wrote that even though the main camp was now only six or seven miles behind them, Bishop Miller had decided he and his company were going to move on and not wait.

When Brigham finished reading the letter, he never said a word, but from the set of his jaw and the hardness of his lips, Heber C. Kimball knew full well that George Miller was heavily on his mind. Finally, Brigham looked up. "I'd like you to come with me to Matthew Steed's tent."

———•◦•———

This time there were no promises of a quick return. There was another letter to take—one filled with sharp rebuke and a command for Miller to wait where he was, Matthew guessed— but it was more than that. Brigham was calling other men besides Matthew. "I've told Miller in no uncertain terms that his job is to prepare the way for us," he said, glowering at the tent canvas. "We cannot spend this kind of time and effort at every river crossing. We've got three choices. Dig down the banks. Make a ferry. Or build bridges."

He turned to Jenny and there was sadness in his eyes. "That's where your husband comes in, Sister Steed. We're not just talking about getting ourselves across; we've still got thousands of people coming behind us. We have got to prepare the way for them too."

"I understand perfectly," Jenny said, fighting to not show her disappointment.

"Matthew is a skilled carpenter, a natural builder. I'm sorry to have to ask this of you, but I need him out there with that advance company. And it could be weeks before you see him again."

Jenny's head came up. "President Young," she said, her voice calm but firm now, "our whole family is hoping and praying that Melissa and Carl will change their minds and come west. If that happens, and Matthew has made it possible for them to reach us more quickly, then you'll not hear one word of complaint from me or anyone else in our family."

For a long moment, Brigham sat there, looking at this young Irish woman who would now have two children to watch over on her own. Then he got up slowly, walked over to her, and took her in his arms. He never said a word, just held her close and closed his eyes and buried his face in her hair.

------———————

Monday, March 23, 1846

It has been more than a week since I have been able to write in my journal. The midday meal is over. Many are sleeping now, including my Will. The weather has been beautiful since crossing the equator, and with the southeasterly trade winds, we are making good time. I should be sleepy too, what with the heat, and a full stomach—from the food, I mean. I am growing noticeably now and thought I felt the first stirrings of life yesterday. Perhaps it is thoughts of the baby that keep me from sleeping. I still cannot believe that I shall be a mother. However, since I am awake, I thought I would catch up in my journal.

We are now in what are called the tropics, that zone which lies both north and south of the equator and which is always

warm and pleasant, warm being a relative word, of course. When
the sun is at its zenith it can beat down unmercifully. During the
doldrums, when there was no wind and no movement to stir the
air, the crew had to rig canvas awnings before we could even
bear to be on deck. In the morning and again in the evening, it
is perfectly delightful. I love to be out on deck with Will and let
the wind catch my face.

I understand better now Will's love of the sea. For the first
few weeks, especially during that horrible four days of storminess
that nearly drove us against the rocky shores of the Cape Verde
Islands, I hated the sea and everything about it. But lately, unless
Will is standing watch, or helping the crew, or working for Elder
Brannan, we walk around the ship and he teaches me what he
knows. It has opened my eyes to what is happening and that
helps pass the time more easily. It also helps to reduce my fear as
we continue south toward Cape Horn, the name given to the
southernmost tip of South America.

This is good because Will says Cape Horn will be the most
challenging part of the voyage. The crew almost whisper whenever they speak of what lies ahead. It is truly the graveyard of
ships, according to them. It will be about the first week of April
when we reach there, but in the Southern Hemisphere, that is
like November. Will says that where the warm waters of the
Pacific and the colder waters of the Atlantic meet, the weather
is often violent. He says the wind can change direction on you
at any moment. Often there will be hail and sleet storms that
can even tear the sails. The waves can seem like mountains
cresting all around you. This leaves me a little anxious but, surprisingly, not filled with dread as I would have been before.

Well, to more pleasant things. For the last week or so, we
have seen some of the creatures of the sea. Often we have por-
poises, or dolphins, for company. This is wonderful. They race
alongside the ship, jumping in and out of the water with great
zest. The children on board line the rails and find great delight

in them. They think they can even recognize some with distinctive marks and have given them names.

Even more delightful are the "flying fish." Yes, you read that right, dear reader. Flying fish. This is truly an amazing sight. They leap out of the water, usually just ahead of the prow of the ship, and fly for great distances through the air before returning to the sea. Some of the sailors told me that if I watched closely I could actually see them flap their wings, but Will explained it differently. He said that they don't actually fly, but sail.

Day before yesterday, one of our number caught one for us all to see. It was quite wonderful. They are a large fish—at least by normal standards back home in Missouri—being almost two feet in length. They have two fins folded up alongside their bodies, but these are not ordinary fins. They extend out like the wings of a dragonfly. They are almost as thin and transparent as those wings too. Once I understood that, then I saw that Will was right. They use their powerful tails to shoot up out of the water, then they extend their "wings," or fins, and sail like kites through the air. Usually it is for short distances, ten, twenty, or even fifty feet. But last evening, just before sundown, we were running nearly into the wind—I'm even starting to talk like a sailor—and a whole school of flying fish started leaping. It was wonderful. Some stayed out of the water for what seemed like a full minute, sailing a hundred, two hundred yards or more. They are so beautiful. As I said before, I am beginning to understand why Will has such a love for the sea.

Some do not share my enthusiasm, however. We have been over six weeks now at sea, and many are finding life more and more monotonous. In a way, they are right, but some do not do anything to try and fight it. For example, the night before we left New York City, at our farewell party, a Mr. Van Cott, who was the president of the local literary society, surprised everyone by presenting Brother Brannan and Captain Richardson with a set of the Harper Family Library. This is a wonderful set of one hundred seventy-nine volumes on just about every subject under the sun—adventure stories, poetry, popular science, travel, history. They are much in demand and have provided a wonderful way for us to pass the time. We read them aloud to each other while sitting up on deck when the weather permits. But some will not bother to read them.

Which reminds me. I did not formerly mention our losses and our gains since departing. We sorely miss the two cows which were brought along to furnish us with milk, butter, and cheese. They were always kept tied up on deck near the stern, but during the terrible storm, they did not survive the pitching and rolling of the ship. I shall never be able to erase from my mind the picture of them being hoisted up and over the side of the ship with block and tackle and dumped into the sea to become food for the sharks.

Speaking of sharks—I know, I know, I promised to speak of losses and gains, and I shall return to that in a moment, but the mention of sharks reminded me. We have one of our passengers, a young man with a new wife, who has found a most unusual way to deal with the boredom. We often have sharks following the ship to consume the garbage that is thrown overboard. This young man lowers himself over the edge of the deck until he hovers just barely out of the reach of the sharks, to see if he can tempt them to snap at him. This sends his wife into a near faint, but he seems not to be concerned overly much about her fears. I think Captain Richardson may put an end to it, for the sailors are mostly superstitious about sharks and find this quite disturbing, as they think he is tempting the fates.

But back to my original point. Sister Sarah Burr gave birth to a healthy baby boy about three weeks after our departure. Appropriately, she named him John <u>Atlantic</u> Burr. He is doing fine and that would be pleasant news indeed if it were not also tempered by tragedy. Two days ago, Sarah's son Charles, who was fifteen months old and who had been ailing for some time now, finally passed away. I could not help but weep as I saw the small form carried beneath a blanket, lifted up above the railing, and allowed to slide into the sea as its final resting place. Sister Sarah is devastated. This is the fifth death we have suffered since leaving New York. This is partly because of the rigors of the journey, I am sure.

But I would not close this entry on such a gloomy note. The deaths have been few. The spirit in our little group is still high. Mothers hold school for the young ones. Many a game is played on the decks, and we are adjusting to sea life. Though I miss Mother and Father terribly and often weep when I think of their bitterness, Will and I are so very happy and that helps make up for it. We spend most of each waking day together, something that I know will not happen once we reach Upper California. We have been greatly blessed by the Lord. We think every night of Will's family and pray for them, wondering if they have reached the Rocky Mountains yet. How we miss them and will rejoice when we are reunited! We thank the Lord each day for life, for each other, and for the gospel of our Savior and Master, which brings us so much joy and peace.

Peter Ingalls ran lightly around the south end of Jenson's bakery shop to the small two-room apartment attached to the back. Even before he noted the wheelchair parked outside the door, he saw a slip of light through the curtains and knew that Kathryn had once again returned home before him. He frowned. That meant she had to get herself out of her chair, onto the crutches, and then inside the apartment. Not that he would have done it for her had he been here. He knew better than that. But he always felt better when he was close enough to catch her should one of her feet catch on the door jam or slip on one of the small rugs that covered their wood floor.

He opened the door and stepped inside, shucking off his coat and hanging it on a peg. The entryway was small, no more than five by five, and had no furniture in it. But then, the whole apartment was only two small rooms—one a narrow bedroom, the other, no bigger, that served as their kitchen, sitting room, and parlor. Kathryn was in the kitchen, leaning up against the small counter, peeling some carrots with a small paring knife.

"Hi," she said cheerfully.

"Hello." He walked over and kissed her on the back of her neck.

She set the carrot and knife down and bowed her head further. "Mmm, I like that."

He did it again. She turned, bracing herself against the counter with one hand, and lifted her head to him. He gave her a warm and lingering kiss.

"That's even better," she murmured, and lifted her arms to put around him.

"How long have you been home?"

"Oh, quarter of an hour. No more."

"How was the tutoring?"

"All right. The children are getting a little restless, what with the weather finally turning warm, but they are still wonderful. They love to learn."

Once Mrs. Reed had determined to hire Peter and Kathryn to provide schooling for her children on the trek, she had decided that Kathryn should start with them before their departure. Peter could not yet. Mr. Reed kept him busy with other preparations, but Kathryn had begun tutoring the children a week before.

"So Mrs. Reed isn't about to change her mind?" Peter said with relief.

She laughed. He was such a worrier. "No. She seems very pleased. She said today that she is so glad that we came to apply for the position." There was a momentary frown. "Though she did ask me straight out if I was . . ." She blushed a little. "Well, if we were going to be parents."

Peter nodded, but said nothing. James and Margret Reed had

hired Peter and Kathryn over the protests of the Donners, who worried about having a crippled woman with them. Margret's answer was that Kathryn's handicap did not interfere with her ability to tutor the children. But if Kathryn were also with child, that would probably tip the scales in the other direction, even for the Reeds. Perhaps the Lord was taking that into account, because thus far Kathryn was not in a motherly way. This worried her a great deal because she feared that the lightning strike that had left her paralyzed may have damaged her internally as well. But for now, at least, there was no cause for concern that the Reeds would have to drop them.

"I was with the Donners and Mr. Reed this afternoon," Peter said.

"And?"

He pulled her in more tightly. "They've set the date."

Her face was instantly wreathed in smiles. "Really, Peter? When?"

"Guess."

She slugged at him. "I'm dying to know, Peter Ingalls. Don't you play with me."

"April fifteenth."

Her eyes widened. Today was the last day of March. That meant . . . She felt her pulse quicken. "But that's just two weeks away."

"Two weeks from tomorrow actually."

"That's wonderful!"

"I know. Jacob Donner said they have already had several responses to the advertisement they've been running in the paper. They think they'll have everything in readiness before too much longer. Also, there's a big wagon train leaving Independence, Missouri, in early May. All are agreed that we must be there in time to join up with it."

Kathryn leaned back in his arms. "Two weeks. I can't believe it could finally really happen."

"There's more good news." He reached in his trouser pocket and withdrew an envelope. He waved it beneath her nose. "Got a letter from Melissa today."

She reached for it. "Really? What does she say?"

He held it just out of her grasp. "You know how we've been worrying that with us not leaving until mid-April we might never catch up with Brother Brigham and the family?"

"Yes."

"Well, Melissa says Nathan sent word back with a man who had to come back to Nauvoo for some teams. As of the twenty-second—that's a week ago Sunday—they had just reached the Chariton River."

"Is that good?"

He handed her the letter, jubilant now. "The Chariton River is barely a hundred miles from Nauvoo, Kathryn. A hundred miles! That's no more than five good traveling days out. I guess the incessant rains have made the roads impassable. Nathan said they were camped at one place for twelve days instead of the one or two they had planned on. And when they do move, it's terribly slow."

Kathryn was thinking now, not opening the letter yet. "But even then, if we don't leave for another two weeks, won't they still be at least a month ahead of us?"

"Maybe not. First of all, think about it. What was our weather like last week?"

Her lower lip puckered slightly. "Wet."

"Yes, very wet. Remember, we even had snow last Tuesday. And rain most of the week. It's been warmer the last two days, but assuming Iowa Territory got the same weather we did, I'll bet they've not made more than another two or three days of progress since the twenty-second."

He stopped for breath, realizing he was sounding like a young boy in his excitement, but not caring. "Second of all, Melissa says that there are still huge numbers of Saints just preparing to leave. Carl thinks that Brigham has only about three thousand with him. He says there are thousands who are getting ready to leave now that spring is finally coming. If Brigham moves ahead too fast, he'll have people scattered from the Rocky Mountains to the Mississippi."

"So you think . . ." She let it trail off. Ever since they had left the family and come to Springfield to try to find another way west, she had worried about being so far behind their family that they would never catch up with them on the trail.

"I think this. If we leave here as planned, we'll be in Independence about the first week of May. Say we take three or four days to rest up and get resupplied. Then we head west up the Oregon Trail toward the Platte River. Mr. Donner let me look at the big map that accompanies John C. Frémont's work. The Platte is the most likely place where Brigham and our people will join up with the Oregon Trail. Mr. Donner thinks it's about three hundred and twenty miles, or about two and a half to three weeks' travel, from Independence. That means we'll be there about the last week of May."

"And how long will it take our people to get there?"

"Even assuming no more delays, it will take them at least four or five weeks to reach that part of the Platte River. That means they'll be there about the first or second week of May, and that's with the very best of circumstances." His mind was fairly racing and his eyes were bright with excitement. "And if there are any delays at all . . ." Then his natural cautiousness took over. "I don't think we ought to get our hopes up, but there is a slight chance we could actually cross paths with them, maybe even meet them once we reach the Platte."

She laughed aloud. "That's wonderful, Peter. I hope you're right. I miss them so."

"Yes, so do I. And I was certain that we would end up having to go all the way to California before we could come back and find them. Now . . ." He grinned so broadly it made the corners of his eyes crinkle. "Well, I don't know about you, but I'm ready to go right now."

The carrots were long since forgotten now. Kathryn threw her arms around her husband's neck again. "Oh, me too, Peter. Me too."

Chapter Notes

The headstrong behavior of Bishop George Miller and Brigham Young's growing frustration with him are found in Brigham's personal history of this time (see *MHBY*, pp. 83–84, 93–100).

Before joining the Church, George Miller, a well-to-do farmer in Illinois, at first thought the religion of the Latter-day Saints was humbug, but he nevertheless took pity on the exiles being driven from Missouri and gave thousands of bushels of grain to the refugees. A little over a year after being converted and baptized, he was called to be a general bishop (similar to what today we would call a Presiding Bishop) in 1841 when Bishop Edward Partridge died. At the time of his calling, the Lord described him as a servant "without guile" who "may be trusted because of the integrity of his heart" (D&C 124:20). Later in Nauvoo, in the October 1844 conference, he was sustained as "second bishop," with Newel K. Whitney being "first bishop."

Converted by the powerful personal presence of Joseph Smith, Miller was a faithful and loyal supporter of the Prophet. However, he did not have those same strong feelings toward Brigham Young. Headstrong and inclined to trust in his own wisdom, he particularly chafed at the Camp of Israel's agonizingly slow progress across Iowa. Brigham Young continually tried to rein in his advance company, but Miller would often not follow counsel, though he did seem to moderate his impetuosity during the latter part of the Iowa journey. After the arrival at the Missouri River, he was part of a group of Saints that ended up about 150 miles northwest of Winter Quarters at a Ponca Indian village, where he spent part of the winter. Miller apparently was convinced that the place for the Church was either in Oregon or, preferably, in Texas with Lyman Wight. When President Young announced in early 1847 the revelation regarding the order of the trek west (see D&C 136) and refused to change the plan to settle in the Great Basin, Miller sent a letter asking to have his name withdrawn from the Church.

He went to Texas for a time and joined the Lyman Wight group. Disenchanted with them, he joined the Strangites for a time as well. He died in

1856, never having returned to the Church. (See Susan Easton Black, *Who's Who in the Doctrine and Covenants* [Salt Lake City: Bookcraft, 1997], pp. 195–97.)

The details of the *Brooklyn's* voyage and of life aboard ship, including the flying fish, the death of the cows, the condition of the water, and the birth of a child who was named for the Atlantic Ocean, all come from the writings of those who participated in the journey (see "Voyage," 46–72).

While camped at the Chariton River during the last week of March, 1846, President Brigham Young used the respite as an opportunity to evaluate what was happening and, more important, what needed to happen. This was their third rest stop since leaving Nauvoo. They had been on the road, not counting the long delay at Sugar Creek, for a month and had barely made a hundred miles. The weather was a major factor, but not the only one. The organization by companies was in severe disarray. Bishop Miller's persistence in forging ahead without regard for counsel was only one symptom of the unraveling structure. Even Parley Pratt, one of the Twelve, whose company included his brother, Orson, another member of the Twelve, kept getting impatient with the continuing delays and moved out ahead of the Camp of Israel. The road between the Chariton River and Nauvoo was filled with stragglers and latecomers trying vainly to catch up to the main company. Men were still leaving to return to Nauvoo for families or for possessions they had left behind.

With the rain and the cold came widespread sickness. There were broken wagons, spent teams, dwindling supplies, inadequate clothing, scarce cash resources. Of the original five hundred wagons, there were now less than four hundred that were operational or still with the main camp.

Brigham's uncanny ability to grasp the large picture, even when it was filled with immense complexity, and his ever-pragmatic approach to things made it clear to him that they could not continue the march west as they were doing now. They had twelve or thirteen hundred miles to go before they reached the Rocky Mountains. And that was only the beginning of the challenge. Brigham Young had between two and three thousand Saints with him in the main Camp of Israel. There were still somewhere between ten to fifteen thousand Saints back in Nauvoo who hadn't even started. They were still trying to get outfits together, sell their property, close out their affairs. Many of those—especially some of the recent arrivals from the East and South or from England—were so poor they were at the bare survival level. Purchasing wagons and teams for them was virtually impossible.

On the twenty-seventh of March, while the rains continued, President Young called a leadership council. They met on Shoal Creek, about seven miles southwest of the main camp on the Chariton. After considerable discussion, a proposal for reorganizing the camp was brought forward and approved. Five days later Brigham and his company of fifty left the camp at Chariton and moved on to the site where the leadership conference had been held. There one of the advance parties had completed work on a sixty-foot-long bridge that spanned Shoal Creek. It was an improvement of immense value. There would be no double teaming the wagons, no ropes winched around men and trees to help the wagons down the steep banks, no wagons mired in the swampy approaches to the crossing. There was much yet to do, so many problems yet to solve. But to some degree, the wisdom of Brigham Young was starting to pay dividends. Even if the rains continued and the streams rose, they would not have to halt at Shoal Creek and wait for better weather.

———•———

Brigham Young stood on the top of the west bank of Shoal Creek. Matthew Steed stood beside him. The low rumble of wagon wheels crossing rough planks filled the air as Brigham's lead company crossed over.

"Well done, Matthew," Brigham said heartily, gazing at the narrow bridge that lay before them.

"It wasn't just me, President," Matthew demurred. "It was Captain Averett who determined that there was no alternative but to bridge it."

"I know," came the response. "Elisha's a good man. I'm glad you decided to leave Bishop Miller and join up with Averett's company instead. This is what an advance company should be doing."

"Well, I wasn't sure if that would be acceptable to you, but I finally decided that what you called me to do was help prepare the trail, not stay with Bishop Miller."

"It is acceptable. Thank you. And thank you for coming back to give me a progress report. I know you need to go rejoin Captain Averett and help with more bridges, but if you stick around a little while longer, your family will be along here shortly and you'll get to see them, if only briefly."

"I won't complain about that." Matthew turned and looked at the bridge and wagons rolling across it one after the other, his mind going back to his frustrations with Bishop Miller. "The difference between Bishop Miller and Brother Averett is that Miller thinks he is the *lead* company; Averett sees himself as an *advance* company. There's a lot of difference."

"Exactly," President Young said gruffly. "Well, with this new organization, Miller won't have any excuse to think he's in the lead anymore."

"New organization?"

"You haven't heard?"

"Well, I heard some changes were being made, but I didn't really get the details."

"We reorganized the companies a few days ago."

"In what way?"

"Instead of going with companies of a hundred families—far too much for one captain to manage—we've decided to split each hundred into two companies of roughly fifty wagons each. Each will have a president and a captain. We also appointed leadership for the whole camp."

"You're still the overall leader, I hope," Matthew said quickly.

There was a soft chuckle. "Yes, I fear that I have no choice in that matter. I will be superintendent for the whole camp. William Clayton will be clerk for the camp, and Willard Richards will be camp historian."

"That's good. Elder Richards is so meticulous."

"Yes," came the thoughtful response. "We are as Israel of old, Matthew. We have left the fleshpots of Egypt and strike out into the wilderness to find our own promised land." He looked at Matthew and his face was very earnest. "That is not just idle talk, Matthew. We are making history here. We are also fulfilling prophecy. We are part of that great gathering of Israel in the last days which the prophets foretold. It will be important to future generations to have good records of what we are about."

Matthew nodded, impressed with the senior Apostle's gravity and with what he had just said.

Then Brigham seemed to come out of his reverie. "Anyway, as far as the companies go, there will be three companies of hundreds, and each of those will have two companies of fifties. Each company of a hundred will have a member of the Twelve to preside over it. I will have the first one. Parley Pratt will take the second, and John Taylor the third."

"That will help," Matthew said, pleased with that news.

"And we've chosen good men to be captains and presidents of the companies of fifties—Brother Ezra T. Benson, Heber,

Albert P. Rockwood, Stephen Markham." He stopped, looking suddenly a little sheepish. "Incidentally, your family will be in my company." The sheepishness turned into a grin. "I ought to have some say in who travels with me, don't you think?"

"Wonderful!" Not only would he get to see Jenny and the children again today, but if they were in the first company of fifty, that meant his family would be closer to the advance company that he was with. "What about Bishop Miller? Is he still a captain?"

There was a momentary frown. "Bishop Miller was appointed the president of the sixth group of fifty, but Brother Charles Crisman will be the captain. Do you know Brother Crisman?"

Matthew shook his head.

"A good man. Levelheaded. I'm hoping that with Elder Taylor as his president and Brother Crisman as his captain, Bishop Miller will be more moderate." President Young then smiled. "Bishop Miller is a good man, a hard worker. He just . . ." His voice trailed off and he turned back to look at the bridge.

"He just needs to learn to take counsel?" Matthew supplied tentatively.

There was a quick, firm nod. "That's the heart of it," he agreed. "Why is it so hard for men to learn to take counsel?" He was speaking more to the line of wagons slowly making their way across the sixty-foot span of bridge than he was to Matthew. "Think of how many would have been saved. Oliver Cowdery. David Whitmer. Martin Harris. Thomas B. Marsh. The list goes on and on. They were some of the truly great in the kingdom. How tragic! How different it would have turned out for them, had they just learned to follow counsel!"

Matthew said nothing, not wanting to interrupt. He sensed that, for whatever reason, Brigham's mind had turned to deeper things and that Matthew had a rare opportunity to be taught at the feet of one of the Lord's anointed.

After almost a full minute, the President turned and looked at Matthew. His demeanor was very grave now. "I don't under-

stand it, Matthew. When a man has the Spirit of the Lord, taking counsel from the priesthood is not a challenge. That is the
key. When we have the light of the Holy Spirit in us, then we
know our duty, and when we know our duty fully, it will be easy
to follow truly those whom God has placed over us to lead us—
as a community, as a people, as the kingdom of God."

He swung around. "You know what the root problem is?"
Brigham finally asked absently. "It's pride. They get so filled
with a sense of their own importance, they lose the Spirit.
They're no longer teachable. They don't believe they need
counsel from anyone."

"Yes, I can see that."

"When you give way to this feeling of self-importance, it's
easy to forget that we all are dependent on God. The Savior
himself warned us that those who exalt themselves will be
abased, and those who abase themselves will be exalted."

Matthew said nothing. His thoughts were filled with the
memory of some of those Brigham had named. They had been
the greats of the kingdom. They had participated in some of the
most exciting events of the Restoration. And now they were
gone. Was pride really so heady a mistress that it took down
even those kinds of men?

"Take Oliver Cowdery, for example," Brigham went on, still
half musing, not realizing he was answering Matthew's very
question. "Do you know what he said to Joseph once?"

"What?"

"This was before he had started to fall away from the
Church. One day he told Joseph, 'If I should leave the Church,
it would break up.'"

Matthew almost hooted, but then realized how tragic that
statement really was. "He really said that?"

"Yes. And he meant it."

"What did Joseph say?"

"I wasn't there, but George A. Smith was. He said Joseph
was incredulous. 'What?' he demanded. 'Who are you? The Lord

is not dependent upon you. Do what you will, the work will continue to roll.'"

"Which has certainly been the case," Matthew replied. "Look at all that's happened in the Church since Oliver left—settling Nauvoo, work for the dead, missionary work in many places, another temple, the move west."

"The kingdom rolls forth like the stone cut out of the mountain, just as Joseph said it would. And because of pride, Oliver is left behind. Sidney Rigdon, who tried to exalt himself and become the leader, is left behind." Brigham was shaking his head slowly. "Think of it, Matthew. Even the Twelve, even those who are ordained to be special witnesses of the Savior, are not immune to the infectious poison of pride. Thomas B. Marsh. William McLellin. Lyman Johnson. John Boynton. William Smith. Not only did half the original Quorum fall away, but most of them turned against the Church and bitterly fought to bring down Joseph. Why? Because they feel like they are wiser and more in tune with God than those called to preside over them. And so they refuse to take counsel."

There was total silence. Even the rumbling of the wagons across the bridge and the shouts of the teamsters as they led them across seemed distant and muted. Brigham stared off and beyond them, his thoughts far away. When he spoke it was with sadness and yet also with a curious sense of strength and conviction. "And do you know what, Matthew? They don't break up the work of God. They only break themselves against it."

He straightened, took a deep breath, and turned back to the bridge. He reached out and laid a hand on Matthew's shoulder. "But thank the Lord, there are many of those who do follow counsel. And you're one of them, Matthew. Before he left, Captain Averett told me that it would have taken him twice as long to build the bridge without your help, dear brother."

"Well, that's hardly the case," Matthew started, "there were a lot of good men who—"

There was a sudden twinkle in Brigham's eye. "Are you suggesting that Captain Averett was not telling me the truth?"

Flustered, Matthew stammered a little. "Well, no, I . . ."

Brigham laughed heartily. "Then just say, 'I'm glad I can be of service, Brother Brigham.' "

"I'm glad I can be of service, Brother Brigham," Matthew responded meekly.

"Thank you. So am I." Smiling, he started to turn away, then stopped. His hand lifted, pointing toward a wagon that was just starting to cross Shoal Creek. "Say, isn't that the Hendrickses' wagon?"

"Hendrickses?" Matthew said, turning. "I don't think I know them."

"Sure you do. James Hendricks and his wife, Drusilla?"

Matthew started to shake his head.

Brigham motioned for Matthew to follow as he strode away. "Come on. Enough of this gloomy talk of people who won't follow counsel. I want you to meet some who do, even when they have good reason not to. This will be something that will cheer and lift up both of us while you're waiting for your family to arrive."

"Tell me again who this is and why we are going to see them."

They were picking their way carefully through the campground, watching for puddles or those patches of ground that seemed to be only damp but which often proved to be a thin crust of drying soil over two or three inches of thick prairie mud.

Caroline looked at Joshua. "James and Drusilla Hendricks. We knew them—or rather, I knew them—in Nauvoo. Remember when your mother formed the Steed family women's council a few years back to help those in need?"

"Yes."

"Well, Sister Hendricks was one of those we helped from time to time."

He shifted the sack of flour that he carried on his shoulder so its weight was more comfortable. "And why this sudden urge to go see them?"

"Matthew said he and President Young saw them crossing the bridge today."

"Oh." There was a wry look. "And will we be visiting all of the families that crossed over the bridge today?"

She smiled sweetly. "No. Just the Hendrickses."

"But . . ." He wasn't really fighting her on this, he was just curious. He had come back from getting water from the river. Matthew was there, talking to the family about a visit he and Brigham Young had made. The moment Joshua came up, Caroline had grabbed him, found a sack of flour and a slab of bacon, and insisted they make a visit before supper. "Why them?"

"You'll see," she replied. "Once you meet them, I don't think you'll have any more questions."

Drusilla Hendricks was outside her tent preparing supper over a small fire. Four children—three girls and a boy, ranging in age from about eight or nine into their teens—were working with her or around the wagon, still unpacking some of their things. A half-erected tent was near the wagon. As they approached, the tent abruptly straightened and Joshua saw another son, a young man of about sixteen or seventeen, behind the tent, tightening the guy ropes. The young man reached down with a small sledgehammer and tapped on one of the tent pegs. Then he walked to the other side and began to tighten that as well.

Mrs. Hendricks looked up at the sound of their footsteps. They were coming from the west, and the sun was low in the sky. She brushed a tendril of hair away from her eyes, squinting against the light. Then, recognizing Caroline, she smiled broadly. "Sister Steed! What a pleasant surprise!"

Caroline walked swiftly around the fire, set the bacon slab on the wagon tongue, then gave the woman a warm hug. "How are you, Drusilla? I was so pleased when Matthew told us you had come into camp today. I wanted to come see for myself."

"Wonderful. It was so good to see Matthew again. What a fine young man he is. Brother Brigham seems to have great confidence in him."

"Yes. We're glad we got to see him before he had to leave. President Young has assigned him to be with the advance company." Caroline turned to Joshua. "I don't know if you have ever met my husband, Joshua."

Joshua swung the flour sack to the ground and stepped forward, hand outstretched. "Pleased to meet you."

"And I you," Drusilla said with an appraising smile. "I've heard a lot about you."

He shot Caroline a look, then grinned easily. "Yeah, I'm the difficult one in the family."

Caroline looked startled by that, but Sister Hendricks picked up on it smoothly. "Oh no. That's not what I mean. And it didn't come from your family. You were talked about quite a bit around town, actually. I heard about how you helped your family build their homes when we first moved to Nauvoo. I heard about your venture in the pineries, and the piano you bought for your daughter after her death. I also heard about your stable burning down and you losing all your money." She laughed lightly, shaking his hand once more before letting it go. "Yes, I've heard a lot about you." Then, seeing his embarrassment, she turned to look at the flour and bacon. "What is this, Caroline Steed?"

"Oh, just a little extra we thought you might be able to use."

"Extra?" came the quick reply. "I know better than that."

"We've got enough," Caroline said. "We want you to have it."

There was a sudden shining in Drusilla's eyes. "Thank you." Then, to hide her emotions, she turned and called the children to her and introduced them to Joshua and Caroline. The last to come over was the older boy, who had finished putting up the tent.

"This is my son William. He's what keeps us all going." She reached out and ruffled his hair as he colored at the praise. "Don't know what I'd do without my William."

Joshua shook his hand and was pleased to feel the firmness of it. The boy looked like his mother, with dark hair and open features. Like many of the older boys on the trail, William was doing the work of a man. Now Joshua thought he understood the reason for their visit. Drusilla Hendricks was a widow. With that realization, any feelings he might have had about begrudging her the food instantly disappeared.

But he was wrong. William stepped back. "It will just take me a minute, Mama, and I'll have the bed in place. Then we can help get Papa into the tent."

"All right," Drusilla said. Then, noting Joshua's puzzled look, she said, "Come over and meet my husband."

As William got a straw-filled mattress and a blanket and ducked inside the tent, Drusilla moved toward the wagon. She walked around to the back of it, with Joshua and Caroline close behind. There the wagon flaps were drawn back and Joshua could see a man lying on a bed. His head came up as they appeared.

"James, you remember Caroline Steed, don't you? And this is her husband, Joshua."

"How do you do?" The man nodded, reaching out to grip the side of the wagon and pull himself up. To Joshua's surprise, it was a major effort and he made it only partway up.

"James, wait a moment. William will be right here."

He nodded and lay back down, puffing a little from the effort. Joshua tried not to stare.

Sensing his puzzlement, Drusilla smiled at him. "I don't know if Caroline told you, but James had a terrible accident back in Missouri."

"I didn't," Caroline said. "But I would like him to hear the story."

Drusilla turned to her husband. "Tell him what happened, James."

But before he could do so, William appeared. "Are you ready, Papa?"

"Yes, son. Help me up."

The boy climbed into the wagon beside his father, then put one hand beneath his back and with the other took his father's arm. Again James Hendricks gripped the side of the wagon. With his son's help he was able to get up to a sitting position, though Joshua saw that William had to pull hard to help get him there.

Drusilla reached in and tucked a pillow behind her husband to help support him. "Joshua and Caroline brought us some flour and some bacon," Drusilla said as she brushed his hair quickly with her fingers.

"I heard," James Hendricks said softly. "Much obliged."

"We're happy to do it, James," Caroline said. "How are you holding up?"

"Well, actually," he said with a brief smile, "better than I thought. Sometimes the ride can get pretty rough, but we make do."

Drusilla was watching Joshua's face. "I understand that you were shot during the battle of Far West, back in 1838."

That caught Joshua by surprise. "Yes, I was."

"Do you remember the Battle of Crooked River that took place a few days before that?" Drusilla asked.

Joshua thought for a moment, then shook his head.

James picked it up. "Some of the Missouri militia had kidnapped three of our brethren and were taking them back to

Jackson County where they threatened they would kill them. Brother Joseph sent a group of us out to rescue them."

Caroline broke in now. "You've heard Nathan talk about this, Joshua. He and Matthew rode with them that night."

"Oh, yes," he said, clearly remembering now. He just hadn't made the association with the name of Crooked River. "This is when you overtook them just at dawn?"

"That's right," James replied, his eyes hooded and distant now. "The sun was in our eyes and we barely saw them. One of the picket guards saw us coming and opened fire. We fired back. It lasted no more than a few minutes, but when it was over, one of our men lay dead and two others mortally wounded." There was a long pause. Then his eyes refocused on Joshua. "I took a ball in the back of the neck." He looked down at himself. "I was paralyzed from the neck down."

Joshua didn't know what to say. From the neck down? And he was out here on the trail, headed for the Rocky Mountains?

William smiled brightly at his father. "But he's doing so much better now, aren't you, Pa?"

"I am." He reached for a cane and began to scoot toward the edge of the wagon. "For a long time, Drusilla had to do everything for me—wash me, bathe me, feed me." There was a deep love in his eyes as he looked at his wife. "I'll bet she had to lift me twenty or thirty times a day. And as you can see, she is not a large woman."

"It had to be done," Drusilla said simply, looking back at her husband with that same love in her eyes. "But God has been good to us." She turned to Joshua. "First of all, William is old enough to be a great help to me now. Also, about a year following the wound, James was able to stand by himself. Now he can move around slowly with just a cane."

"Very slowly," he said proudly, "but after my lying motionless in bed for nearly a year, we take that as a small miracle."

He was to the edge of the wagon box now. Drusilla and

William stood beside him, one on each arm, and helped him down.

"Can I help?" Joshua offered awkwardly.

"No, I'm fine," James replied.

"Your bed is all ready, Pa," his son said, steadying him on one arm as he started forward.

As James made his way toward the tent, wife and son walking beside him, Joshua saw that he was able to make his own progress, but it was pretty shaky. Now finally Joshua understood. Drusilla Hendricks was not a widow, but as far as having a man to take her west—drive the wagon, pitch the tent, cut firewood, round up oxen, or do the hundred other things that were part of the daily regimen—she might as well have been.

"We won't stay," Caroline said. "We've got to get back and start supper too."

Drusilla nodded. "Thank you again for your generosity and kindness," she said.

"Yes, we certainly do thank you," James said.

"You are more than welcome," Joshua replied without hesitation. "If there is anything else you need, you let us know."

———————

As they made their way slowly back to their own campsite, Joshua was deep in thought. The image of the pale, thin man walking hesitantly toward his tent was a vivid picture in his mind.

"Tell me what you're thinking," Caroline said.

He turned to her. "I can't believe it. They're out here? How can they possibly get by?"

"That's why I wanted you to meet them. If ever there was a woman who will be sainted, it is Sister Drusilla Hendricks. She's not much bigger than a willow slip, but for the last eight years she's provided for her family, cared for her husband. William is finally old enough now to help, but back in Nauvoo, William was only ten. Can you picture lifting James over and over, day after day? I watched her do it one day. I could tell it took every ounce of her strength."

"But why did they come west? This is insane!" He was deeply troubled by what they had just seen. A good part of what disturbed him was the happiness in Drusilla's eyes. There was no self-pity, no bitterness at the fate that had dealt this kind of a hand to her.

"Because they believe it is the Lord's will for them," Caroline answered quietly.

"You think the Lord expects that?" he exploded. "The man can barely hobble. Surely the Lord would forgive him if he just said, 'It's too much.'"

"I'm sure he would. That's not the point."

He blew out his breath in exasperation. "I know how you people feel about doing what is right. But . . . Wouldn't it have been wiser to stay in Nauvoo until we at least know where we're going?"

She looked at him in genuine surprise. "Wiser? How do you mean?"

That frustrated Joshua all the more. "At least they would have a home, some protection."

Caroline was looking at him strangely. "Why didn't you think it was wiser for me to stay back there?"

That caught him from behind. "Because . . . Well, I was worried."

"Do you think that the enemies of the Church would take pity on James because he is a cripple?"

He started to nod, then stopped. If they didn't take pity on women and children—something he himself had been unwilling to do—then a crippled man probably would not be much different. "But this has got to be so hard for them."

"Let me tell you about Drusilla, about how she has managed to get along without a husband to be the breadwinner. She doesn't like to talk about herself, but one night while we were visiting in their home, your mother pulled this out of her. When she finally got to Nauvoo after getting James out of Missouri, she had only fifty-six dollars. With that she rented a house, bought two bedsteads, four chairs, five falling-leaf tables. She kept one of the tables for herself, gave one to Brother Lewis for helping them move to Nauvoo. She sold two to Sister Emma Smith for some provisions."

Caroline's face had softened with the memory, and her eyes had a touch of shininess to them.

"Some of the brethren gave her and James a lot and put together a log house for them. With what little money she had left she hired a man to put on a roof and build a chimney. She and another woman chinked and plastered it themselves. To support her family, she took in boarders and did washing and ironing. If you think about it, you might remember her at some of the celebrations in town. She would make ginger beer and gingerbread, then she and her children would sell it on public days to the crowds."

Caroline glanced at her husband and saw that he was listening intently. "She made gloves and mittens in the winter and sold those." Now her voice went suddenly husky. "I clearly remember that night we were there. She told us that she made extra mittens so that she could give them as tithing."

Joshua said nothing. He seemed withdrawn into his own thoughts.

"Do you know what is most remarkable about Drusilla Hendricks? She doesn't think she is remarkable in any way."

Finally he nodded. "I could see that."

"Do you wish I hadn't taken flour and bacon to them?" Caroline asked. "I know we don't have any extra to spare."

He looked surprised. "You think I would resent that?"

"No, and I'm glad. But you do think they are wrong for being out here, don't you?"

For a long moment he thought about that. Then he shook his head. "I don't know if it's wrong or not, but that doesn't change the fact that they are two very remarkable people."

Chapter Notes

While there is no specific account contemporary with the time shown here where Brigham Young speaks about the importance of following counsel, the sentiments he expresses to Matthew are drawn from things he said later in life (see *Journal of Discourses*, 26 vols. [London: Latter-day Saints' Book Depot, 1854–86], 12:126).

George A. Smith—cousin to the Prophet Joseph, a member of the Twelve, and First Counselor to President Brigham Young from 1868 to 1875—is the one who reports that Oliver Cowdery once stated his belief that if he left the Church it would fail (see *Journal of Discourses* 17:199).

Drusilla and James Hendricks were part of the first group to start west from Nauvoo. Their story as told here is an accurate portrayal of their situation. The description of how Drusilla supported her family while in Nauvoo comes from her own words as recorded in her life story. (See Leonard J. Arrington and Susan Arrington Madsen, *Sunbonnet Sisters: True Stories of Mormon Women and Frontier Life* [Salt Lake City: Bookcraft, 1984], pp. 29–30.)

I can't imagine where he has gone to," Caroline said. "He just said he was going to cut some firewood."

"When was that?" Nathan asked.

"Almost two hours ago."

He sensed that Caroline was trying to be nonchalant about it, but there was just a touch of anxiety in her voice.

Solomon seemed to note it too. He grinned at Caroline. "Knowing Joshua, he probably saw someone he knew, or thought of something else he needed to do first."

"Probably," Caroline agreed.

Brigham's company had left Shoal Creek Camp the day before, April third, traveling in the rain fourteen miles to reach what they called the Hickory Grove Camp. There was a small stream and an extensive stand of timber there to give at least some shelter. Some of the Steeds were now walking upstream, or north, along the west bank of the creek. They had come nearly half a mile from their camp, passing the last of the encampment's tents five minutes before. Above them, through the trees, the sky was overcast, but it was high and thin—thin enough to show that the sun was almost directly overhead. Back in camp they were beginning to start the fires in preparation for the midday meal. And the Steeds had virtually no firewood. On their arrival, they had gathered only enough for supper and breakfast. So Joshua had left shortly after breakfast with two oxen and one wagon to gather more.

"Maybe he crossed over to the other bank," Josh volunteered.

Nathan shook his head. "No point, unless he saw someone." The creek was only a couple of feet deep, though twenty or so feet across, and fording it would be no challenge. But there was no need for Joshua to go over. Then Nathan had second thoughts. "However, there's been a lot of people getting firewood on this side. Maybe he thought there might be more over there."

Solomon nodded and motioned to Josh. "Come on. We'll go across and search on that side."

They cut to the right and quickly disappeared in the trees. Nathan looked at Caroline. "Why don't you stay right along the creek bed here? I'll go see if he might be over this way. Go another five minutes, then wait. I'll come to you."

She nodded, and even as Nathan moved away she lifted her head and called out. "Joshua!"

Nathan angled to the left, working his way through the trees. In less than a minute he could barely hear Caroline's voice anymore. So much for calling out. Unless they got right on top of him, Joshua wouldn't hear them, especially if he was chopping or stacking wood. So Nathan peered ahead, watching for tracks or movement, listening for any sounds.

He was puzzled more than worried. Once they got farther west, where the Indian tribes still ran free, there would be more cause for concern at a time like this, but not now. An accident was possible, but Joshua was not some inexperienced traveler.

Solomon was most likely right. Joshua had probably seen someone or gone back another way. He might even be back at the
camp by now.

Nathan came to where he could see the trees thinning out
and giving way to open prairie again. He turned straight north,
making better time now through the more scattered timber,
moving as silently as possible as he listened intently for the
sound of an ax or the lowing of an ox. When he finally saw the
movement, back to his right, deeper in the trees, he froze, staring at the spot where he thought he had seen something. There
was nothing for several seconds; then there it was again. A tail
had swished, momentarily flashing against the surrounding
trees. In the speckled and subdued light of the forest, the
brindle-colored oxen blended in almost perfectly. Had the one
not moved, Nathan would have gone right on by. Now he could
see the wagon behind it. They had stripped the canvas cover off
the lightest wagon and unloaded it enough to take a good load
of firewood. The wagon was nearly full.

He lifted his hand, about to shout, then dropped it again.
There was no other movement—no swinging of an ax, no thud-
ding as wood was tossed up on the stack. A slow grin stole across
Nathan's face. Joshua had fallen asleep. That was the only
explanation. For that, he would deserve a ribbing. Moving even
more carefully than before, Nathan crept forward.

He had gone only a few steps when he saw Joshua. He was
not stretched out somewhere but rather was sitting on a fallen
log, his back to Nathan. His head was down, his chin in one
hand. For a moment, Nathan thought he might have dozed off,
but then his head came up and stared out into the trees ahead of
him. Then it dropped again. His hand moved, reaching for
something on his lap. There was a momentary flash of white. He
was reading something.

Nathan felt a sudden sense of being an intruder and he
changed his mind about trying to startle his brother. "Joshua?"
He called just loudly enough for his voice to reach him.

Joshua shot to his feet, jerking his head around. "Nathan!" He fumbled quickly, not turning his body, as if he were shoving something inside his coat. Finally, he turned around, looking a little sheepish.

Nathan went forward, walking more swiftly now. "Hi. Are you all right?"

"Yeah," Joshua called back, forcing a laugh. "You startled me." He buttoned the bottom of his jacket, even though the air was not that chilly, then reached down and picked up the ax that was lying at his feet. He walked to the wagon, meeting Nathan there.

Nathan gave him a strange look, but Joshua only smiled blandly. "I was just getting ready to leave. Sat down for a minute to rest."

"Looks like you're done," Nathan said, noting the full wagon and the ground littered with chips and small branches that Joshua had cut from a fallen log.

"Yep. That should last us for a while, don't you think?"

"I would think so."

Joshua put the ax beneath the wagon seat, then walked to the head of the oxen. "What are you doing out here anyway?"

"Looking for you." Nathan again looked at him closely. "Do you know what time it is?"

There was a momentary start and Joshua looked up at the sky, where the sun was nearing its zenith. "Oh!" He shook his head. "It's getting later than I thought." He shrugged, recovering swiftly now. "Sorry. I lost track, I guess."

Nathan nearly said something. He was also almost certain Joshua had been reading something, but there was nothing in his hands now. If he had been reading, he didn't want Nathan to know about it. Nathan decided to let it pass. "Caroline is over by the creek. Solomon and Josh are on the other side."

"My, my," Joshua said, chiding just a little now. "I wasn't that late."

"I know. We thought maybe you could use some help. Caroline said she wanted to get out and walk."

"And she was worried just a little, I'll bet," he answered.

"Yes, that too." Nathan jerked his head toward the east. "I told her to stay close to the creek. I'll take the load in if you want to go find her."

"Sure. Thanks."

"You'll hear her as you get closer. She's been calling."

"Okay. See you back at camp."

Joshua swung around again and moved off, not turning back. Nathan watched him curiously. In a moment he disappeared into the subdued light, and finally Nathan shrugged. He walked to the oxen. "All right, boys, let's get going. You've got people waiting to get a meal started."

Joshua stood motionless behind a large hickory tree until he could no longer hear the sound of the wagon. With a quick movement of his right hand, he reached inside his coat and retrieved the book that he had jammed up under his arm. For a moment he stared at the dark stain on the cover, then looked up again, staring at the spot where he had last seen Nathan. Had his brother seen that he was reading? He thought about that, then shook his head. Nathan had been behind him. There was no way he could have. But he would have to be more careful from now on. The last thing he needed was to be interrogated by an overeager family. He was curious, that was all. Over the past few days he had read here and there in the book, browsing more than reading. But the encounter with Drusilla and James Hendricks had left him wondering what it was that drove them.

He stepped out from behind the tree, looking once more to make sure Nathan was gone. The forest was silent. Reaching carefully around to the back of his trousers, he tucked the book into the waistline, then pulled his coat down lower in the back.

Satisfied, he spun around and started walking again. He raised his head. "Caroline! Caroline! It's me! I'm over here."

———•———

It was expected that spring would bring rain to the Great Plains. That was as sure as mosquitoes along the Mississippi or falling leaves in autumn. But the spring of 1846 brought rains like no one had ever seen, at least in the memory of any white man. It was as though Iowa Territory saw the burgeoning stream of refugees pouring across the river and onto her prairies as a personal threat and fought back with the only means at hand—the weather. It would rain for days on end, stopping the companies dead. But the Saints would not turn back. The moment the roads began to dry, they were out again. They had not learned their lesson. So once again it would start to rain.

They were stopped for twelve days at Richardson's Point, ten days at the Chariton River. Finally, on the first day of April, the order came to move west again. The first and fourth companies of fifty moved out about nine a.m. But not all were ready, and it was not until the night of the second that all of the companies reached the next camp on Shoal Creek, just six or seven miles west of the Chariton River. That night the wind started to blow, signalling the next storm. This time Brigham wouldn't give in. They had to keep moving. So on the morning of the third, they pulled their coats around them, lowered their heads, cinched down the wagon covers, and moved out, slogging straight into the teeth of the storm.

It proved to be one of the worst of days in what was becoming a never-ending march of miserable days. It rained and blew hard all day. Oxen and mules sunk up to their bellies in the bogs. Even the slightest rise of land required double and triple teaming. Some teams became mired as they were going *down* the far side of hillocks and ridges. Incredibly, they made fourteen miles, one of the longest marches since they had left Nauvoo. But by nightfall, when they reached Hickory Grove, about a mile from the east fork of Locust Creek, dozens of wagons had been left behind, mired deeply.

Finally Brigham saw there was no point in battling the inevitable. Once again, as the rains came down in blinding sheets, Brigham ordered a halt. The next day, Saturday, April fourth, saw continued rain in the form of scattered showers. Most rested in camp, but several teams were sent back to help retrieve those who had been stranded the day before. The next day, the fifth of April, was Sunday. It dawned cold and clear, but most of the camp would stay put this day. That afternoon Brigham took advantage of the respite to ride out a few miles west and survey the area around the east and middle forks of Locust Creek. He returned to the main camp about sunset and announced that they would be moving out tomorrow at sunrise. But once again it started raining during the night. Nevertheless, on Monday morning part of the camp moved about three miles west, crossing the east fork and the middle fork of Locust Creek and stopping on the west bank of the middle fork. Here they began pitching their tents. Their spirits were lifted when near sundown the sky cleared and there was a beautiful sunset. They should have been wiser.

As darkness fell, the clouds came scudding in and the wind began to rise. About eight o'clock the heavens let loose in such fury that it would prove to be the worst storm seen thus far. Lightning and thunder crashed all around, shaking the trees and making even the ground tremble. Tents were torn loose and blown down. Wagon covers were ripped away. Stock panicked and stampeded. Bedding and clothing were instantly drenched. The rain came in horizontally, peppering bare skin like pebbles flung from a boy's flipper.

It was April sixth, 1846, the sixteenth anniversary of The Church of Jesus Christ of Latter-day Saints.

It cleared nearly as quickly as it had come, but it was followed by a severe drop in the temperature. By the morning of the seventh, there was snow on the ground and the thousands of puddles had become miniature ice ponds. Locust Creek rose six feet into a raging, muddy torrent, blocking any passage. Once again, man recognized the superior force. For the next ten days the Saints would hunker down in the Locust Creek Camp to wait for a kinder and more gentle response from the weather that seemed to be fighting them at every hand.

It was nearly ten o'clock on the morning of April eighth when Josh came splashing through the water and mud in search of his father. The weather had improved somewhat—the rain was intermittent now and not nearly as heavy as it had been— but it was still very cold and windy. Nathan, Joshua, Solomon, and Derek were out with the stock, letting them graze on the browse of the heavy willows along the Locust Creek bottoms.

Nathan was prodding at the neck of one of his oxen. The animal was bent on heading directly into the roiling waters of Locust Creek, and Nathan was trying to persuade it otherwise. Derek called to him, and when Nathan turned, his brother-in-law jerked his head in the direction of an oncoming figure. When he saw his son, Nathan gave the ox one tremendous whack with the palm of his hand, which finally turned it away from the stream, and then he trotted over to meet Josh.

"Is it Mama, son?"

"Yes. She wants us to find Sister Sessions."

The others came in around father and son now too, faces anxious. "Is it time?" Solomon asked.

Josh nodded. "I think so. Mama wants us to find the midwife."

"Is she all right?" Nathan asked, handing his ox goad to Derek.

"She said she's fine. Not to worry. Just get Sister Sessions."

"All right," Nathan said, taking his son by the elbow. "Let's go."

Patty Sessions was known all over camp, as she had been in Nauvoo, as being the best midwife among the Latter-day Saints. She was the wife of David Sessions, a wealthy farmer who had joined the Church back in 1835, one year after Patty had been baptized. Patty and her family had come to Kirtland in 1837 just in time to leave the city in the hands of the apostates before going to Far West. And then in 1839 they were driven to Nauvoo. Caring, cheerful, competent, Patty was a source of great comfort to Nathan. He stood back with the rest of the men, watching as she directed the Steed family women like a sergeant at arms—empty Nathan's tent, prepare a bed, boil water, find clean dry cloths and dry bedding, no mean feat after days of incessant rain.

As she turned to go back into the tent, she stopped and looked over to Nathan. There was a quick, warm smile. "It will be all right," she called. "Everything's going to be fine."

Nathan felt the knot in his stomach loosen just a bit. Maybe it was just her way of trying to reduce his tension, but he didn't think so. Lydia had thought the baby would come the last week of March. They were now into the second week of April. That was always cause for concern, and yet Lydia had been doing remarkably well. She kept telling Nathan that she was probably just too early in her calculations. Nevertheless, there had been their "silent baby" born back at the Morley farm outside of Kirtland in 1834. Then they had lost little three-year-old Nathan to the ague during that first summer at Nauvoo. Both had devastated Lydia. Nathan lay awake nights now worrying about what another tragedy might cost her.

With a jerk, he turned to Matthew, who had recently rejoined the family for a time. "Let's start chopping some firewood. There's no sense just standing around waiting."

———⋅•⋅———

It was shortly after two p.m. when Patty Sessions stepped outside the tent, looked around until she spotted Nathan, then waved for him to come over. He dropped the ax and trotted over to face her. His heart dropped as he saw the gravity on her face, but as he reached her she broke into a broad smile. "It's over," she said. "Lydia is just fine. The baby too."

"What is it?"

There was a soft chuckle. "That's not for the midwife to say. Why don't you go in and see for yourself."

He took her hand and wrung it fervently. "Thank you, Sister Sessions."

"No," she said quickly, still smiling, "thank *you*. Thank you for having confidence in me."

He nodded and slipped inside the tent. Lydia's head turned and her eyes opened. Her face was drawn and pale, but she was radiant with joy. Cuddled up against her left arm was a tiny bundle of white. He moved swiftly to her side and dropped to his knees, taking her hands. "How are you?" he whispered.

"Fine."

"Really?"

"Yes. Tired, but fine."

He looked down. "What is it?"

Her eyes followed his, her mouth softening. "It's a girl, Nathan. It's a little girl."

"Wonderful!"

She laughed softly. "Actually, she's not so little. Sister Sessions guesses she'd weigh in at about nine pounds." She reached down and pulled back the blanket.

For a long moment, Nathan just stared. Lydia was right. The little face was round and fat, the cheeks looking almost as though they were stuffed with food. Her skin was still red and flushed from birth but smooth and without flaw. Her eyes were closed, but long dark lashes showed against the cheeks. Her head was covered with black hair, almost an inch long, and very thick. Gingerly he reached out and touched it. It felt like silk. "Oh, Lydia," he breathed, "she's beautiful."

"I know." Tears had welled up in her eyes. She smiled through them, reaching out to squeeze Nathan's hand. "I know."

———————

Josh's head appeared suddenly in the tent door. "Brother Brigham's coming."

Nathan and Lydia both looked up in surprise. "Here?" Lydia blurted.

"Looks like it." Josh withdrew again.

"I'll bet Matthew sent word to him," Mary Ann said. She was in one corner, sitting beside Emily, who was rocking the baby back and forth, cooing to it softly.

"Quick, Nathan, get me my hairbrush."

Smiling, Nathan complied. He wanted to argue with her, tell her she didn't need anything. He couldn't remember her ever looking more beautiful. She had slept for two or three hours this afternoon and awakened much refreshed. But he knew better than to dispute with her over this and crawled quickly to the chest and retrieved the brush for her.

"Is the baby still dry?" she asked Emily as she began to brush her hair with long, quick strokes.

Emily felt beneath the blanket. "Yes, Mama."

"Maybe Brother Brigham is just passing by." She lifted her hair and began to twist it. "Nathan, get me my whalebone hair clip."

He gave his mother a look, but Grandma Steed only smiled, so he went to the trunk again.

Outside now they heard Josh's voice. "Good evening, President Young."

"Good evening, Brother Brigham." Elizabeth Mary, Josiah, and little Joseph, who would all be sleeping in the wagon tonight, sang out their greeting together.

"Good evening, children. I understand you have a new-comer at your house."

"Oh," Lydia said, piling her hair into a bun and jamming at it with the clip Nathan had gotten her. "He is coming here."

"You look wonderful, Lydia."

"You do," Mary Ann agreed. "You look fine."

There was a rap on the canvas flap, and then it pulled back. Nathan stood up and walked over to greet the senior Apostle. "Hello, President."

Brigham reached out and took his hand, pumping it vigorously. "I hear congratulations are in order," he exclaimed, looking past Nathan to where Lydia now sat straight up in her bed. "Evening, Sister Lydia. Evening, Mary Ann."

As Brigham came in, Josh followed him and let the tent flap drop again.

"Good evening, Brother Brigham," Mary Ann answered. Lydia just nodded demurely.

"How are you?" Brigham asked, moving around Nathan to kneel down beside Lydia.

"Very well, all things considered."

"That's what Sister Sessions said too. I'm glad."

"So she's the one who told you?" Nathan asked.

"Well, that and Matthew came over, as proud as if he were the father himself." He peered more closely at Lydia. "You look really good, Lydia." Without waiting for a response, he swung around to Emily and pointed to the baby. "So is this her?"

"Yes," Emily said proudly. She twisted her body so that the baby's face was visible.

"My, my," Brigham said, reaching out to take the baby from Emily. "She's like a little china doll! And so tiny." He pulled the blanket back further. "And would you look at that hair!"

"That comes from Lydia's side of the family," Mary Ann laughed. "The Steed family babies get nothing like that."

The tent door opened again and the other children trooped in. They weren't about to miss a visit from President Young. He patted the ground beside him. "Come here, you young'uns, and tell me about this new baby sister of yours." As they settled in around him, he looked at them with sudden solemnity. "What are you going to call her?"

They all turned to look at their mother for permission to speak.

"You can tell him," Lydia smiled.

"Patricia," Elizabeth Mary said shyly. She would be eight soon, and of all the children she looked the most like her father. She was also the one who had most hoped for a little sister.

"Patricia Ann," five-year-old Josiah said.

"But we're gonna call her Tricia," little Joseph, not quite three, sang out, wanting to be heard too.

"It's for my grandmother on my mother's side," Lydia explained. "She was always my favorite grandmother."

"Little Tricia Steed." Brigham turned and winked at Emily. "I think she's going to look just like you," he said.

Emily positively beamed. "I think so too. Look at her chin. And her eyes are going to be dark, I think."

"That's still too early to tell," Josh said.

"I know," Emily said tartly. "But Mama thinks they'll go dark too, don't you, Mama?"

"Could be," she said, pleased at her children's pride in their new sister.

The Apostle turned to Nathan. "Well, one bit of good news, for you anyway. I took a small group of men out to scout out the road ahead. We'll not be going anywhere for another day or two."

Nathan felt quick relief. He had assumed that, with the weather, they wouldn't be moving on, but hearing the confirmation of that took away some anxiety. There was no way he could be moving Lydia for another day or two, even if they had to stay behind the rest of the company. "So the roads are still pretty bad?"

Brigham pulled a face. "Not really. We only found one mud hole."

"Only one?" Nathan said in surprise.

There was a quick impishness in the gray-blue eyes. "Yes, but it was six miles long and about half again that wide."

They all laughed at that. Brigham turned back to the baby and stroked her hair with the side of one finger. "So little Tricia Steed. A pretty name for a pretty girl." He turned to Joseph. "But aren't you going to call her Locust Creek Steed?"

There was momentary shock, then the children tittered. "Locust Creek!" Josiah groaned. "That's not a name for a girl."

"Oh?" Brigham said gravely.

"You silly," Joseph said. "You don't name girls that."

"But why not?" Brigham looked at Elizabeth Mary. "Didn't you hear about Sister Jacobs?" He glanced at Lydia. "That's Zina Huntington Jacobs, wife of Henry B. Jacobs." He looked back at Elizabeth Mary now. "She gave birth to a little boy about two weeks ago, while we were crossing the Chariton River. So they named the boy Chariton."

Elizabeth Mary looked openly dubious. Even Emily wondered if he wasn't teasing them.

"That's true," Mary Ann said. "I saw the baby myself. And they're going to call him that too."

"So, here we are at Locust Creek," Nathan broke in with a deadpan look at his younger children. "Maybe Locust Creek Steed is a better name than Tricia. We could call her Loki or something like that."

"Oh, Papa," Elizabeth Mary said, with an air of infinite patience.

"Maybe you're right," Brigham went on. "Maybe Tricia is better."

"I think so," Josiah and Joseph said together, not really very amused with the other possibility.

Brigham looked over to Lydia. "Did you hear that Sister Stewart gave birth yesterday as well?"

"No, which Sister Stewart?"

"Maria Stewart, wife of Brother Rufus Stewart." He frowned a little. "Unfortunately, she wasn't quite as lucky as you. They were still coming into camp night before last in the midst of that terrible storm when she started into travail. She had no choice but to continue walking. They were almost two miles away from any shelter. You know what Locust Creek has been like?"

"Yes," Lydia said. They could still hear it roaring even now, and the water had subsided substantially since the rain had stopped.

"Well, Rufus saw a vacant house that would provide her some shelter, but they had to cross the creek to get to it. He led her across on a narrow log."

Lydia groaned in empathy. If the pains had started while she was making her way across the raging water . . . She shuddered.

"Anyway, they made it safely, and early yesterday morning she gave birth to a healthy baby boy."

"I know Sister Stewart," Mary Ann said, as the others shook their heads. "I'll go see her tomorrow."

Brigham looked back at the children and his sly grin was back. "I don't think she's going to name her baby Locust Creek either."

They giggled now, knowing that they were being teased.

"Well," Brigham said, handing the baby back to Emily, "I'd best be going. We're so happy for you. She is a beautiful baby."

"Thank you, President," Lydia said, deeply pleased that he had come when there were likely a hundred things shouting for his attention.

As he stood up he turned to Nathan. "There is one more bit of good news, besides there being only one mud hole, I mean."

"What's that?"

"We got word from the advance company. They've made a contract with one of the settlements ahead. They want us to split three thousand rails at fifty cents per hundred."

"Really!" Nathan exclaimed. "That is good news."

"Yes. They'll make payment with one milk cow worth ten dollars and the rest in bacon at five cents a pound."

"That is great. Count on us for help."

"I knew I could." Now Brigham turned to Mary Ann and his face was serious again. "I'm afraid I'm going to have to send Matthew back out again. Once this weather breaks, we're going to need more bridges and maybe even a ferry or two."

"He's ready whenever you say."

"I know. And I'm grateful for that."

He put his hat back on and stepped to the tent flap. "Well, again, my congratulations. You've got a wonderful daughter there, Lydia. We're very happy for you."

"Did Brother Brigham give you any idea what this is all about?" Nathan asked Matthew.

"No. Actually it was one of his sons who brought the word. All he said was that President Young had called a special council meeting."

"And he asked for us specifically?" Derek said.

"That's what he said."

"Including me?" Joshua said with some skepticism. "You're sure he said he wanted me to come too?"

They were riding their two horses—Derek and Nathan doubled on one, Joshua and Matthew on the other. Heber C. Kimball's company was still back at the Hickory Grove Camp, three miles behind them. William Clayton and other leaders were even farther back than that. Hence Brigham had called for the council meeting to be held at Hickory Grove. So now the Steed men—with the exception of Solomon, who was staying to tend camp—made their way east again.

Matthew's head bobbed emphatically. "Yes, Joshua, he specifically requested you."

"Do they know that I'm not a member of the Church?"

"I would think so," Matthew responded cheerfully. "Brother Brigham certainly does."

Every member of the Quorum of the Twelve who was currently in the general vicinity of Locust Creek was present, seated on chairs or boxes or barrels directly in front of Heber C. Kimball's main wagon. William Clayton, clerk for the camp, was there. Nathan saw that the two bishops were also there. Newel K. Whitney and George Miller were seated on the far right, just beyond the two Pratt brothers, Orson and Parley, who were both members of the Twelve. The rest of the group consisted of about thirty-five or forty others, including the company captains and presidents, most of whom Nathan knew personally or at least knew by sight. But the rest of the men—some he knew and some he did not—seemed to have no specific reason for being there. Such as himself and the others in his family.

But they didn't have long to wait to find out why. Brigham Young looked around the group, almost as if he were counting, then leaned over and said something to his longtime friend and fellow Apostle. Heber nodded, and Brigham stood up. The group instantly quieted.

"Brethren, thank you for coming. We appreciate you taking time away from your families on this Sabbath day to attend to matters of great importance. We shall not keep you long, but I would request your careful attention to the matter which we have before us."

He stopped and let his eyes sweep around the group. The weather had finally tempered somewhat. It was still cool and a pretty good breeze blew out of the west, but the overcast was high and thin and promised to burn off as the day progressed.

"As you know, brethren," Brigham continued, "for the past week or two we have been moving in a southwesterly direction. Where we are camped now is no more than two or three miles from the Missouri border."

A low murmur rippled through the group. This was not news to anyone. In fact, for the past few days they had been following a track covered by Mormons once before. In 1838, during the siege of Far West, word came that those who had participated in the Battle of Crooked River would be arrested and shot. Nathan and Matthew, who had been part of that skirmish, were among the twenty or so who slipped quietly out of Far West and headed north toward the border between Missouri and Iowa Territory. Nathan and Matthew had eventually turned back, feeling impressed to return to their family, but the rest had crossed into Iowa Territory, then turned east until they reached Illinois. Now they were following that same route—though in the opposite direction. But even after eight years the mere mention of Missouri, and knowing they were this close to old battlegrounds and old and terrible hatreds, was enough to raise their anxieties.

Brigham let it die out again before going on. "We have done this because we hoped to find settlements where we could find work and trade for grain. I don't need to tell any of you, without corn, without wheat, without some oats and barley, we are soon going to be in very serious trouble. The oxen and cattle are doing well on the browse here along the bottomland, but our horses are failing. Our mules are failing."

Many were nodding at that. And while the hunting had been good and supplemented the food supply, even the people could not live on venison and turkey and prairie chicken alone. They had to have flour, and flour was in desperately short supply. This was one of the reasons they had traveled in a southwest direction, to get closer to the more heavily settled areas in the state of Missouri.

"As you well know," President Young went on, his voice sober and low now, "feelings in Missouri still run high against us. If we venture farther south to trade, we increase our risks." He stopped for a moment to gather his thoughts. "But that is not all. As you know, our progress has been very slow." He grimaced, as though he had just bitten into something bitter. "If we continue at this rate, we will make the Rocky Mountains sometime around the middle of July—in the year *eighteen forty-eight!*"

That hit the group like a slap in the face. Summer of forty-eight? More than two years hence?

He held up his hands at the nervous laughter and the gasps of shock. "I know, I know. Once this abominable weather finally breaks, we'll do much better than that, but that is only one of our problems. Think about how many of our brothers and sisters are still back in Nauvoo and the surrounding communities. Less than a quarter have escaped the grasp of our enemies, enemies who, by the way, were promised that we would be gone by the time the first grass was on the prairies. Have you looked around, brethren? Have you looked under your feet? What do you see?"

Now many were nodding. It was true. It might feel like spring would never come, but it was, and eventually the weather had to turn and spring would be here in its fulness. The first glimpses of green shoots pushing upward through the black mud had started in the last day or two.

"Many of those thousands back in Nauvoo are still not ready to leave. Many are so poor they will be lucky if they can pay the fee for ferrying across the river. What will they eat as they follow us? If we are short of grain with as few as we have with us here, what shall it be like when there are ten or twelve or fourteen thousand more?"

He let that sink in. If his purpose was to sober the group, he was successful in that, Joshua thought. Almost to the point of despair. And yet this was not just alarmist thinking. Brigham was exactly right. How could another ten to fifteen thousand people come through what they had seen so far and survive?

Nathan's thoughts were running along a different line. How did Brigham Young bear up under such pressure? Nathan often lay awake nights worrying about Lydia giving birth or about how low their supply of flour was getting. And he was responsible for less than thirty people. The President had a hundred fold—no, five hundred fold—that many more to worry about. How many times did he lie awake nights worrying about giving birth to the whole kingdom? about settling an entire community in a wilderness? No wonder he was grave. No wonder he did not smile as easily as he had done in times past. No wonder he was noticeably thinner, down forty or fifty pounds, Nathan estimated.

"I've not come simply to complain, my friends," Brigham finally said. "These are real problems, and I wanted you to be aware of how weighty they are so that you can better understand what we would like to propose to you here and now. We have been holding council meetings, trying to determine what is best. We have come to some decisions and have some recommendations. I should like to put those before you now."

He glanced at Heber Kimball, who was nodding his encouragement. Only a couple of inches taller than Brigham, Heber was far more stout, looking much like a large cooper's barrel with a coat and shirt on. He often liked to say that he was the only man he knew whose chest measurements were the same from front to back as they were from side to side. His eyes were dark and quick to sparkle with humor. But they could flash with fire when he was exercised, as he was now. In a time like this, he was a source of great strength to Brigham Young.

"Brethren, this is not a time for many words," Brigham went on. "We are in need of reevaluating our plan of action. We question the wisdom of moving farther toward our old enemies. We must find a way to care for those coming behind us. Therefore, I should like to give you in brief outline form what the council is recommending. You will be asked to sustain these proposals with your vote when we are finished, since all of you will be affected by them one way or another. I would appreciate your most careful attention."

It was not as if he had to ask, Joshua thought wryly. There was not one drooping eye, not one lagging span of attention. Virtually every man was leaning forward, straining to hear.

"Number one. Beginning tomorrow we shall change our route of march. We shall turn northwest instead of southwest and move away from Missouri."

That won him an instant rumble of relief and approval.

"Instead of aiming to cross the Missouri River into Indian Territory at St. Joseph, Missouri, as we thought, we shall now set our sights on those trading posts farther up the Missouri near what is called Council Bluffs, Iowa Territory."

The rumble deepened, but Brigham rode over it loudly. "Number two. We shall ask Brother Elisha Averett and his company to stop their work on the construction of additional bridges over Locust Creek and to concentrate on fulfilling any unfinished work on contracts with the Iowans so that we can get additional grain. Then they shall prepare to leave as soon as possible. Number three. All those going on from here will be asked to leave behind as much corn and grain as can be spared. There is a mill on the Grand River, and we shall ask Brother Averett's company to seek work there upon arrival and to take their payment in meal and flour if possible.

"Number four. Certain men, including your President and most of the Twelve, shall proceed tomorrow at all possible speed toward the Grand River. There they shall search out a spot for a suitable farming settlement."

He had to stop, for the group of men erupted with excitement. The Grand River! Where was that? Fifty miles or so? Maybe a hundred? A farming settlement? For whom? What did that mean for the march west?

"Brethren!" Heber roared. That cut it off like a knife. He smiled to show that he was actually pleased with their excitement. "There will be time for questions once we have outlined the proposal. Let the President continue."

President Young smiled and then went on. "Number five. Selected men and their families will accompany the Twelve to this farming settlement. There they will fence in a field two miles square, or about thirteen hundred acres. They shall build twenty log cabins, plow the acreage they have fenced, and plant spring crops at this 'way station' on the trail."

This time he let it go. As the group exploded into a hundred conversations, he turned and smiled at Heber and the rest of the Apostles, who were nodding with pleasure. They had expected no less a reaction. When it finally died, he went on more calmly now.

"Please note that I said selected men *and their families*. Since this will take some time, we do not expect the men to leave their families behind. For example, from my company we will be asking the Steeds to be part of that advance group. All in their families will accompany them."

As many heads turned to look at them, Matthew slapped his leg. "Yes!" he exclaimed in an exultant whisper. "This time I don't have to go alone."

Hearing that, President Young turned. He smiled sadly. "Sorry, Matthew, but you will go ahead with Brother Averett's advance party. But we shall not be far behind you." Without waiting for Matthew's reaction, he continued. "Item seven. The main bulk of the Camp of Israel will remain here on Locust Creek until they can come on successfully. Some will wait until the new settlement can be established and put into place. There is relatively good feed here, and as the grass continues to come forth, it will get better. That will give us a chance to recruit our teams and strengthen them for the next leg of the trail.

"Finally," Brother Brigham went on, speaking easily now, "once we have reached the Grand River and have started the new settlement, approximately one hundred wagons will press on to the Missouri River. There they will search out a place for another settlement. As quickly as possible, they will resupply themselves and start west for the Rocky Mountains. In this way it is hoped that they will reach our final destination early enough to put in crops and build shelters for those who are to follow. But it is clear now that we cannot take all of our people to the Rocky Mountains this season. Therefore, the majority of our people will winter over either at the settlement on the Grand River or at the Missouri River bottoms where there will be food for the people and our stock."

"My word," Joshua breathed. "They really have thought this through."

"Yes," Nathan answered. "This is a major change of plans."

"Now," Brother Young called out once the noise had diminished again, "there is one last thing. From among those who will be staying here we'd like you captains to select a few men as scouts. Their task will be to retrace the trail over which we have come and find the best routes from Nauvoo to Locust Creek and from Locust Creek to the Grand River. We do not wish the thousands who are yet to follow to have to face the same hazards we have faced, to traverse the same places we have traversed in all cases—" He winked broadly. "In many places the bogs are already so full of abandoned wagons there isn't room for any more."

The men roared at that, but it was bittersweet laughter. More than one had left material possessions behind in the myriad mud holes that had marked their march west from Sugar Creek.

There was a long pause, then the President concluded. "That is the proposal, brethren. It has come only after careful council together. All of you who feel to support your leaders in this proposal, would you raise your right hand to the square."

Nathan gave Joshua a strange look as the older brother's hand came up automatically along with everyone else's. Joshua saw the look and was puzzled. "What?" he mouthed.

Nathan shook his head. Common consent was a pivotal principle in the Church. It pleased him that Joshua accepted it without even thinking.

"Thank you, brethren," Brigham said. "We'll formally dismiss now, and then you can ask your questions. We'll ask Brother Willard Richards to close our meeting and invoke the Lord's blessing on what we have just determined to do."

Chapter Notes

If one counts back to the first day wagons began leaving Nauvoo, 4 February, by 7 April 1846 the Saints had been on the road for sixty-three days of travel but had come only 118 miles. That meant they were averaging less than two miles per day. As in other chapters, the author has tried to accurately represent the details of the weather, the campsites, and what was happening day by day along the trail as recorded in the various journals (see *CN*, 6 April 1996, p. 10; also *Iowa Trail*, pp. xviii–xx).

Zina Huntington Jacobs, who became the third general president of the Relief Society in 1887, gave birth to a son on 22 March 1846. The birth took place in a wagon while she and her husband were waiting to ford the Chariton River. They named the boy Henry Chariton Jacobs. (See *Iowa Trail*, p. xviii.) Chariton Jacobs remained faithful throughout his life and eventually was made a patriarch in the Church (see *LDSBE* 3:421–23).

Maria Judd Stewart, wife of Rufus Putnam Stewart, also gave birth to a son under the circumstances described here. No name is given for the son in the account. (See *MHBY*, pp. 126–27; *Iowa Trail*, p. xx.)

By the middle of April it was becoming painfully clear to Brigham Young that their original plans for a quick dash to the Rocky Mountains were not realistic. It is a witness to his great vision and leadership abilities how quickly he accepted that reality and adapted to meet the needs of his people in the wilderness. (See *William Clayton's Journal* [Salt Lake City: Clayton Family Association, 1921], pp. 17–18; and *CN*, 20 April 1996, p. 7.)

Concerning the Saints' stay in the Locust Creek area and their proximity to Missouri at this point during the trek west, William G. Hartley has written, "On 6–15 April the companies camped by Locust Creek, three miles above the Missouri border." However, he goes on to explain, "several diary entries support the possibility that their Locust Creek encampments were a few miles farther south, in Missouri, below the disputed boundary line between Iowa Territory and Missouri." ("The Pioneer Trek: Nauvoo to Winter Quarters," *Ensign* 27 [June 1997]: 35, 43 n. 13.)

Chapter Twelve

The scene was one of total pandemonium, but if one looked more closely, it was pandemonium that was controlled and channeled and organized. Nine wagons, lined up in three rows of three each, filled the hilltop on the west side of Springfield on Wednesday, April fifteenth, 1846. Men were shouting to each other as they yoked up the oxen or saddled horses. Dogs raced in and out, barking and yelping, sensing the excitement of their masters. Young boys were in the nearby meadow, barking and yelping almost as incessantly as the dogs as they tried to keep the milk cows and the beef cattle in some semblance of order. Women and girls shuttled back and forth between the wagons, making sure everything was secure or that the baskets of food were near at hand. The Reeds' twelve-year-old daughter, Virginia, was already mounted on her pony, which was prancing around the assembly. Virginia looked as though everything that was happening was under her direct supervision.

Kathryn McIntire Ingalls sat on a stool in the back of the first of the three Reed wagons, the wagon that everyone was coming to call the "pioneer palace car." The cover of the over-sized wagon was pulled halfway back, so it was open to the warm spring sunshine and to a view of all that was happening around them. Beside Kathryn, half reclining on a feather mattress, was Mrs. Keyes, mother of Margret Reed and grandmother to the Reed children. "Isn't it wonderful?" she exclaimed, almost clapping her hands together. "This is so exciting."

"Yes!" Kathryn agreed with warm enthusiasm. She felt it too. The long-awaited day had finally come. She and Peter had been packed for three days now. It was almost nine o'clock. The Donners, who lived a short distance out of town, had come in the previous night. The Reeds had joined them first thing this morning. The morning was nearly half done already. *On with it!* Kathryn thought. *No more delay. Tell the boys to move the stock up. Get the teamsters up here "a-geeing" and "a-hawing" to their oxen. Let the wagons roll!*

But of course it wasn't up to her to give that command, and so she sat, trying to contain her impatience. Margret Reed, Kathryn's employer, was still over with Tamsen Donner, helping her sort the last of her things. Kathryn turned. Peter was there in her view, checking the yoke on the last pair of oxen on the last wagon. Mr. Reed was cinching the girth on the saddle of his prized gray racing horse.

At another sound, Kathryn turned back. Margret Reed was approaching the wagon. "We're done, Mother. I think we're ready."

"Well, *we* certainly are, aren't we, Kathryn?" Mrs. Keyes said.

"I've been ready for a month now," Kathryn groaned.

Mrs. Reed laughed. "Good. I'll tell Eliza to round up the children."

As Mrs. Reed moved off, Kathryn turned to survey the nine wagons that would constitute their train for now. She shook her head, knowing what was in them. That still amazed Kathryn.

When she thought of her own family and friends, the Saints in Nauvoo scraping together everything they had to get enough to get them across the river, what she saw here was astounding. This wagon train would be one of the most amply equipped to ever leave the state, she decided. She and Peter would be traveling in the lap of luxury while her family fought for survival. The only comfort came in knowing that going this way left two less people for their family to have to worry about.

The difference was money, pure and simple. There was no other explanation. George Donner was a very well-to-do man. Twice widowed, "Uncle George," as everyone called him, was sixty-two years old. He had spent a lifetime being a very successful farmer. He and his first wife had raised a family who were all grown and married now. According to Mr. Reed, Uncle George had left each of those children from the first marriage with prosperous farms of their own. That said all that needed to be said, didn't it? Some years before, he had married for the third time. Tamsen Donner was a mere whiffet of a woman—she was barely five feet tall and weighed no more than a hundred pounds—and was nearly twenty years Donner's junior. But in that tiny frame was a lot of spunk. Born in Massachusetts, she had come west to be a schoolteacher and gotten married. Her first husband had also died, and after a time she married George Donner. He was still raising two daughters from his second marriage, and he and Tamsen had begotten three more daughters of their own. All five girls would be going west with their parents.

In addition to one whole wagon filled with food, the Donners were taking a load of what Peter called "geegaws"—beads, knives, and other trinkets to be given as presents to the Indians and laces and silks to be traded with the Mexicans in California. Tamsen was also taking along a supply of schoolbooks, paper, brushes, watercolors, oils, and other supplies needed for the girls' seminary she planned to establish once they reached Upper California. Mr. Reed had also let it be known that Uncle George was carrying plenty of gold so they could purchase whatever land he wanted once they got there. And Mrs. Reed had whispered to her mother and Kathryn just last night the rumor that Mrs. Donner had sewn ten thousand dollars cash into one of the quilts. Ten thousand dollars! Kathryn could barely comprehend such a sum.

For that matter, what must the Reeds have spent to get ready? she wondered. They were traveling first-class as well. Take this wagon, for example. James Reed had paid a man to specially build it for him. Larger than a normal wagon by maybe a third again, it had an entrance on the side with steps that folded up or extended down, a second level on each end to provide sleeping quarters, and a small iron stove for cooking and for when the nights turned cold. And that was only this wagon. Reed also had two other wagons filled with food, tools, and personal effects. Kathryn had helped pack the dresses for Virginia and Patty. Peter had helped get the boys' clothing ready. When they compared notes later, they guessed that in just clothing alone, what the Reeds were taking would have come close to outfitting a full wagon back in Nauvoo.

And the food! They had almost sixteen hundred pounds of flour, boxes of smoked sausage, barrels of salted cod, tubs of lard, three or four cans with a hundred pounds of sugar in each, bags of rice, cans of coffee and tea, raisins, salt, spices, dried fruit, potatoes and carrots packed in boxes of sawdust. Then there was all the paraphernalia that it took to maintain life on the trail— pots, kettles, dishes, butter churns, cheese presses, eating utensils. There were the tool kits, the spare parts, the tar buckets and water barrels. They had two extra wagon tongues and four extra axles, all slung beneath the wagon boxes of their three wagons. Buckets and boxes and pens of chickens were tied to the sides to the point that each wagon looked like the carriage of some traveling huckster.

Jacob Donner, head of the third family, was no less well-off, though Kathryn did not know his family as well. "Uncle Jake," like his brother, was a kindly and industrious man, but seemed far less robust and healthy. When Kathryn learned that he was only two or three years older than George, it shocked her, for it seemed more like ten or twelve years' difference. But his outfit was as well stocked as—

Kathryn turned as she heard children's voices approaching the front of the wagon. Eliza Williams was herding the three younger Reed children toward them, speaking softly to them to keep them moving. She looked up and saw Kathryn. "Mrs. Reed said they're nearly ready to go. She wants the children in the wagon."

"All right, children," Kathryn said, pulling herself to her feet by holding on to the side of the wagon. "Come up now. I have your places all ready."

First Eliza handed up the youngest, Thomas Keyes, who was three. He was Kathryn's personal favorite. Thoughtful but unfailingly cheerful, he was bright and very observant. He had won her heart one day shortly after the Reeds had hired them. After watching her get up on her crutches, he came to her and whispered in her ear, "If you need something, Miss Kathryn, let me know and I'll get it for you." And thus far he had been true to his word. She pointed to his place near the front wagon seat, directly behind where his father would sit, then whacked him gently on the rump as he scooted past her.

Next came Martha, whom they all called Patty, though Kathryn had not yet discerned why. At eight, she was already every bit the lady, just as her mother was. Her clothes were purchased from Springfield's best shops, and she wore them with just the right touch of primness and modesty. She knelt down beside her grandmother. "Oh, Granny," she cried, "it's time!"

"Yes, Patty," Mrs. Keyes said, taking her hand. "Isn't it exciting?"

Last up was James Frazier Reed, Jr. This one was all boy. Though only five, he was forever out with the men, checking the harnessing, eyeing the stock, or kicking at the wagon spokes to make sure they were dished correctly. His parents always called him James, but Kathryn had taken to calling him Jamie, which in her Irish line was a more favored nickname than either Jim or Jimmy. Having been born in the north of Ireland himself, Mr. Reed did not seem to mind, and though he never used the name himself, he never corrected Kathryn when she did. To no one's surprise, Jamie crawled past his brother and onto the wagon seat to await his father's signal to move.

Kathryn laughed. "Going to drive us all the way to California, Jamie?"

"Aye," he shot back with a grin.

"And he'll probably beat the rest of us by a month," Eliza said.

Kathryn chuckled. That was very likely. She looked at Eliza. "Are you all set?" she asked.

"Yes. I'm in the next wagon. Baylis will be leading that one mostly."

Kathryn nodded. Baylis Williams was Eliza's half brother. Both single—Eliza was thirty-one and Baylis was about twenty-five—they were going as part of the Reeds' staff, just as Kathryn and Peter were. Eliza, who for years had been a domestic for the Reeds, would be the cook for the family and help Kathryn with the children—tending them, not tutoring them, for Kathryn suspected that Eliza, who was very hard of hearing, did not know how to read. Baylis was an all-around utility and fix-it man, and would help with the driving and herding of stock. Like the Ingallses, the Williamses would receive their board and a journey across the plains with no investment required of them other than their labor. Baylis spoke proudly of finding land of his own once they reached California, and in this he was encouraged by Mr. Reed.

There was a sound behind her and the wagon rocked a little. Margret Reed had returned and was climbing up. Peter was right behind her. He folded the steps, which fit ingeniously in beneath the wagon box, and shut the small door.

Kathryn beamed. Peter wore a wide-brimmed hat and carried the long ox whip over his shoulder. One did not "drive" oxen in the way that one drove a team of horses. There were no reins and harnessing in the usual sense. Oxen were "yoked" to the wagon through a series of hitch ropes or chains which led from the great yokes that sat on the animals' shoulders to the wagon tongue. No one sat in the wagon seat to drive them. Instead, the ox driver, usually called a "bullwhacker," would walk alongside the animals, directing them with soft commands—"gee" to turn them right, "haw" to turn them left—or the crack of the whip above their heads. Peter would be leading the four yoke that pulled the big wagon. And with his hat and boots and whip he looked like the real thing. Knowing of his preference for books and printing type and writing poetry, it amused her greatly to see him in this role. It also made her very proud. He had spent a lot of time on his own learning how to handle oxen.

"Are you ready?" Peter asked Mrs. Reed.

She looked to each of the children, who nodded enthusiastically. "We are," she said back to Peter.

Just then Mr. Reed rode up on his horse. He leaned over, reaching for the wagon cover to pull it back over the hoops.

"Oh no, James," Margret said. "We want to see everything. If it gets too dusty, then we'll close it."

"All right." He looked down at Peter, who had moved to the head of the lead yoke. "Uncle George will lead out. We'll be next. Just fall in behind them."

"Yes, Mr. Reed."

Reed turned to where Jamie sat in the wagon seat. "You ready, son?"

"*Yes, sir!*"

Reed laughed, then spurred his horse and rode forward to join George Donner. For a moment the two of them surveyed the whole scene; then Donner lifted his hat and raised it high. "Ready?" he called.

All up and down the line things went quiet.

He stood up high in the stirrups. "Upper California, here we come!" He gave a whoop and waved his arm at the lead teamster.

There was a cry and the man cracked the whip sharply. With a creak and groan, the first wagon began to move. One by one Donner's three wagons moved out, rolling down the road that led to the southwest.

As the last of Donner's wagons passed, Peter raised his whip. The handle was short—no more than fifteen or eighteen inches—but the lash was a good ten to fifteen feet long. His arm flashed back, letting the black braided leather uncurl behind his head in a sinuous movement. Then he snapped his arm sharply. In a blur of motion the whip shot forward, cracking with a sharp *pop* directly over the ear of the near ox in the lead yoke.

"Away with you, Duke!" he shouted. "Dig in there, Boss! Let's go! Let's go!" The whip flashed, then cracked again, this time over the second yoke. "Giddap there, Bright. Lean into that yoke! Come on, Charlie. It's time to move. Giddap, boys!"

Margret Reed turned to look at Kathryn and laughed merrily. "Not bad, I'd say."

At that moment Peter turned his head and looked at Kathryn. One hand came up and he touched his finger to the brim of his hat. His face was sober, but the triumph in his eyes was absolutely unmistakable.

Kathryn clapped her hands, applauding wildly. "Bravo! Bravo!"

Melissa Rogers reached out and grabbed Carl's arm. "Look. I think that's Wilford Woodruff."

"Where?"

"There. Just coming out of the temple."

Carl Rogers looked to where she was pointing. They were still half a block away from the temple grounds. There were half a dozen men and three or four women just coming down the front steps. He wasn't sure which of the men she was looking at. "Could be. Why? Does that surprise you?"

"Yes. He's been in England. Don't you remember? Brother

Brigham sent him there to preside over the British Mission not long after Joseph's death."

Carl gave her an odd look and clucked softly to the horse, keeping the carriage rolling along smoothly. "Actually, Melissa, I don't pay much attention to where the various Apostles and leaders of the Church are at any given time."

She barely heard him. "I'm sure that's him. Yes. And there's Phoebe beside him. Oh, Carl, let's go say hello."

"Why?" he asked bluntly.

"He may have some word of the family."

"Not if he's been in England."

"But I don't know if he has. Perhaps he's been out on the trail and has some news."

Carl shrugged. It was a beautiful, warm spring day. They were on their way out to a farm east of town to purchase some baby chicks that would become young fryers by summertime. There were no orders at the brickyard for today, and young Carl was minding the dry goods store. The rest of the children were left with a teenage neighbor so that Melissa could ride out with him. There was no set schedule and no particular hurry. Why not? He pulled lightly on the reins, turning the horse toward the other side of the street.

They reached the gate to the temple yard just as the group was coming through it. "Elder Woodruff!" Melissa called.

Wilford Woodruff was in the rear, talking earnestly with one of the other couples. He looked up, squinting a little.

"It's Melissa Rogers," she called as they pulled to a stop.

"But of course," he said, waving now. He pushed his way through the others, who stepped aside for him. Phoebe came right behind him. "You all go on ahead," Wilford said. "We'll be along shortly."

Carl and Melissa climbed down from the carriage as the Woodruffs reached them. The Apostle was smiling broadly. "How good to see you again!" he said, taking Melissa's hands.

Carl leaned toward him, his mouth opening to say, "Carl

Rogers, Mr. Woodruff," but before he could say a word, Wilford took his hand and gripped it tightly. "How are you, Carl? You're looking well."

"I'm fine, thank you." He was surprised and pleased to be remembered.

"How's the brick business?" And then, at Carl's look, he frowned. "You're still making the best bricks in town, now, aren't you?"

Carl shook his head. "Not much anymore." A few years ago it was his yard that furnished the bricks for the fine two-story Woodruff home on Durphy Street.

"I was by your home just a few days ago," Carl said now, warming to the memory. "I'll bet you're glad to be back to it again."

Phoebe's eyes clouded a little. "We are, but it won't be for long."

"Have you sold it?" Carl asked, genuinely surprised.

"It appears that we will," Wilford answered. "We are very fortunate. I have had an offer for a twelve-acre parcel I own out east of town and my house and lot. Six hundred seventy-five dollars."

Carl gave a low whistle. "I know it's worth far more than that, but some people are only getting a pittance of what their property is worth."

"We've heard," Phoebe broke in sadly. "We just hope it goes through. We've heard of people trading off their homes for a yoke of oxen, or even something like a bed quilt."

"Well, people know they've got us over a barrel," Wilford said. "We don't have much choice but to take what we're offered. I don't know why we were so fortunate. Maybe the Lord knows that without a sale, there would be no way for us to purchase a wagon and teams and join the others."

Melissa's face fell. "So you're just back from England?" she asked. "You've not been out on the trail yet?"

"No, no," Wilford said. "I wish we were on the trail. We're

anxious to see President Young and my other brethren in the Twelve again, but it will take us some time to get ready."

"We were hoping you might have some news of my family."

Wilford shook his head. "So they've gone, have they?"

"Yes."

"What about Joshua and that wonderful wife of his, did they go too?"

"They did," Carl said. "I don't know if you heard about Melissa's father."

The Apostle's face instantly fell. "I did. Elder Hyde was telling me about that tragedy with Benjamin trying to save his granddaughter. He was a man of unusual grace and courage."

"I know." Melissa managed a smile. "We miss him terribly, of course, but with Mother being alone, Joshua decided to go with her. And then, much to our surprise, about a week later he came back and got Caroline and the children and they all went."

"Wonderful!" Wilford said with great enthusiasm. He gave Carl a keen look, then slapped him on the shoulder. "And what about you, Brother Carl? Why don't you get yourself a team and a wagon, and come on with us when we cross the river? I'm sure there'll be a need for a brickyard wherever we're going."

Carl was not offended. He had too much respect for the man to respond in that way, and there had been a half-joking tone to the invitation. "Someone's got to stay and watch over things here," he said easily.

Now Wilford frowned deeply. "All jesting aside, Carl, things are not looking good. Brother Young—Joseph Young, Brigham's older brother, who has been left in charge of the Saints here— he was telling us last night that our old enemies have not gone away. They're still prowling around, talking brashly and waving their rifles and their whiskey bottles."

"There's always a few who want to stir up trouble," Carl admitted. The conversation had taken a serious turn and he was starting to feel uncomfortable. "But you can't jump at every shadow."

For a long moment, Wilford's eyes held Carl's. "I don't want to seem pessimistic, my friend, and you know that I respect your right to choose what course you wish to take, but if things turn ugly here, which they very likely could, the fact that you are not one of us may not be enough."

"I appreciate your concern, Mr. Woodruff. I truly do. But we'll be fine. We're just going about our business, not doing anything to rile anyone up." He glanced at Melissa, who was staring at the ground. "We'll be fine."

"I hope so. There aren't many finer people than you two, and it would sorrow us greatly to see you have any hardships. And you know that we'd be right pleased to have you and your family travel with us to rejoin your family, if that was what you chose to do."

Carl's voice was cool now. "Can I ask you a question?"

"Of course."

"How many wives does Brigham Young have traveling with him?"

Melissa took in a breath sharply. Phoebe's head jerked up. Wilford was taken aback too, but immediately smiled. "I'm not sure, not having been here. Maybe ten. Maybe more."

"And Heber Kimball?"

"Several," Wilford said steadily, not flinching from the anger that was flashing in Carl's eyes now.

"How many others have more than one wife going with them out there, Mr. Woodruff?"

"Carl!" Melissa said it in a low, soft rebuke. He didn't look at her.

"I don't know," Wilford Woodruff said softly. "Several, I would think."

"Then I don't think we'll be thinking about joining up with you and the others." Carl took a quick breath. "I mean no offense, Mr. Woodruff—"

"No offense taken."

"And I have the greatest respect for you personally, but that one thing alone makes it impossible for me and my wife to consider being part of what is happening."

"I understand."

"If there's anything you need," Carl said, forcing some warmth back into his voice again, "a line of credit at the store, help in getting your things packed—anything—let us know. We'd be pleased to be of help."

"Thank you. We're much obliged." He shook hands with Carl again. Then he gave Melissa a quick hug. "We'll take your love to your family when we go. And any letters, if you'd like."

"Oh, yes," Melissa said. She stepped back from him, still not meeting his eyes. "Thank you, Brother Woodruff. Thank you, Phoebe."

"How good to see you both again!" Phoebe said warmly. "We shall see you again before we leave, I'm sure."

They waved and walked slowly away. Carl watched them go, then turned back to his wife. She was still looking at the ground.

"I'm sorry if I embarrassed you, Melissa, but they might as well know the real reason. I'm not going to just give all these honeyed phrases that sound good."

"I know."

He peered at her, reaching out to lift her head. "You're not changing your mind, are you?"

She pulled away. "No."

"But?" he pressed.

"But I'm frightened, Carl. What's it going to be like when everyone is gone?"

"It will be quiet and peaceful and very, very normal. There won't be nearly as big a city, but it will be all right." He stepped forward and put his arms around her, pulling her in against him. "Really, Melissa. We'll be just fine."

She nodded. "I know." Then she looked up at him. "If you don't mind, Carl, you go on ahead. I'll just walk home. I don't feel much like a ride anymore."

For a moment there was a flash of irritation, but then he

understood. In spite of it all. In spite of the plural marriage, in spite of the fear of going a thousand miles into the wilderness for nothing, there was always the family. The Steeds were a family with powerful ties to each other, and for Melissa all those were severed now, at least in terms of immediate association. So finally he just nodded and kissed her on the cheek. "I understand," he said. "I'll be home before supper." And with that, he let her go, climbed back into the carriage, and drove away.

Chapter Notes

Though at this time the group of emigrants who left Springfield, Illinois, on 15 April 1846 were not formally known as the Donner Party, about thirty-two people were in the company that left then. (It should be noted, however, that a few people in addition to this—such as George Donner's son, William, and Margret Reed's brothers James and Gersham Keyes—accompanied the group during the first part of the journey to help them get on their way.) The names, ages, and other details of those who went—including the two Donner brothers and their families, James Frazier Reed and his family, and the various people they had hired to help them—are drawn from history, with the exception of the material about Kathryn and Peter Ingalls, who are of course only characters in the novel. (See George R. Stewart, *Ordeal by Hunger: The Story of the Donner Party* [Boston: Houghton Mifflin Co., 1988], pp. 14–19; Walter M. Stookey, *Fatal Decision: The Tragic Story of the Donner Party* [Salt Lake City: Deseret Book Co., 1950], pp. 60–62; Eliza Poor Donner Houghton, *The Expedition of the Donner Party and Its Tragic Fate* [Chicago: McClurg, 1911], p. 8; Virginia Reed Murphy, "Across the Plains in the Donner Party (1846)," in Kristin Johnson, ed., *"Unfortunate Emigrants": Narratives of the Donner Party* [Logan, Utah: Utah State University Press, 1996], pp. 266, 268.)

After presiding over the British Mission during 1844 and 1845, Wilford Woodruff set sail from Liverpool in January 1846. He arrived back in Nauvoo on 13 April 1846, and was able to sell his property for the price noted just two days later (see *Wilford Woodruff's Journal, 1833–1898*, typescript, ed. Scott G. Kenney, 9 vols. [Midvale, Utah: Signature Books, 1983–85], 3:38–39).

They had come only about four miles since morning because of the late start they had made leaving the camp at Locust Creek. Now, with the sun high in the sky, Brigham Young sent word back along his company that they would "noon" here. A small creek with steep banks meandered through the rolling expanse of prairie land that was otherwise devoid of tree and bush. As the word came back, the advance company, led by Brigham Young and Albert P. Rockwood, fell out of line and moved up and down the creek to let their animals drink and to refill their water barrels.

Nooning was the word they used to describe the midday stop. Used to give the animals a chance to rest and graze and the people an opportunity to get something to eat, normally the nooning stop lasted an hour and a half to two hours. Because they had not gotten off until after nine o'clock, word was passed back that today the stop would be no more than an hour. This was not a real problem. Usually the noon meal was a cold meal anyway—hardtack, dried fruit or raisins, maybe some bread and cheese. Mostly the people rested, along with the animals, before moving on again. The Steeds ate quickly, then went to the wagons and squeezed in as best they could to try and grab a quick nap.

Nathan and Josh had volunteered to watch the oxen, which had been unhitched from the wagons. It was not that they worried about them straying too far during the short stop. Rather, it was a new problem which had come to plague them. It was the same reason why the people crowded into the wagons rather than spreading blankets or straw mattresses out on the prairie as they usually did when the weather was dry. The concern was snakes. The three days of warm weather which had finally come over the plains produced a mixed blessing. The roads were drying out, the creeks were subsiding to normal levels, and the campsites were no longer unbearable swamps. And the prairie rattlesnakes were coming out of hibernation.

At first there had been only one or two, and they were sluggish enough to present no real threat. But the previous afternoon, when the temperature had approached seventy, the serpents had started appearing with alarming frequency. For those walking close to the wagons, there wasn't any real danger. The noise of the moving company frightened the snakes away. At rest, when all was quiet, it was a different matter.

The real problem was the stock. Out in the deeper grass one could be almost on top of one of the rattlers before the low buzzing sound sent an instant chill up the back. That meant problems for the grazing animals. Two oxen had been bitten the previous day; three more and a horse had gotten it this morning. The prairie rattler was a smaller snake, usually only a foot or two long, and its bite for a large animal was not typically fatal. But it could make a full-grown ox sick enough that it could no longer pull a wagon or even keep up easily with the rest of the herd. If it was bitten more than once, death could result. Right now the Saints didn't need that kind of setback.

Nathan moved ahead of the animals slowly, thumping the grass with the shovel handle he carried. The oxen were bunched behind him, heads down, munching contentedly, as if they knew that he and his son were keeping them safe. Nathan looked to his left. On the other side of the animals Josh walked along, whistling a tune and beating a shovel on the ground in time to the beat of it.

"Anything?" Nathan called.

"I've seen a couple slither away. How about you?"

"Only one."

His son nodded. "Uncle Joshua was telling me that out on the Sante Fe Trail they saw rattlesnakes that were six and seven feet long and thicker than a man's arm."

Nathan pulled a face. He hated the snakes and couldn't imagine what it would be like to deal with something so much bigger than these. "Yeah," he said. "He told me that too."

"He said they called them diamondbacks because of an unusual pattern of markings on their skin."

"I saw a skin of one of those in Independence once. A teamster had brought it in from Mexico. No question about why they call it that. The pattern was made up of almost perfect diamonds all along it."

"Joshua says that if a diamondback strikes your horse, it could die if you don't do something about it real quick."

"Well, thank heavens we don't have to worry about diamondbacks out here."

"Worry about what out here?"

Both father and son turned to see Lydia coming toward them, picking her way through the grass, watching carefully where her feet were stepping.

"Diamondback rattlesnakes," Josh said clearly. He was still intrigued with the whole idea of something that big and that dangerous.

There was a quick shudder. Lydia had overheard her son's conversation with his uncle about the big snakes and it had left her skin crawling. She didn't want to think about it. "How are they doing?" she asked, gesturing toward the oxen as she caught up with Nathan.

"Fine. They do good on this old dried grass. I'm glad we traded off the horses. They don't fare nearly as well on this kind of feed."

Josh called over to his parents. "Looks like they're starting to hitch up, Pa."

Nathan turned. Across the creek, men and boys were pushing their oxen back toward the wagons. He could see the banner that marked Brigham Young's wagon and saw that someone was already hitching a yoke to one of his wagons.

"All right. Let's turn them around and take them back." He raised his hands and moved toward the oxen, calling softly. They hesitated for a moment, then began to turn. "You go out in front, Josh," Nathan said to his son. "Your mother and I will bring them along."

"Watch for snakes," Lydia called anxiously.

"Yes, Mama."

Nathan decided to take her mind off the rattlers. "Is Tricia asleep?"

"Yep. She ate like a little piglet and then promptly fell asleep again."

Nathan grinned, proud and pleased. Little Tricia was proving to be as easy to handle as she was beautiful. She ate greedily about every two hours. Fortunately Lydia's milk was ample, and they could already see that the baby's fat little cheeks were rounding out even more than when she was born. She also had a double chin now. Delay the feeding much beyond the two-hour mark and she squalled angrily. But once fed she either went right back to sleep or lay awake with her eyes open, perfectly content to watch what was going on around her.

Lydia raised her arm and pointed eastward, back over the way they had come. "Oh, look, Nathan!"

He turned to where she was pointing. "What?"

"Look at the color of the hill there."

And then he saw it too. The gentle rise that started fifty or so yards from where they were rose to the skyline. It was in full sun, which was slightly behind them now. A very subtle shading of green could be seen here and there through the golden brown. It wasn't dramatic yet. The much higher grass of last summer was still the dominant color, but there was no question about it. The new grass was coming up and would soon replace last year's dead crop. They had seen the new shoots coming up everywhere beneath their feet the last few days. But this was the first time when you could actually see it on a hillside.

"It's beautiful."

Nathan nodded, knowing that she meant far more than what the eye was taking in. The beauty was in the promise that it held. It meant that the worst of the cold, wet weather was behind them. It meant that more forage for their stock—even the horses—would soon be plentiful. It meant that the roads would be dry and hard again. It meant making twelve or fifteen miles a day instead of two or less. "Yes, it is," he agreed.

As they drew nearer to their wagon, a movement caught his eye, and he saw that Emily and Rachel were sitting on the tongue of Nathan's wagon, laughing and giggling together. Lydia laughed softly. "I don't think those two slept very much."

"The Barker boy?" Nathan guessed.

"Of course." The Barkers were traveling just a few wagons in back of the Steeds, and their sixteen-year-old son kept managing to lose control of the milk cow. She would invariably come forward enough—with a little encouragement from the boy, Nathan was sure—that Barker could smile shyly at the two cousins when he came to retrieve her. The last time, he had even worked up sufficient courage to say hello. For two fourteen-year-old girls, that was adventure enough to keep them breathless and giggly for several days.

As they moved the animals back toward their wagons, Nathan looked around. It was another warm day. The wind had been blowing steadily out of the south since the previous night, and it was warm and humid, probably nearing seventy once again. It felt wonderful and would help them make good time for the rest of the day. He slipped one arm around Lydia's waist. "It does feel good to have spring finally here, doesn't it?"

———◆———

As soon as the animals were hitched up, the Saints were on their way again. The wagons fell into single file to cross the creek at the one spot where the banks gently sloped down to the water. Once across, they spread out somewhat again. When a wagon company of this size rolled along, especially when they were crossing open prairie and there were no well-established roads, they did not all stay in one long, single-file column. They would spread out, sometimes covering a front half a mile wide, each subgroup within the group picking their own route so as to avoid one another's dust and also to avoid packing down the prairie sod so tightly that it was like driving across large cobblestones. That also helped when they nooned, since all the stock would not be competing for the same grass. Since they had come across the creek, the usual order of march had mostly disintegrated. It turned out that the Steeds became their own little group, with Solomon's wagon in the lead and the others following close behind. While they were not farthest out in front by any means—President Young's group was clearly in the lead— the Steeds were along the ragged front line of the march.

"Papa! Look!"

Rachel's cry brought Nathan's head up with a jerk. He and Solomon were out in front a few yards. They walked steadily, heads down, shovel handles poised, watching for snakes. For a moment Nathan saw nothing. He turned to look back at Rachel.

She was pointing out ahead of them but slightly to the left, toward the southwest. Then he saw it. About a half mile away, a thin line of gray smoke was rising upward from behind the next gentle rise. It was light enough in color that it was hard to see it clearly against the sky. Nathan lifted a hand and shaded his eyes.

Joshua and Derek came running up to join them. Nathan's son Josh was only a few steps behind. "Is it . . . ?" Derek said, squinting and leaning forward.

"Yes," Joshua said flatly. "Something's burning."

"What is it, Solomon?" Jessica called.

"Is it just a campfire, Uncle Joshua?" Rachel asked nervously.

Joshua and Solomon looked at each other. Solomon shook his head. "I didn't see anyone camped out ahead of us."

"Me neither."

Josh shook his head. "Not camped, but I did see a couple of wagons to the south of us a few minutes ago." He frowned. "If they were carrying coals in a bucket and it somehow spilled . . ." He didn't finish.

Joshua grunted angrily. His first thought had been Indians. It was well known that farther west the Indians would start grass fires out ahead of the white man's trains to drive away the buffalo and to leave the invaders' animals no forage. But they weren't in Indian Territory yet. There had been absolutely no word of any Indians in their vicinity, so that was highly unlikely. The sky was clear, so it was not dry lightning. But coals? Some families did not like to start a fire each night with a flint. So they would shovel the hot coals of their fire into a bucket, cover them with a layer of ashes to insulate them, then hang them on a hook on the outside of the wagon. If the wagon had been jarred sharply enough, it could have knocked the bucket off its hook.

Even as they watched, the column of smoke doubled in size and turned darker. The wind gusted. It was blowing straight into their faces and Nathan got his first whiff of smoke. In what seemed like only another moment, the column of smoke became a wall of dirty gray, flattening out as it moved toward them in the wind. Suddenly a man appeared on the top of the rise ahead of them, frantically waving his arms. "Fire! Fire!" came the faint cry.

That did it. Nathan leaped into action. "Josh! Derek! Get the wagons together. Wet blankets and quilts and sacks." They turned and ran to the wagons. Nathan lifted his shovel. Joshua stuck his head inside his wagon and brought out a gunnysack. Then he darted around to the water barrel and shoved the sack into it.

Solomon raced to his wagon and grabbed a blanket. As he shoved it into his water barrel, he shouted to his wife. "Jessica! Have everyone get rags and wet them. Tie them across their faces."

Joshua stopped only for a minute to touch Caroline's arm. "Get the younger children into the wagons." He swung away. "Josh! Derek! Pull the wagons into a tight circle." All up and down the line now they could hear shouts and see people running. He jerked his head around and groaned. The smoke was a massive wall now.

Nathan, Joshua, and Solomon came together near Solomon's wagon. They stopped, gaping. Still about a half mile away, the first flames had crested the rise, and they could see the bright yellow-orange ribbon weaving and dancing and leaping and spitting great clouds of smoke. The sight of it changed Nathan's mind.

"There's no sense going out to help those other wagons now," he cried. "It's either blown past them, or—" He shrugged that off, not wanting to think about it. "I think we'd better make our stand here."

"Agreed," Joshua said. "We can start cutting a fire line. Get the wagons behind it."

Nathan shook his head, not in disagreement but in discouragement. "We'll have to work fast. With the wind, the sparks will be flying."

"I know," Solomon replied. "But we can—"

"Nathan! Joshua!"

They turned. A man on horseback was coming at a hard run

toward them, waving his hat. It was Albert Rockwood, their captain of fifty. He pulled up sharply, the horse's hooves sliding on the thick prairie grass. "Brigham wants us to pull in closer. Fight it together."

"Can we get back across the creek?" Derek called. He and Josh were already pulling the wagons in closer together.

"No! There's already a solid line of wagons trying to get across the ford. Everywhere else the banks are too steep to cross. We've got to fight it here."

"What about a counter fire?" Nathan said suddenly.

Rockwood whipped around. "A counter fire?"

"Yes. What if we start a fire of our own? Put a circle of men around it. Do a controlled burn so it doesn't threaten those behind us. Then we could pull the wagons back into the burned area."

"Yes!" Joshua said, grabbing at Nathan's arm. "That would give us a real firebreak. It's moving mostly north. If we can let it go around us, it will miss the rest of the company and go on."

Rockwood gave a curt nod and grabbed the reins. "Good idea! I'll tell Brigham!" He wheeled the horse around and pounded away.

"Let's go! Let's go!" Joshua shouted at the family, pointing north. "Get those wagons up to join with Brigham's group. Mark! Luke! Get the saddle horse and the milk cow. Tie them to one of the wagons."

Nathan ran back to his wagon. He looked up at Lydia and his mother, who sat side by side on the wagon seat, their faces pale, their eyes frightened. "We'll be all right. Just hang on." Josh was waiting by the head of the oxen. Nathan looked at him. "I've got to get the flint and tow from the wagon. Then go, Josh. But don't let the animals panic. The fire will spook 'em."

"Yes, Papa."

Nathan darted around to the back of his wagon, pawed through a box there, and came up with the flint, the steel, and a wad of tow. "Go!" he shouted at his son. Then he raced away.

He saw Joshua at the back of his wagon and swerved to join him. Joshua straightened and Nathan saw that he had his fire-starting kit as well. Without a word, they broke into a run, heading for the wall of fire that was bearing down toward them.

"I figure we got less than ten minutes," Joshua said, between breaths.

"It'll be enough," Nathan answered. "The wind will work for us too." Now the smell of smoke was heavy in the air, and they could see light ash blowing in the wind. He shook his head, hoping that his time estimate was right.

They ran hard for maybe five or six hundred yards. All along, wagons were swinging around. Men and boys were racing to herd in loose stock. Women were running alongside, dousing sacks and blankets in the water barrels. Children were tying wet rags across their faces.

"Here come's Brigham," Nathan shouted, pointing. The President and more than a dozen men were running toward them. Nathan stopped and dropped to one knee. He placed the wad of tow on the ground and began striking the flint against the steel with short, hard strokes.

Joshua did the same, calling out the plan to Brigham and the others even as they ran up to join them. Brigham started barking out orders like a general on the line of battle. "You and you. Get clumps of grass. Make torches. We'll fire the grass all along this line." He waved his arms. "You brethren, you move right along with it. Don't let it go south. The wind will take it away from us, so it should be no problem."

"How far should we let it go?" someone called out.

Brigham considered that for a moment, peering east. He grabbed one man by the shoulder. "You head back across the creek. Have them put a line of men along the east bank to watch for sparks. If we don't let it get out of hand, the creek will stop it from going farther that way." The man turned and raced away.

Tow is made up of the short, soft fibers that are pulled off during the hackling of flax. It is dry and highly flammable. On

Fighting Fire with Fire

his fourth strike, Nathan's flint sent a bright yellow spark off the steel and into the tow. He instantly dropped to all fours and blew on it softly. A tiny wisp of smoke curled upward. He blew again. There was a soft puff and the tow burst into flame. "Got it!" he cried. He grabbed a handful of dried grass and laid it gently on top. It caught and started to crackle.

"Mine's going!" Joshua yelled beside him.

"All right!" Brigham shouted. "I want half a dozen men. Use the grass as torches. Make a line of fire all the way to the creek. The rest fall in behind. The wind will take it north, and that's what we want. As soon as the fire has moved away from you, follow it in. Stamp out the hot spots."

He swung around to where women and children watched from about thirty or forty yards away. "As soon as we signal," he called, "bring those oxen and wagons into the burned area. Anyone not driving a wagon or herding cattle, get a blanket or a sack and come help beat down the fire. And you women! Watch your skirts. Don't get too close to the flames."

Nathan was taking the makeshift torches from the men and shoving them into the fire. "All we need is a space big enough to pull all the wagons into it."

One by one the men lit their torches and raced away. Nathan grabbed a handful of grass, jerked it loose, and made his own torch. In a moment, he was off and running, stopping every few feet to stick the burning clump down into bunches of grass until they caught.

It was a remarkable sight. Lydia stood up on the seat of their wagon, watching anxiously. One moment it was a clot of men gathered around the kneeling figures of Nathan and Joshua. In the next it looked like a band of warriors racing outward, smoke streaming from their hands, on their way to torch the enemy camp. In moments a second fire was burning along a hundred-yard front. The wind whipped it quickly into a crackling, roaring inferno, pushing it north away from them. Dozens of men and women moved in behind those with the torches, beating and slapping at the fire with shovels and brooms or with dripping sacks, rugs, blankets, or aprons.

She turned. The main fire was coming just as quickly along a half-mile front now that stretched from southeast to northwest. It was no more than a quarter of a mile away now. She wanted to cry out. They were standing on an island of brown that was quickly being consumed on either side of them.

Lydia stiffened, staring at the line where the men were starting the second fire. Among the racing, darting figures was a smaller person in a dress. She stared. What was a girl doing there? Then through the swirl of smoke she saw the flash of red hair. She couldn't believe it for a moment. Then she cupped her hands and started screaming. "Nathan! Nathan!"

Nathan watched the thick grass catch the flame from his torch and eagerly begin to spread. Through the melee he suddenly heard Lydia's voice and straightened. She was pointing frantically at a spot beyond him. "What?" he shouted.

"Savannah!"

He spun around, not sure what she meant. Then he saw. Savannah had a torch of her own and was moving steadily along with the men, thrusting it down into the clumps of prairie grass. "Savannah?" It came out as an astonished question. He whirled. "Joshua!"

His brother looked up, three or four men down the line from him. Nathan jabbed his finger in Savannah's direction. "It's Savannah!"

There was a startled oath, then Joshua dropped his torch and started to run. When he reached her she was bent over, pulling off clumps of grass to form a new torch, since hers had burned down too close to her hand.

"Savannah!" he cried. "What in the world are you doing here? Get back to the wagons."

"I want to help, Papa."

He grabbed her by the shoulders and turned her around. Only then did he see that in bending down she had swept the skirts of her dress around and into the licking flames. The cloth was smouldering and showing black spots.

He jerked her away from it, then stomped on it until he was sure it was out. She watched, half-horrified, half-fascinated.

"This is no place for you," he snapped. "You get back to your mother and help her there."

"But Papa!"

"You heard me," he roared. "Now, go!"

Meekly she nodded and started back to where the wagons were waiting.

Watching it all, Lydia sank back down to the wagon seat, greatly relieved. Thankfully, Caroline was at the back of her wagon and had seen none of it.

Brigham's figure suddenly stepped out of the smoke. He was waving at them with quick, frantic motions. "Bring the wagons forward," he shouted.

"Let's go, Josh," Lydia said to her son. She turned. Emily and Rachel, as well as Mark and Luke Griffith, were with their loose stock. "Stay close!" she called.

All around, everyone leaped into action. The older boys and some women turned the wagons and started toward the new fire line, fighting to keep the bellowing and lowing oxen from breaking away from them. Women and children ran after loose stock and herded it in toward the wagons. Small children were running back and forth with wet strips of cloth for those on the line to tie across their faces. Women doused towels, rugs, blankets, quilts, and sacks in the water barrels, then passed them up to the waiting men and women on the fire line. There was no bucket brigade. Each wagon carried a small barrel of water for drinking, but there was not water anywhere near sufficient to fight the fire directly. Three or four buckets per wagon and the barrels would be empty. The smoke from the main fire was rolling in heavily now, burning the eyes and searing the throat.

Behind them about two hundred yards, the last of the wagons which were near the creek were frantically going back across.

Those still east of the creek were drawn up in a line of defense, with shovels and blankets ready in case the fire jumped the stream.

Nathan worked between Albert Rockwood and Joseph A. Young, Brigham's oldest son, who was almost twelve now. Derek and Joshua were just beyond that. Brigham Young and others of the party were on the other side of them. Brigham ran back and forth along the edge of the blackened, smoking prairie, stomping and slapping at flare-ups or spots that still smoked too heavily. He bellowed out commands, directed traffic, shouted encouragement.

"Watch out!"

Nathan wasn't sure who yelled, or whom they were yelling at, but he spun around anyway. He was not quick enough. There was a momentary rattle, a gray blur, and then something struck his boot hard just above the ankle.

"Snake! Snake!" Rockwood gave Nathan a hard shove and began pounding furiously at the ground with his shovel.

Nathan's blood went instantly cold. He dropped to one knee, clawing at his pant leg. Instantly Joshua and their captain were at his side. "Did he get you?" Joshua cried. "Are you bit?"

Nathan, half-dazed, pulled the trouser leg up, then stared at the two parallel marks where the leather boot had been scored by the fangs. "No," he breathed. He lowered his pant leg, trying to stop the trembling in his hand. "Thank heavens for strong leather."

"Rattler! Rattler!" Somewhere down the line a man was shouting.

Brigham was to them now too. He looked grim. "The fire's driving them out." He cupped his hand to his mouth. "Watch for snakes. You men with shovels. Keep an eye out. Throw them back into the fire."

He looked at Nathan and Joshua and grinned. "Don't know if Brother Joseph would approve, but there's not time to think about that." And with that, he swung back to the task of bringing order to the chaos all around him.

Still shaken, Nathan stood motionless for a moment. He turned. The air was thick with smoke, and that, added to his burning eyes, made it difficult to see. Then he grunted in satisfaction. He could see that Solomon and Josh had the two lead wagons of the Steeds into the blackened area. The others were coming on hard behind them. They would be all right now. He lifted his shovel and broke into a run, seeing a tongue of flame licking its way southward through a thick clump of grass.

As he stomped it out, he heard someone come up behind him. He turned. It was Brigham Young. He was looking north, where the flames were now a good two hundred yards away. To the east the fire had died, denied by the creek of any further eastward advance. "I think we did it," Brigham said.

Nathan nodded, turning to look the other way. All the wagons were into the black now. So were the animals. Beyond them, still roaring in fury, the main fire was now less than a hundred yards away. But suddenly it didn't seem frightening anymore. When it finally reached where they now stood, it would find nothing more on which to feast. He looked back to Brigham. "Yes," he said softly, "I think we did."

On the ground it was nearly full dark now, except for the flickering light of the small campfires which spread out in any direction. The western sky was still a pale velvet purple tinged with the softest of yellow-orange, but night was almost fully upon them. Mary Ann Steed sat back, leaning against a chest that Joshua had gotten for her. She was alone for the moment. The mothers and older children were getting the younger children to bed. Nathan and Derek were off with the stock. The rest of the men were at the wagons, securing things for the night.

After their scare with the fire, Brigham had decided to stop where they were. The fire-scorched prairie was several hundred yards behind them now. The soot-blackened faces were washed; the blankets and quilts that had been used in the battle against the fire were hung on wagon tongues and over tent ropes to dry. But the people stayed near their wagons, tending small fires that were banked and dying now that supper was over.

Mary Ann wondered if this reticence was an instinctive reaction to the fire of that afternoon. When it was all over, everything had turned out okay. No wagons were lost. No one was injured, except for a few superficial burns among the fire-fighters. When Brigham Young called a halt, he had dubbed the place Camp Rolling Prairie. And that it was. They were still out in a vast sea of grass. The prairie was like a frozen sea, with great swells and gentle troughs of undulating endlessness. And maybe the thoughts of a sudden breeze carrying a spark into the grass and starting the ordeal all over again was heavy on everyone's mind. Or maybe it was just that the day's crisis had left them exhausted and drained and they had only enough energy to sit around their fires and contemplate the day.

She certainly was drained and exhausted. In six months Mary Ann Morgan Steed would celebrate her sixtieth birthday. Tonight she could feel every one of those years. It was the bone-deep weariness that did not quickly go away with a good night's rest. If they had called for a dance, she would have gone and watched, envying the boundless energy of youth. But to sit here quietly with the family was even more appreciated.

She looked up. Nathan and Derek were coming toward her with several other men. In the deep shadows she could not see who they were. But they were talking and one of them suddenly laughed. It was deep and rich and she recognized that it was Heber Kimball. Heber's company of fifty had come in at about two o'clock. Others had straggled in until almost six. Then she heard Brigham Young say something in response. She sat up, brushing down her skirts and fussing momentarily at her hair.

As they came into the circle of light, she started to rise, but Brigham stepped swiftly to her. "No, no!" he said, laying a hand on her shoulder. "You stay right there."

As she settled back down, he dropped beside her, making

sure she wouldn't feel like she had to be on her feet. Heber came over too, reaching out his hand. "And how is one of my favorite people?" he boomed pleasantly.

"I'm fine, Brother Kimball."

"Good. Good." He too sat down on the thick grass, folding his legs until he was comfortable. The other men followed suit, encircling the fire as they found places to settle in.

Mary Ann was surprised at who had just graced their campsite. There were five members of the Twelve—Brigham and Heber, Willard Richards, Parley Pratt, and John Taylor. The latter two were a surprise, since she had heard they were camped a few miles ahead of the group here at Rolling Prairie. William Clayton, camp clerk, was beside Brigham Young. The rest were either company captains or presidents—Albert Rockwood, Howard Egan, Ezra Benson, Charles Rich. She felt a sudden twist of anxiety. Was this a formal visit? Had they come to call one of the family members to another assignment?

Seeing her face, Brigham laughed. "Now, Mary Ann," he said gently, "don't you be getting all worried. We had just finished up a meeting with all the captains when Nathan and Derek happened by. We decided we just might come and pay you all a visit."

Embarrassed by his perceptiveness, she nodded. "What a pleasant surprise."

Brigham chuckled, but as if to prove that they weren't there on official business, he said nothing more, just sat back beside her and listened to the men talking. The sound of their voices brought the others out of their tents, and soon all but the younger children were seated around, laughing and visiting informally. They spoke about the fire. There was still excitement in their voices and a little awe at what they had experienced. Then the conversation moved to the other companies that were still behind them, or those who had not even started as yet. The mood sobered as a discussion arose about those still left in Nauvoo and how soon they might be starting out to follow them. But that quickly lightened again as Heber began telling a story of trying to shoe one of his oxen. Since an ox could kick like a mule, and since it had a hard time balancing on three legs, the best way to shoe an ox was to turn it upside down with its legs in the air. Heber had tried to do that all by himself, and soon they were all holding their sides as he described what he had gone through to do it.

As the laughter subsided and the conversation quieted somewhat, Brigham looked at Mary Ann more closely. "How are you doing?" he asked quietly.

"I'm doing fine," she said immediately.

He smiled. "Yes. Somehow I thought you'd say that. Are you really?" His eyes held her gaze and penetrated deeply.

"Yes," she responded more slowly. "I'm tired, of course, but who isn't after a day like today?"

There was a brief nod. His face was somber in the firelight. "I was thinking about Ben today, Mary Ann. What a privilege it was for me to have known him."

His comment was so unexpected that it caught her off guard. There was a sudden glistening in her eyes. "It was a privilege for me to have been his wife."

There was a soft chuckle. "If he were here right now, you know what he'd say, don't you?"

She laughed too, nodding through the tears. "He'd get all gruff and say that he was the lucky one."

"Exactly. And that's part of what made him the man he was. He never lost that sense of humility that is so much a part of those who truly love God."

"I know," she said, grateful now that Brigham had turned the conversation that direction. Though she was reminded of her grief at losing him, it was as if he had called Benjamin to her side for a moment and she could feel his gentle and comforting presence. It filled her with a great sense of peace.

Brigham looked over at Lydia, who was sitting beside Nathan, leaning against him. "I guess you know that your husband is the hero of the day," he said.

Nathan looked surprised. Lydia just nodded. "I was very proud of him."

Joshua was bobbing his head vigorously. "That idea to use a counter burn was brilliant. By the way, President, what did you mean by that comment today that you hoped Joseph would approve of us throwing the rattlesnakes into the fire?"

"Oh, that?"

Josh raised his hand. "I know, President Young. Papa told me."

"Then tell him, Josh. Tell your Uncle Joshua about Joseph Smith."

Josh turned his body so that he faced his uncle more squarely. "It was while Pa was on Zion's Camp. That was in . . . ?" He looked at his father.

"Thirty-four," Nathan answered. "The spring of eighteen thirty-four."

"Yes. Well, on the march one morning, some men woke up and there were rattlesnakes nearby."

"Nearby is right," Nathan agreed. "Some had curled right up against us to get warm."

"Ooh!" Emily shuddered.

"When some of the men were about to kill them," Josh continued, "Brother Joseph rebuked them. He said something about how would men and animals ever lose their hatred for each other if we killed them all the time, or something like that."

"That's pretty close," Brigham said.

"Then he got a stick and carried them away from the camp," Josh finished.

"That's right," Nathan said, smiling at his son. "You remember it well."

"Well," Brigham drawled, now speaking to Joshua again. "I still believe that Joseph's point was a good one, but today I didn't think we had a lot of time for making our peace with the animal kingdom. So I hope Brother Joseph understands."

"I hope it burned them all up," Elizabeth Mary said, bringing a laugh from all of them.

Brigham decided to change the subject. "We are grateful to Nathan for his quick thinking today, but we probably ought to offer a few words of thanks to the Lord as well. That could have been a disaster for us."

"Amen," Nathan said fervently. Others were nodding, faces sober as they remembered those tense few minutes earlier in the day.

"For all the difficulties," Willard Richards came in, "for all the challenges of mud and rain and broken wagon axles, the Lord has truly been with us."

"Amen," several said now in unison.

Brigham straightened, turning to his clerk. "William, this would be a wonderful time for your song." He turned to Mary Ann. "Brother Clayton received some good news from Nauvoo."

"Really?" Mary Ann said, turning to the Englishman. "What was it?"

"Well," Brother Clayton answered, "one of the brethren received a letter and in it there was news of my Diantha. She had a fine, fat baby boy."

"Really?" Rebecca spoke up. "That's wonderful, William. How is Diantha?" Because Derek and William Clayton were both Englishmen, the Ingallses and the Claytons had become good friends back in Nauvoo.

A momentary shadow crossed William's face. "Not as well. She has the mumps and is troubled by the ague, according to the report, but all in all, they say she is doing better than when I left her."

He turned to the others. "All of you may not know, but because Diantha was with child, and because she was so ill, I was forced to leave her behind with friends to care for her. As soon as we find a suitable resting place somewhere along the trail—I hope in the next week or two—President Young has said I can send for her and the baby."

Rebecca nodded at that. Along with other Church leaders, William Clayton was one of those who had been asked to take plural wives. Diantha was the youngest of his four wives. She was slight of build and fragile by nature, and when she found she was with child, it only aggravated her tendency toward illness. As clerk to the Church, William Clayton served as scribe to Brigham Young and the Twelve. He kept a journal of the trail and tried to estimate the mileage for each day. He was also charged with the overseeing of several wagons which contained the Church's property—histories, sacred manuscripts, record books, artifacts, temple furniture, and the like. When Brigham and the main body of the Twelve finally crossed the Mississippi River, he agonized about going on ahead and leaving Diantha behind. But with rumors that the armies were near and that they had warrants for the arrest of all the Church leaders, he finally decided the safest thing for his family was for him and his other three wives to leave with Brigham, find a place where they would be safe, and then quietly send back to Nauvoo and get Diantha out.

Rebecca knew that he worried constantly about Diantha. He had not heard recently of her condition. Knowing how depressed and discouraged he had been, she could only imagine how relieved he must be to have finally heard that things were all right back in Nauvoo.

"So," Brigham prodded, "tell them what happened."

Clayton seemed embarrassed. "Well, as you know, I'm a musician."

"Well, now," Mary Ann said with a smile, "there's an understatement if I ever heard one." William Clayton was a member of the William Pitt brass band. He was an accomplished player of the violin, the horn, the drums, and the pianoforte. He had been one of those who had earned critically needed funds by arranging concerts in the various Iowa settlements along the route. They also frequently played in the evenings for the Saints.

"But I am not an accomplished songwriter," he went on. "I've written a few songs, but I'm much better at playing what others have written."

"But you wrote a song?" Caroline asked. All of them were listening intently, and it was clear that not even all the other men had heard this account as yet.

"When I learned of the birth of my son, though I was still greatly concerned about Diantha's health, I felt to rejoice at the news that she had finally had the baby and that he was fat and healthy and well. I decided to name him William Adriel Benoni Clayton." He chuckled. "That ought to be name enough for any boy. Anyway, after I heard the news yesterday morning, the feeling of joy and gratitude lay heavy upon me. Desiring to express the feelings of my heart, I went off by myself. When I returned two hours later, I had composed a song."

"Do you have it with you, William?" Heber Kimball asked.

"No, but I do not need it. I know the words by heart."

"Then sing it for us," Willard Richards exclaimed. He looked around at the others. "It's a wonderful song."

"Yes, William," Brigham said quietly, "after today, I think it would be appropriate for you to sing it for us all."

He nodded and got to his feet. "I wish I had thought to bring my violin."

"You have a wonderful voice," Derek exclaimed. "Just sing it for us."

"All right." He hesitated for a moment, looking around at his audience. "The music comes from an old English folk tune—Derek and maybe Jenny will likely know it well. It's long been a favorite in the British Isles. It's called 'Good Morning, Gossip Joan.'" He was enjoying himself now. "Fortunately, someone here in America rewrote it into a song you may be more familiar with. It's called, 'All Is Well.'"

"Ah, yes," Mary Ann said. "I know that song."

"Well, I have kept the title but revised the tune somewhat to fit the rhythm of the words. But the words are all new."

"Brother William is far too modest to say this," Willard Richards said, "but he felt strongly inspired as he wrote."

William's head lowered slightly. "Yes, that's true. The Spirit rested upon me and I felt the words flowing from the power and inspiration of the Lord." There was a wry smile. "With that glowing introduction, you may find the whole thing quite a disappointment."

"Sing it," Brother Brigham commanded.

"Yes, sing it," several others called out.

He walked to the edge of the circle, and dropped his hands to his sides. His head came up and his eyes half closed. Then in a clear, sweet tenor voice he began to sing.

> Come, come, ye Saints, no toil nor labor fear;
> But with joy wend your way.
> Though hard to you this journey may appear,
> Grace shall be as your day.

The notes floated across the camp. All around them, voices hushed. Laughter stopped. Heads turned toward the dark figure who stood near the Steed campfire.

> 'Tis better far for us to strive
> Our useless cares from us to drive;
> Do this, and joy your hearts will swell—
> All is well! All is well!

If William Clayton was mindful of his audience, it no longer showed on his face. It was as though he were back at Diantha's side, comforting and congratulating her.

> Why should we mourn or think our lot is hard?
> 'Tis not so; all is right.

Why should we think to earn a great reward
If we now shun the fight?
Gird up your loins; fresh courage take.
Our God will never us forsake;
And soon we'll have this tale to tell—
All is well! All is well!

Finally now his chin lowered again, and he looked squarely at those who watched with rapturous, upturned faces.

We'll find the place which God for us prepared,
Far away in the West,
Where none shall come to hurt or make afraid;
There the Saints will be blessed.

His voice rose joyously.

We'll make the air with music ring,
Shout praises to our God and King;
Above the rest these words we'll tell—
All is well! All is well!

He stopped. The last notes died away. Not a sound broke the silence. For a moment, Mary Ann wondered if he was through. But he did not move. She saw in the faint light that tears were streaming down his face. But when he finally started again, there was not the slightest quaver to his voice. He sang out clearly and triumphantly. It was a cry of faith and affirmation and covenant.

And should we die before our journey's through,
Happy day! All is well!
We then are free from toil and sorrow, too;
With the just we shall dwell!
But if our lives are spared again
To see the Saints their rest obtain,
Oh, how we'll make this chorus swell—
All is well! All is well!

William Clayton stood silently for a moment, then looked around, smiling faintly. He slowly sank down to sit on the ground. No one moved. No one spoke. Above them the stars were like a great glittering cape across the sky. Around them the night seemed impenetrable but safe. Finally, Brigham cleared his throat. "William, I want you to make copies of that song. I want it passed around the camp." He stopped, deeply moved. "I want every Latter-day Saint to learn those words and start singing them to each other. Thank you, William, for bringing us a gift from above."

Chapter Notes

Once the weather turned warmer and drier, two new challenges began to plague the Saints—rattlesnakes and prairie fires. References to both begin to crop up in the journals at this time. Brigham makes mention of a fire on the sixteenth of April about noon. He says that it "burned over doing no damage." (*MHBY*, p. 134.) Several journals also mention a fire on the seventeenth. This was in the evening and was fought "with whips [probably wet blankets and sacks] and water" ("Diary of Lorenzo Dow Young," *Utah Historical Quarterly* 14 [1946]: 136). For purposes of the novel, only one fire is described and it is placed on the sixteenth.

In his journal, under date of Wednesday, 15 April 1846, William Clayton wrote the following while camped at Locust Creek in Iowa Territory: "This morning I composed a new song—'All is well.'" Thus was born a hymn that became the most beloved of songs sung along the trail and an anthem that came to symbolize the spirit of the Latter-day Saints throughout the world. The details of its coming forth and of William Clayton come from contemporary sources. (See *CN*, 6 April 1996, pp. 6, 12; Paul E. Dahl, "'All Is Well . . .': The Story of 'the Hymn That Went Around the World,'" *BYU Studies* 21 [Fall 1981]: 515–27.)

Somewhere on the plains of Iowa—April 18, 1846 (Saturday)

My name is Rachel Steed Griffith Garrett. I was born on the 24th day of January in the year of our Lord, one thousand eight hundred and thirty-two. I am now fourteen years of age. My mother is Jessica Roundy Steed Griffith Garrett, and my father (actually my stepfather, but he is as good as any real father could be) is Solomon Garrett. Perhaps later I can write more of my life story and tell you why my mother and I have all those names, but for now I want to begin with the present.

Two days ago we had a terrible fire on the prairie. We were out where there was lots of grass, and the wind was blowing hard. The fire was large and moved very fast. I was very scared and wondered if someone would be killed or if some of our wagons would be burned. But Heavenly Father blessed us. We started another fire, then drove our wagons into the burned area. The other fire just went around us and we were safe. But that night, after we were in camp, my cousin Emily Steed and me (Emily is not only my cousin, she is also my very best friend) talked about what would happen if we had died in the fire or maybe if we are killed by Indians as we go west. We have not had a chance to get married and have children, so there would be no one who would know that we lived. We decided to keep journals and write about ourselves so that if we die, someone will know about us. Mama gave me her journal and said I could write in the back of it. I promised I won't read hers, and she promised she won't read mine.

I may not get to write every day. There is no way to write in the daytime when we are traveling. Even if I rode in the wagon, which I don't, it would be too bumpy to write anything. And when we make camp, there is so much to do—getting the tent up, starting the fire, cooking supper, helping Mama churn butter or get little Miriam and Sol to bed. (Miriam is my baby sister. She's two, almost three. Sol is Solomon. He's named after my father. He's just a year old.) By the time we're done, it's usually dark. Lamp oil and candles are scarce. So unless Mama or Papa keep a light on, I have to wait. I wanted to start yesterday, but couldn't because there was so much to do when we reached camp. Maybe on a rest day—like a Sunday—I can write more about my early life and catch up on what has happened since we left Nauvoo, but for now I'll try and write something every day.

Yesterday, two children in camp died of the measles. I didn't know them, but the whole camp was sad. Lots of children have the measles right now. And mumps. (Miriam has the mumps and rode in the wagon all day yesterday.) They buried the children outside of camp, then drove the wagon back and forth over the graves so the wolves can't tell where they're buried. I will ask Heavenly Father in my prayers tonight to take the children home to him.

Pleasant Point—April 19, 1846 (Sunday)

Pres. Young named our camp here Pleasant Point. This is another beautiful day—the fourth in a row now. Everyone is happy. Mama says spring is here for sure. It is so nice to walk around camp without sinking in mud. We had sacrament meeting today and almost everyone in camp came. Papa said there were about 600 of us. It was a good meeting. Brother John Kay and William Pitt from the band sang a song about the exodus. Then we all sang Brother Clayton's new song, "All Is Well!" Everyone sang loudly and I felt little goose bumps on my arms when they sang. Mama says that happens sometimes when you feel the Spirit. Uncle Nathan talked to Pres. Y. afterwards and he said he had never felt a sweeter spirit since we started. I'd like to ask the Pres. if he got goose bumps too, but I wouldn't dare. Emily says she will for me. I forbade her to do it.

This afternoon, some messengers arrived from Nauvoo. They had a whole bag of letters that were passed out. Grandma Steed got a letter from Aunt Melissa and we all gathered round to hear it. Melissa and Carl are doing fine. They say many people are getting ready to leave the city now that the weather's getting better. One thing was not good news. M. says they got a letter from Kirtland saying that Carl's mother had died. That's sad. Their baby Mary never got to go to Kirtland, so she will never see her Grandmother Rogers.

After we finished the letter, we started talking about the rest of our family who aren't with us. We all pray for Will and Alice, who are at sea somewhere. We also pray for Peter and Kathryn. They should have left Springfield by now, so we hope we'll meet them soon on the trail.

I knew the good weather was too good to be true. It has started to rain again and I shall have to stop now.

Hog Creek—April 21, 1846 (Tuesday)

We stayed in camp all day yesterday, but I was too busy to write. We washed clothes and cleaned out the tents. Miriam is still quite sick with the mumps. She looks like a chipmunk, but Mama says she thinks she is past the worst. We left camp this morning. It has rained off and on all day. Not hard, but the mud is back. After we got here to camp, someone accidentally lit some gunpowder. It exploded and started a grass fire, but it was wet enough that it was put out quickly. After the fire of the other day, though, a lot of people got quite excited.

Uncle Matthew and other men built a simple bridge over the creek and we camped on this side (west). Tonight some of the hunters found two wild hogs and killed them. So we're calling this the Hog Creek Camp.

Garden Grove—April 25, 1846 (Saturday)

It has been four days since I've gotten a chance to write. There has been too much to do or I was too tired by the time chores were done. I will try and remember what has happened. On Wednesday, we reached a very pretty spot and the leaders named it Pleasant Grove. Pres. Y's horse was bitten by a rattlesnake that day. He caught the snake and killed it. Then he did something very strange. He cut the snake into pieces and put the raw meat on the wound. The snake meat drew out the poison and the horse was fine. I asked Uncle Joshua if he had ever heard of something like that. He said he'd heard of the Indians doing such a thing, but had always wondered if it was true.

Except for a move of only one mile in the evening, we stayed in camp on Thursday while Pres. Y and others rode ahead to reach the Grand River where the settlement will be. Some others caught up with us. It rained hard during the night and it is cold and muddy again. The hunters are finding quite a bit of game—a deer, some prairie chickens, and a wild turkey. One of them shot what they call a prairie dog. Ugh! Papa says they're just a ground squirrel and probably taste like a squirrel. I said I didn't want to eat anything that was called a dog, even if it was a squirrel. Emily says she would rather waste away and die first. But there is hardly any flour in camp anymore so the meat the hunters find is important.

I thought I would write about what it is like out here so that my grandchildren will know what I went through. Actually this is Josh's idea. (Josh is Emily's older brother.) Emily told him that we're writing journals now and he said that our children and grandchildren are going to want to know more about us than whether or not it rained on this day or that. I think that's a good idea so here goes. I shall pick a good day to describe for my future readers.

The bugle blows at 5:30 each morning. I don't know who blows it. One of William Pitt's band members I guess. Then we have to be up by six o'clock. First thing is always prayer. We do this as a family in our tents. Then while the men get a fire started—if we're lucky and it didn't rain, there will still be a few coals from the night before—the girls and the women start breakfast. The younger boys and girls get the little children dressed. Mothers with little babies have to feed them, so they help when they can.

Breakfast on the trail is usually simple. Most often its just mush with a little milk or sugar. Sometimes we have just bread and milk topped with a touch of sugar if there is any. If there is meat, the men like fried bacon or ham, or thin steaks. When there is no meat, we eat a lot of lumpy dick. When I tell you how we make it, you won't wonder any more why it's called that. For lumpy dick, you fill a kettle with milk and put it over the hot coals. You have to watch it real close so the milk doesn't scorch. The minute the milk starts to boil, you start to put in flour, just a little bit at a time. You don't stir it in. You have to kind of poke and mix it. You don't want it to become slick and smooth. You want it to be lumpy. (See, I told you it would make sense.) You do that for about fifteen minutes until it's quite thick, like cereal.

Eat it with sugar or thick cream while it's still hot and it's very good, though I get tired of it quickly.

When we noon, or stop at midday, we usually eat a cold meal—bread, cheeses, dried fruits, beef or venison jerky, and hardtack. Hardtack is like a biscuit, only harder. We eat a lot of it for two reasons. First, it never spoils. If you keep it dry, it will last for months. It doesn't have any yeast in it. Second, it is easy to make. You just get flour, salt, and then add just enough water to make the flour stick together and make dough. Then you roll it out flat, cut it into squares, bake it on both sides, then eat it. It's called hardtack because it's like chewing on the bark of a tree, only tastier.

Supper is the biggest meal. Unless it's raining hard, we always build a fire and cook supper. Things we eat a lot are rice and baked beans and stew. Stew is especially good if the hunters have shot a rabbit or a squirrel. Especially good is when they get a prairie hen or a wild turkey. With the stew we eat corn bread or johnnycake. (Those are about the same thing only corn bread has yeast and is baked, johnnycake is cornmeal mixed with water or milk and cooked on a griddle.) For dessert, we may have sugar cookies or gingerbread. Sometimes we have pilot pudding. Pilot pudding is easy to make. You take some bread and break it into a bowl, then pour boiling water over it. Then you drain off the extra water, put sugar and cream on it, and eat it while it's hot. It is very good. If the cow has just been milked and there is fresh cream, one of my favorite desserts is to skim the cream off the top of the milk where it is the thickest, then spread it on a piece of white bread or corn bread like it was butter and sprinkle a little sugar or cinnamon on it. Mmm. I'm hungry just thinking about it.

Once breakfast is over, we clean up the camp while the men get the stock and hitch them to the wagons. The older boys take the tents down and fold them up. Usually we start out between eight or nine o'clock. Though traveling is the hardest part of being out here, it is also my favorite part. I love to walk alongside the wagons or up beside the oxen. Papa is teaching me how to drive them by calling out to them. Papa never whips the oxen. He says it only frightens them the more. Usually I have chores to do, such as to grease the axles if they start to creak, or to watch the smaller children. That's very important now that the rattlesnakes have started to come out everywhere.

I love the prairie. Now that spring is coming, it is so beautiful. We walk for miles and miles and see nothing but grass and flowers waving gently in the wind. It is like being on an ocean, with the hills rolling gently like waves, and the breeze rippling through the grass. When we reach a high spot, you can look forward and back and see wagons and oxen and horses and sheep and dogs and pigs and children and women all strung out along the trail. It is a grand sight and never fails to make me stop and look. At the creeks and rivers, we pile up like sheep trying to get through the narrow gate to the sheepfold. And as we cross, it is all pandemonium. Men holler, the oxen bellow, the wagons rattle and splash, the children squeal as they have water fights, the women hike up their skirts and wade across if it isn't too deep.

I won't say any more about the mud and the rain, I have talked a lot about that already. It is part of our trip, but now that spring is here, it won't be a problem nearly as much anymore.

Well, back to the news. That same afternoon—Thursday— Pres Y. and the others returned to camp. They found the place on the Grand River where we shall build a settlement for those who are still coming. They are going to call it Garden Grove. We all came here yesterday. Everyone is excited. This will mean we can stop for a while. We will build fences and cabins and plant grain for those who are still to come. Also there is a mill on the river. Pres. Y. says the local settlers are willing to hire some of the men and they will pay us in flour and seed grain. Oh, a piece of warm bread with butter and honey sounds more heavenly than I can express in words.

Uncle Matthew is back with us again, at least for now.

Garden Grove Camp—April 29, 1846 (Wednesday)

What a beautiful place. It *is* like a garden here on the Grand River. I'm glad they're calling it Garden Grove. It has rained a lot since we arrived on Friday. The camp is a great bog, just like so many times before, but work goes on anyway. Rain or not, everyone seems happier. More people are coming every day now. Papa, and all my uncles—Joshua, Derek, Matthew, and Nathan—and my cousin Josh (Emily's older brother) have been working for local people or splitting rails to fence in land for plowing. But we haven't gotten any grain yet. The river has risen so much with the rain that the gristmill can't work. So we will have to wait a little longer for bread. One sad thing. Pres. Y. told the men that they have decided to try and sell the Kirtland Temple and the Nauvoo Temple so they can get enough money to help the rest of the Saints come west. Everyone knows it had to happen, but it still made everyone gloomy. Mama says it is like they are selling a piece of us. I wanted to cry but didn't because I didn't want the little ones to think something was wrong.

Speaking of the little ones. Miriam is better now. She was sitting up and laughing this afternoon. Thank you, Heavenly Father, for answering our prayers.

———•———

Melissa Rogers was in the back room of the Steed Family Dry Goods and General Store, taking inventory of the bags and boxes and barrels. It didn't take long. There wasn't much that was left. For that matter, the shelves out front had a lot of empty space as well. The store was just a shadow of what it had been a year ago when it had been one of the hubs of Nauvoo, drawing many people in to visit and talk as well as to shop.

She closed the ledger book and sat down on a stool. Was it her? Was it the fact that she and Carl were known to have turned their backs on the Church? Did people resent the fact that they had kept the Steed family name on the store even though there were no more Steeds in Nauvoo?

Immediately she shook her head. No, it wasn't that. At least it wasn't a major factor. People were still friendly and kind. People still greeted her pleasantly on the street and treated Carl with respect. It was just the times. The population of Nauvoo was emptying quickly now. Since the weather had turned more pleasant, the ferries across the river were running full almost every trip. And the demand for supplies had been so heavy for the last six months that they simply could not keep up with it. That had started a vicious downward spiral. Much of what Lydia and Caroline had done prior to their leaving had been to buy and sell by bartering. Cash was a rare commodity nowadays. Unfortunately, the things most commonly taken in trade were things which those leaving for the West did not need. To turn around and sell or trade them off again in a city whose whole focus was going west was not a highly profitable way to run a store. And without profit, without cash in hand, there were very few suppliers who were extending credit to businesses in Nauvoo. So the supplies dwindled and the customers with them.

It made her sad. Not for the money. Lydia and Caroline had given them the store on the promise that someday she and Carl would pay them something for it. In a way, they were out nothing so far. Rather, it was that she had found a strange fulfillment in the store. She wasn't sure exactly why. Maybe it was being able to account for each thing and to have a place for it until it was sold. Maybe it was being out of the house and meeting people for part of each day. Maybe it was pure nostalgia, a way to keep in touch with the family that were now gone. There had been many happy hours spent in this store on the corner of Knight and Main Streets.

"Mama?"

The door pushed open and her oldest son was there. Carl had just turned fourteen yesterday. Like his mother, he loved the store and had become her mainstay in running it. With all the schools closed—Melissa was teaching all of her children at home now—there was nothing else to take his time. Except the brickyard. To his father's great disappointment, young Carl did not care for the brick business at all. David and Caleb were there almost every day. Carl would go only if his father specifically asked him to. But he reveled in the dry goods business and was meticulous in helping his mother make it work.

She stood. "Yes, son?"

"There's a man out front asking for you."

"Oh? Do you know who he is?"

"No. He looks familiar but . . ." He shrugged.

"All right." She followed him out of the storeroom and down the narrow hall. To her surprise, Wilford Woodruff was standing near the counter. He turned at their approach.

"Good morning, Sister Rogers."

"Good morning, Brother Woodruff. Have you met my son, Carl?"

"Met him, but didn't introduce myself." He stuck out his hand. "Wilford Woodruff, Carl. I'm pleased to meet you."

Carl shook his hand, then took the book from his mother's hand. "I'll finish the inventory of what's upstairs, Mama."

"Thank you."

They watched him leave again; then Melissa went around behind the counter. "How can I help you today?"

"Phoebe is hoping that you might have some red thread and a packet of small needles."

"I think I do," she said, moving down the counter and sliding open a glass door. She fought the temptation to watch him as she walked, to see if his face gave any clue as to what this was all about. If he had simply wanted needles and thread, he could have gotten them from Carl.

She brought out a small ball of red thread and a package of three needles. "Are these small enough?"

He took them and looked at them, then smiled sheepishly. "She said small. If these are small, then I'm sure they'll be fine."

"Okay. The thread is five cents, the needles, fifteen."

He fished in his watch pocket and brought out some coins. "You wouldn't have any licorice candy, I suppose."

"Actually, I do have a few pieces left. Would you like them?"

"Yes. I'll surprise the children."

She got them, wrapped them in some waxed paper, and laid them down beside the needles and thread. "That will be twenty-five cents altogether, then."

"Good." He slid the money across to her. But he made no move to pick up his purchases. He was looking down at them, not meeting her gaze.

"Is there anything else, Brother Woodruff?"

He looked up. "Melissa, you've been on my mind a great deal since you and I and Carl talked the other day."

"Oh?"

"Yes. I understand Carl's feelings perfectly, and I understand why he wants to stay."

"He feels pretty strongly about it," she admitted, keeping her face impassive.

He decided to change the subject. "I heard that he just got word that his mother passed away."

"Yes. A letter came from his brothers a couple of weeks ago. We knew her health was failing, so it was not a great shock."

"But still a loss, I'm sure."

"Of course."

"Will Carl be going back to Kirtland, then?"

Her eyes flickered momentarily, betraying her surprise at the question. "No. We had planned to make a visit there this summer to see his mother. Now that she's gone, Carl says there's not much there for us anymore. His brothers are running the business. Carl would only be a complication."

"I see."

She waited, sensing there was more than that on his mind.

"Melissa"—he was suddenly all business—"we, the Church leadership, received a letter from Governor Ford a few days ago."

She saw that his hands were very still now. "He wrote to inform us that he can no longer send out state militia to keep the peace here in Nauvoo."

She felt her heart drop. "What does that mean?"

His head came up. Anger flashed in the eyes that were so pleasantly blue and usually filled with kindness. "It means," he said flatly, "that he is washing his hands of the whole situation. It means that he's giving notice to our enemies that there will be no more interference." His brows knit together in a deep frown. "It means that the situation here could grow worse very quickly."

She nodded, feeling a little numb. "Is that why so many are leaving all of a sudden?"

"Yes. There's great fear among our people. Memories of Carthage and Yelrome are heavy on everyone's minds. The men responsible for those depredations are still out there and they're still howling for blood."

"Carl says we'll be all right." It came out woodenly, as if she were forced to say it.

"I know that he thinks that."

"But you don't?"

"Melissa, hatred against our religion is only a cloak for deeper motives here. Don't get me wrong. The hatred is real, all right. But there's something much deeper, and for you and Carl, more threatening."

"What?" she asked in a small voice. She had been lying awake every night for the past week, long after Carl was asleep, worrying about this very thing.

"It happened in Kirtland. It happened in Jackson County. It happened in Far West. And it's happening again here now. Our people come in and begin to settle a place. We are industrious and orderly. We take pride in doing things right. We build homes and barns, we clear and plow the land, we plant crops." His voice turned suddenly bitter. "And if we're driven out, well, what a coincidence. There's all that valuable property just left behind. If you have no scruples whatsoever, you can pick it up for nothing. If your conscience is pricked a little because you know that you're engaged in highway robbery, then you may be willing to pay ten cents on the dollar."

"You're lucky to get ten cents on the dollar," she murmured.

"That's right. And all the while the state and county governments either stand by and refuse to help, or else they become part of the mob."

"And you think that's what is coming here?"

For a long moment he looked at her, his eyes sad and filled with compassion. "I am certain of it," he finally said.

She had a sudden thought. "What about Emma? I saw her day before yesterday. She absolutely refuses to follow Brigham Young. And she's certain that she will be fine."

"So am I."

Her head came up. "But . . ."

"Emma Smith is the widow of the Prophet Joseph Smith. If she turns her back on the main body of the Saints, that is a real feather in the caps of those who hate us. As long as she doesn't change her mind, I think they will leave her alone so she can serve as an example."

"But Carl isn't even a member."

"Carl has a brickyard. You and he hold the deeds to two of your family's homes. You now own this store."

She looked away. That was a compelling argument.

When she finally turned back, he was picking up his purchases. "Melissa." There was deep sorrow in his voice.

"Yes?"

"Come back!"

Her eyes widened.

"I know what's bothering you, but you are not happy. Not really."

She flared, suddenly angry and defensive. "I am happy! Carl is a wonderful husband. I have wonderful children. We're doing fine . . . we're getting by all right. I am happy."

He nodded slowly. "Yes, of course. I didn't mean that. Let me put it a different way. You are not at peace. Nor have you been for some time."

"I . . ."

"You know that's true," he said softly. "I remember back in Kirtland how strong your testimony was. Come back, Melissa. Until you do you will not have peace."

She was faltering, finding it hard to collect herself. "Carl wouldn't—"

"This is not about, Carl, Melissa. It's about you. You and the Lord." He slipped the purchases in the pocket of his coat and started to turn. Then, on impulse, he reached out and laid a hand over hers. "I'm sorry, Melissa. It's not my place to speak so plainly." He took a breath. "But if your father were here—" He stopped as instant tears sprang to her eyes. His own eyes misted up. "If he were here, you know what he'd say, don't you?"

She didn't answer. She couldn't face those eyes now. She stared down at the money.

"Don't you?" he asked again, his voice so low she barely heard it.

After a moment, she nodded slowly.

He withdrew his hand and straightened. "Thank you for the needles and thread. And the candy. Phoebe will be pleased."

She still didn't look at him. "You're welcome."

He walked to the door and opened it. But he stopped again and turned. "We shall be dedicating the temple this evening."

That brought her head up. "What?"

"Yes. In a private ceremony. But tomorrow there will be a public dedication." There was a long silence. Then, "Will you come?"

She looked up. Her cheeks were wet now and her vision blurred by the tears. "I'll try," she finally whispered.

"Good." He stepped through the door, shut it softly behind him, and walked away.

"Carl?"

He was seated on the chair by their bed, pulling off his boots. He looked up.

"They're dedicating the temple tomorrow."

He stopped and his foot lowered back to the floor. "Oh?"

She nodded. She sat in bed, the covers pulled across her waist, leaning back against her pillow. She began tracing some of the stitching on the quilt with her little finger.

"I thought they already dedicated it last fall."

"Only the part of it that was finished. This will be the whole building."

"Oh." He waited, and when it became obvious she wasn't going to say more, he went on undressing. He washed his face in the basin, toweled it off, then blew out the lamp. When he was in bed, he too sat up against his pillow. "Are you saying you want to go?" he asked.

She wanted to hesitate, make it sound like she was still struggling. But she couldn't. She couldn't be dishonest with him. "Yes," she said simply.

"Why?"

"I . . . I'm not sure."

"Not that I object," he said evenly. "If that's what you want, do it. It just surprises me."

"It surprises me too, Carl. But the temple has meant so much to my family. Papa and Nathan and Matthew and Derek all worked so long on it. I remember those nights when Mama and the rest of us sat around sewing, making curtains and chair cushions and other things for the endowment rooms."

"It's fine, Melissa. If you want to go, go."

She thought she could detect disappointment, but no anger. "Are you sure?"

"I'm sure." He burrowed down beneath the sheets, pulling the pillow down with him.

"What about the children?"

He thought about that for a moment. "If they want to, fine. But I wouldn't like you forcing them, Melissa."

"I wouldn't do that, Carl."

He reached out and touched her. "I know. I just wanted to say it."

"I guess that you—"

"No," he said flatly.

"You hauled a lot of rock up there, Carl."

"I've got a big day at the yard tomorrow."

"All right." She too lay down now, staying on her back, looking up at the ceiling. They hadn't had a big day at the brickyard now for six months. Almost a full minute went by before she spoke. "Thank you, Carl."

"You're sure you know what you're doing?"

"No, I'm not. But . . ."

"You don't have to explain, Melissa. I said it's fine, and I meant it."

Chapter Notes

The details of life on the trail as given in Rachel's diary come from the various journal accounts for this time period (see *CN*, 20 April 1996, p. 12; 27 April 1996, p. 12; 4 May 1996, p. 10).

With Wilford Woodruff back from England and the main body of the Saints preparing to flee Nauvoo, final work on the temple went forward at a frantic pace. Finally, on the evening of 30 April 1846, the temple was dedicated in a private ceremony for a small group of Church leaders. Brother Joseph Young—senior president of the Seventy, brother to Brigham Young, and the one who had been left in Nauvoo to preside over the people there—gave the dedicatory prayer. The following day, 1 May, the public was invited and a second dedicatory service was held. Elder Orson Hyde of the Twelve offered that dedicatory prayer. In his journal entry for 30 April 1846, Wilford Woodruff recorded: "Notwithstanding the many false prophesies of Sidney

Rigdon and others that the roof should not go on nor the house be finished and the threats of the mob that we should not dedicate it, yet we have done both." (See *Church History in the Fulness of Times* [Salt Lake City: The Church of Jesus Christ of Latter-day Saints, 1989], p. 317.)

Chapter Fifteen

Joshua poked his head inside the tent. "Caroline?"

A muffled voice called from outside. "I'm back here."

He withdrew his head and walked around back of the tent. Caroline and Savannah were there but had their backs to him. They were bent over, and he could hear a wailing and knew it was coming from Livvy.

When he came around enough to see what was going on, he smiled. Caroline had borrowed a small tub from Nathan, and Livvy was being given a bath. Not yet two, Livvy was small for her age, but she still filled up the tub, and her boney knees were jammed right up under her chin. Her mother was scrubbing at her neck and down her back, rubbing the flat bar of rough lye soap carefully across the skin.

The wailing stopped as Livvy looked up and saw her father. Then there was a horrified howl. "Daddy! Not dressed!"

"Oh!" Properly chagrined, he turned away and stared pointedly at the empty sky. "Sorry."

Caroline laughed at her daughter. "Don't you think that your father has seen you without clothes before, Livvy?"

"Not dressed, Mama."

"Oh, all right." Caroline handed the soap to Savannah. "Here, you finish, and I'll talk with your father so he doesn't have to turn around."

Savannah took the soap. "Hold still, Livvy," she said in exasperation. "You're only making it last longer."

Caroline came over, wiping her hands on her apron. "That child," she said, not without some pride. "Talk about a mind of her own."

"Just like her namesake," Joshua said, grinning.

Caroline tossed her head. "Olivia was never like this, not when she was this young, anyway. This one knows exactly what she wants and doesn't want and you'd better not cross her."

"Maybe the Lord sent us a strong-minded one because of what she's going to have to do in the next few years."

That brought Caroline up short, as much for the fact that he had said it as for what he had said. She gave him a long, searching look. "I suppose you're right. I'd not thought of it like that before."

The thought had just popped into his head and he hadn't meant it to be something profound. He got on with what had brought him in search of her. "Brother Ezra Benson came by a few minutes ago."

"Oh?"

"Yeah. Word has come in that there is a family mired down somewhere on the trail. They don't have anyone to help them get out, so Nathan, Derek, and I are going to go out with Brother Benson to give them a hand."

"All right. Do you know how far back they are?" She was thinking about supper, which was still a few hours away.

"Four or five miles is all, but they say they're mired in deep. Don't wait supper for us, we'll probably be late."

"All right." She reached out and touched his arm. "Thank you for being willing to help."

He looked surprised. "Do you think that only Mormons help their brethren?"

A slow smile stole across her face. "No, but I thought it was only Mormons who called each other 'brother.'" She went up and gave him a quick kiss. "Be careful."

"I will." He turned. "Livvy, Papa has got to go out and help some people. Can I come kiss you good-bye?"

There was a cry of horror. "No, Daddy. Not dressed."

"Can I blow you a kiss?" he chuckled, looking at Caroline. "Eyes closed?"

He shook his head at Caroline. "I promise." He squeezed his eyes tightly shut, turned around, and blew a kiss in Livvy's general direction. Then he opened his eyes and looked squarely at her. "I think you're kind of cute, actually."

"*Daddy!*"

Laughing, he gave Caroline a quick hug, then walked away.

They rode along at a leisurely pace. It had rained again for several days and was threatening even now, and the roads were still a mess, but the days were warmer and the air pleasant. Also, they were not anxious to tire the teams before they reached the stranded wagon. Ezra Benson and Nathan were on saddle horses and led two big workhorses on tethers behind them. Joshua and Derek drove a light wagon pulled by two other draft horses. In the wagon was the harnessing that would be used for the teams once they got there. They moved steadily but not briskly.

For a time they talked about conditions in Garden Grove and about how slowly the work was going, what with all the rain. Then Nathan decided he wanted to learn more about this man whom he knew only casually. It was evident that Brigham Young held him in high regard and was relying on him more and more in various leadership capacities. Nathan was curious for himself, but he also had another purpose in asking. He wanted Joshua to hear stories about how others had come into the Church.

"Ezra," he began, "what was it that brought you out west? Aren't you from Massachusetts originally?"

Ezra nodded. He knew that his accent, with its flat nasal A's and the adding of an *r* sound to words that ended in A, gave away where he was from, but he didn't mind. He was proud of his New England heritage. Massachusetts was one of the original thirteen colonies and had been instrumental in the founding of the country. The independence, industry, and thrift that were all part of that heritage were nothing to be ashamed of, and Ezra knew they were qualities that had made him what he was. He was a man solidly built, with bold features and a direct manner. He was two years younger than Nathan's thirty-seven years, and four years younger than Joshua.

"So tell us how you came to Illinois," Nathan persisted. "Unlike most of us, you weren't a member then, were you?"

"No, I knew nothing about the Church when I first arrived. That was in '37. I just had a yearning to come out west. I had tried my hand at several things before then—farming, I owned a hotel for a time, my brother-in-law and I tried a cotton mill. I was even postmaster in one town. But I had this restlessness, this desire to go west. I see now that it was the hand of the Lord working on me, but back then I just had itchy feet. Pamelia and I finally came out to St. Louis, bought a small stock of goods, then started up the Illinois River, not sure where we wanted to go or what we wanted to do."

"By a stock of goods, do you mean for a store?" Joshua asked.

"No, more for our own use, something to live on until we got settled."

"So where did you go?" Derek asked.

"Well, I bounced around here and there, but finally in the fall of '38 I heard that Quincy was an up-and-coming town, so I moved there and started looking for a home."

"Fall of '38," Nathan broke in. "So that was just when the first of our people started coming to Quincy out of Missouri."

"That's right. I had heard about the Mormons by then, about

what a strange people they were, but I didn't find them that way at all. In fact, as I listened to some of their teachers, and learned about their being driven out of Missouri, I was quite impressed. That winter I boarded with a Latter-day Saint family, and my opinion of them as a people only rose the higher. When they moved north and started turning that swampland into a city, that really impressed me. Then one day, in the summer of '40, there was a debate held in town. A Mr. Nelson had challenged the Mormons to debate their beliefs with him. He was a minister in the area, as I remember. Anyway, I was curious, and so I went to hear it. Joseph Smith was also there, but others were appointed to speak for the Mormons. I can still remember how much I was impressed with him, though—with his humility, his plainness."

"Impressed but not converted?" Joshua inquired, interested now in the story the man was telling.

"Nope, not then. I thought the Latter-day Saints won the debate handily—as did most of the town—and made Mr. Nelson look foolish. I was convinced that the Mormons were believers in and committed to the principles of the Bible, unlike what their enemies were saying."

"So?" Derek prodded as Ezra seemed to retreat into his own thoughts.

"Well, my wife and I commenced attending the Mormon meetings. Then one day after we had returned from one of those meetings, Pamelia sat me down. I remember this very clearly. She got down the Bible, turned to the book of First Corinthians, and read me a passage from chapter twelve, verse twenty-eight."

"Which says?" Derek asked.

"That God has set apostles and prophets in his church. Pamelia told me she firmly believed that Joseph Smith was a prophet. I could tell that she was convinced of the truth of the doctrines, and the word went forth that we were believers in Mormonism.

"And that's when things got interesting, I'll tell you. Some of our friends thought that we were about to 'sell out to the devil,' as they called it, and they worked like the devil to get me to join another church in hopes that that would persuade us not to become Mormons. Their efforts were to no avail, however."

"So that's when you decided to join the Church?" Derek said.

"Not quite. I still wasn't ready. But before long, Pamelia told me that she was going to be baptized."

Joshua thought back to those days in Nauvoo when he and Caroline had struggled over the same kind of disparity in their beliefs. "And what did you say?" he finally asked.

Ezra looked thoughtful. "Well, I was a bit taken aback. But I was not opposed to the idea. I finally told her if she would give me a week, then I thought I could be ready."

"And you were?" Nathan said.

"I prayed a lot and thought about it a lot, and yes, on the following Sunday my wife and I were baptized. That was July nineteenth, eighteen hundred and forty. There was a big gathering that day down on the riverbank. People had come to try and talk us out of it. When we came up out of the water, some of the people started shouting, 'The Mormons have got them now.'" There was a deep, infectious chuckle. "Couldn't argue with that. We just had different opinions about what being got by the Mormons meant for our eternal salvation."

"No regrets?" Nathan asked, glancing at Joshua, who seemed to have lost interest now.

"No regrets," came the firm reply. "I always wanted to come west." Now he laughed aloud. "And look at me now."

The family—a father and a mother and three young children—had mired in almost to the wagon box. Their two yoke of oxen were up to their bellies and could only swing their heads back and forth and bellow mournfully. Throughout the day others had passed and given the family their sympathy, but no one had stopped to help. Most of those still out on the trail were desperately short on supplies and already had exhausted their teams. They would tell others when they got to Garden Grove, they promised, but if they stopped, all it would mean was that more families would be stranded.

The four newly arrived men worked for nearly an hour to dig out the oxen, then to clear the thickening mud around the wheels. While Ezra and Nathan hitched the draft horses to the mired wagon, Derek and Joshua waded in and out of the slough, lightening the load by carrying out the family's heavier possessions. The father wanted to help, but he was fighting a severe cold and was already close to exhaustion, so they made him sit with his wife and children and watch.

As they brought out the last load and set it down beside the couple, Joshua smiled at them. "That should do it. The rest of the stuff is light enough that it shouldn't matter."

"Thank you so much," the mother said. "I don't know how we could ever have done it."

Just then Nathan called. Joshua and Derek both turned. The four draft horses were now harnessed to the wagon. In addition, both Nathan and Ezra Benson had ropes tied to the wagon and wrapped around their saddle horns. "We're ready," Nathan called.

"All right," Joshua said with a wave. Then he turned to Derek. "One more time into the slough, my boy. Do you want to drive the wagon or push it?"

Derek was poker faced. "You drive. I love the feel of mud between my toes."

Joshua grunted, then waded back into the bog, headed for the back of the wagon. "On second thought, you drive. Why should you have all the fun?"

Derek laughed and waded in too, moving to the front and then climbing up onto the wagon seat. He picked up the reins. "Whenever you're ready," he hollered.

There was a shout and the cracking of chains and harness-ing. "Go, boys! Get up!" Derek hollered, snapping the reins. Nathan and Ezra Benson spurred their horses, and the ropes to their saddles snapped taut.

For a moment it was as though the four horses were trying to pull an oak tree up by the roots, but then suddenly there was a sucking sound and the wagon began to move forward. Out of the corner of one eye, Joshua saw the family on their feet, all of them shouting and hollering in excitement. And then the wagon jerked away from him, nearly pulling him down with it, and it was free.

———•◦•———

Nathan and Derek hitched the couple's oxen back up to their wagon while Joshua and Ezra Benson reloaded the family's things on it. When it was ready, they sent the family on their way, promising to catch them once they got the harnessing put away and their own team hitched back to the wagon they had brought with them. It was almost dark now, and there was no sense making the family wait while they got themselves ready.

"The Lord bless you," they called back, waving to them as they moved up the rutted, muddy road that led to Garden Grove.

The four men waved back, then turned to work. As they folded the harnessing and laid it in the wagon, Brother Benson stopped for a moment, watching as the wagon disappeared over the next rise. "I was going to give them my lesson on how to lighten the load until I saw how little they have. They're practi-cally without any food at all."

"I saw," Joshua said. "And unfortunately, there isn't going to be a lot of flour waiting for them. Not until this rain stops and the water subsides again."

But something Benson had said caught Nathan's attention. "You have a lesson on how to lighten the load in a wagon?"

"I do," he averred. "Works every time. Guaranteed."

"Let's hear it," Derek said, curious now too.

"Let's get loaded and on our way, then I'll share it with you."

They worked swiftly, and in five minutes they were under way again. This time the two extra workhorses were tied on lead ropes to the back of the wagon. Joshua and Nathan drove the wagon, and Derek and Ezra rode the saddle horses.

"All right," Nathan said. "Let's hear it. Teach me how to lighten a load."

"Well," Ezra said with a droll smile, "it's not really my lesson. I learned it from President Young."

"We're listening."

"It happened back at Richardson's Point. You remember what a miserable time that was?"

"That we do," Joshua said fervently. It was getting harder to separate out one place of misery from another, but Richardson's Point was quite memorable.

"It was the ninth day of March. Pamelia was heavy with child and had been having a difficult time. That night she finally gave birth." He frowned deeply. "I'll never forget that night. There was so much rain and mud. We had nothing but a tent as a place of refuge. We finally had to cut piles of brush and bring them into the tent and make a bed so we could keep her dry." Now the corners of his mouth smoothed and his eyes softened. "Thank the Lord, all went well and she brought forth our little Isabella.

"Anyway, when it came time to move out again, the ground was so soft and miry that the wagons were sinking up to their hubs."

"We remember," Nathan said. "We remember it well."

"Well, I had six hundred pounds of flour in my wagon, along with a few bushels of meal."

"Six hundred pounds?" Joshua blurted.

He shrugged. "That's what we were told to bring. I was fortunate in that I had sufficient money to purchase that much flour and a wagon to carry it in."

"So you were really loaded," Derek suggested.

"Yes. But the roads were so bad, my teams could make no progress at all. Finally, I went to Brother Brigham. I told him I would have to tarry there until the weather improved and I could get on further. But he wouldn't hear of it. He said I mustn't stop. He wanted me to stay with him and the rest of the camp. Then he asked me what I had in my wagon. When I told him, he got that funny little look he sometimes gets and said, 'Brother Ezra, I have just the solution for you. Bring your flour and meal to me, and I will lighten you up.' "

"Did he take some of it in his own wagons?" Derek asked in surprise. Brigham Young had a large group traveling with him, and Derek couldn't picture him having much extra room.

"Well, not exactly," Ezra drawled. "When I got the flour over there, Brother Brigham called John D. Lee over—he was in charge of supplies—and he says, 'Brother John, Brother Benson here needs some help in lightening his load. So I'd like you to take this six hundred pounds of flour and the bushels of meal and divide it among the camps. If my calculations are correct, that should be about fifty pounds of flour and a half bushel of meal for each camp.' "

"He didn't!" Joshua said, staring at Benson to see if he was joshing them.

"He did," Ezra laughed. "I just stood there with my mouth open for a moment or two."

Derek was nodding. "So that's where that came from. You remember, Nathan? We got it that night. Fifty pounds of flour and a half bushel of meal. It was a godsend."

"I do remember." Nathan was smiling too.

"Well, you can thank good old Ezra T. Benson for it," Ezra said with a grand bow.

"Did he leave you with anything?" Joshua asked, his voice filled with disbelief.

"Yep. Me and Pamelia and the children got fifty pounds of flour and a half bushel of meal for our sojourn in the wilderness, just like everybody else."

"And you let him do it?" Joshua cried.

"Of course." And there it was. Simple statement. No anger. No resentment. No recriminations. And what was just as astonishing, neither was there any pride, any sense of great sacrifice for the cause. Benson was simply telling them what had happened to his flour.

"And you know what?" Ezra went on, sobering now. "I got back in my wagon and we rolled along like there was nothing to it. And every time Pamelia and me would come up on some wagon stuck in the mud, we'd just sing out and say, 'Go see Brother Brigham. He'll lighten your load.'"

———◆———

It was nearing eleven o'clock when Nathan pulled off his boots, lifted the flap to his tent, and slipped inside. It was pitch-black, and he stood there for a moment, listening to the soft sounds of children sleeping. Hoping that no one had moved anything since he had been in here earlier in the day, he stepped carefully to the side, sat down, and pushed his boots into the corner where they would be out of the way. He undressed swiftly, then crawled slowly along the bed, taking care not to bump Lydia's sleeping form, which he sensed more than saw. As he lifted the covers and slipped beneath them, there was a soft "Hi."

He reached out and found her hand. "Why are you still awake?" he whispered. "Is the baby all right?"

"She's fine. Everything's fine."

"Just couldn't sleep?"

There was a soft chuckle in the darkness. "No, I wanted to stay awake until you got back."

He hadn't expected that. Nursing the baby two or three times a night took a lot out of her, and usually she was asleep within minutes after the lights were blown out. "You shouldn't have."

"Oh, yes, I should."

"Why?"

"Who else would there be to wish you happy birthday."

There was silence for a moment, then an answering chuckle. "It's not my birthday."

"Today is April thirtieth."

"It is?" He hadn't thought about what calendar day it was for some time now. It was Thursday, and it was April. Out here that about sufficed.

She slid over closer to him and touched his face. He lifted one arm and she slid into his embrace. "I'm sorry I didn't think about it until after you had gone."

"You thought about it before I did."

"But I've never forgotten your birthday before."

"We've never been in quite this kind of situation before." Then he groaned. "Our anniversary was on the thirteenth."

"I know," she said sweetly.

"Oh, Lydia, I'm sorry."

"You had a few things on your mind that day."

"I did. What was going on?"

"The same thing as the day before and the day after and every day since."

"Why didn't you say something, Lydia? I would have felt bad, but not as awful as I feel now some three weeks later."

There was a muffled laugh. "Tricia was just five days old that day. We were preparing to leave Locust Creek, as I remember. To be honest, I didn't realize that it had passed until two days later myself."

He caressed her cheek gently. "Not quite the glamorous life I promised to give you, is it?"

She came up on one elbow and kissed him softly. "It's not what you promised, but it's everything I hoped for."

Chapter Notes

Ezra Taft Benson, commonly called Ezra T. Benson, was the great-grandfather of Ezra Taft Benson, thirteenth President of The Church of Jesus Christ of Latter-day Saints. Details of his life as given here are taken from published biographical information (see *MHBY*, pp. 246–50; *LDSBE* 1:99–102; and Ivan J. Barrett, *Joseph Smith and the Restoration: A History of the Church to 1846* [Provo, Utah: Brigham Young University Press, 1973], p. 468). While serving as a counselor to William Huntington at Mount Pisgah, he received a letter from President Young appointing him to the Quorum of the Twelve. He was ordained to the apostleship on 16 July 1846 at Council Bluffs, Iowa.

The story of Brother Brigham lightening Ezra T. Benson's load by giving away his flour as told here is based on Brother Benson's own words (see *MHBY*, p. 258).

Alice slipped an arm around Will's waist and leaned against him. She shivered momentarily as the wind caught her hair and tugged at her woolen bonnet. He smiled and opened his coat, pulling it around her. "Cold?"

"Not really. Just a brief shiver. With the baby, I'm always either too hot or too cold."

He reached out and laid a hand on the roundness of her stomach. "So," he said with great solemnity, "would you say that means it's a boy or a girl?"

She laughed. He asked that question no matter what the comment she had made. ("I'm tired tonight, Will." "Does that mean it's a boy?" "I don't feel very hungry right now." "So is that how it is with girls?")

She loved it that he was so excited about the life that she could now feel within her. There had been days when she had not done so well, especially coming around the Cape when the seas had gotten very rough, but all in all she was doing fine.

"Well?" he pressed.

"Well, what?" Her mind was on to other things.

"If you're cold, is it a boy or a girl?"

"Definitely," she answered. Actually, though she was glad for a coat at the moment, it was not as cold as it had been. Tomorrow would be the first of May, which in the Southern Hemisphere meant that winter was coming. But they were sailing north again, up the western coast of the continent, and the weather that was just coming was softening as they moved into a more temperate climate.

She turned and peered into the darkness, looking off the starboard side, or eastward. Above them, the sky was thickly overcast and they could see no stars or moon. Up or out—there was nothing to see but endless darkness. She laid her head against his chest and snuggled in against him. The chill had passed, but she wasn't going to let him know that. He put his arms around her.

"You think Captain Richardson is lost?" she asked softly, not wanting any of the crew to overhear her if they happened to be near.

He instantly shook his head, frowning into the night. "Not for one minute. And I think Elder Brannan needs to sit down and reprimand a few of the looser tongues on board."

His answer did not surprise her. "They're not sailors like you, Will. The thoughts of being lost at sea are frightening to them. And it's been so long now."

His mouth softened and he laid his cheek against her hair, sensing that for all the outward bravery, there was some deep-held anxiety here as well. "Yes, it has. Come Monday, it will be three months since we left, three months since we've touched on land. That's even hard on a sailor, let alone you land creatures."

She laughed. She had come to love the sea, but she didn't yet have Will's absolute joy in it. If ever there was a son of Poseidon, here he was.

"I talked to the captain tonight," he went on. "He showed me on the charts. We're about a hundred miles south of Valparaíso and about seventy-five miles offshore. That's too far to see land, but it's there. You've got the whole continent just out of sight beyond the horizon. If this south wind holds, he thinks we'll make port tomorrow night, or by daybreak on Saturday at the latest."

"And you believe him?"

"Yes, Alice, I believe him. Abel Richardson is a fine captain. Perhaps not quite as competent as the man I first sailed under, but I have full confidence in him."

"Good. We are in desperate need of replenishing our supplies."

"I won't argue with that," he muttered. "One more drink of that slime they call water and I'll consider swimming to Valparaíso."

She pulled a face and shuddered. Before departing New York, the ship's crew had filled huge hogsheads with fresh water from Croton Lake. Most of that was gone now. They were being held to one pint of water per person per day—half that for a child. Not that that was all bad. The thirst could be terrible, but it had to be before you could work up enough courage to drink something that was so thick and ropy that it had to be strained between your teeth. "The taste is horrid!" she exclaimed. "I'm not sure I'll ever be able to get that terrible taste out of my mouth."

He nodded. The water was only the half of it. Rats now infested the ship everywhere, and the people slept with blankets stretched tightly in front of their bunks to keep anything from crawling over them. The remaining food stores were infested with cockroaches, weevil, and half a dozen other species of small vermin. Eternal vigilance was the cost of eating a meal without unexpectedly crunching into something.

He reached down and lifted her chin. "They say that Valparaíso is beautiful. In Spanish its name means Valley of Paradise."

She looked up at him and smiled. "Paradise is something I could use a touch of right now. Did you ever stop there, Will?"

"No. When we went to China, we went around Africa because we were leaving from Europe. But all sailors talk about their favorite ports, and Valparaíso is one of them. They say that the city sits at the base of the Andes Mountains and that the mountains rise straight up out of the plains. They're high enough to make you dizzy." He touched her face. "Beautiful or not, it will give us a chance to be on land again. There'll be fresh water, plenty of grain, good meat, fruits, vegetables."

"Mmm," she murmured. "How about a pile of mashed potatoes and thick gravy, with a bowl of green peas on the side?"

"Now, is this a meal for a boy or for a girl?" he asked soberly.

She laughed and poked him in the stomach. "Maybe I'll just have one of each to spite you."

"Spite me?" he said in surprise. "How about *delight* me."

She went up on tiptoes and kissed him. "Would you be delighted if it was twins, Will?"

He leaned in closer, his eyes eager. "I would. Do you think it is?"

Laughing merrily, she shook her head. "No, I don't. Come on, Will. We'd better go below and get some sleep."

———✦———

"Will! Will!"

He opened one eye, peering at the dark shape that loomed above him in the dim light. Only gradually did he realize it was his wife and that she was already dressed. Both eyes fluttered open and he sat up, careful not to hit his head on the bunk above him. "What is it? Are you all right?"

"Yes." She took his hand. "Captain Richardson wants everyone up on deck."

He swung his feet around and hopped down onto the cold planking. "What's the matter?" He could see light streaming down from the hatch above. "What time is it?"

"Half past seven. You were a sleepyhead this morning. Come on. A lot of the people are up there already."

He pulled his pants on quickly, then shrugged into his shirt. "What's it all about?"

"I don't know. He just sent word that he wants everyone up on deck."

Will finished dressing, then slipped on his boots. They went to the ladder that led up out of the hold and he let Alice go first. It was steep and often wet, and he wanted to be behind her in case she slipped. When they came through the hatchway and onto the deck, they had to squint against the brightness of the light. Though the sun was not quite up yet, it was a clear day and the sky was bright. A crowd was already gathered near the front of the ship. Will saw that Captain Richardson was up at the point of the bow, watching the people in front of him. They were talking excitedly and some were pointing. Will stopped and grabbed Alice's arm. "Look!" he said.

There it was. The ship was still running in a northerly direction, but something had dramatically changed since yesterday. There was no longer an endless flat horizon of sea to the east. In its place, about fifteen or twenty miles away, Will guessed, was a solid black wall of mountains, stretching north and south as far as one could see in either direction. The sun had not cleared its dark mass as yet, but some of the higher peaks were catching its rays and the whole range was backlit dramatically.

"Oh!" Alice said, stopping at the sight.

"Well, well," Will breathed.

"What is it?"

"The Andes Mountains."

Before she could respond to that, Captain Richardson called out. "All right, folks. Gather in close." The crowd quieted immediately as Will and Alice pushed in to one side. The captain did not look pleased, though he smiled briefly at Will. "It's been brought to my attention"—he gave a sharp look in the direction of Samuel Brannan—"that some on board are of the notion that I have lost my way, that I have no idea where Valparaíso is, or Chile itself, for that matter."

Several heads dropped and eyes turned away from his accusing glance. He turned and looked eastward. "Well, yesterday afternoon we made a minor course change so that you can see for yourselves whether there is any truth to that rumor."

One arm came up now, taking in the whole range of the Andes in one sweeping gesture. "Does this answer your questions? You know what they are, don't you?"

"The Andes," someone cried out.

"Yes. And below them is the coast of Chile." His arm came up again, this time to point to a spot to the northeast. "See that one massive peak there? The one that has the sun full on it?"

People leaned forward, peering eagerly. Will saw it immediately. It stood alone and majestic, surrounded by lower massifs but solitary in its towering height. It was like a great, jagged pyramid of stone. The sun was fully on it and the snow-covered ramparts were dazzling to the eye. It was an awesome, spectacular sight.

"Know what that is?" the captain asked, not trying to hide his irritation now. "That, my friends, is *Aconcagua!*"

There was a moment of silence; then the voices began to murmur. "Acon-what?" "What is that?" "Which one is it?" "I can't see it, Mama."

Alice looked at her husband, who was nodding slowly. "What is it, Will?"

"Aconcagua is the highest peak in South America. In fact, some say it is the highest spot in all of the Americas."

"It's beautiful!" she whispered.

Captain Richardson heard her comment and turned to them. "Twenty-three thousand feet high," he cried, "or nearly so. The snow never leaves its summit." Now he spoke to the rest of the crowd. "And do you want to know what is most important about Aconcagua?"

Every head turned to him.

He smiled thinly. "The port of Valparaíso lies at the foot of that mighty mountain."

There was another moment of silence; then several clapped their hands together and there were cries of excitement.

He raised his hands, shouting over their noise. "We should be in port by this time tomorrow morning."

This time it was in total unison. One great, mighty cheer rose from the decks of the ship *Brooklyn* and filled the morning air.

———•———

It turned out that Captain Richardson was wrong, not as to their location, but as to their projected landing time. It had nothing to do with his abilities as a sailor or with his knowledge of the sea. It was just part of life for a seaman.

Will should have known it. He grabbed at a line as the bow of the ship dipped sharply and plunged into the angry sea. It shuddered from stem to stern as tons of water crashed over the decks, slapping at Will's body like an angry animal. He turned his head and shut his eyes against the stinging, salty water. By noon yesterday, while everyone was still charged with excitement at the sight of land, one of the brethren, a man in his fifties, had started complaining about how his lumbago was aching. Will had thought nothing of it at first. He too was filled with excitement at the thought of finally making landfall. But he should have known better. You could feel it in the air—that heaviness, that almost oppressive feeling which signaled a coming storm.

By suppertime, the ship's barometer was dropping like a rock and confirming the man's complaints. The tops of the Andes had disappeared beneath an ominous mass of clouds which extended across the whole northern sky as well. Spots of light rippled here and there. That and the distant rumble of thunder gave one the feeling that some far-off armies were having a mighty artillery duel. By nightfall, the south wind had shifted almost one hundred eighty degrees and was blowing stiffly out of the northeast. That was the worst possible news. The captain had tried tacking for a time, using the wind to zigzag back and forth, inching forward a little with each turn, but soon the wind was too strong. The passengers were sent below and the hatches battened down. Will had volunteered his help, which Richardson gladly accepted.

By midnight, they were in a howling gale and were being driven south again, back down the coast toward the Cape. All night they fought the battle, pulling in the canvas, working in the rigging, so that the storm didn't tear the sails apart, and yet keeping enough canvas up to control the ship. Dawn had come three hours ago, though it was hard to tell. The sky overhead was almost black, and the light was muted and dim, more like twilight than daylight. The captain had finally given up and was letting the ship run before the wind, even though it was driving them farther and farther from Valparaíso.

There was a shout and Will turned his head. Back on the fo'c'sle, standing at the great wheel, the bosun was waving at him to come over.

Will raised a hand in acknowledgment, braced himself for the next crashing wash of water, then darted across the deck as the ship pulled itself up the next mountainous wave. When he reached the ship's officer, the man merely pointed. "Captain Richardson would like you in his cabin."

"Thank you." Letting his body follow the rolling motion of the ship, Will made his way to the passageway that led to the captain's cabin. He knocked, and the door was immediately opened.

There were four men inside in addition to the captain. Richardson was seated at his desk with a large chart in front of him. The first mate was standing beside the door and it was he who had let Will in. The other three men were Samuel Brannan and his two counselors in the presidency of the company of Saints. Brannan was standing beside the captain, leaning over and peering at the chart. The other two men stood back, one holding on to a chair that was fastened to the deck, the other grasping a beam in the overhead bulkhead trying to steady himself. They both looked a little green and totally miserable.

"Come in, Steed," the captain said.

Will stepped inside and the first mate shut the door behind him.

"We're having a conference," Brannan said, lifting his head. "We could use another sailor's expert opinion."

Will moved over to the desk and the first mate followed him. The two counselors did not move from where they were, obviously willing to just listen rather than to give themselves over to the rolling of the ship. Will's practiced eye ran over the chart, immediately identifying what was shown. It was a large chart, two feet by three feet, with north being on the top of the narrow width. The whole right side of the chart showed the coastline of South America. He leaned closer and saw dots marking the sites of Santiago and Valparaíso.

Richardson looked up at Will and Brannan to see if they were watching, then jabbed a finger at the map. "I figure that we were to here yesterday." He was tapping a spot less than half an inch below Valparaíso. "Now"—he tapped a spot almost two inches below it—"I figure we're somewhere about here."

Will shook his head. It was discouraging but the captain was probably right. They were running before the wind now, probably making five or six knots, and had been doing so for almost eighteen hours. So a hundred and fifty to two hundred miles below Valparaíso was probably right. He felt a great wave of discouragement. The storm was bad enough for morale, but to know they wouldn't be making landfall immediately would be devastating to Alice and all the rest.

"So what does that mean?" Brannan asked quietly. He too was subdued by the news.

"It means," Richardson said bluntly, "that we are in a crisis. There's no way we can make Valparaíso now with this wind against us. Judging from the nature of the storm, I'd say we've got another two or three days before it blows itself out." He stopped and looked at Will and the first mate. "Would you agree?"

"Yes," said the officer.

Will nodded. "At least."

"By then we'll be a week or more out of port, and that's assuming the winds turn favorable. As you know, our water and food stores have reached critical levels. We don't have enough to see us through another week or ten days."

There was silence in the room. The situation was grim and everyone knew it.

"I have a possible solution," the captain said finally.

"What?" Brannan demanded, eager for any sliver of hope.

The seaman bent over the chart. His finger still touched the spot which marked their present position. "We have a north-easterly wind, which is contrary to where we need to go. But . . ." He paused for effect. "But what if we let it drive us in a south-westward direction"—his finger moved across the chart and stopped where there were three small, irregularly shaped circles in the vast expanse of ocean—"to here?"

Will leaned forward, peering carefully. In small letters above the three circles were the words *Islas Juan Fernández*.

"Where is that?" Brannan asked, leaning over and touching shoulders with Will.

"The Juan Fernández Islands," the captain said with satisfaction.

"What are they," Will asked, "about three or four hundred miles off the coast?"

"Closer to four hundred," the first mate replied.

"What's there?" Brannan asked. "Can we make it?"

"That's where the wind is driving us right now," Richardson answered with a quick nod. "If we let her run, I think we can make landfall in three days at the most. And what's there? Well, the best answer I could give to that would be to tell you that these are the islands where a man named Alexander Selkirk was marooned for four years back in the early seventeen hundreds. Later, an English writer made his experiences the basis for a—"

Will's head jerked up. "Robinson Crusoe!"

The captain was smiling. "Yes, *Robinson Crusoe* by Daniel Defoe. The Juan Fernández Islands is where it all happened."

Brannan straightened slowly. "So we could get supplies there?"

"Of course," the first mate exclaimed. "Don't you remember? The place was a paradise. Fresh water. Fruits. Wild animals. Selkirk lived there for four years and did fine."

Now Brannan was smiling. "So that would solve our problem?"

"It would solve several problems," Richardson said happily. Then he sobered. "Mind you, Mr. Brannan, I'm not asking for your permission to change course. That's a captain's prerogative. But I wanted you to know what I have decided. I think it's the best solution, all things considered."

Brannan looked at Will.

"The captain's right," Will said without hesitation. "It's a good solution."

The leading elder of the Mormon company swung around to look to his counselors. They were nodding, still pale but obviously pleased. Finally Brannan turned back to Richardson. "Thank you, Captain, for letting us know of your plans. We shall inform the passengers. *And*," he went on quickly as the captain was about to answer, "I shall convey to our people our utmost confidence in your judgment. You shall have no more complaints from us as to your course of action."

"Thank you, Mr. Brannan. I would appreciate that."

"Is there *anything* I can get you, Alice?"

She moaned softly, then opened her eyes. "Yes."

"What?"

"Give me your sea legs and your iron stomach and you have the baby." She tried a smile, but suddenly gagged. Will grabbed the pail and held it out for her. She went up on one elbow and retched again and again.

When she was through, she dropped back to the pillow again. Will set the pail down. He might as well have not bothered. Alice had eaten nothing for the past two days and had reached the point where she was having the dry heaves.

He reached over and stroked her forehead, feeling the clamminess of the skin. "I would if I could," he murmured. "Do you know that?"

"Yes." She touched his hand briefly, then let her hand drop back again to lie limply at her side. "I know you would."

"The wind has started to die a little, Alice. I think the storm is starting to blow itself out."

"Try a dagger."

He reared back, caught off guard by that. "What?"

"The wind," she said, the tiniest hint of a smile playing around the corner of her mouth. "If it's dying, help it out."

Now he understood and he laughed softly. How he loved this woman, so miserable and so brave all at the same time. "Maybe by tomorrow morning."

Her eyes closed and he couldn't tell if that had encouraged her or discouraged her. Her lips moved.

He leaned closer. "What was that?"

"How soon the islands?"

"The captain thinks by Monday morning. Not tomorrow but the next day."

"Good." She squeezed his hand weakly.

He squeezed back but said nothing more. If she could sleep again, so much the better. He laid his head on his arm and closed his eyes as well, ignoring the creaking of the timbers and the crash of waves overhead. It was not much, but he could feel that the battle between the ship and the sea was lessening.

"Laura!"

The cry of a man's voice brought Will up with a jerk. He swung around. Sister Laura Goodwin was standing at the foot of the steep ladder that led out of the passenger hold. Across the room, Isaac Goodwin was climbing out of his bunk. "Laura, wait! Let me help you."

The Goodwins were a couple that Will and Alice had come to like very much. Though Laura Goodwin was considerably older than Alice—she had seven children and was carrying her eighth—when she learned that this would be Alice's first baby, she had taken the younger woman to her as though she were one of her own. It had been a great comfort to Alice.

Will stood and turned to see what was going on. Laura stood at the foot of the ladder, peering up at the hatchway cover, looking very ill. "Got to have some air," she mumbled.

"Wait," Isaac called. "Let me get my boots on and I'll help you."

If she heard, she gave no sign. She grasped the rope railing and started up the ladder. Will leaped to his feet. The hatch above her head was battened down, but salt water from the storm above dripped steadily through the cracks. The ladder was wet and slippery with encrusted salt. Will would not let Alice go up it without his being right behind her. There had already been a couple of nasty falls, and those were in good weather.

"Sister Goodwin," he called, starting around one of the eating tables toward her. "Wait!"

"Need air," she said, looking up at the hatch above her. She was climbing up the ladder now, half in a daze.

"Laura, no!" Isaac had one boot on, but forgot the other. He was coming as fast as he could from the far corner, almost losing his balance with the pitching and rolling of the ship.

Will was closer and was moving quickly now. "Come down," he cried. "Let me get the hatch for you."

She was at the top of the ladder now, reaching up with one hand to fumble awkwardly at the fasteners above her head.

"Laura!" Isaac shouted. "Hold on!"

At that moment, a wave hit the bow of the ship, sending a shuddering jolt all along the beam. It threw Will hard enough that he slammed against a chair, his shin striking the crossbar. He yelped in pain. Isaac Goodwin flew sidewards and hit the bulkhead.

There was a cry. Will, bent over and holding his shin, jerked up. Laura Goodwin was dangling in midair, one foot barely on the step, the other flailing wildly. One hand clutched at the rope railing; the other was clinging to the hatch fastener. He hurled himself toward her, but not quickly enough. The ship lurched again, fighting its way upward against the driving power of the sea. The movement snapped the ladder roughly. Laura Goodwin's other foot slipped on the wet wood. She screamed, them plummeted downward, hitting the deck with a sickening thud.

"No!" It was an agonized scream from Isaac Goodwin.

Will reached her and dropped to one knee. She was on her back, her face twisted with pain, her eyes wild and filled with shock. Then Isaac was down beside them. "Laura! Are you all right?"

There was a quick, almost imperceptible shake of the head. "Needed air," she gasped.

He took her hands. "Don't speak." Others were coming to help now.

"Let's get her into her bunk," Will said.

Isaac nodded numbly. "It will be all right," he said to his wife. Her eyes were closed now, her teeth clenched tightly against the pain.

Sam Brannan was suddenly there. "All right," he said, taking command. "Let's have six men, three on each side. Easy, now."

Laura screamed as the men put their arms underneath her.

Her husband grabbed her hands and held them tightly. "We're going to get you to the bed, Laura. Hang on."

"The baby! The baby!" She was screaming and sobbing and writhing. She jerked one hand away and clutched at her stomach.

"Go," Brannan said to the men. "Careful, now."

As they lifted, she screamed again, then bit down hard on her lower lip. In the far corner, her other children were whimpering in terror, arms outstretched toward their mother.

Pausing to keep their balance, bracing themselves each time the bow dipped and drove down into the waves again, the men moved across the passenger hold, Isaac holding his wife's hands and guiding them, Laura grunting and gasping with the pain.

Carefully they placed her in the cot where she normally slept. The men stepped back as the member of the company who served as their doctor moved in beside her.

Isaac Goodwin, totally stricken now, looked around. "Thank you."

"What else can we do?" Brannan asked.

His chin dropped and his eyes looked away. "You can pray," he said.

———————

The first thing Alice was aware of was that there was a faint light coming through the cracks in the hatchway. The second thing was that the violent pitching and yawing of the boat had stopped. It was still rolling in the swells, but this was normal, this was to be expected. A tremendous sense of relief washed over her. The storm was over.

She turned her head. In the faint light of the one lamp they kept lit in the compartment she could see Will. His eyes opened slowly, and for a moment he stared at the bottom of the bunk directly above them. Then he turned and saw her. He smiled. "Do you feel that?"

"Yes," she whispered. "It's wonderful."

He turned on his side and took her into his arms. "I told you it was going to blow over."

She pulled a face at him. "Are you ever wrong?" she chided.

"I was only once."

She kicked at his leg. "And when was that?"

"When I waited so long to ask you to marry me."

"Now, there's the right answer," she laughed softly, kissing his nose. Then memory returned and sorrow with it. "I wonder how Isaac is doing."

Will shook his head. "The whole family is taking it very hard."

"Will the captain honor her request?"

Will nodded again. "Yes. It's very unusual. Sailors are very superstitious. It makes them very nervous to have a dead person on board, but where we're so close to landing, the captain said he will do as she requested."

As Laura Goodwin had grown worse and worse through the afternoon and into the evening and it became evident she was dying, she became obsessed with a fear of being buried at sea. She had always hated the endless ocean and especially the sharks that followed the ship scavenging on the garbage. She begged her husband to promise her that he would not let the crew do that to her. Finally, Will had gone to the captain and interceded in her behalf. Captain Abel Richardson was a good man, a religious man, and he had proven to be a decent man. They both knew how the crew would react to this bit of news, but he had agreed almost immediately. He returned personally to the hold and promised Sister Goodwin that her wishes would be granted. It was the first peace she had had since the fall from the ladder. A few minutes later she lapsed into sleep, then into a coma; and then she slipped away just before nightfall.

It left the Saints in a deep pall, for the Goodwins were widely respected. Now instead of a wife and eight children, Isaac had seven motherless ones.

Will kissed Alice firmly, deciding not to let her dwell on this. "Come on," he said. "Let's get dressed and go up top."

"Yes," she said eagerly. "I would like that."

Five minutes later they pushed the hatch open and Alice climbed through it and onto the main deck. Will was right behind her. It was a glorious day. The sun behind them was up a short distance above the eastern horizon and held the promise for a warm and pleasant day. She tipped her head back, breathing deeply, rejoicing in the solidness of a deck that barely moved beneath her feet.

Will touched her shoulder. "Look," he said.

She turned around toward the bow of the ship, then gasped. Directly off the port bow, some fifteen or twenty miles away, the expanse of the sea was broken with what surely had to be one of the loveliest scenes Alice had ever laid eyes on. Rising up out of the water were massive emerald green peaks. The tops were wreathed in mist that made them seem as if they were crowned with a white garland.

"Oh, Will!" she said.

"Yes." He too was struck deeply by what they saw. "Isn't that a sight?"

"The Juan Fernández Islands," a voice called from behind them.

They turned. The first mate was at the wheel of the ship, with Captain Richardson standing beside him. It was Richardson who had spoken. "The one you see there is the biggest island. It's called Robinson Crusoe Island."

Alice turned back. "It's beautiful."

"Yes," Richardson said again, pleasure deepening his voice. "And we should be dropping anchor around noon today."

"I can't wait," she cried.

Will looked up at the two seamen. "Isn't today May fourth?" he asked.

The captain nodded. "It is."

"Then it's three months to the day since we left New York City."

They both looked surprised for a moment. "That's right," the first mate said, "it was February fourth, wasn't it?"

"Three months at sea without a single break," Richardson said. "I think it's time for a stop, don't you, Mrs. Steed?"

She threw her head back joyously, tossing her hair. "I do indeed, Mr. Richardson. I do indeed."

Approaching Robinson Crusoe Island

Chapter Notes

The ship *Brooklyn* was nearing the port of Valparaíso, Chile, at the end of April 1846 when a severe storm drove them back again. The travelers being in critical need of resupply—the description of their water supply and the vermin-infested food comes from the account of one of the company— the captain turned and ran with the wind, setting sail for the Juan Fernández Islands, the place which provided the basis for Defoe's classic novel. (See "Voyage," pp. 57–58.)

Shortly after sunup on the morning of 4 May 1846, exactly three months to the day after leaving New York Harbor, the *Brooklyn* came in sight of the Juan Fernández Islands. They reached the harbor and dropped anchor about one p.m. of that same day. The main island had only two Chilean families (eight people) who lived in primitive huts in a leisurely subsistence style of existence. "The island abounded in untended fruit trees, continually reseeding vegetables, and animals (goats, hares, and pigs) which ran wild from previous settlements." ("Voyage," p. 58.)

During the storm that drove the *Brooklyn* back from Valparaíso, Laura Goodwin, who was carrying her eighth child, lost her footing on slippery wood and was thrown down a companionway. She went into premature labor, developed complications, and finally died. She begged her grief-stricken family not to bury her at sea. The captain complied with her wishes and she was buried on the island soon after their arrival. (See "Voyage," pp. 58–59.) She was one of the eleven passengers who died before the journey was completed.

Garden Grove Settlement, May 4, 1846 (Monday)

It has been five days since I last wrote in my journal. Emily says it has been even longer for her. Today we promised each other we would write no matter what. This morning the sun was shining when we came out of the tents. It has been sunny and warm all day. The sky is still clear, even in the west. Wonderful! It has rained much since we arrived at Garden Grove. Yesterday during worship services President Young spoke to us. He said that it is the word of the Lord that we should plant crops at this place, and that some should go ahead and start another settlement so those still coming will have food to eat. Today, Papa and the other men split rails most of the day. The north field is all fenced now. Hardly any food left in camp.

Garden Grove Settlement, May 6th (Wednesday)

Rained most of the night again. It stopped raining in the morning though and the men went right back to work. If it is the word of the Lord to build this place, they want to be obedient, even though Papa worked on an empty stomach. He wasn't the only one. The bridge over the river is coming along fine. Pres. Y worked with the men on it. Afternoon, stormed again—very hard! Many trees were blown down, one fell on a cow and another on a mule. Almost everyone in the camp had to hang on to their tents with all their might, the wind was blowing so hard. There was hail too. I started to complain about the weather at supper time but Emily gave me a lesson on murmuring. "Rachel," she said, "do you know why they call it murmuring?" Then she told me that it is a word that sounds like what it describes. And that's what we do when we murmur. We mumble under our breath and it sounds like mur-mur-mur. I don't want to murmur. It was very miserable today though. That's not murmuring, that's just recording the truth.

I just had a strange thought. I wonder if Noah ever murmured.

Garden Grove, May 7th, 1846 (Thursday)

Joy! Joy! Joy! Some of the brethren returned from northern Missouri where they had gone to trade. They brought 35 bushels of wheat and 4 bushels of cornmeal. Much rejoicing in camp. One of the horses which was bit by rattlesnakes died.

Garden Grove Camp, May 8, 1846 (Friday)

Wheat and meal given out this morning. Mama and Grandma and Aunt Lydia baked bread in the Dutch oven. It was so good! The camp commissaries (the men who get supplies for us) loaded up wagons with furniture, beds, saddles, harnessing, and anything else that could be spared for trade. Brother Brigham says to get rid of our feather beds and get something more practical. The wagons left for Missouri again. Fence around the south field done. Saw Jeremy Barker today. He smiled at me!!!!

296

Garden Grove, May 9. (Saturday)

No rain! Four more log cabins were raised for those coming behind.

———•———

Melissa Rogers waited until supper was over; then, as the children got up to clear the table, she spoke to her oldest. "Carl. I'd like to speak with your father. Would you take the children outside for a while? You can do the dishes later."

He looked surprised, but nodded immediately. "Yes, Mama."

The other children whooped with pleasure and shot away.

Once they were gone, Melissa turned to her husband. She jumped in without preamble. "A woman came in the store today. She told me about what happened to Andrew Ray yesterday."

He nodded but said nothing.

"Did you know about that?"

He nodded again. "I heard word of it."

"Were you going to tell me about it, Carl?" Now there was a slight bite to her voice.

He considered that, then shrugged. "I probably would have mentioned it eventually."

"Eventually?"

"There's no use in getting yourself all worked up over this, Melissa. It was an isolated incident that happened outside of town."

"Tell me what you heard."

"I don't think—"

"Tell me, Carl."

He leaned back, seeing she was determined. "Evidently Mr. Ray has been trying to sell his farm so he can go west. He's had some offers but nothing he would consider. So he's been holding on. Yesterday some ruffians—riffraff from the river probably—came to his farm."

"And?"

He could see there was no sense softening it. She probably had heard it all anyway. "And they dragged him from his home and beat him pretty badly."

"With an ox goad?"

He sighed wearily. "Yes, they used an ox goad and jabbed his skin several times."

She was angry now. "Several times? The word I heard was *repeatedly*."

"All right, so they jabbed him repeatedly. But he'll be all right."

"And did you learn why they did it?" she pressed.

"They want to drive him off his farm before he can sell it."

"So they can take it over?"

"Yes."

"I thought you said they were riffraff from the river. Riffraff don't know about taking over some Mormon's farm."

"You don't know that."

"And you don't know but what they were some more of Illinois's more upstanding citizens, do you?" The sarcasm was heavy in her voice.

He shrugged.

"This is just what Elder Woodruff said would happen."

"Look, Melissa. It was outside of town. It was—"

"An isolated incident?" she finished for him. "Haven't there been other reports of mob harassment in the past few days?"

He leaned forward, seeing that she had worked up a real head of steam over this. "Melissa, I know what you're thinking. And I won't say there is no cause for concern. But a group of us who aren't members of the Church—including several of those who have recently purchased homes and businesses here—are talking about forming a group. It will give us a chance to stick together, to negotiate without it looking like we're part of the Church."

"Yes," she snapped. "And these wonderful non-Mormons you're talking about are the same ones who built a tenpin alley opposite from the temple."

His eyes narrowed a little. "So?"

"They're also the ones bringing in groggeries all over the city. Is that what you want for Nauvoo, Carl?"

"No, I—"

"There's hardly a night that goes by now that you can't hear the drunkards going up and down the street, whooping and hollering. We never had that before, Carl. Is this what your group is going to protect?"

She stepped back, a little surprised by her own vehemence.

Carl watched her for several seconds, still taken aback by the strength of her feelings. Finally he decided it was safer to stick to the original question of safety and security. "The enemies of the Church just want the Mormons out, Melissa. That's what they're after. They just want the Mormons out."

"I'm a Mormon," she retorted. "Does that concern you at all?"

"Come on, Melissa. You know what I mean." He felt a touch of anger of his own now. "Having that temple dedication the other day didn't help. The enemies of the Church are saying that's proof that the Saints are not leaving, that they've reneged on their promise to leave."

"Their promise to leave? No, Carl!" She flung it back at him. "You make it sound like we are leaving for a trip somewhere. It makes it sound like we got tired of Nauvoo. My family didn't 'decide' to leave. They were driven out, Carl. And some of those men who will be making up this little group of yours are the very ones who are glad to see them go because they have profited from their leaving."

"I don't know what's got you so worked up all of a sudden, but—"

She stood, pushing back her chair. She leaned forward, hands on the table. "I want to say this, Carl. I know that I am largely to blame for how you feel about the Church now. I—"

"I've never felt wonderful about the Church," he shot back.

"I know. But I'm the one who turned you so bitter over plural marriage, because I hated so much what was going on. I'm the one who said I didn't want to go west, even when the family was leaving. I know all that, Carl, and so I'm not blaming you. But you need to know. I'm scared, Carl! I'm afraid that Wilford Woodruff is right. I don't think we're safe here."

"I—"

She rode over him, wanting it done, wanting it said clearly this one time. "I won't bring it up again, Carl. I made my bed the way I thought it should be. Now I've got to sleep in it. But just so you understand, if you ever change your mind, if you ever have second thoughts about leaving, you don't need to ask me. I'll be ready."

"What if I say we're leaving but we're going back to Kirtland?"

Her face was filled with weariness and sorrow and surrender. "You know I'll go wherever you decide to go, Carl. I will go with you."

"But that's not where you'd like to go?" He was feeling a little sick. He had known that something had been eating at her for some time now. But he had no idea it was this deeply felt.

"No, Carl. If you're asking me, I want to go west. I want to find my family and be with them." There was a long pause. "I want to be with the Church."

———— ·◆· ————

Alice Samuelson Steed stopped as she and Will reached the beginning of the makeshift dock that ran a short distance out into the harbor. The large rowboat from the ship had just arrived to take the last load of the passengers back out to where the ship lay at anchor. They were fourth or fifth in line, but she suddenly stepped aside and let the others pass. Surprised, Will followed suit. "What?"

"Oh, Will," she said, turning and letting her gaze sweep up

and up the verdant peaks that rose like green-shrouded fingers thrust from a pool of perfect turquoise blue. For one born and raised for her entire life in St. Louis, Missouri, the sight was still completely overwhelming to her.

"It's beautiful, isn't it?" Will murmured.

She let her eyes drop to the metal and palm frond huts along the curve of beach. This was where the few permanent inhabitants of Robinson Crusoe Island lived. She pulled a face. The small settlement was like a scab on otherwise healthy flesh, a bruise on a perfect piece of fruit. Man's part of this island was shabby and dreary and rundown, but God's part . . . Ah! She lifted her eyes again. God's part was incredibly fine. "More beautiful than anything I've ever seen," she said, remembering that Will had spoken to her. "I wish we could stay longer."

"I do too. But they say that the Sandwich Islands are just as beautiful."

She frowned slightly. "Do we have to go there, Will? It's so far out of the way. Can't we just sail for Upper California now that we're resupplied?"

He shook his head. "There's an old saying among sailors. You follow the wind and you follow the cargo. The southeast trade winds blow all the way across the Pacific from here. If we head straight up the coast we'll be bucking the northeasterlies. And part of what is paying for our voyage are those five hundred crates of freight we have to deliver at Honolulu."

"Hono-what?"

"The port there in the Sandwich Islands. It's on the island of Oahu."

"If you never came this way, how come you know so much about it?"

"The Sandwich Islands are one of the major stops on the China route from America. Many of the men I worked with had come this way before. They say that almost six hundred ships a year stop at the islands. It's also the base for the whaling crews that hunt in the North Pacific."

She gave him a teasing look. "So if we can't buck the north-easterlies, how do we get from the islands back to California?"

He chuckled. She had become half a sailor herself. "If you sail a northern route from the islands, you pick up the westerly trades."

"Oh." She should have known better than to challenge him. She understood that—the winds and the cargo and the way of sailors—but it still meant another long detour from their destination. They had sailed almost all the way to the coast of Africa, then all the way around South America, then four hundred miles out from Chile. Now they were going even farther out into the Pacific.

"The Lord works in mysterious ways, doesn't he?" Will said, bringing her out of her thoughts.

"In what way?"

"We all felt so bad about the storm, about being blown back from Valparaíso."

"Oh, yes," she said, understanding perfectly now.

Valparaíso might mean the Valley of Paradise in Spanish, but it could not possibly be any more paradisiacal than this. And that was not the only blessing that had come from their second-choice landfall. In Valparaíso they would have had to pay port fees and shell out top dollar for whatever supplies they needed. Here they had found fresh water just two rods from the beach. The crew had cleaned out the large hogshead water barrels, then filled them with eighteen thousand gallons of fresh water. They had picked tons of fruit and laid it out to dry. From the sea they caught, then salted, hundreds of barrels of fish. Cords of fire-wood—driftwood picked up along the beaches—were bundled and brought aboard. In short, they had resupplied at a fraction of the cost and had been privileged at the same time to stay in this beautiful setting. Valparaíso might be beautiful, but it couldn't match this, of that she was certain. Will was right. The Lord had truly blessed them through what they had first thought was a tragedy.

It was a lesson to be learned, she told herself. As it said in the Doctrine and Covenants, "You cannot see with your natural eyes what the Lord thy God has in store for thee." And elsewhere in that book it said, "Be still and know that I am God." In the future, when the storms blew and she became deathly sick, she would remind herself of that: "Be still and know that I am God."

"I don't suppose there's time for one more bath in the stream," she said dreamily.

He laughed. "I don't think so."

On the day following their landing, after they had buried Laura Goodwin, the whole company had trekked the short distance to the stream gushing down from the mountains. The men and boys formed a line in the thick trees to stand guard and the women and girls went on another hundred yards where there was a deep pool. There they washed off the filth and grime and sweat and seasickness with which they had lived for three months. There had been the water basins on the ship, the washing of the body as best one could with rags, but no chance for a real bath. Alice could not remember anything in her life that was comparable to feeling clean again. They bathed and swam and washed their clothes and frolicked like children. Once they were done, the women returned to the beach and the men had their turn. By nightfall, when they gathered around a large bonfire on the beach, it was as if the whole company had been reborn. They sang and danced and offered prayers of rejoicing.

"Well," Will said, reaching for her elbow, "this is the last boat. I think we'd better get on board."

They turned and walked onto the dock where the boat was waiting. Samuel Brannan, who was supervising the loading, had seen them stand aside. He smiled as he took Alice's hand and helped her down into the boat. "If you didn't know the Lord was calling us on, it would be right down tempting to stay, wouldn't it?"

She nodded vigorously. "I could have stayed here fifty days instead of five."

"At least," Will agreed.

Alice grimaced. "I think I've never faced such supreme temptation in my life, Elder Brannan. I sure hope where Brigham Young is taking us is half as pretty."

Garden Grove, May 10, 1846 (Sunday)

Still no rain. Spring is here! It's wonderful!!!! Two Sabbath meetings were held today—worship services in the morning, sacrament meeting in the afternoon. Pres. Young says it is the first Sabbath since we left Nauvoo that wasn't interrupted by rain. He also said that the camp here will soon break up. Some will go west looking for a new settlement site. Some are being sent back with teams to Nauvoo to get their families and bring them here. Garden Grove will be home for others, since some will have to stay and tend the crops and help the others when they get here. Don't know what we will be doing. Uncle Matthew thinks he may be asked to go ahead with the others.

Peter Ingalls undid the last yoke, waved to the boy who was herding the rest of the oxen so he would see they were coming, then slapped the animals on the rump and sent them on their way. He picked up the yoke and started for the wagon, checking it as he walked to see if there were any cracks in the heavy carved wood.

As he came around the lead wagon of the Reeds, he saw that Kathryn was down on the ground, bracing herself against the fold-down steps, looking back up into the wagon. As he came closer, Peter looked into the wagon and could see that Margret Reed was struggling a bit to help her mother sit up. He laid the yoke against the wagon wheel and hurried up to Kathryn's side. "Can I help you, Mrs. Reed?" he said.

She looked down at him and nodded. "Yes, thank you, Peter. I'd like to get Mother so she can sit up."

He went up the stairs lightly, squeezing past Mrs. Reed to the old woman's side. "Here, Mrs. Keyes, let me help you."

"I'll be fine," she said in a quavering voice. "Just give me a minute."

"Mother, let Peter help you. He's strong."

There was a sudden, coy smile. "I know he is," she said impishly. "And if I was about fifty years younger, I'd give Kathryn a run for her money."

They all laughed at that. "Why, Mrs. Keyes," Kathryn said in mock horror, "I had no idea you had intentions for my husband."

Peter slipped an arm behind the elderly woman's back. "Actually, I've been a little smitten with you as well, Mrs. Keyes, but we ought not to talk about that in front of my wife."

"Oh, you!" she said, delighted that he would play back with her.

"Come on," he said, taking most of her weight against his body as he got her into a sitting position. "I'll bet you're glad that we're stopping over for a while, aren't you?"

"I certainly am."

They were all concerned about Mrs. Keyes. She had been in frail health when they began, and these first weeks on the trail had weakened her noticeably. And they were only now to Independence, Missouri. They still had over fifteen hundred miles to go! No one said it, but there was great fear that she would not last much longer. Peter wondered if she knew, and suspected the answer was yes. But she was a plucky woman, and he supposed that if death came it would be no more tragic out here than sitting in a rocking chair back home in Illinois.

Surprisingly, Mrs. Reed was strengthening with each passing week. When Peter and Kathryn had first heard about the Reeds, they were told that Mrs. Reed was an invalid with an invalid mother. That had proven only half right as far as Margret Reed was concerned. She was in poor health, often suffering from headaches, and seemed ever fighting a cold or some other ailment. That was one of the reasons Mr. Reed decided to take her to California. Both of them—wife and mother-in-law—were also the reason he had ordered a special wagon built. He would see that their journey was as comfortable as possible. No one was surprised that the trail was weakening a woman in her seventies. But everyone, including Mr. Reed, was amazed that it seemed to be putting strength into Mrs. Reed. Her color was much better now. She sometimes walked alongside the wagon or would take Virginia's pony and ride out ahead with her husband.

"There," Peter said as he propped two pillows behind Mrs. Keyes. "You just sit there and rest, and we'll get some supper going."

"Thank you."

At that moment Margret's daughters, eight-year-old Patty and twelve-year-old Virginia, came up to the wagon's entrance. They'd been out walking, inspecting their new campsite. Looking up at her mother now, Patty said, "Mama, if you and Peter and Kathryn want to come outside, I'll stay here with Grandma."

Kathryn smiled at Patty's thoughtfulness. Ever since they had left Springfield, young Patty had taken it upon herself to look after her grandmother.

"That would be nice, Patty," said Margret. She turned to Mrs. Keyes. "Will you be all right, Mother?"

"Of course I will—especially if I have my Patty here with me."

Patty stepped up into the wagon to join her grandmother, and Peter and Margret came down out of the wagon to stand by Kathryn and Virginia.

Margret Reed looked across the campground that was filled with wagons and horses, oxen and mules, and carts and men. They could see the buildings of Independence about a half mile away. "Do you know how long we shall stay here, Peter?"

It was said with longing. She was looking forward to a break from the trail. And she knew that her aged mother would appreciate having two or three days respite from traveling in the wagon, which, in spite of its elaborate springs, still provided a jolting ride.

"I don't, Mrs. Reed. I know Mr. Reed is over conferring with the two Mr. Donners right now. I suppose part of that will depend on when the larger train leaves. That's their hope, to join the larger party." He frowned. "Unfortunately I don't see another train. Right now we're the largest group here. Perhaps they haven't arrived yet."

She nodded. "So we might have to wait for them?" she asked hopefully.

"That's a good possibility."

"That would be wonderful. And don't we need to get more supplies? Isn't this the last real outfitting place for a while?"

"A long while," Peter affirmed. "Independence is the end of civilization in this part of the world. From now on it's strictly wilderness."

"What about Fort Laramie?" Kathryn said.

"Oh, there're trading posts along the trail," he said, "but no more towns like this one. We need to get the essentials here. And that too could take some time."

Virginia spoke up. "Papa already sent Baylis Williams and Mr. Herron into town to see what they could buy."

"Good."

Kathryn reached inside the wagon and got a three-legged stool; then, using only one crutch, she brought it over to Mrs. Reed, who turned in surprise. "Kathryn, for heaven's sake, I should be getting *you* a stool."

"I'm not paying you to help me, Mrs. Reed. It's the other way around."

"Well, thank you. You come sit down too for a time. We'll let the men get a fire started before we start worrying about supper."

———◆———

It was nearly sundown. Walt Herron and Baylis Williams had still not returned from town, and the other two men were off somewhere helping Mr. Reed, so Peter had gotten the fire going, even though as a teamster, that was not part of his job. He didn't mind, and often pitched in to help the others.

Now he had a good bed of hot coals and was assisting Eliza Williams—sister to Baylis and the Reeds' hired woman—in getting a kettle full of a rich, savory stew hung over them. Virginia Reed was also helping out.

"Did you know we got others who want to join us?" Virginia said suddenly.

Peter looked up in surprise. "For supper you mean?"

"No. On the trail."

Mrs. Reed and Kathryn stopped and turned their heads. Peter sat back on his heels.

"Where'd you hear that, Virginia?" Kathryn asked.

"While I was getting water from the creek. I met some of the ladies."

Peter smiled. Virginia was a young woman who was full of life and energy. She always knew more about whatever was going on anywhere in the camp than anyone else. If she heard it, it was probably true. "How many?"

"Don't know for sure. There are at least two family groups. An Irishman—he's got a passel of young'uns—and then there are some Dutchmen." She lowered her voice at that, as though she were speaking of something dangerous.

"Anyone else?" Mrs. Reed asked, amused at her daughter's store of information.

Virginia shrugged.

"That's interesting," Peter said. Her information wasn't really news, it was just interesting. There was safety in numbers out on the plains. And the more healthy working men in a train, the better the chances of moving forward at a good pace. The plan had always been to join up with a larger train. The fact that others wanted to do the same was not too surprising.

He heard someone call his name and stood up to look in the direction of the sound. It was James Reed, standing near the back of one of the Donner wagons. He was waving his arm. "Peter, can you come over here?"

"Yes, Mr. Reed," he shouted back. He turned to Margret

Reed. "I'll be back and help with supper as soon as we're through."

She waved a hand. "See if you can talk Mr. Reed into coming back with you."

"Yes, ma'am." He trotted away, circling a little so as not to spook the animals that were grazing nearby. In a few moments he joined Mr. Reed, who waited for him.

"We've got some news," he said, laying an arm on Peter's shoulder as they turned and started for the wagon. "I'd like you there to hear this. It will make a difference as to what we do."

"Yes, sir. What is it?"

"Come on over here and sit down."

In the circle made by the Donner wagons several men were already seated. In addition to George and Jacob Donner, Peter saw that most of the teamsters and hired men were there as well. Two more men were just coming from the herd, led by George Donner's lead driver. There were also several men whom Peter did not recognize.

Once everyone had found a place to sit down, George Donner stood up. As was his manner, he jumped right into what was on his mind with no preamble or introduction. "Let me start right out by saying that we've got some people here who would like to travel with our party until we can join with a more substantial train. We'll make introductions in a minute, assuming you're of a mind to accept them. If not . . . well, then, there isn't much point in introducing them."

Peter tried not to smile. George Donner was not rude, at least not intentionally. He was just direct, not given much to small talk. Some found that disconcerting, though personally Peter liked it. The strangers didn't seem offended but were nodding at his words. And out here on the trail a simple but effective democracy prevailed. All would have a say in who traveled with them.

"My brother and me," George went on, "along with Mr. Reed, feel inclined to recommend that we accept them. Can't ever have too many people in a train once you leave civilization. Besides that, these people are well equipped. They have plenty of supplies, good teams, serviceable wagons. We'd like to put it to a vote."

Reed leaned forward slightly. "Tell us what that would mean for wagons and teams," he suggested.

Donner grunted. "Seven or eight more wagons and seven more working men."

The man who sat on the end of the group of newcomers raised his hand. "My son is fourteen and full grown. Make that eight working men." There was a definite lilt to the man's speech, and Peter guessed this was Virginia's Irishman.

Uncle George, as everyone called him, looked around the circle. "All in our party who are in favor of accepting these additions to our train raise your hand."

Every hand came up. He nodded in satisfaction. "Welcome, then," he said to the newcomers. "You are now free to travel with us. Each family head will have one vote, same as the rest of us. Why don't you introduce yourselves to those who haven't met you yet."

The man on the end started out. Peter had been right. His name was Patrick Breen and he had come from Ireland some years before. He was traveling with a wife and seven children and a single man, Patrick Dolan, who was a friend and had his own wagon.

Virginia had been wrong about the so-called "Dutchmen," however. They were actually Germans. To Peter's surprise, the one called Keseberg, a tall, virile-looking man, looked very well-to-do. So did another man named Wolfinger, who was traveling with the Kesebergs.

When they were done, Donner got right back to business. "Now, Mr. Reed has a problem to lay before us." He turned. "James?"

Reed stepped forward, smiling warmly. "We are pleased to have you travel with us," he said to the new men. "We all want to go to the same place and get there as quickly as possible, so I think we can help one another do that."

All around the circle, heads were nodding.

Continuing, Reed gazed around the circle. "There is a problem, however. We learned this evening that the wagon train headed by Colonel William Russell with which we hoped to join up left Independence headed for California about a week ago."

There were cries of disappointment and a groan or two. Reed nodded. "I understand it has grown into a big train—almost fifty wagons and still growing." He let that sink in for a moment. "I talked to some men at the courthouse. They strongly recommend that we catch up and join in with them. They're not sure there will be another group that large leaving here this season. It's already mid-May. Therefore, as the Donners and I have discussed this, we would propose spending tomorrow stocking up and making preparations, then moving out first thing Tuesday morning—"

He stopped again. This time it was mostly groans, and they came from the men in their company who had barely unhitched their oxen just an hour or two before. "I know, I know," he said. "We'd planned to rest for two or three days here, but if we're going to catch them, we need to leave as soon as possible, and we'll have to push right along to overtake them. But I think it's the wisest move."

Keseberg shrugged. "The problem is with your group, Mr. Reed," he said. "We've been here for over a week waiting for someone to come. We're ready."

"Mr. Breen?" Reed asked.

"We just got in yesterday, but we'll be fine."

Reed looked around the circle for a moment. "Those in favor of rolling out first thing Tuesday, then?"

Once again every hand came up, some reluctantly, but they were up.

"Then it's done. Let's go to work. There's a lot to do before then."

As the men rose to their feet and began to talk, Peter turned away. This was not going to be good news for Reed's wife and mother-in-law. Nor for Kathryn either. She was doing well, but he could tell she was tired too. They all needed a substantial rest.

"Peter?"

He turned back. Reed was motioning to him. "Wait for a moment. There's something else you need to know. I'll walk back with you."

———◆———

"Who?"

Peter touched a finger to Kathryn's lips. Their tent was just a few feet away from the Reeds' wagon. When he spoke, he spoke softly, but he pronounced the dreaded words slowly and distinctly. "Lilburn W. Boggs."

For a moment he could tell it still hadn't registered; then she gasped audibly. "Not . . . ?"

"Yes. Former governor of the state of Missouri. The man who called out the militia against the Mormons." He blew out his breath. "The man who signed the extermination order against our people."

"He'll be traveling with us?"

"It's very likely, yes. Apparently he'll be joining up with Colonel Russell's group, just as we plan to do. He and his son and a whole party from Jackson County are headed to California. According to Mr. Reed, several of them are known Mormon-haters."

Kathryn had come up on one elbow to stare at Peter in the darkness. Now she dropped back again. "I can't believe it. Governor Boggs. After all these years." He could almost feel her shiver at the thought.

Peter sighed. "Mr. Reed said he was surprised at how strong the feelings against the Mormons are here in Independence, even after so long."

That brought another question to mind. "Did you tell Mr. Reed that we are Latter-day Saints, Peter?"

"No. But I'm sure he knows. He never talks about it, but . . ."

She was nodding in the darkness. She had felt the same thing with Mrs. Reed. When Kathryn and Peter had come to Springfield with the purpose of signing on with one of the emigrant parties going west, they had decided they would never hide their Church membership. But neither would they flaunt it. If they were asked, they would answer and answer honestly. Otherwise they simply did not talk about it. But several things Mrs. Reed had said over the past several months had made Kathryn wonder if she knew. Thankfully, it seemed to make no difference to the Reeds.

"How did he come to tell you?" she asked.

"As the meeting broke up, he took me aside and said there was something that he thought I should know. Then he told me."

"But he didn't say anything about us being members of the Church?"

"No. He just told me. Said he thought I'd want to know." He was thinking back. Mr. Reed's announcement had taken Peter so much by surprise that he hadn't listened too closely to the rest. "He did say something like, 'Don't worry about it. There won't by any problems. I'll see to that.'"

"Which means he does know we're Latter-day Saints."

"I think so."

"In a way that's good."

"Yes. He could be a powerful friend if we ever need him." He took a breath. "But that's not all the bad news."

"No," she cried. "What else?"

"News of our people is filtering down from the northern counties."

"Really?" she exclaimed, coming up on an elbow again.

"Yes. Evidently some Latter-day Saints have been coming down into the northern settlements trying to trade goods for grain and food."

"Is there news of—" Her voice had gone tight.

"No, no one in particular. Mr. Reed didn't know enough to ask specifics. It's just that . . ."

"What, Peter?"

"The latest word is that our people are only about halfway across Iowa Territory now."

"No!"

"Yes. That means that we are now out ahead of them. And we leave again in two days."

"How can that be? They left Nauvoo in February."

"They're having a terrible time, according to the reports."

"What does that mean for us, Peter?" This was even more depressing than his other news.

He let out his breath in a deep sigh of discouragement. "I'm not sure. We'll just have to hope we get more news as we move west." He was trying to put the best face on it, but she knew this wasn't good. She didn't have the heart to ask him about it further, however.

Chapter Notes

After a welcome five-day stay in the Juan Fernández Islands in which the *Brooklyn* company was able to resupply both food and water, they set sail again on 9 May 1846. Instead of going north to California, the ship continued northwestward to the Sandwich Islands, later to be called Hawaii. (See "Voyage," pp. 58–59.)

The references to the tenpin alley (a forerunner of bowling) and the grog shops that had sprung up in Nauvoo at this time come from a letter written by John Taylor (see David R. Crockett, *Saints in Exile: A Day-by-Day Pioneer Experience,* vol. 1 of *LDS-Gems Pioneer Trek Series* [Tucson, Arizona: LDS-Gems Press, 1996], p. 305).

The emigrant party led by George and Jacob Donner and James Reed left Springfield, Illinois, on 15 April. They did not arrive in Independence, Missouri, the final outfitting center for the Oregon-California Trail, until 10 May.

Some of those who would eventually become part of the Donner-Reed party and participate in the tragedy that befell them in the high Sierras joined the Donners somewhere about this time. However, it is not always clear exactly where and when that took place. For convenience, several are shown here as joining the Donners on 10 May at Independence, Missouri, though it may have been a few days later and a few miles beyond Independence. All the names used here are actual people who were members of the Donner Party. (See George R. Stewart, *Ordeal by Hunger: The Story of the Donner Party* [Boston: Houghton Mifflin Co., 1988], pp. 20–22; Walter M. Stookey, *Fatal Decision: The Tragic Story of the Donner Party* [Salt Lake City: Deseret Book Co., 1950], pp. 84–88.)

It is known that Lilburn W. Boggs, ex-governor of Missouri, was in the same train as the Donners and the Reeds for a time. He evidently left Independence not long before the Donners and caught up with Colonel Russell's train on 15 May. Later, Boggs and his group did not take the southern route taken by the Donner Party but stayed with the main part of the Russell train on the better-known northern route of the Oregon-California Trail, which went by way of Fort Hall (near present-day Pocatello, Idaho). Thus he was not part of the ordeal suffered by the Donner Party.

Chapter Eighteen

Garden Grove Camp, May 12, 1846 (Tuesday)

This is my first entry in my "new journal." I said before that I would be writing this in the back of Mama's journal. But day before yesterday, when Mama saw how much I am writing and how much she is writing, she decided we are going to fill up her book too fast. So yesterday Papa traded some molasses with Sister Carter and got two dozen sheets of foolscap for me to write on. Anyway, in case this ever gets separated from the first part, my name again is Rachel Garrett. I turned fourteen on January 24, 1846. I am the oldest daughter of Jessica and Solomon Garrett. (Actually Solomon is only my stepfather, but I explained that in the other journal and you will have to read it there.)

This has been a sad day in a way. A decision was made that will split our family, at least for a time. President B. Young and the Twelve have made some assignments. Four of the Twelve were asked to leave immediately with their three companies—

Elders Parley Pratt and Orson Pratt are traveling together—to go ahead and find a place for another settlement like Garden Grove. It didn't surprise us to learn that Matthew was asked to go with Elder Parley Pratt's advance party. Jenny is sad, but she expected it. They left yesterday afternoon. But today, the council decided that Pres. Y. is going to take a group and go too so that they can help build that settlement quickly. To our surprise, Uncle Nathan and Uncle Joshua were asked to go with him. They will leave tomorrow morning on their saddle horses and leave their families to come on later with Uncle Derek and my cousin Josh to help them. The rest of the family will wait a few days before going on, so by the time they reach the new settlement, things will be ready for them. I asked Mama why their families couldn't go too, since some families are going with Pres. Y. She said she thought it might be because our teams have been doing so poorly and need to recruit their strength somewhat. She also wondered if Pres. Y. wants more men to help build the settlement before all the families come. Then she reminded me that when our leaders ask us to do something, even if it's hard, you do it without having to understand everything.

Having Nathan and Joshua gone for a week or so is still not the saddest news, though I can tell that Aunt Caroline and Aunt Lydia are very sad. The saddest part is that our immediate family—especially Papa—has been asked by Pres. Y. to stay here in Garden Grove to help get things ready for those who are still coming. That means our family will be the only ones among the Steed family group to stay for more than a few days. But I won't be staying and neither will Luke. Mama and Papa have decided I should go with Lydia and the others. With Nathan gone, Lydia will need help with the baby and the other children. Luke will go with Aunt Caroline to help drive their wagon. Josh is old enough—he's almost fifteen now—to drive for Aunt Lydia and his own family, but Aunt Caroline has no one, so Luke will become the teamster for her. Papa has been teaching him how to handle the oxen ever since we left Nauvoo. He's a year younger than Josh, but does very well. He is so proud to do this all by himself!!! He's already calling himself a bullwhacker.

Mark—who is still not even twelve yet—is not happy. He keeps begging Papa to let him go too, but Papa says no. It helped a little when Papa said he will let Mark start learning how to drive our team so he can become a bullwhacker too.

As I think about it, I'm not— Have to quit. Pres. Young and his brother Lorenzo D. Young are outside.

Nathan waited until all the family had gathered around the campfire, including the small children. He stood beside Brigham. Brigham's younger brother, Lorenzo Dow Young, had taken a seat on a length of log and was content to be in the background.

Rachel was the last to come, darting out from the tent and walking quickly to sit with her family. "Sorry," she murmured to Nathan, "I was writing in my journal."

"Good for you, Rachel," Brigham spoke up. "That's very important. As you know, our beloved Brother Joseph felt very strongly about recording our history." He turned and let his eyes sweep across the campground with its myriad fires and the white wagon tops looking like giant cotton balls in the dwindling light. "And this is history too. We are the Camp of Israel, and future generations yet unborn will be forever grateful for records which chronicle this event."

Rachel blushed deeply. She had not said it as a way to draw attention to herself but as an apology for keeping President Young waiting. Emily Steed, who sat beside her mother, was staring at Rachel with wonder and envy. She and her cousin had started out keeping journals together, but Rachel was so much more diligent than she had been. Emily had written maybe four or five entries all told since they had promised each other to write whenever possible. She looked up at Lydia. "Mama, I'm going to do better with my journal," she whispered.

"That would be good, Emmy."

"Well," Nathan said when it was clear Brigham was through, "I happened to see Brother Brigham and Brother Lorenzo while I was fetching water. Since there is only one topic of conversation around every campfire this night, I decided I would ask the President if it's true, or if it's just another one of those rumors that gets started in the camp."

"About the valley, you mean?" Solomon asked.

Nathan nodded. "When I mentioned that we had heard about it and wondered if it was really true, Brother Brigham said he would stop and talk to us all."

Brigham was nodding. "You know what they say. 'Rumor runs in ten-mile strides while Truth is still getting out of bed.' It never ceases to amaze me how susceptible our camp is to this kind of thing."

Joshua raised his head a little. "So it's all a rumor, this story about your vision of the valley?"

"No, no," Brigham said hastily, "I didn't mean that. I was just saying how quick we are to believe anything we hear. I'm not sure what all is being said, and if it's not being embellished a little in the telling, I'll be surprised, but no, the story is basically true."

Emily couldn't contain herself. "You actually saw where we're going, President Young?"

Nathan held up his hands. "Why don't we just let President Young say what he has to say. Maybe then we can ask some questions."

Emily colored slightly, not because of her father's reply, but because she had been so bold as to speak out as she had.

Nathan moved over to sit with his family as Brigham moved around so he could see everyone a little better. "A lot of people are saying it was a vision," the Apostle began. "It happened while I was lying down, though I didn't feel as though I was asleep yet."

"Does it matter?" Lorenzo Young asked. "Dream, vision—as long as it's from the Lord, isn't it the same thing?"

"Of course," his brother agreed. "What matters is what I saw and the feelings that followed."

The adults sat very still, watching their leader. Even the little children were attentive.

Brigham leaned forward, his gray-blue eyes filled with a strange intensity. "It was a marvelous thing. I was shown a large valley—a very large valley. It was as though it were a grand panorama and I could look down upon the whole of it. Somehow I knew that it was in the midst of the Rocky Mountains and that it was our new home."

"What did it look like?" Mark Garrett blurted out.

"Let President Young tell it," Jessica said with a smile to her son.

You could see in his eyes that it pleased Brigham that the children were as excited by his account as the grown-ups. "Well," he said slowly, savoring his memory of the scene, "it was surrounded by high snowcapped mountains, not just on one side, but on both sides. There were many trees on the mountains. They were green and beautiful. I could see many streams coming down from the mountains to water the valley."

"Really?" Mary Ann breathed, caught up with his description to the point that she was almost seeing it in her mind.

"Ah, Mother Steed," Brigham sighed, "it was a beautiful sight. And as I gazed upon it, I knew that it was large enough to hold our people. I was also given to know that it is far enough away from civilization that we shall be free from our enemies. No mobs will come in the night to burn property and whip and kidnap our people as they have everywhere else. It will be a place of safety and refuge. There we will build our homes, and there we will make a city."

He stopped, far away in his thoughts now. No one spoke. Finally he came back to them. "Anyway, that was it. It didn't last very long, but the images of what I saw will be in my mind forever."

"That's wonderful," Lydia exclaimed. "Imagine, no more Far Wests. No more tragedies like Haun's Mill. Could we really find a place where we have peace?"

Brigham straightened now. "We could and we will, Lydia. Of that I have not the slightest doubt." He looked around. "Now, do you have any questions?"

"How far is it?" Josh asked, raising his hand and speaking at the same time.

"Far away," was the answer. "I was not told exactly how far."

"Were you shown where it was?" Rebecca asked.

"No, not exactly."

"But it is in the Rocky Mountains?" Caroline asked.

"Definitely." A look of frustration crossed his features. "I fear that there are still some of our people who think Brother Brigham has stepped off the cliff and is tumbling helter-skelter, head over heels across the plains of Iowa with no idea where we are going. But I tell you, that is not the case. Joseph knew more than ten years ago that we would be going to the Rocky Mountains. You remember that, Nathan? You were there that night, as we were getting ready for Zion's Camp."

"I do."

"Joseph startled us all." Brigham laughed softly. "He had a habit of doing that. We were talking about going to Zion, and all of a sudden he said something like, 'You don't begin to understand our destiny. We are only a little handful of priesthood here tonight, but this church will fill North and South America—it will fill the world. There will be tens of thousands of us who will gather to the Rocky Mountains.'" Again Brigham drifted away into his thoughts. "We were astonished at his words and weren't sure what they meant or how their fulfillment could even be possible. Not then, at least. But that wasn't the only time he talked about it. He knew that we were going west. Now his prophecy is being fulfilled."

He leaned down, looking directly at the children. "So, we may not know exactly where it is," he said, "but when I get there, I'll know it for sure, so there's no need to worry about Brother Brigham getting us all lost."

Christopher Ingalls, Derek's firstborn, who was now almost seven, nodded gravely. "I never thought you were lost, Brother Brigham."

Brigham laughed in delight. "Why, thank you, young man. I wish everyone had your faith." He turned to Nathan. "Well, we'd best be getting back."

"Thank you, President," Nathan said.

"Oh, yes, thank you," Mary Ann added. "Thank you for taking the time to stop by and share that with us."

They rose now and gathered around him. Brigham waved a general farewell to the adults, but took the time to shake hands with each of the children. As he was doing so, Nathan sidled up to Joshua. "Well?" he said.

Joshua gave him a bland look. "Well what?"

"What do you think of that?"

"Do you think I don't believe him?" he asked curtly.

Nathan looked surprised. "No, I didn't mean that. I just wondered what you thought."

Joshua watched Brigham shaking hands with his own children now. Savannah's eyes were glowing, and Charles stood there like a peasant boy finally privileged to meet the mayor of the town. "I think Brigham Young is a great leader," he said carefully. "Maybe, for this task, even better than Joseph."

"Hmm," Nathan said, looking at him oddly.

"And what is that expression supposed to mean?"

"I didn't ask you what you thought of Brigham Young, I asked you what you thought of his vision."

"Oh." There was an awkward moment, and then Joshua shook his head. "I think he had an experience of some kind. Sometimes when you're between wakefulness and sleep, things can seem very real to you."

"But you don't think it was a vision? You're not sure he actually saw where we are going?"

Now Joshua surprised Nathan a great deal. "No, I'm not sure.

On the other hand, I want to believe him. Is that worth any-thing?"

That so caught Nathan by surprise that he just looked at him. Joshua chuckled and clapped him on the arm. "It's good to know I can still sneak up on you now and then, little brother." And with that he walked over to say good-bye to the two Young brothers.

The coals of the fire glowed a dull red-black in the darkness. Only a few flickering flames still remained. Joshua leaned half back, looking up into the sky. Here and there he could see a few stars, but it was mostly overcast and smelled like there might be rain before morning. Finally he turned his head and looked at his mother. He was surprised that she had stayed out. Once Brigham and Lorenzo Young were gone, the family had talked for a few more minutes, then had a family prayer and retired to their tents. Mary Ann sat down by the fire instead. Seeing that, Joshua waved Caroline on and sat down beside his mother.

They had sat together in comfortable silence, staring into the dying flames, both lost in their own thoughts. He could see she was tired, but he also sensed that she wanted to be with him out here. With the rigid schedule of trail life, these opportuni-ties didn't come very often. It was a cool night for mid-May, but cool was not cold. Finally the winter's chill was being pushed back.

"What are you thinking, Mother?"

"About your father."

"Oh." That wasn't a great surprise. Nights always seemed to bring his memory closer to the surface. He sat up straight, watch-ing her eyes in the firelight. He would have guessed they would be sad. Instead, from what little he could see, they were filled with a quiet peace.

"And what were you thinking, Joshua?" she asked.

He shrugged. "About you and Papa, I guess. I had always heard about people grieving for someone," he said. "I never fully understood what that meant until now."

She nodded slowly. "God said that it was not good for man to be alone, and so he made man and woman for each other. Now I know just how profoundly true that is, Joshua. It's like . . ." She groped for a way to express what she was feeling. "I don't know. It's like a part of me is gone—not an arm or hand or something external, but some part of the inner me. I am no longer whole."

He watched her, wishing he could better see her face and into her eyes, but knowing somehow that the darkness protected her and that that was one of the reasons she was willing to speak of these things. He smiled faintly in the darkness. "I remember one night. We were all having supper at your house. You and Papa were clear across the room from each other. There was lots of noise, everyone was laughing and talking. But I was watching you, and I saw something come into your eyes. I turned to see what you were looking at." His voice went suddenly husky. "And there was Papa with that same look in his eyes. Something passed between you—I don't know what—but it was as if you two were completely alone in a room speaking quietly to each other."

"Yes," she said, and now he knew that tears were close. "That's why I grieve. Not because he's dead, because I know that he isn't, but because he's gone and I am not whole."

Joshua straightened and slid closer to her, so their shoulders touched. He didn't speak, and she seemed glad for it. Two or three minutes passed in silence. The fire was almost gone now. The sounds of the night were muted and distant around them.

"You grieve too, Joshua, but for different reasons."

Her words startled him. He peered at her, but her face was only just distinguishable in the light from the glowing coals. "I miss him too, Mother, but not in the same way you do."

"I wasn't talking about your father, Joshua."

It took all he could do not to flinch with the pain that shot through him. He looked away, not trusting himself to speak, not wanting to if he could. Mary Ann didn't look at him, didn't say anything further, but after several moments she reached out and took his hand in hers and held it softly. After a long time, he finally lifted his head. "I think of her every day, Mama. I watch Rachel and Emily giggling about this boy or that and I think . . ." His throat constricted and he stopped and took a quick breath. "Olivia will never have that."

"Joshua, I—"

"Not ever, Mama," he whispered. "Not ever! She can never sit in front of a mirror and have Caroline brush her hair. How she would have loved Lydia's little Tricia! Now she will never see her." There was a choking sound. "And her father can never take her in his arms and say, 'I'm sorry, Livvy. I'm so, so terribly sorry.'"

"Joshua, don't."

"Why? Do you think not saying it makes it more bearable?"

"That's what I meant," Mary Ann said gently. "You are grieving too, but my grief comes from love. Yours is born of guilt."

He pulled free of her hand, accusing her with his stare in the darkness. "I loved Olivia, Mama!" he cried in a hoarse whisper. "I loved her!"

"I know that, Joshua." She reached out and touched his arm. He was stiff and unmoving. "I know you loved her, but your pain is coming mostly from hopelessness. If you knew that Olivia still lives, as surely as I know that Benjamin still lives, you would still grieve, but it would not be filled with guilt."

"It was my stupidity that killed her, Mama," he burst out.

"No," she whispered fiercely, "it was not. It was evil men, trying to harass an innocent Mormon family, who killed her, Joshua. You loved your daughter. What you did was what you thought was best for her."

His head dropped. Now his voice was dull, without life. "If only I would have listened to her."

She sat back. "I think it's time you stopped just reading that Book of Mormon and started praying about it."

His head came up slowly. "What did you say?"

"Oh, Joshua," she said, the love welling up inside her, bringing her close to tears again, "you have it, don't you?"

"Have what?" he stammered.

She shook her head. "From the time you were a little boy, I could always tell when you weren't telling the truth. I watched you that day when Nathan asked you if you'd seen Lydia's Book of Mormon."

He didn't know what to say.

She suddenly stood. "I'm very tired, Joshua. Thank you for being with me. We need to do this more."

He stood too, still in a little bit of a whirl. She had known right from the beginning?

She stepped up to him, went up on the balls of her feet, and kissed him softly on the cheek. "You can't just read it, Joshua," she said into his ear. "You also have to ask."

Lydia looked up as the front flap of her tent opened and a flash of sunlight lit the tent. She was seated on the floor, feet beneath her, folding clothing from the wash she and Mary Ann had done earlier in the day. Joshua's head poked through the tent flap. "Hi."

Surprised, she smiled up at him. "Good morning, Joshua. Nathan went out to saddle the horse. He's all ready other than that."

"I know. I saw him go. Do you mind if I come in?"

That caught her by surprise. She had just assumed that—"Of course not. Come in. There's a stool in the corner."

He stepped inside but remained standing. "That's all right. This won't take long." He reached inside his shirt and withdrew something. Curious, she tried to see what he held, but he dropped his hand too quickly for her to see what it was. He took a breath, then another, his face flushing a little.

Thoroughly intrigued now by his obvious discomfort, she set the clothes aside. "What is it, Joshua?"

"I owe you an apology."

"An apology? For what?"

He lifted his hand, palm up.

She stared at it for a moment, not comprehending. It was a Book of Mormon, but . . . She stood up and moved to Joshua, peering more closely at the book. He held it up so she could see the back of it. There was a soft gasp. There was no mistaking the darkened corner. It was *her* Book of Mormon.

"I took it," he said simply. "That day when I stayed behind to dry out the bedding. I saw it there . . ." He thrust it toward her. "I should have said something sooner."

She was too shocked to move. Finally she forced her gaze away from the book and to his face. His dark eyes were somber and hooded. "You had it all this time?"

"Yes."

"I . . ." She shook her head. She took it from him and pressed it to her breast. "I'm so glad to find it. Thank you, Joshua."

"I'm sorry, Lydia. It was wrong of me to do it. It was worse not to let you know when you thought you had lost it. I was going to say something, but then everyone would have known and—"

And then her joy at seeing the book gave way to something else. Her eyes met and held his. "Have you been reading it?"

For a long moment they stood there, eyes locked. Then slowly, ever so slowly, he nodded.

If she had been caught by surprise before, now she was absolutely astonished. "You have? You really have?"

"Lydia, I'm going to ask you not to say anything to anyone about this."

She turned away for a moment, setting the book down, her thoughts tumbling wildly, and then she swung back. Joshua? It had been he who took her Book of Mormon? "Does Caroline know?"

"No. I just found out last night that Mother guessed that it was me. But no one else knows. Not Caroline. Not Nathan. No one but you and Mama now."

"But why?" she cried. "Why haven't you said anything? Of all people, Caroline should— Why now, Joshua?"

"Because Nathan and I are leaving in a few minutes. I've kept it long enough."

The implications of what he was saying began to override her amazement. "Did you finish it?" she asked very softly.

"No."

"How far did you get?" She was almost whispering, as though she were suddenly in a cathedral.

"I was in the book of Alma."

"That far!" She clasped her hands together in pleasure. "That's wonderful, Joshua." She was still a little dazed. "Why now, Joshua? After all of these years of us trying to get you to read it. Why now?"

He had suspected she would ask him that question. "Partly curiosity, I guess. I look at some of these people—Drusilla Hendricks, Ezra T. Benson. I see what they are willing to go through for their faith." His shoulders lifted and fell. "I'd like to understand it better."

"And?" she asked after a moment.

He pretended not to understand. "And what?"

She stepped forward and took his arms, then shook him gently. "Tell me, Joshua. What are your feelings about it?"

He had expected this question too and wanted to be honest with her. "I'm not sure. Some of it I like. There are some beautiful things in there. Other times I don't like what I'm reading, or don't understand it. I have a lot of questions."

"Oh, Joshua. I can't believe what I'm hearing. You're actually reading it." She was so excited now, she shook him again, barely aware that she still held his arms. "What passages did you like?"

He thought for a moment, then answered. "There's a place where one of them—Nephi, I think—talks about himself, about how he feels."

"What does he say?"

"He feels like he is unworthy. He talks about how weak he is."

"Yes," Lydia breathed. "That is one of my favorite parts of the whole Book of Mormon."

She retrieved the book, turning the pages quickly, scanning. Then she held it out, pointing to a place on the page. "This?"

He looked, nodded, then took it from her. He read in a low voice, but one that captured all the emotion and pathos that Nephi had tried to express. "'O wretched man that I am; yea, my heart sorroweth, because of my flesh. My soul grieveth, because of mine iniquities. I am encompassed about, because of the temptations and the sins which doth so easily beset me.'" He closed the book. "That's the one."

She snatched the book from him and found the place quickly again. "But don't stop there, Joshua. Go on." She held it out, but he didn't take it. So she read it for him. "'Awake, my soul! No longer droop in sin. Rejoice O my heart, and give place no more for the enemy of my soul.'"

He looked away. "I don't understand what all of it means, but it is beautiful."

Suddenly Lydia was embarrassed. "I'm sorry, Joshua, here I am going on like a young girl. I haven't even thanked you for telling me." She waved the book. "And for bringing this back to me. I was so disturbed when I thought I had lost it."

"I know. I don't know what possessed me. I guess I was afraid to let—" He stopped, his face troubled now. "Will you not say anything to Caroline? I don't want to give her any false hopes, Lydia. You know what she'll think. And then when nothing happens, it will be a bitter disappointment to her."

"Are you sure nothing will happen?" she asked, trying to make it sound as if she were merely teasing him.

He shrugged. "Joshua Steed getting religion? Doesn't sound like much of a possibility to me." Before she could respond to that, he went on. "Will you not say anything, Lydia?"

She nodded slowly. "I won't tell a soul without your express permission, but I urge you to tell Caroline, Joshua. She needs to know."

His mouth pulled down into a stubborn line. "Maybe so, but not yet."

She nodded, not necessarily agreeing, but understanding. "Then at least tell Nathan, Joshua. You'll have time together over these next few days. Talk to him. If you have questions about what you're reading, you can ask him."

There was a droll smile. "You think his heart can withstand that kind of a shock?"

She laughed gaily. "I'd like to find out. Oh, Joshua. I can't tell you how happy I am." Then on impulse she thrust the book at him. "I don't want it back, Joshua."

"What?"

"Not yet. Take it with you. Without your family these next few days, you'll have more time to read. Finish it. Then you can bring it back to me."

"No, I—"

She pressed it into his hand. "Yes! I want you to keep it." She tossed her head back and laughed. "Besides, if it shows up now, Nathan is going to want to know where I found it. How would I explain that without telling him everything? Please, Joshua."

He took the book back, looking down at it.

"I'm not asking for any promises, Joshua. There are no expectations. Just take it, okay?"

He smiled sardonically. "I thought I was supposed to pray about it too." Then, before she could answer, he turned away. "Well, Nathan will be ready to leave. I'd better go. Thank you."

"Why me, Joshua?"

Again there was that enigmatic shrug. "It's your book."

She shook her head immediately. "No. You could have just left it somewhere for me to find." Now her face filled with wonder. "You wanted to tell me. Why?"

He thought about that for a moment, realizing that he hadn't really answered that question for himself. "I guess because of all the family, I thought you'd understand more than the others."

"Yes," she said softly, remembering back so many years before when Nathan had tried to get her to read this book with the leather cover. "Yes, I do understand, Joshua. And that's why it's so important that you keep reading. And that you pray about it. It wasn't until I read it all the way through and asked Heavenly Father if it was true that I came to know." She smiled, embarrassed a little by her own fervency. "Who knows, maybe it will come easier for you than it did for me."

There was a short bark of bitter laughter. "It's not the same for you, Lydia. You were never . . ." He stopped and looked away.

"I was never what?"

"Never mind. I'd better go before Nathan comes back."

She grabbed at his arm. "I was never what, Joshua?"

A deep gloom had settled over him. "You were never as bitter as I was."

"Maybe not, but I was bitter, Joshua. I hated Joseph Smith. Remember that day in Palmyra when the crowd had cornered Emma and was mocking her? I was right there, cheering them on."

His head came up slowly. "You call that bitterness? How about sticking a pistol in your father's face and coming so close to pulling the trigger that you still have nightmares about it? Or how about getting blind drunk and beating your wife until she is forced to flee with an infant baby? Were you ever that bitter? Did you ever drive women and children barefoot out of their homes into a winter's night like I did in Jackson County?" His face was twisted with contempt—self-contempt. His voice dropped to a mere whisper. "Did you have your own brother bullwhipped until his whole body was a mass of bloody flesh?"

Now she understood. How many times had she run her fingers over the scars on Nathan's back and chest and marveled at the emotions that had driven Joshua that night? She wanted to reach out to Joshua now, to somehow touch *his* wounds and heal them. But she didn't know how. She was close to tears now. "You've changed, Joshua. That's not you anymore."

He shook his head, despair filling his eyes. "If I had changed, Olivia would be here with us now." And with that, he swung around and plunged out of the tent, leaving her to stare after him in sorrow and wonder.

It was the year of our Lord, one thousand eight hundred forty-six. In retrospect, it would prove to be one of those years that later historians would label as "pivotal," "monumental," "a watershed year."

It was a year when a poem called "The Raven," written by a neurotic genius named Edgar Allan Poe, a man who had flunked out of West Point, was being quoted all across the nation; when poetry by Henry Wadsworth Longfellow and John Greenleaf Whittier was being published in the East. West of Boston, a man by the name of Henry David Thoreau dwelt in a small cabin he had built on the shores of what would come to be known to the world as "Walden Pond." In New York City, a man by the name of P. T. Barnum was shocking society—and making them pay dearly for it—as he displayed what he called "all that is monstrous, scaley, strange, and queer" to vast audiences. A song, "Jim Crack Corn, or the Blue Tail Fly," was published and quickly became an American folk classic.

At an industrial fair in the nation's capital, an inventor by the name of Elias Howe demonstrated an amazing new sewing machine that did the same amount of work in a manner of minutes that it took a woman hours to do by hand. And it did it better! The first telegraph lines were strung between Washington and Baltimore. A dentist in Boston, having learned that inhaling a fluid called sulfuric ether rendered one unconscious, became instrumental in establishing its use as an anesthetic for surgical operations. A rotary "lightning press" was patented in New York City that could run ten thousand sheets per hour. A portable, hand-cranked ice-cream freezer was invented by a woman in New Jersey.

Alexis de Tocqueville, a French statesman and philosopher who visited America in 1831, was greatly impressed with the new democracy but noted that Americans were "slaves of slogans." In 1846, the slogan on everyone's lips was "Manifest Destiny." Coined by a New York publisher the year before, Manifest Destiny was a phrase that captured in two words the belief that it was the will of Divine Providence for the American democracy, with its constitutional form of government, to reign from sea to sea, from the Atlantic to the Pacific.

At the beginning of 1846, the United States had expanded westward not even half the width of the continent. James K. Polk, a virtual political nobody, rode the wave of Manifest Destiny to the White House with his cry of "54-40 or fight," a promise to make Oregon Territory part of the United States or go to war with Great Britain. Thankfully, Britain was not in a mood for battle and a compromise was reached giving the U.S. everything south of the 49th parallel, which would eventually include Washington, Oregon, Idaho, and most of Montana. England got to keep everything north of that line, including Vancouver Island, British Columbia, and the vast wheat fields of what would become the province of Alberta.

The rest of the western continent—a vast, largely unexplored and unsettled territory—was controlled by Mexico and known as Upper California and New Mexico. Ten years before, the Republic of Texas had won its independence from Mexico by defeating Santa Anna's forces at San Jacinto. Ever since, the two "nations" bitterly disputed over what constituted the southern border of Texas. Then Texas became a state of the Union, and the border dispute became the concern of the U.S. government. President

Polk offered to buy California for $25 million and New Mexico for $5 million, but the offer was refused. Angry, the president ordered a two-thousand-man army into Texas—or Mexico, depending on whose border one accepted. An angry Mexican government sent an army across the Rio Grande. When the brief skirmish was over, eleven Americans were dead.

On May eleventh, an outraged President Polk sent a war message to Congress declaring that Mexico had "shed American blood upon American soil"—a statement of truth only if you accepted the U.S. definition of the border. An outraged Congress passed an act declaring war with Mexico, and on May thirteenth, 1846, the president signed it into law. Once again in its short history the United States of America was at war with a foreign power.

Chapter Notes

The original Book of Mormon was not divided into the chapters and verses found in modern editions, but the scriptures discussed by Lydia and Joshua are now 2 Nephi 4:17–18, 28.

Brigham Young's vision of the valley described here was reported in the memoirs of John R. Young, son of Lorenzo D. Young. When word of the vision circulated through the camp, John R. recalled, it "formed the most entrancing theme of our conversations, and the national song of Switzerland became our favorite hymn: 'For the strength of the hills we bless thee, Our God, our fathers' God.'" (See CN, 18 May 1996, p. 10.)

John R. Young's report seems to imply that the vision took place about this time on the trail. President George A. Smith reported that Brigham Young, apparently before the Saints left Nauvoo, had a vision in which he saw Joseph Smith and in which the Prophet showed Brigham what is now known as Ensign Peak, just north of Salt Lake City (see *Journal of Discourses*, 26 vols. [London: Latter-day Saints' Book Depot, 1854–86], 13:85–86; see also Susa Young Gates, *The Life Story of Brigham Young* [London: Jarrolds Publishers, n.d.], p. 86). It is unclear whether these reports, that of John R. Young and that of George A. Smith, refer to the same vision or to two separate visions. For the purposes of the novel, it is assumed that the vision referred to by John R. Young took place while the Saints were in Iowa.

The prophecy about the gathering to the Rocky Mountains declared to those preparing to leave on Zion's Camp was given in 1834 and was reported by Wilford Woodruff (see Ivan J. Barrett, *Joseph Smith and the Restoration: A History of the Church to 1846* [Provo, Utah: Brigham Young University Press, 1973], p. 278).

The details of various happenings in the United States during 1846, including the declaration of war against Mexico, come from two sources (Timothy Foote, "1846: The Way We Were—and the Way We Went," *Smithsonian*, April 1996, pp. 38–42; and James Trager, *The People's Chronology: A Year-by-Year Record of Human Events from Prehistory to the Present*, rev. ed. [New York: Henry Holt and Co., 1992], pp. 440–43).

Parley Parker Pratt had celebrated his thirty-ninth birthday on April twelfth, less than a week following the sixteenth anniversary of the founding of The Church of Jesus Christ of Latter-day Saints. For nearly sixteen of those thirty-nine years he had been a member of the Church. Within days of his baptism in upstate New York, he had received a call to go to the western borders of the United States on a mission to the Lamanites. Since then he had left his home many times in the service of the Lord—to Upper Canada, to the eastern United States, to England. Now he was on a different kind of mission. On this morning of May sixteenth, 1846, he was one of the company sent ahead by President Young to find the Grand River, in Iowa Territory, and then choose a site where a second semi-permanent settlement for the Saints could be established.

The Grand River, which was estimated to be about two hundred miles west of Nauvoo and about two-thirds of the way across Iowa, shouldn't be that hard to find, he thought. If you kept moving west, surely you would come across it sooner or later. But things were not as simple now. Since Brigham Young had made the decision not to take the Saints into Missouri, they had left the road and turned to the northwest. Guided only by compasses, they moved across the fertile but trackless prairie. Each new stream, lined with trees or underbrush, and usually with steep banks or swampy ground on both sides, presented a new challenge for the wagon train. The crossing of even the smallest creek could turn out to be a fiendish task that exhausted teams, tried men's tempers, and broke equipment.

They had been on the road for five days now, and still there was no sign of the Grand River. By the previous night, the group had grown quite discouraged. Had they miscalculated? Were the reports they had received incorrect? Or worse, were they striking off in a direction that just might miss the river altogether? One degree off course could take you right past the river without ever seeing it. Parley discounted that one. Their compasses were reliable, and the reports said the Grand River went another fifty miles north of their intended crossing. But the gloom in the camp had been real nevertheless. So while the others were still rising and preparing breakfast, Parley had saddled his horse and ridden out to see what he could see. He had come three, maybe four miles. The sky was thinly overcast, but the light was full enough and the air perfectly clear.

He went up in his stirrups now, peering ahead, letting his eyes scan the western horizon carefully, looking for any signs of a river. Up about a mile ahead, a little north of due west, he could see what looked like small groves of trees dotting a series of gently rolling hills. There was no distinct tree line that gave promise of a river, but that was to be expected. A river as substantial as the Grand would flow along a floodplain below the bluffs.

Feeling a stir of excitement, Parley sat back in the saddle and kicked his heels into the horse's flanks, pointing the mare's head at the highest of the hills before him. She broke into an easy lope and he leaned forward and let her run.

When he crested the bluff about five minutes later, he reined in abruptly. There was a sharp intake of breath. Differing shades of green—the yellow-green of new grass, the deeper hues of brush and shrubbery, and the richness of trees in full leaf—were mingled with a sprinkling of reds, yellows, blues, and purples of a thousand prairie wildflowers. The river snaked through it, brown from recent rains. It was a remarkable sight, and he drank it in with breathless excitement.

Enthralled, he clucked softly and his horse moved forward. There was a sudden movement. Two deer, startled from their morning's browsing, bounded away. A moment later he saw a flash of gray in the underbrush. Peering more closely, he saw that it was a wolf watching him warily. In a moment it was gone, like a momentary puff of smoke taken by the wind. He took a deep breath, savoring the air and the scenery. It was as if he were looking down upon an exquisitely groomed English park.

He reined in again, and for a long moment just sat there, totally transfixed. Then, unbidden, an Old Testament image came to his mind. When Moses and the children of Israel moved up the east side of the Jordan toward the promised land, the Lord had directed Moses to the peak of a mountain that overlooked the river and the land beyond. Moses had recorded that from that mount he could see the promised land, eastward and northward, southward and westward. He named it Mount Pisgah.

With a flood of joy, Parley Parker Pratt removed his hat and lifted it high in the air. "This is Mount Pisgah," he cried. "This is where we shall make our next place of rest." He did not ride down farther. He had seen what he needed to see. With a whoop of elation, he turned the mare around and headed back toward the camp.

———◆———

The afternoon sun, combined with the monotony of the endless trail, was taking its toll on Nathan. After several days of on-again, off-again rain, the sun felt so good. His eyes kept drooping and his head bobbing as his horse plodded steadily along beside Joshua's. It was May eighteenth, their sixth day since leaving Garden Grove. They had started out pretty good, making a total of twelve miles the first two days. But then the rain began again. They made only five miles the third day, and four the next. Yesterday it was bad enough that they had barely gone two miles before camping again. But the weather had cleared, and Nathan guessed that they had come about another eight or nine miles already. Being on horseback, had they been alone the two of them could have made a lot better time. But in a wagon train it was not the fastest man who set the pace but the slowest. And so they rode alongside the rear wagon, reins hanging loosely to let the horses pick their own way.

"Nathan?"

Nathan's head came up and he forced his eyes open. Joshua was not looking at him and so had not seen that he had brought him back from the verge of falling asleep. "Yes?"

There was a long silence. Nathan waited, coming fully awake, curious now.

"I've been reading the Book of Mormon."

Nathan stiffened so abruptly that his horse flinched beneath him, startled by the sudden movement on its back. "You what?" he finally managed.

Joshua was looking at him and grinning now. "I told Lydia I was worried about whether your heart could stand this or not."

"You're reading the Book of Mormon?" Nathan repeated slowly.

"That's what I said." Joshua was greatly amused.

A hundred questions came in a rush to Nathan's mind. "How long?" he finally settled on.

"Since I took Lydia's book from the tent several weeks ago."

Nathan's eyes widened. "That was you?" he exclaimed.

Joshua's smile broadened and now he was laughing softly at Nathan. "Yes, that was me. And yes, Lydia knows. I told her before we left Garden Grove. And no, Caroline doesn't know anything about this. Only you and Lydia and Mama know. Are there any other questions?"

Nathan wanted to rub his eyes, make sure that he had come fully awake. Finally all he could think of to say was what he was feeling. "That's wonderful, Joshua!"

"Thank you." Now Joshua's face pulled into a partial scowl. "I don't want you jumping to conclusions. I am not ready to become a Mormon. Not by a long shot. Don't know if I ever will be. I'm just telling you this because I have some questions. Lydia said I should let you know so I could ask you about them, that is, if you're willing."

"Willing?" Nathan blurted. "I am so thrilled right now, you're lucky I haven't jumped on your horse and started pounding you on the back."

Now any trace of Joshua's former humor was gone. "That's what I mean. That's why I hesitated telling you and the others. You're going to think this means a lot more than it does."

Nathan sobered now too, understanding fully what lay behind that concern. "I know, and I'll control myself. But if you think I can hide the fact that I am absolutely delighted with this news, then you've got your head stuck in a jug."

"Delighted is all right," Joshua conceded. "I just would like to take this at my own speed, all right?"

Nathan nodded. "I'll tell you what. I will let you take the lead. I won't ask you anything, I won't push you in anyway. When you're ready to talk, I'll be here. If you're not ready, I'll wait. Fair enough?"

Gratitude showed in Joshua's eyes. "That would be the way I would prefer it. I'm not sure what I'm even doing on this path, Nathan. And right now it feels awfully slippery to me."

"I understand. You've got the lead. It will probably take every ounce of self-control for me to behave myself in this, but I will, Joshua. I promise."

Joshua was looking at him directly now, debating whether to say something else.

Nathan suspected what it was. "I won't tell anyone unless you say I can. You have my word."

"Thank you."

"I do think you need to tell Caroline, though. I'll just say that much."

He looked glum. "That's what Lydia said too. And you're both right, of course. It's just that . . ."

"It will be a bitter disappointment to her if nothing comes of it," Nathan finished for him.

"Exactly."

Nathan said nothing. This was something Joshua would have to work through in his own mind. Nathan watched him out of the corner of his eye. He was looking away from Nathan, deep in thought. Nathan fought back the almost overwhelming urge to say something more, to ask a dozen questions. This was going to be hard, he suddenly realized. Joshua had dropped a cannonball out of the sky directly onto his head, and now he wasn't even supposed to say "Ouch."

Almost ten minutes passed before Joshua turned to him again. "So are you up to a few questions?"

Nathan felt a leap of exultation. "I think so," he said calmly.

Joshua reached back and lifted the flap on his saddlebag, then fumbled inside. In a moment he withdrew Lydia's Book of Mormon.

Nathan shook his head slowly. "So you had it all the time?" he said softly, more to himself than to Joshua.

There was a grunt but nothing more as he opened the book. Nathan saw that he was using a piece of rawhide string as a bookmark. He found his place, then closed the book again. Awkwardly now, he began to speak. "I'd like to say a couple of things first."

"All right."

"I may ask some questions that upset you, but I have no desire to offend. I just—"

Nathan cut that off with a shake of his head. "There's nothing you can say that will offend me. If I can't handle it, then I
shouldn't be talking with you."

"Good." Joshua seemed pleased with that. "The second thing
is, I won't be a hypocrite."

"A hypocrite. In what way?"

"Joining the Church just to please everyone. Going along
like I accept everything. Acting the part of a believer when
there're too many things I don't believe."

"No, you would not be like that, Joshua. I know that. So
what is it you can't believe?"

Joshua opened the book now. "Like this, for example. I was
reading this last night." He ran his finger down the page until he
found what he wanted. "This is in Alma. But it's someone
named Am-u . . ." He fumbled with the pronunciation.

"Amulek?"

"Yes. He's preaching and here's what he says." He began to
read, using emphasis to alert Nathan to the things that were
bothering him. " 'Behold, I say unto you, that I do know that
Christ shall come among the children of men, *to take upon him
the transgressions of his people*, and that *he shall atone for the sins of
the world*; for the Lord God hath spoken it; for it is expedient
that an atonement should be made; for according to the great
plan of the Eternal God, there must be an *atonement* made, or else
all mankind must unavoidably perish.' " He stopped, put the string
back in, and shut the book. "There's more, but let's start there."

"Okay. What's your question?"

"This atonement, this idea that a Redeemer was chosen
before the world to come down and take our sins upon him,
don't you find that inconsistent?"

"Inconsistent?" That was a word that took Nathan by surprise. "In what way?"

"You really think one person could take away another's sins?"

"I do."

"You can't change the past, Nathan."

"I beg your pardon?"

"You can't change what has already happened."

"I don't disagree with that. What has that got to do with taking away someone's sins?"

"Okay, let me put it this way. You know what I've done in the past, what I've been."

"Yes, but you've changed, Joshua."

"Of course I have," he shot back. "That's what you all keep telling me. So that will make my point even more. The fact that I have changed doesn't change what I *did*. It doesn't make it go away."

"No, it doesn't."

He nodded, seeing that Nathan was concentrating, trying to understand what he was saying. "Even if Christ did suffer, like you say he did, what good does that do for things that are already done? It doesn't—it can't!—change one thing."

"Oh, Joshua, but it does."

"No! Listen, let's say that I repent, that I change my life, get a new heart, all the things that you people call it. You say Christ will take my sins upon himself and everything will be made right."

"Yes, and I think I can explain how."

"And I say, that is impossible. It's trying to change what has already happened."

Nathan leaned forward on the saddle horn, determined not to jump in too quickly until he really saw what was in Joshua's mind.

Joshua took his silence as a sign of partial victory and went on. "Sure, someone can say to me, 'It's all right, Joshua. You're forgiven.' But what does that change? Fourteen years ago, in a drunken fit, I went after my wife. She had an infant at that time. That didn't stop me. I hit her, Nathan. I hit her hard."

"I know, Joshua," Nathan said quietly. "If you remember, I arrived in Independence just a day or two after that. I saw her face."

"Yes, I remember." Bitterness twisted his mouth now. "And I'm supposed to believe that if I repent, it will be like nothing ever happened? That's ridiculous. Then Jessica would still be my wife and Rachel my daughter. What happens to Caroline and Solomon and all the rest?"

"I never said it makes things like it never happened, but it can—"

But Joshua was not about to be detoured. "If I truly repent, will the Savior take away those scars on your back and chest and make the skin smooth again? No!" And then just that quickly, the flat hardness, the rigidity, was gone and there was a forlorn note in his voice. "If I were to go to the nearest creek right this moment and be baptized, would it bring Olivia back?"

"No, it won't bring Olivia back," Nathan said softly.

"Then what's all this talk of redemption, then? I don't give a fig about having someone look all somber and say, 'Joshua, your sins are forgiven.' You find a way to put things back the way they were, and then I'll be there standing in line to praise your Savior for what he did." Joshua frowned suddenly as he saw Nathan's expression. "What? Have I offended you with that comment about the Savior?"

"What you said saddened me, Joshua, it did not offend me."

"Saddened you?" He was suddenly bristling. "I don't need you feeling sorry for me."

"Who said I was feeling sorry for you?" Nathan shot right back at him. "I wasn't even thinking about you. I was thinking about Olivia. And suddenly I was sad."

"Oh." Joshua looked a little embarrassed. He took a breath. "Anyway, that's it. You call it redemption. I don't believe that true redemption is possible."

"You've thought pretty deeply about this, haven't you?"

"Well, the Book of Mormon is full of references to the Atonement and to Christ as our Redeemer. So yeah, I've thought a lot about it."

"All right, let me try and answer that for you." Nathan

paused, trying to decide how best to begin. "First of all, there's a difference between redemption and restoration. What you're talking about is restoration, putting things back as they were before. That is not what redemption is. Christ is the Redeemer because he paid the price for our sins, Joshua. In his sacrifice he took the pain of our sins upon him, he took the effects of our transgressions upon himself."

"Isn't the fact that Olivia is dead one of the effects of my transgression?"

Nathan took a breath, frustrated that he couldn't find the words. "Yes, but—"

At that moment there was a cry from up at the head of the line. "Rider coming in."

Both Nathan and Joshua stood in their stirrups, peering ahead. Then Joshua dug his heels into the horse's flanks. "Let's go see who it is," he said as his horse went into a brisk trot. Nathan kicked his horse into a trot as well, relieved for the interruption. This would give him some time to think through how to answer Joshua's concerns.

The rider turned out to be Lorenzo Snow, sent to them by Parley and Orson Pratt. Nathan and Joshua and several other men of the company gathered around Brother Snow as he dismounted and strode to President Young. His face was filled with excitement. "We found it, President," he said before he even reached him. "We found the Grand River and a beautiful place for our settlement." He described it quickly, not trying to hide the excitement in his voice, moving his hands in grand sweeping gestures as he talked.

"This is good news, Brother Snow," Brigham said when he finished. "How much farther is it?"

"About four miles. We should be there in an hour."

"Very good."

"President?"

"Yes."

"Elder Parley Pratt is the one who found the place. He has a name he'd like to suggest." Lorenzo explained quickly about Elder Pratt's feelings on seeing the river and how the Old Testament example of Moses had come to his mind. "He'd like to call it Mount Pisgah," Lorenzo concluded.

Brigham was silent for a moment, considering that; then he smiled. "If it was good enough for Moses, I think that's good enough for us. Mount Pisgah it shall be."

————◆————

For Melissa Rogers, it started out only as a walk through Nauvoo to enjoy the first really warm spell in almost two weeks of unsettled weather. Carl had the three boys with him, delivering a rare load of bricks to Carthage, and wouldn't be back until tomorrow. By three o'clock, there had been only two customers in the store the entire day, so she got out Mary Melissa's baby carriage, got a bonnet for herself and Sarah, and locked the store. She didn't even bother putting a note out explaining why she had closed early.

Mary Melissa, who would turn two in July, loved to ride in the carriage and chattered gaily as Sarah, now seven and a half, pushed her along the boardwalk and pointed out things of interest—a beetle pushing a piece of leaf in the dust, a mongrel dog with four puppies trailing along trying to snatch a meal as she walked, a passing wagon pulled by a horse and a mule hitched awkwardly together. Melissa was barely aware of her children as she walked along. Everywhere her eyes were drawn filled her with foreboding. Nauvoo was a city in the process of dying. The public dedication of the temple on the first of the month had galvanized the opposition. The Mormons were not going to leave after all, went up the cry; otherwise why were they dedicating their temple? Rumors swarmed as thickly as mosquitoes along the riverbanks. Men were being caught and beaten outside the city. Haystacks had been burned, cattle shot. It was Missouri and

Carthage and Warsaw and Yelrome all over again. Carl, openly disdainful, said that if one story in ten were actually true it would surprise him. She had retorted that even if only one story in twenty were true, she was growing increasingly more terrified.

The weather had at last turned warm, at least for a time. The roads were drying again, and Nauvoo was on the move. She felt like weeping as she passed house after house that stood deserted. Here and there was scattered furniture in the front yard, along with boxes of personal goods—abandoned when the wagon filled up and there was room for nothing more, the owners not even bothering to return them to the house. Across the street stood a two-story frame home with a front window broken out and the door ajar. It was like a gaping corpse. Amid the abandoned, deserted homes were the others with wagons and teams standing out front and with people scurrying back and forth with boxes and barrels and bedding.

As they reached Parley Street, Melissa was amazed. The lineup for the ferry at the west end of Parley Street, where the ferry landing was, stretched back for half a mile, almost all the way to Durphy Street. Wagons of various sizes stood in three parallel lines. Oxen, mules, and horses stood with heads down and eyes half-closed. People milled around talking. Many lay on the grassy shoulders of the street. Some were soundly asleep.

She shook her head, finding the sight astonishing. All these people, and that was with the ferry running day and night for the last week. And the word was that the ferry at Fort Madison, upriver a few miles, was also going around the clock. No wonder the city seemed deserted.

She raised a hand against the afternoon sun. Though it was almost a mile from where she stood, she could see the bluffs that marked the Iowa side of the river. It looked like a hillside of teeming ants. Tiny black figures moved everywhere. The wagon covers appeared to be seedpods carried on the backs of the tiny insects to some unseen anthill.

"Mama?"

She turned. "Yes, Sarah."

"Is everybody in Nauvoo going?" she said.

Everyone but us. But she didn't say it. She just smiled. "No, Sarah, many people are going, but a lot are staying, just like us."

"Oh."

Melissa couldn't tell if Sarah was disappointed or relieved. "And there are people moving in too. We won't be alone."

"Papa says the new people are making a group so they can be strong."

"Yes, that's right. They're calling themselves the 'new citizens.'" She didn't add that the primary motive behind that designation was a fear that the anti-Mormons might not distinguish between Mormon and non-Mormon when they came in looking for a chance to expropriate property.

Melissa had turned back toward the bluffs now, her eyes looking for something other than the people who swarmed over them. But she was too far away to pick it out. Perhaps if she was actually down at the river's side. Then a thought struck her with such power that it nearly took her breath away. She rocked back a little. And then, before her rational side took control again, she turned to Sarah. "Sarah, let me push Mary Melissa. Stay right with me."

The ferryman just stared at her, wondering if she had had too much of the sun.

She bit her lip, fighting not to scream at him. "I have money."

He shook his head in disbelief, gesturing toward the line that stretched back from the river. "It ain't a question of money, ma'am."

"Look, I have to get across. I have no wagons. Just the three of us. And we'll be coming back later today."

"Coming back won't be any problem at all," he said shortly. "You can have the ferry to yourself if you want. But these people have all been waiting for hours. I can't—"

A man beside the last wagon loaded on the ferry was listening. "We can squeeze her on with us," he called.

"Oh, thank you," Melissa cried. She turned back to the ferryman.

He finally nodded. "The baby carriage will have to stay here. I'll keep it there by the hut. That'll be seventy-five cents for the round trip."

She reached inside her pocket and withdrew the small purse. She gave him a dollar. As he reached for the box where he kept the fares, she shook her head. "Thank you for letting me go."

The spring grasses had nearly obscured the gravestone, and if she hadn't known to look for the solitary oak tree, she likely would not have found it. While Sarah and Mary Melissa played tag, Melissa patiently cleared the grass away. When she was done, she looked up. "Sarah?"

"Yes, Mama?"

"Why don't you and Mary find some wildflowers for Grandpa's grave."

"Yes, Mama." Immediately they set off. It would not be a hard task. The hillside was covered with yellows and purples and pinks.

She turned back, raising a hand to wipe away the dust from the letters etched into the stone.

Benjamin Steed
Born: May 18, 1785
Died: February 9, 1846
He found joy in the service of the Lord.
He was beloved of his family.

As she reached the last line of text, she spoke it aloud. "'Good-bye until we meet again.'"

The children returned with arms full of flowers. "That's wonderful, Sarah. Grandpa will be so pleased." She took them and laid them carefully across the mound, now grass covered.

Surprisingly, she was not crying. She felt a deep peace and understood now the urgency of her need to come here.

"I miss him, Mama," Sarah said.

"I know. I miss him too," she whispered. Mary Melissa nodded gravely, though her memories of her grandfather were already dimming. Melissa looked up at Sarah. "We'll have to be starting back soon. Why don't you and Mary Melissa play a little more. I'll call you."

"Yes, Mama." She took her sister by the hand and moved away, understanding her mother's need to be alone.

Melissa turned back to the gravestone. "I'm reading the Book of Mormon again, Papa. I wanted you to know." She brought her knees up and hugged them tightly. "Carl is a little dismayed. He doesn't know exactly what's happening." There was a soft laugh. "To be truthful, neither do I."

She closed her eyes, letting the memories of days gone by wash over her. How she longed for one more chance to move into those wonderful arms and feel his breath upon her hair as he told her that she would always be his little Melissa. Then she decided that if that was not possible, then this was second best. She looked up. "I'm back, Papa. I don't think Carl will ever leave Nauvoo, so you'll have to tell Mama if you can. I've been away from the Church, and from my testimony, but I'm back now."

Chapter Notes

When Elder Parley P. Pratt returned to his camp and announced to the others that he had found the Grand River, he jubilantly reported what he wanted to call their new settlement there. They agreed, as did Brigham, and thus the name of the second way station along the trail became Mount Pisgah. (See Parley P. Pratt, *Autobiography of Parley P. Pratt*, ed. Parley P. Pratt, Jr., Classics in Mormon Literature [Salt Lake City: Deseret Book Co., 1985], pp. 307–8.) Mount Pisgah was about 191 miles from Nauvoo. Elder Pratt found Mount Pisgah on 16 May 1846. Brigham Young's company arrived there two days later on 18 May.

Once the temple was publically dedicated on 1 May 1846, a great urgency to remove from Nauvoo swept the remaining Saints. That urgency was partly driven by the rising tide of opposition from the enemies of the Church. On 10 May, Wilford Woodruff spoke to three thousand Saints at the temple, his last public address in Nauvoo. He used a text from Ecclesiastes (see 3:1), "There is a time to all things; and for every purpose under heaven there is a season." (See *Wilford Woodruff's Journal, 1833–1898*, typescript, ed. Scott G. Kenney, 9 vols. [Midvale, Utah: Signature Books, 1983–85], 3:47.) The Saints interpreted that as a call to leave immediately. Large numbers responded, and the second of three major departure waves (in what would come to be known as the spring exodus) took place. (See *Iowa Trail*, p. 64.) By the end of June, over twelve thousand Saints would be gone and on the trail somewhere between Nauvoo and the Missouri River, leaving less than a thousand behind.

I have another question."

Nathan looked up. He had a small mirror propped in the fork of a tree and was shaving. Joshua was bent down in front of their small morning fire, stirring a pot of mush. "We didn't get a chance to finish answering your first one," Nathan said to him.

"That's all right," Joshua replied. "This one kind of goes along the same lines."

"All right. I'm about done here."

They had gotten to the Grand River the previous afternoon about an hour before sundown, but there had been little chance to continue their discussion. Matthew, who had gone ahead with the advance party of Parley P. Pratt, was there and they were able to have supper with him. They invited him to come and camp with them, but his group was charged by Brigham Young with other assignments, including finding a suitable place and getting a bridge across the Grand as quickly as possible, and so he felt that he needed to stay with the rest of his group.

After supper, assignments had been given out. Nathan and Joshua, along with several other pairs of men, were given the task of splitting rails for fencing. With that, and since they did not have a wagon to put in a circle with the others, they decided to move their campsite closer down to the river where there was a promising stand of trees. They set to work with axes and hatchets to build them a small lean-to, and worked feverishly until after dark to get it completed. By then it was time for lights out and they gratefully collapsed onto their bedrolls. Nathan wanted badly to remind Joshua that he hadn't finished answering his question, but Joshua seemed to have forgotten the whole matter, and Nathan, determined to be faithful to his promise to let Joshua set the pace on all of this, said nothing. So having Joshua raise the topic now this morning was pleasing to Nathan.

He finished scraping off the last of the shaving soap below his neck, then wiped the straight razor on the small towel. He folded it up and put it in its case, retrieved the mirror, then walked back to the fire. "All right, I'm ready."

Joshua nodded, but got out two bowls and the small can of sugar. They had no milk, but with water from the little brook that gurgled nearby and some bread, it would be all right. Once the food was served, Joshua inclined his head toward Nathan, who offered a short prayer of thanks. Only when they had settled back and were eating did Joshua begin. "All right, here's my question. As I said, it's related to the one I asked yesterday."

"I'm listening."

He paused, the spoon midway to his mouth. "The Book of Mormon speaks a lot about God's mercy, about Christ's mercy."

"Yes, it does."

"So what is that supposed to mean? Tell me about mercy."

Nathan thought for a moment. "Well, mercy is one of God's attributes. One of the reasons I love the Book of Mormon is that it reminds us that God is not just some strict, autocratic deity who destroys anyone who dares to disobey him or sends people to someplace where they will burn in hell for all eternity. I think he wants us to know that he is a merciful God, a Father who loves his children and wants what is best for them."

"And how would you define mercy?"

"Love. Compassion. I guess, in a way, the very idea of mercy is to receive something we don't deserve."

"All right, here's my question. If God is merciful, as you believe, where was mercy on that sunny October afternoon at Haun's Mill?"

Nathan hadn't seen it coming, but it really wasn't a great surprise to him.

"You think about it. Why was John Griffith caught in the blacksmith shop that day? He was about as good a man as I've ever known."

"Yes, he was."

"And that little boy? the one that tried to hide under the bellows—"

"Sardius Smith?"

"That's the one. Would you like to tell me how merciful God was when he let that man reach in with his rifle and blow that boy's head off?" He was getting a head of steam now. "I wouldn't expect God to step in and wipe out the whole mob riding in that day, but couldn't he at least have warned John? You people talk a lot about listening to the promptings of the Spirit. So why didn't the Lord tell them to get out of there?"

Nathan set his bowl aside, no longer hungry. Joshua had ridden into Haun's Mill the day following the massacre. He had seen the bodies laid out for burial in a newly dug well. He had seen Jessica's shattered hand where a ball had passed through the door panel and then her palm. He had seen the body of ten-year-old Sardius Smith.

Joshua's voice was heavy with bitterness now. "Where was mercy that day on the ferry? Tell me that. Tell me why a piece of river scum is allowed to spit tobacco juice into the eyes of your oxen and drive them mad with pain. Why wasn't it that man who got knocked off and drowned instead of Pa?" He stopped and looked away. "Why not me, even? That would make some sense at least."

"Joshua, I—"

"No, I'm not just feeling sorry for myself. You've got to admit it. When you compare my life to Pa's, it would have been more merciful if I had drowned and not Pa." He set his half-empty bowl of mush down and reached beside him. What he brought up was Lydia's Book of Mormon. Nathan was a little surprised, for he had not seen it there in the grass. Joshua tapped the book now with one finger. "You want to know what's ironic, Nathan? How's this for irony? You all are so excited to have me read the Book of Mormon, but it's the Book of Mormon that is raising all the questions in my mind."

Nathan sighed wearily. "No, it's not, Joshua. It's your life that's raising the questions; the Book of Mormon is just helping you find words to express them."

There was real anger now. "So, is that your answer?"

"Of course not. I'm just saying that the Book of Mormon is only helping you give voice to your questions."

"Well, it is doing that for sure. So, where are the answers?"

"In the Book of Mormon as well. And in the Bible. All of the scriptures actually."

"I'm waiting."

"Look," Nathan said. "We're supposed to be ready to work here in a few minutes. What do you say we clean up breakfast, then we can talk while we work?"

Joshua nodded. "That's fine." He got his bowl again, quickly ate the last few bites of bread and cereal, then washed it down with water. Nathan ate more slowly, considering the implications of what Joshua had said. If Joshua had not been there, he would have lifted his eyes to heaven, or bowed his head. But he could not, so he simply looked at the porridge before him and deep within let the words ring out. *O Lord, help me.*

They didn't get to talk until midafternoon. When they reached the stand of trees they had selected the night before, they found two teams of men there already working. Brigham Young and Heber Kimball were anxious to get the first acreage fenced, plowed, and planted, so they had reconsidered the assignments and pulled men off the crew for building cabins and sent them down to help split rails. Joshua was amused by Nathan's obvious frustration at not being alone. But they set to work without comment, working just a few yards from the other teams.

At the midday meal break, they all ate together, so there was no chance to talk then either. Joshua's amusement deepened. At about two o'clock Heber came down to the site with the wagon that was hauling the rails up onto the bluffs. Nathan waved him down.

"Yes, Nathan," Heber said when he joined them.

"I've been thinking," he said, "there is another good stand of trees about a half mile downriver from here. Joshua and I could start there. Then, as the fence moves south, we'll have a second location that's closer to where the rails will be needed."

Heber turned and looked, pulling on his lower lip. "That's not a bad suggestion. You want another team to come with you?"

"Oh, no," Nathan said casually, "we'll get it started at least, see how it looks." He looked away from Joshua's smirk. "If we need help, we'll send word."

"All right. We'll come back in a few hours and see how it looks."

As Heber went back to the wagon, Joshua turned and went by Nathan. "You are one sly dog," he said under his breath. Nathan merely smiled.

Splitting rails was not a job for weak men. After picking one of the straightest trees, they had to hew it down. Then they went along the trunk, making it "clean," or trimming off all the branches. They would prop up one end with a thick branch to give them room to cut it, then go to work with the two-man saw.

Once the first log was cut, they worked separately. One man would continue felling trees and cutting lengths of logs, while the other did the actual splitting. Currently, Nathan was acting as splitter. In a while they would trade positions, in order to give a particular set of muscles a rest.

Splitting rails off a green tree trunk was hard work, and no good woodsman would ever try to do it with an ax alone. For one thing, the ax blade could get bound up so tightly in the green wood that it was almost impossible to pull it free again. Second, eight feet of green wood didn't simply split off with a single blow. So a series of wedges—"gluts," as they were called—were driven into the log along a straight line. This was not done with the ax. Hammering the wedges with the head of an ax was a quick way to destroy a valuable tool. Instead they used a "beetle."

The beetle, which derived its name from the Old English word meaning to "beat," was a long-handled hammer with a heavy wooden head shaped like a miniature barrel. The head was made by sawing off a thick piece of oak limb and then binding it fast with iron hoops, banded on while they were red hot, then doused in cold water to make them shrink and cut tightly into the wood and hold it tight enough to stop it from splitting. A hole was then drilled through the center of the head and a handle tapped into it, and the beetle was ready. Weighing ten to twelve pounds, the beetle was a powerful tool.

Nathan moved along the length of the log, holding the beetle right up beneath the head as he tapped in each of the gluts along a straight line, about a foot apart. Once he had the gluts in, he stood and started in earnest, swinging the beetle again and again, hitting the gluts with solid thuds, moving down the log and smacking them each in turn, then starting over again.

Behind him, the final piece of log fell off and Joshua straightened, letting the saw hang loose in his hand. Sweat poured from his forehead, and he wiped at it with a rag from his pocket. He stood there, legs apart, breathing heavily as he watched Nathan work. "You ready for a break?" he called when Nathan paused for a moment.

"Yeah. Be right there."

Nathan moved to the end of the log and started again. The hammer swung back over his shoulder, and then in one smooth motion he would grunt and bring it up and over in a blur of speed. The gluts were in almost six inches now, and hitting the heads squarely took concentration.

Whumph! One step to the left. Hammer swings back. A low grunt. Up and over comes the head of the beetle. *Whumph!*

Nathan had developed a rhythm now and moved like a machine. As he reached about two-thirds of the way down the log, there was a sudden crack and a six-inch-thick piece of log snapped free, letting the gluts drop to the ground. He straightened, wiped at his brow with his sleeve, then let the beetle slip from his hands to rest against the log.

Joshua was at the wooden water bucket. He had the dipper filled and drank deeply. Then he refilled it and handed it to Nathan, who drank greedily, letting the water spill down his chin and onto his shirt. "Now, *that,*" he exclaimed, finally stopping for air, "that is good stuff."

Joshua took the ladle, filled it once more, and drank deeply again. He filled it a fourth time and gave it to Nathan. Finally, both satisfied, they moved over to the log Joshua had just finished cutting and sat down beside it, putting their backs against it.

It was nearing four o'clock in the afternoon. In the two hours since they had changed locations, they had dropped and trimmed three trees and split almost three dozen rails off from them. They were ready for a break.

Joshua tipped his head back and closed his eyes. Nathan watched him for a moment, then ventured a question. "You want to talk, or would you rather just rest?"

There was a sardonic smile. "After you went to all that work to get us alone?" he said. "I think we'd better talk."

Nathan was not feeling guilty in the least. "Good," he said, and leaned back too. "I'd like to start with some basic concepts. Then, if they don't answer your questions, we can pursue it further."

Joshua nodded. "I still have this nagging worry that you're getting your hopes up over all this, Nathan."

"I do have high hopes," Nathan agreed, "but I don't have high expectations. If you choose not to become a member"—there was a sudden, boyish grin—"we'll just tie you to the whipping post until you change your mind. Fair enough?"

Joshua laughed and shook his head. "Only a Mormon would think that was fair."

"All right. You asked some questions about why God does things the way he does them—why he isn't more merciful, why life doesn't seem fair, how we can talk about redemption if it doesn't change anything. So I'd like to start by talking about God."

"All right."

"Let me ask you a question. When Walter Samuelson sold you out, he virtually ruined you financially."

"Not virtually. He did ruin me."

"Some people would have taken revenge on him—set fire to his warehouses, maybe beaten him up some night. I suppose that some men might have even set about to try and kill him."

"I know men that would," he agreed.

"But you didn't. Why not?"

"Because . . ." He stopped, pondering that. "I thought about it actually. Not the killing, but I considered ways of getting even."

"But you didn't carry them out. Again I ask, why not?"

"I don't know. I guess I understood his anger. I guess I didn't want to stoop to become like him. Remember what Pa always used to say? 'When someone does you wrong, there's only one way to get *even* with them, and that's to drop down to their level and become like them.' It didn't seem worth it."

"But you could have, if you had wanted to."

"Yes." He knew Nathan was making a point here, but he didn't see it yet.

"Would you agree that this is partly because of your nature? You are a man of integrity and goodwill, so even though you *could* have done terrible things to Samuelson, you *chose* not to because it was contrary to what you are."

"I suppose that's one way to put it."

Nathan leaned back, looking satisfied. "That's how it is with God."

Joshua cocked his head. "Say that again."

Nathan now being eager, his words came out in a rush. "It's not that he *can't* do all the things you would like him to do—strike down the mob coming to Haun's Mill, stop the man with the rifle before he shoots Sardius Smith, shove that tobacco-spitting scum into the river instead of Benjamin Steed—but that he *won't*."

Joshua came forward a little now. "But if he can do something about those things and won't, doesn't that say something about what kind of person he is?"

"Like maybe he doesn't care?" Nathan offered.

"Well, that's one possibility. Or maybe he doesn't hear us. I know you picture a God who is a personal being, a Heavenly Father, as you call him, who watches over his children like a doting parent. What if he is nothing more than a Great Clockmaker? He made our world and all that's in it, then wound it up and put it on the mantel. Now he's off to other things."

Nathan was nodding now. "But if he is a caring, loving person, he wouldn't act in that way? That's what you're thinking, right?"

"Yeah, something like that. It's either that or you have to say that he doesn't have the power to change things. That's a possibility too. He would like to do something, but he can't."

"I submit that there's another explanation for why he works with us as he does. I submit that by his very nature he *won't* do certain things. Not that he *can't*, but that he won't." He could see that he had piqued Joshua's interest now, so he went on quickly. "By nature, God is perfect in his every attribute. He is not only loving and merciful, he is *perfectly* loving and *perfectly* merciful. He is a just God, but he is more than that, he is *perfectly* just.

He has perfect power, perfect knowledge. In everything, he is perfect. That's what makes him God."

"All right," Joshua said slowly, clearly thinking that through. "So what?"

"So think about it. If he is perfect, then every part of his character has to be in perfect balance, perfect harmony. For example, he can't be so filled with love that he ignores what's right and wrong. Justice is part of his nature too. He can't overlook evil simply because he loves the person who commits the evil. Does that make sense?"

"I'm not sure."

"Well, let's say Savannah does something you feel is deeply wrong. You punish her. Does that mean you don't love her?"

"No, I punish her because I *do* love her. I want what's best for . . . her . . ." His words petered out, not because he disagreed with Nathan, but because he finally saw where Nathan was going with this.

"Exactly. And will Savannah always see it that way, that you're doing this for her, because you love her?"

He had to concede. Nathan had tied it up neatly. "No, sometimes she will be angry and say that I don't love her. I can remember once when she was just two or three, I took a hunting knife away from her. She got angry with me and said that I hated her."

"Ah," Nathan said slowly, pleased with his answer. "And so, if God wants what is best for us, sometimes he may do things that make us think he doesn't hear us, or that he doesn't care?"

Joshua had to give it to him, though it came a little grudgingly. It was a logical explanation. "I can see that is a possibility," he finally said.

Nathan tried not to look too elated. "Good. Now, here's a second important point, and again, let me use an example. Why was it you and Pa fought so bitterly back in Palmyra?"

"Because we thought differently."

"No. You and I thought differently too, but we didn't fight like that. Melissa and you were always very close, but she disagreed with much of what you were doing. So why did you and Pa have such a clash?"

His eyes were thoughtful. "I guess because he tried to force me to do what he thought was best for me. I didn't like that."

Nathan nodded in satisfaction.

Joshua smiled at him. "All right, I've made your point. So what is it?"

"Now that you look back on it, do you think that what Pa wanted for you was better for you than what you wanted for yourself?"

"No question about it."

"So doesn't that make it all right? If what I'm trying to make you do is actually good for you, why can't I force you to do it?"

"Because you have no right to choose what is best for me. Maybe I'll make some dumb mistakes—like I did, by the way— but that's what freedom is all about. I don't want you telling me what I have to do to be good."

"You don't want me lashing you to a hitching post and whipping you until you agree to become a member of the Church?"

He shook his head slowly, his mind starting to expand on the implications of that. "No."

"There has been more than one religion that has tried that very thing. That's why the Founding Fathers wrote the Bill of Rights."

"Agreed."

"You call it freedom, Joshua. The Lord calls it 'moral agency.' In the Church we believe that an inherent part of our eternal nature is the desire, the will, the longing to be free, to have choice, to be allowed to carry out those choices. This agency is so fundamental that we believe we cannot be happy if it is taken away from us."

"I agree. Slavery is not a very happy condition."

"Exactly. So think about agency and God for a moment. God, understanding that inner drive, that inward part of our nature, made it part of his plan to give us agency. Agency is so sacred, so important to our happiness, that the Father has determined that he will never violate it."

"If I believed that, it would certainly make me feel better about God."

"If I thought God did anything else but that, that he would force me to do his will, I would have trouble worshipping him. We cannot be happy when we are forced to do someone else's will."

He stopped but Joshua merely watched him, his eyes thoughtful.

"Part of God's respect for agency is related to happiness," Nathan continued, "but there's something else just as fundamental. Force takes away morality."

"Say that again."

"Force takes away morality. Let me explain what I mean. Suppose I put a gun to your head and make you kneel in prayer. Does that make you a spiritual person?"

"No, that's obvious. You have to want to do something like that or it's meaningless."

"Precisely my point. If there is no choice, then you cannot talk about doing right or wrong. There must be agency in order for there to be morality—goodness or badness."

Joshua lay back on his elbow, chewing on his lip, deep in thought. Nathan waited. This was so important for what had to follow.

"So you're saying," Joshua began, speaking slowly as he thought through what was in his mind, "that God can't force us—"

"I suppose he could," Nathan broke in. "He's got all power. That's why I started with the first concept about God's nature. He can, but he won't."

"Because it would be contrary to his nature."

"Right!" It was hard for Nathan not to cry out aloud. Joshua was getting it. "So, now let's go to your question about mercy. Suppose in his desire for mercy God stopped that man from spitting tobacco juice at my oxen. He *could* do that, but why *wouldn't* he?"

"Maybe he should," Joshua said, though not with any conviction. "Is Pa's life worth that man's freedom?"

Nathan leaned forward, very earnest now. "So what you want is selective agency. You're free to do what you choose up to a point, then someone will step in and stop you."

"Well," he began, then stopped.

"We all tried to convince you that Olivia was not lying to you about her relationship with Joseph Smith," Nathan said very slowly now, "we tried to show you that what you were doing was not right. How did you feel then? I know now you wish that someone would have stopped you, but then?"

There was no answer to that, not, at least, that he could put into words. It was still too searingly painful. He decided to answer it in a different way. "If God is God, why can't he just make us so we're not that way, so we're not stubborn or stupid or selfish?"

"Because then it is his choice, not yours, Joshua. You, of all people, ought to understand why he can't do that."

He finally nodded. "All right. I agree. I'm not sure I like it, but I understand what you're saying." He straightened suddenly. "I'm going to have to think on that."

Nathan stood up, wanting to say so much more, but sensing he had just heard Joshua call for a halt. "That answers your second question about God's mercy, but not the first one about redemption. When you're ready to talk about that, let me know."

Joshua hauled himself up. "I will." He looked around, then stretched lazily. "I'd say we've got about two hours. Think we can finish splitting everything we cut before Heber comes back?"

Nathan surveyed their work site for a moment. "I think so. You want me to take the beetle or work the gluts?"

———•◆•———

It was late afternoon of May nineteenth. Peter Ingalls, walking at the head of the four yoke of oxen that pulled James Reed's "pioneer palace car," was thinking about the last week. It had been exactly that, one full week, since they had left Independence, Missouri. They had made good time in those seven days, not stopping for the Sabbath in their urgency, resting their teams only as absolutely necessary, as they sought to catch the main wagon train out in front of them. Reed and the Donner brothers estimated they were now about one hundred miles or so west of the border of the United States, somewhere out in that unnamed territory that the local Indians called Kansas. Peter was getting a little concerned. They had found good grass for the most part, and plenty of water along the Kansas River or the creeks that emptied into it, but they were pushing the animals hard. Even the best of oxen needed to stop every six or seven days to recruit their strength.

He heard the sound of children's laughter, and turned his head. Mrs. Reed had borrowed her daughter's horse and now rode up ahead with her husband. Kathryn had the children in the wagon, supposedly giving them their daily lesson. But from the peals of giggles coming from the wagon, he guessed they had more likely wheedled a story out of Kathryn. Through the open wagon cover Peter could see Mrs. Keyes. Her head was back and she was smiling. That said something about Kathryn's influence, because Mrs. Reed's mother was not doing well now at all. Peter smiled and turned back to the front. That was good. Since both Mrs. Keyes and Kathryn had no choice but to ride in the wagon, they had grown quite close. Mrs. Keyes adored Kathryn, and Kathryn seemed to feel a special affinity for the older woman. The laughter and smiles were proof enough of that.

Peter heard the shout from up ahead. He squinted a little, then saw that George Donner's lead teamster was waving his hat and pointing. Peter lifted his eyes, and felt a sudden jolt of excitement. His eye immediately caught the splashes of white amid the green foliage of the river bottoms about two or three miles ahead of them. It was a wagon train, and, judging from the number of wagon covers he could see, it was a big one at that.

Catching Up to the Russell Wagon Train

Ahead he saw James Reed put spurs to his horse and join the two Donners. They conferred for a moment, then Reed raced ahead. Peter turned his head. "I think it's them," he called.

There was a scuffling sound; then Kathryn and the children were at the front of the wagon. "Who?" young James said.

"The Russell train," Peter said jubilantly. He was grinning widely. "One week. It only took us a week to catch them. And they were originally eight or nine days ahead of us."

Reed returned in three-quarters of an hour. He was in an ebullient mood as he came loping up. By then Margret Reed was back in the wagon with her mother. She came to the wagon's door at the sound of the horse. As Reed swung down and tied the reins of his horse to the wagon wheel, he was beaming triumphantly. "It's done, Margret," he cried, striding to where he could reach up and take her hand. "They voted unanimously to accept our group."

"Wonderful, James."

"Yes, it is," he enthused. "There are about a hundred fighting men down there, nearly fifty wagons."

Peter nodded. Only the most powerful Indian band would dare take on a train of this size.

"How about women?" Mrs. Keyes asked. "Do they have many women?"

James Reed smiled up at his mother-in-law. "They have about fifty and some children as well. You'll have lots of company, Mother." Reed looked back to his wife. "We've done it, Mrs. Reed. We've found our train. This is the last big hurdle. Now we're on our way to California."

Chapter Notes

The Donner-Reed group left Independence, Missouri, on 12 May 1846. A substantial wagon train led by Colonel William Henry Russell had left Independence about eight or nine days before that. Anxious to have the safety of the larger train, the Donners and the Reeds pushed hard and found the Russell train a week later somewhere near Topeka in present-day Kansas. They were accepted unanimously and thereafter traveled with members of the larger group until they reached what was known as "the parting of the ways" in present-day Wyoming. (See Walter M. Stookey, *Fatal Decision: The Tragic Story of the Donner Party* [Salt Lake City: Deseret Book Co., 1950], pp. 63, 74–75.)

It was a beautiful day in what had become an almost never-ending string of beautiful days. The trade winds were steady and the *Brooklyn* was under full sail. She cut through the water effortlessly, sending a spray off the bow and into the wind. No wonder they called it the Pacific Ocean, Alice thought as she came through the hatch onto the deck and looked around. It was enough to pacify even the most troubled heart.

It was not a big surprise for her to find Will near the prow of the ship, leaning over the rail, his face to the wind, letting the beads of spray strike him full in the face, then licking the salty water off his lips with relish. He had gone up to help put up the awnings for the afternoon school that was held on deck. She had stayed behind to help clean the passenger hold. As she came out of the hatch and saw that the awnings were up, she immediately turned to the front of the ship, knowing that's where he would be.

Will heard her footsteps and turned. "Are you done?"

"Yes. You too, I see."

"Uh-huh. It doesn't take long anymore."

She moved up beside him, close enough that their shoulders touched. "So what have you been thinking?"

"About Hawaii."

"Hawaii?"

"Yes, that's what the natives call the Sandwich Islands."

"Really? What does it mean?"

He shrugged. "The first mate says it comes from *Hawaiki*, the legendary homeland of all the Polynesians."

"Has he been to the islands before?"

"Several times. He was on a whaler before he joined with Captain Richardson."

"Are there lots of whales around Hawaii?"

"Not always. Most of the whaling is done way north of there, in the Gulf of Alaska."

"Oh." She leaned forward so her face could catch the wind too. "So why do they call them the Sandwich Islands, then?"

"Well, again, according to the first mate, Captain James Cook, who discovered them, named them after the Earl of Sandwich, who was Lord of the English Admiralty at the time Cook sailed."

"I like Hawaii much better."

"So do I. And I love the Polynesian names. We'll dock in the harbor at *Honolulu* on the island of *Oahu*, which is not far from the island of *Molokai*. There are also islands called *Maui* and *Lanai* and *Kauai*. There're smaller ones too, but I don't remember their names. The king who united the islands over thirty years ago was called—" He had to stop for a moment to make sure he had it. He had been so charmed by the name that he had made the ship's officer repeat it until he could get it right. "*Kamehameha*."

"Oh," she said with a laugh, "that's lovely. Say it again. More slowly, please."

"Ka-may-ha-may-ha."

She laughed, then bowed slightly, swirling her hand as if to royalty. "I'm very pleased to meet you, your majesty Kamehameha."

"Well, actually now it's Kamehameha the Third, one of the sons of the original king. Before he took the dynastic name, he was called Kauikeaouli."

She clapped her hands. "Oh, yes, Will. I see why you love them. They sound like poetry." Then she gave him a closer look. "How do you know all this?"

His shoulders lifted briefly. "I ask a lot of questions."

She nodded, more serious now. "You like to learn about places where you're going, don't you?"

"Sure. I find it fascinating."

"So how much longer?"

"Well, today is the twenty-third. The captain is predicting landfall about the third week of June, so a little less than a month."

She groaned. It seemed like a year since they had left the Juan Fernández Islands, even though it had been only two weeks ago. And New York seemed like an eternity ago. "That long?" she mourned.

"Yep. But if it's any solace to you, Captain Richardson plans to stay there for a week to ten days."

"Good. Why is that?"

"He has the cargo to unload, as well as restocking with food and water before we turn east again."

"And then how long will it be?" It came out with longing. She could hardly imagine being on land without having to count the days until they sailed again.

"About a month after that."

She moaned again. "So when, then?"

He calculated swiftly. "About the end of July or the first week of August, depending on how long we stay at Honolulu."

Her hand stole down to her stomach, now visibly round even beneath the layers of her clothing. She was due to give birth near the end of September sometime. "I don't want to have to name our son 'Atlantic' or 'Pacific,' Will."

He laughed. Shortly after the great storm which had hit them within a few days of departing New York, Sister Sarah Burr gave birth to a son. They named him John Atlantic Burr. And just recently, Phoebe Robbins, who had lost two of her sons during the early part of the voyage, gave birth to a little girl. At the midday meal Brother Robbins announced that she would be called Georgiana Pacific Robbins.

Then suddenly Will realized what she had said. "You think it's a boy?"

For the first time she decided not to put his question off. "Yes, I do, Will."

He swung around. "Truly! You really mean it?"

She was pleased at his excitement. "Yes, I think so."

"That's wonderful. Let's think of some names."

She laughed merrily and leaned against him. "I think we have plenty of time, Will."

———— ••• ————

Brigham Young's company arrived at Mount Pisgah on the afternoon of Monday, May eighteenth. They had come to create another way station, and by Saturday, just five working days later, they had done a remarkable amount of work toward that end. Two or three hundred acres were fenced now, and most of that was plowed. Wheat, corn, and barley were going in right behind the plows. There were five cabins or sod huts now completed and eight more in various stages of completion. Work on a sturdy bridge across the river was under way. They were also constructing a gristmill. Dozens of small plots were already spaded and planted with garden vegetables. Not only was Mount Pisgah a place of remarkable beauty, it was also, unlike Garden Grove, completely free of rattlesnakes. That alone made it almost a paradise. So what had been the week before uninhabited wilderness was now a significant community.

The first of the wagons of those who had stayed behind at Garden Grove started arriving on Wednesday. At first it was just a few here and there. By Friday it was a steady trickle. By Saturday they were coming in an almost endless stream.

———————◆•◆———————

The sound of wagons caused both Joshua and Nathan to stop work for a moment and look to where the road dropped over the eastern bluffs and into the Grand River floodplain. It took them only a moment to see that there were no Steed wagons among the six that came into sight and they immediately lost interest. They didn't really expect their family for another day or two, but they always stopped to look.

Joshua leaned on the beetle, looking down at the pile of rails they had completed since the wagon had last come for them. In five days they had become quite proficient, and Nathan, who always liked to track things like that, said they had cut almost five hundred rails, enough to make about a half mile of fence.

Joshua reached down and pulled on a long piece of prairie grass. When it came free he began to chew on its soft, sweet stem. "Nathan?"

"Yes?"

"What do you think we should do?"

Nathan frowned. He didn't have to ask what Joshua meant. It was the number-one topic of discussion in camp right now. President Young had already chosen the leadership for Mount Pisgah. To Nathan's pleased surprise, Father William Huntington was chosen as president, and he had chosen Ezra T. Benson as his first counselor and Charles Rich as his second. Other families would be chosen to stay here in Mount Pisgah, just as Solomon and Jessica would be staying at Garden Grove for a time. Their job would be to prepare things for the thousands yet to come. If the Steeds were chosen as one of those, then there would be no further question, but neither Joshua nor Nathan thought they would be.

The question that weighed heavily on Brigham's mind was the Rocky Mountains. May was almost over and they weren't even across Iowa Territory yet. That meant they still had more than a thousand miles to go, five times the distance they had already come! On Wednesday, two days after their arrival, Brigham called a council meeting. The rain had started again by then, so they gathered in the post office tent. Heber C. Kimball, in his usual direct manner, started the meeting by stating that at their current rate of travel and with the present numbers of teams, there was no way they were all going to make it over the mountains this season.

That started a vigorous discussion. No one disagreed with the assessment, but what to do about it was not so clear. After almost half an hour of listening, President Young stood. "Brethren, I have a possible solution. I would propose that the Twelve and a few others blaze the way ahead to Council Bluffs on the Missouri River. There, if all goes well, we can purchase additional supplies, establish a third way station, then push on with a vanguard company across the Rockies. Hopefully we could get to the valley in time to put in crops. Next spring that group would return to guide the rest of the people to our new home."

It was quickly agreed that this was the only practical answer. The bulk of the Saints would stay in the area at Council Bluffs, Mount Pisgah, or Garden Grove to raise crops for next year's journey. Only those who had good teams and sufficient provisions would be allowed to continue west.

Though not the best equipped of families, the Steeds met Brigham's criteria for the vanguard company. And that selection would not be strictly by assignment. If they wanted to go, they could go. But not the whole family. A vanguard company would be almost exclusively men. Speed would be of the essence. And therein lay the question. Should Nathan and Joshua, and perhaps Matthew, go on with the vanguard company and winter over, leaving their family behind? Or should they leave that to others?

Nathan shook his head slowly. "I don't know. I'm torn both ways. What are your feelings by now?"

Joshua looked around, his eyes taking in all that had been done in the last few days. This was a lovely place. Parley Pratt had not exaggerated. It would not be an unpleasant place to settle in for a time. But . . . He pulled the piece of grass from his mouth and flipped it away. "I was never very good at standing in place, Nathan."

"Yeah, me neither," he said glumly. The thoughts of plopping down here and waiting until spring were thoroughly depressing. Now that they were on the move, he wanted to keep moving. On the other hand, splitting up the family was a totally un-attractive option. "I think we wait until the family gets here, and then hold a family council."

"You're right," Joshua agreed. "Everyone needs to be in on this discussion and—"

He stopped. Nathan was looking past him, peering intently at the oncoming wagons which were now just about seventy-five yards east of where they stood.

Joshua turned too. "What is it?"

"I think that's John Taylor," he said. "There, at the head of the first wagon." Then, with a shout, he started toward the road. "Elder Taylor! John Taylor! Is that you?"

"We brought a whole sack of letters," Elder Taylor said to Nathan. "One was from your sister."

"Melissa?" both Nathan and Joshua said together. They were walking beside Elder Taylor as they moved slowly toward the main encampment.

"Yes," Elder Taylor said, "but we gave it to your mother."

"So you saw them?" Joshua asked eagerly. "How far out?"

"They were packing up getting ready to leave Garden Grove. They told us to tell you they should be here Monday afternoon."

"Wonderful!"

"It is so good to see you," Nathan said, laying a hand on Elder Taylor's shoulder. Nathan had accompanied Parley P. Pratt on a mission to Upper Canada in the spring of 1836. The first place they stayed was in the home of a recent English emigrant. The rest had become history. John Taylor and his wife eventually joined the Church and referred many of their friends as well, including Joseph Fielding and his two sisters, Mary and Mercy. So the friendship between Nathan and the Taylors went back many years and was strengthened even more by the natural affection that ties a missionary and his proselytes together.

The Apostle was smiling at him. "Had you heard that Melissa came to the temple dedication?"

Nathan stopped. "She did?"

"Yes. Wilford Woodruff is back from England now. He went and saw Melissa at the store and told her there would be a public dedication. To his surprise, she came."

"Did Carl?" Joshua asked, as surprised as Nathan.

"No, but Melissa brought the children."

John Taylor frowned, and there was clear anxiety in his eyes. "Things are not good for those who are staying in Nauvoo, Nathan. I worry about them."

"We have heard that our old enemies are getting more and more impatient about us leaving. Are more of the Saints getting out of there?"

"It seems the whole city is on the move," he replied. "Guess how many wagons we counted that had crossed the Mississippi and were waiting on this side of the river to get under way."

"How many?"

"Over four hundred."

Joshua gave a low whistle. Nathan just shook his head. Four hundred. That was about the same number as their total company, including those in Garden Grove and in between.

"And I've been counting the numbers of teams we have passed on the trail. I thought President Young would want to know."

"How many?" Nathan asked.

"Not counting the four hundred at Montrose and Sugar Creek, we easily passed another eight hundred wagons between here and there."

"Twelve hundred wagons!" The very thought of that was staggering.

"At five or six people per wagon," Joshua calculated quickly, "that's six or seven thousand people. Oh, my!"

"At least," Elder Taylor agreed. "Nauvoo is like a ghost town. I would say that by the time June is here, there will be less than a thousand of our people left in the city." The Apostle smiled at Nathan. "Would you like some good news that you will find quite depressing?"

Nathan gave him a strange look, and Elder Taylor just laughed. "When did you actually leave Sugar Creek?"

Nathan thought back.

Joshua spoke up. "It was March first."

"Yeah, that's right," Nathan agreed.

"And today is the twenty-third of May?" Elder Taylor queried.

"Yes."

"So it has taken you two months and three weeks—almost three months—to get to this point?"

"That's right. In another week it will be a full three months since we started."

There was a smile mingled with just a touch of sadness. "Most of the companies are covering that same distance in about three weeks."

Nathan's mouth fell open. "Three weeks?"

"Yes. I'm really not trying to gloat. We have been traveling with a light wagon and carriage, but we have come from Nauvoo in about two weeks. I tell you this because those thousands of people behind us are going to be here much sooner than you think."

Nathan let out his breath slowly. Three weeks! And yet, strangely, he felt no regrets, no envy. Those coming now would never know what they had endured. But they had been the first, and they had paid the price. If it smoothed the way for those to follow, then there was a deep satisfaction in that. He looked at his old friend. "President Young will need to know all of this, Elder Taylor. He is going to be very glad to see you."

"Yes. I am anxious to see him again. Also Leonora came on with others when I returned to Nauvoo. I am most anxious to see her again too."

———◆———

Joshua lay on his back, staring up at the interwoven lattice-work of willows that made up the roof of their simple lean-to shelter. He slapped at a mosquito that buzzed near his ear, then rolled over onto his stomach. Directly in front of his nose lay Lydia's Book of Mormon. It was closed. It had been closed since Nathan had left to have supper with Parley Pratt and the Taylors. Once he had left, Joshua had fished the book out of his saddle-bags and tossed it on the bed, and there it had lain ever since.

It was a perfect time for reading. He and Nathan had chosen to make their shelter out away from the main encampment so that they would be close to the trees where they were splitting rails. It was not likely that someone would happen by unexpectedly. There was at least another three-quarters of an hour during which there would be sufficient light to read by. But still the book lay there, closed and silent.

"Keep the book, Joshua. Read it until you're done."

"You need to tell Caroline, Joshua. Of all people, she should know."

"It's your life that is raising the questions, Joshua. The Book of Mormon has only helped give voice to those questions."

He sat up abruptly, wanting the voices in his mind stilled. He was reading. Not as much as before. The man-killing schedule Brigham had put them on greatly restricted that, but he was more than two-thirds through the book now. And he was no closer to an answer or to a resolution of his questions than he was when he and Nathan set out from Garden Grove eleven days ago now.

He had not gone back to Nathan with further questions since that day they talked while splitting rails. He could tell it was costing Nathan dearly, not to be able to prod him a little, but thus far he had been completely true to his promise. It was Joshua's lead, and Nathan would not push him. That was not without its drawbacks. Sometimes he would not have resented a little push. It was hard to jump in just out of the blue and start asking questions.

"It's not enough to just read, Joshua. You have to ask."

Well, he retorted to himself, that was not without its own problems. Three times now he had determined that he would try to pray, and specifically that he would pray about the Book of Mormon, as both his mother and Lydia had strongly suggested. But each time, when he actually started to open his mouth, he just couldn't bring himself to do it. Once he had even found a place behind a clump of brush and knelt down. Before he could actually pray, he ended up feeling so ridiculous that he jumped up and stalked away. He had sworn aloud, at himself and at his family, and vowed he wouldn't make that mistake again.

Abruptly he grabbed the book, rolled over, and shoved it back inside his saddlebags. He retrieved the rifle from its scabbard and sighted down its barrel. Now there was a thought to solve this malaise he was in. He looked up at the sky. The sun was just going down. That gave him another thirty or forty minutes of daylight. The perfect time for hunting. Cheered by the thoughts of occupying his mind with something besides religion, he turned back to the saddlebags and began rummaging for his powder and the bag of lead balls. As he did so, he began to whistle to himself some unknown tune.

He found three does and a yearling—probably a young spike—stripping buds off the willows right at the river's edge. They were no more than twenty or thirty yards from where he was. Perhaps they heard the scrape of the branches against his shirt. Maybe it was their incredible sixth sense of danger. Through a screen of underbrush, he saw their heads come up with a frightened jerk, ears cocked forward, their bodies frozen, poised for flight. So perfectly did they blend into the deepening shadows, that had it not been for that sudden movement, he wouldn't have seen them at all. Then he would have stepped out into the open and spooked them for sure. As it was, he was still mostly hidden from them. He stood there, as motionless as they, poised on the balls of his feet, barely breathing. After almost a full minute of staring in his direction, they finally decided that whatever it was they heard was not a threat and they turned back to the willows.

He relaxed, letting himself sink slowly down into a crouch. Slowly, ever so slowly, he slid the muzzle of his rifle through the screen of underbrush. Then he sat back on his heels, letting his eyes scan the trees behind them. Where there was a group of does, there was a good possibility that they would be escorted by something more than this young male. He was sure of the sex of the yearling now, seeing the stubby little knobs that marked the beginning of his antlers. He was too young to qualify as the protector of this group. But if there was an old mossy-back buck, he would be far more cautious than his womenfolk. That's how they got to be old enough to carry those magnificent racks of antlers. And for that, he would wait.

He was close enough that he could see their fur—light brown now, with summer coming—ripple as they tried to ward off the swarms of mosquitoes that were thickening as the air cooled. Their white tails flipped up and down, flashing like naval semaphores when they turned their rumps toward him. Every few seconds they would stop. Their ears would come forward, and they would stare at some spot along the river before returning to their eating.

He waited almost five minutes before he saw it. There was a movement in the trees that lay beyond the flat meadows along the river. It was so nearly imperceptible he wasn't even sure but what it was the flash of a bird's wing. Another full minute went by. The gloom was deepening rapidly, and he knew that if he waited much longer, he would have to be content with taking one of the others, or go home empty-handed.

Then, just like that, it was there. Again there was a brief movement, and then another deer stepped out from between two trees and into the clearing, moving ever so slowly. If the other four saw it, they gave no sign. Neither did he seem the least interested in them. When the new deer turned his head, Joshua gave a satisfied grunt.

A deer's antlers begin to grow in the spring, usually in April or early May. They start as stubby knobs on the top of the animal's head and then, for the next several weeks, grow rapidly. By August they are fully grown, though still in the "velvet stage," semi-soft and covered with a fuzzy sheath. But as fall approaches, the velvet covering is quickly rubbed off, and the antlers become the bone-hard racks that are worn through the winter before they fall off and the whole process starts over again. Since this was late in May, the buck's antlers were still in the first stages of growth. Nevertheless they were far enough along that Joshua could see that this animal had significantly more than the stubby knobs on the yearling. They were already four inches long and very thick at the base. Judging from that, he guessed this one was eight, or maybe nine, years old, well into his prime.

Carefully, moving so slowly as to make no sound or move the brush in any unnatural way, Joshua lifted the rifle. He aimed the front sight so it pointed at the neck, just ahead of the front quarters. He took a breath, let it out slowly, breathed again, let it out halfway, then squeezed slowly.

The crack of the rifle was like the explosion of a cannon in the evening quiet. The buck jerked around violently, leaped once into the air, then crumpled as his forelegs buckled beneath him. The other four deer shot away in great bounding leaps, tails flashing white. Three crows burst into the air from a dead cottonwood, cawing angrily at this intrusion on their privacy.

Joshua straightened and pushed out from his blind. The buck was down now, legs shaking in its final death throes. He nodded in satisfaction. A clean shot. No suffering. No having to track the blood stains, then losing them in the darkness.

———•—•———

He thought about going for Nathan. He didn't dare leave the carcass out for the whole night. Wolf sightings had not been uncommon. This would be too tempting to leave unattended. But then he decided it was not likely that Nathan had returned from dinner yet, so he set to work on his own. He would clean it out, get it propped open so that the meat would cool, and then he would find Nathan to help him drag it back to camp. Glad that he had sharpened his knife that morning on Heber Kimball's grindstone, he bled the deer carefully, then opened up the stomach. Once it was cleaned, he dragged the body a short distance from the entrails, then propped open the body cavity with two sticks so that it could cool. Leave an animal too long in its own body heat and the meat could turn pretty "gamey."

He was whistling again now as he worked, finding a deep satisfaction in the evening's success. When he finished, he moved the few yards to the creek and washed the blood off his hands and knife. As he stood, wiping the blade of his knife against his trouser leg, he turned and looked at the deer. In the dragging of the body away from where he had cleaned it, he had left the neck twisted a little, so it was looking at him. For a moment it looked as though it were simply lying down, resting.

And then, a strange thing happened. The song he was whistling died on his lips. He moved slowly back to the slain deer, staring down at it in sudden morbid fascination. A quarter of an hour ago this had been a living thing. It had stepped out of the forest, a thing of beauty and magnificence. Now it was dead.

Slowly he put the knife back in its case. He squatted down again, directly in front of the animal. The large brown eyes had not closed in death but stared sightlessly back at him, locked forever open by that shattering blow from the ball. He reached out and touched the brown fur. It felt stiff, and beneath it he could feel the flesh already cooling. What was it that was gone now? When the buck had stepped out of the trees it had life. It had intelligence. It sniffed the air for danger. It scanned the forest for any threat. It had done so for years now, pitting its natural caution against the cunning of the wolves and the threat of winter storms and the predator known as man. Then Joshua's shot had taken him down. In seconds the life—whatever it was—was gone. What was it that was different now? Outwardly there was little difference—if you ignored the fact that Joshua had cleaned the animal. The head was the same shape, the velvet antlers still there, but the eyes were as dead as though made from glass. The fur was the same color and texture, but it was no longer alive and shimmering with movement.

He knew what Nathan would say if he were to ask these questions of him. He would talk about the spirit. Did a deer have a spirit? Or did it just have life? *Just life?* His brow furrowed. Life was a miracle whether it was spirit or not. And he had just ended that miracle. He felt no guilt. That wasn't it at all. Food was a constant problem for the Saints. Tomorrow they would cut up the meat and distribute it among the men working at Mount Pisgah. The fat around the deer's stomach was thick, and Joshua knew that the steaks and roasts cut from its flanks would be marbled with veins of fat as well. Working men needed that for strength and endurance. So what he was feeling wasn't guilt. Rather it was a sudden, strange fascination.

Then Joshua visibly started. With a jolt he realized what it was that he had been whistling to himself for the past half an hour or more. It was the song that Savannah had been playing that last day back in Nauvoo. It was "Olivia's song."

A great sadness washed over him. Olivia too had once been filled with laughter, love, intelligence, vibrancy. Wasn't that what was meant by life? Nathan had once said that the body was just an outward shell, the house in which the spirit lived. It wasn't the "house" that was Olivia. It was whatever it was inside her. That's what made her what she was, what he had come to love.

And then, with the same blinding swiftness that had cut down this beautiful animal, her life too was gone. But gone where? Was she still out there somewhere, as Caroline so firmly believed? He wanted to believe that, but . . . He shook his head. Wasn't that, in a way, the ultimate demand on God? Wasn't that the ultimate request? that his daughter still be allowed to live on somewhere after death?

Then, unbidden, his thoughts turned to his father. Just before the funeral, as hundreds streamed past the open coffin to pay one last tribute to Benjamin Steed, several people, including his own mother, had made a comment something like this. "That's not Benjamin." It had irritated him at the time. Of course it was Benjamin. Of course it was the man who had lived such a rich life, then given it without a moment's hesitation for his granddaughter. But now Joshua understood. What lay before him now was no longer the beautiful white-tailed deer that had come out of the trees. It was just a body. The deer was gone.

For a long time he sat there, letting the darkness slowly envelop him. Finally, with a sigh from deep within, he got to his feet. He looked around. There was no moon as yet, and only the last vestiges of twilight gave him any sight at all. There was no sound of voices or laughter. He was too far away for that.

He walked away from the deer a few steps, moving back to the river's edge. He stood there for almost a minute, staring down at the water; then finally, slowly, he sank to his knees. For a long moment, there was nothing, no movement, no sound. Then at last his lips began to move, and in a murmur so low that the sounds of the river's current overrode it, Joshua began to speak.

"O God."

He stopped. The last time he had prayed had been while he was still living with his family back in Palmyra almost twenty years ago now. And even though he could remember some of the words and phrases from back then, they seemed so alien to him now.

"I don't know if you're there. And if you are, I don't know that you would have any cause to listen to me."

An overwhelming feeling of being the fool rushed over him. His tongue felt heavy and thick. What was he doing? Here he was kneeling on the ground, talking out loud to himself, as if he were some crazy man or something. He opened his eyes, starting to rise, looking around quickly to make sure no one was watching, silently vowing that he would never, ever make this mistake again. But then as he got to one knee, his eyes fell upon the deer. It was still propped up a few yards from where he was, the large lifeless eyes gazing at him steadily.

He sank back down and closed his eyes. "O God. I don't know what to say. I don't know how to ask you for anything. But I want to know if my Olivia is still alive. I'm so sorry for the things which I did that led to her death. I was such a fool. If only I could know that she's not gone forever. And Papa too. I would like to know about him too. Mama and Nathan and Caroline and all the rest say they know he's still alive. I don't know how they know, but if that's possible, I would like that too."

For the third time the words ceased and his eyes opened. He wasn't fighting it anymore. He just didn't know what else to say. Finally, he lowered his head for the last time, staring at the ground before him. "I'm sorry for what I am. I wish there was a way to make it different." And then, after another moment of silence, he finished lamely, "Amen."

It was almost midnight by the time they got the deer back to their lean-to shelter and hoisted it up high enough between two trees to keep it away from wolves, foxes, raccoons, or any other creatures that might want to sample the fattened flesh. Once it was safe, they started to prepare for bed. Nathan stayed outside for a time, and Joshua knew he was saying his prayers. He did it out alone so that Joshua would not be embarrassed by it. When he came back he undressed quickly and crawled inside his bed-roll. There was a deep sigh of pleasure. "Now, that feels good."

"Yes, it does."

"Brigham came by the Taylors' wagon tonight. There's going to be a worship service tomorrow. They estimate we're up over three hundred wagons already. Probably more than a thousand people."

"I would guess that's pretty close."

"In addition to worship services, it will give Brigham a chance to speak to everyone about what he's thinking."

"They need to know." Joshua was chuckling inwardly now. He could tell that Nathan badly wanted to ask if he planned to go to the meeting, but was holding back. Then he decided it wasn't fair to play with him in this way. "Yes," he said.

"Yes, what?"

"Yes, I'd like to go to the meeting."

Nathan laughed softly. "You don't miss much, do you?"

He smiled in the darkness. "When you split logs with a man, you get to know his mind."

"I wish that were true."

There was no answer, and the silence was suddenly heavy and awkward.

Nathan made a sound of mock pain. "Sorry. Comment with-drawn. I wasn't—"

"No apology necessary," Joshua cut in.

They lay there, listening to the sounds of the night—the crickets just outside their shelter, the lower-pitched chorus of frogs coming from the river, the soft hoot of an owl somewhere above them. Both were very tired; both were far from sleep. After almost five minutes, still wide awake, Joshua turned his head. "Nathan?"

"Yes?"

"There's something you ought to know."

"What?"

He searched for words that would not sound utterly foolish; then he decided to just say it straight out. "I know now that Olivia still lives somewhere. And Papa."

Nathan's eyes half closed. It was as though someone had jabbed him, only the sensation was not pain but pure joy. "Really!" And then after a moment, "Can I ask how you know?"

"It's a long story. It happened while I was cleaning the deer, but . . . I finally asked God."

Nathan had to swallow hard twice as the enormous implications of that statement hit him. "That's wonderful, Joshua."

"I know. I don't understand it all. I'm not even sure how it came. But I know."

"Then that's enough for now," Nathan said softly.

"Yes." Nathan could hear the wonder in Joshua's voice too. "Yes, it is for now."

Chapter Notes

The *Brooklyn* sailed from Robinson Crusoe Island off the coast of Chile on 9 May. They would not land in Hawaii until 20 June. There were two children born during the voyage who were named as indicated in this chapter, though the Robbins baby was born a little later than is shown here. (See "Voyage," pp. 53, 59–60.)

After having returned to Nauvoo for a short time to attend to some business, John Taylor arrived at Mount Pisgah on Saturday, 23 May 1846. His report of how many wagons he had passed between Nauvoo and Mount Pisgah was electrifying to the Church leadership and spurred them on to even greater efforts to prepare for those who were to come. (See *CN*, 25 May 1996, p. 12.)

The formal count on Sunday morning showed just over three hundred and fifty wagons at Mount Pisgah, with over a thousand people. In spite of the large number, Brigham called for a general worship service, starting at noon. When the bugle sounded, announcing that it was time, Nathan and Joshua walked together up the hill toward the main encampment.

The business portion was brief. Brigham said little about pressing on to the Rocky Mountains with a vanguard company that Nathan and Joshua did not already know, then asked each family to discuss their circumstances and needs. Then he started the meeting. Nathan found it interesting that President Young set the theme for the meeting by speaking on the plan of salvation. All of the other speakers followed suit. From time to time Nathan would cast a sidelong glance at his brother to see if he could tell what Joshua was thinking, but though Joshua listened attentively, there was no reaction at all.

As they walked back to their campsite, it was almost all that Nathan could do to stop from asking Joshua what he thought, but remembering his vow, he steered the conversation to what had to be done before the family arrived. If John Taylor was right, they would arrive sometime tomorrow. That left a lot of work to be done. They discussed possible campsites, where to graze their animals, how much firewood they would need. Then, as they ate, they talked again at some length about whether or not to go west with the vanguard company. As before, they decided that until they could bring it before the family, they couldn't determine which course to take.

When the meal was over and the dishes washed in the brook, Nathan went inside the lean-to and started rummaging through his gear.

"What are you looking for?" Joshua called.

"My pen and some paper. I thought I'd write Melissa and Carl a letter in case someone is going back to Nauvoo."

"I thought you still owed me the answer to one question."

There was silence; then a moment later Nathan stuck his head out of the shelter to look at him with some surprise.

"Well," Joshua said, waving Lydia's Book of Mormon, "do you or don't you?"

"I do. Just a minute." When he reappeared a moment later, he had his own Book of Mormon. He came down and sat across the fire from Joshua. "All right."

"Do you even remember what my question was? It's been over a week now."

"I do. You were bothered by the concept of redemption. You wanted to know how something bad could be atoned for, or paid for, if nothing in the past could be changed."

"Very good. So, do you have an answer?"

"I do, but whether or not it will satisfy you remains to be seen. This is pretty heavy doctrine. Simple in a way, and yet very profound."

"Try me," Joshua said dryly.

"All right. We talked about agency, about why God allows us the freedom to choose, even though some people will choose to do bad things, even very bad things. The problem is, this is not fair for others. Papa drowns because an evil man made a terrible choice. Jessica loses a husband because other men choose to try and drive us out of Missouri. That's not fair."

"Who ever said life was fair?"

"But wait," Nathan said quickly, "remember that God is perfectly just. If not, then he is not God. I'm not saying that all things will turn out to be perfectly fair in this life. Not at all. But in God's eyes, this life is only a tiny part of our existence. So as long as it is made right, then justice is done."

"So you're about to tell me your answers are not answers for this life."

Nathan pointed a finger at him and wagged it a little. "Don't be putting words in my mouth, Joshua. Just hear me out. I want to show you how payment can be made and justice done."

Chastened, Joshua nodded. "Go on."

"Before, I used an example of how you deal with Savannah to teach you how God deals with us. Let me do that again, only let's use Charles this time." Nathan hesitated for a moment, knowing he was about to move onto very sensitive ground. "Before I do that, I want to ask you some questions. They may be a little painful."

"Go ahead," he said warily.

"Do you consider yourself worthy of Caroline?"

"No." It came out flat and without equivocation.

"Why?"

"Because of what I was. What I've done."

"But you've changed."

He sighed, suddenly tired of it all. "Maybe I have changed, but those things haven't changed. That's what I'm trying to tell you. The past will always be there, no matter what I do now."

"I understand. And since Caroline has nothing like that in her past, it's not fair that she should have to have a man who did do those terrible things. Is that it?"

There was a brief nod, his eyes not meeting Nathan's now.

"And part of why you feel so terrible about Olivia is that it is so unjust that she should suffer for your mistakes, right?"

It was barely a whisper now. "That's it exactly."

"So there's our dilemma again. God is merciful, and because you've truly changed he wants you to be with your family forever. But you say that your change of heart doesn't take away the past. In other words, it isn't fair—or just—that Caroline and Olivia should have to deal with a father and husband who has been far less than they have been."

Again there were no words, just a brief movement of the head.

"All right, now to my example with Charles. Let's suppose that he is playing stickball with some of the boys. They are in a field across the street from a general store. Charles knocks the ball with a solid hit. It soars out of the field, across the street, and right through the window of the general store."

There was a bemused smile. "That sounds like Charles, all right."

"So here we have a interesting situation. The storekeeper has lost an expensive glass window. He wants to be paid for its replacement. He wants justice. And that is only right. But you are the father. You want mercy for your son. This wasn't a malicious act. He's only six. He wasn't thinking. He didn't understand the consequences of his actions. Should he be blamed and punished? And if so, how can he possibly pay the damages? He earns no money, has no resources of his own." He stopped and waited a moment before saying, "Do you see the conflict now between mercy and justice?"

"Well, I probably would have put it in different terms, but yes."

"So how do you resolve it so that both mercy and justice are satisfied? Would you make Charles go to work at the store until the debt is paid?"

"He's only six," Joshua protested.

"And that wouldn't be very merciful, would it? So be merciful to Charles. Just tell the storekeeper that Charles is only a boy and that he—the storekeeper—will have to replace the window himself."

"No, that's not fair either."

"Now you're beginning to see why the Book of Mormon says that mercy cannot rob justice. That would not be right."

"What if I paid it?" Joshua suddenly said.

"Ah," Nathan said softly.

Joshua shook his head ruefully. "Every time you say 'Ah,' I feel like I just stepped into a trap. Ah, what?"

"That's your answer, Joshua. If you pay the storekeeper, will he be satisfied?"

"Of course."

"He won't insist that Charles actually make the payment?"

"No, not unless he's a dolt."

"One more question, then I'll make my point. If you pay for the window to the satisfaction of the storekeeper, is everything all right now?"

Again Joshua sensed he was being led, but there was only one answer to that. "Yes."

"But you haven't changed the past," Nathan said quietly.

Joshua saw it now and it hit him with full force. It showed in his eyes and around the corners of his mouth.

"Nothing in the past has been changed, Joshua, but mercy has been shown and justice has been satisfied." Nathan went on, slowly now, choosing his words with great care. "Suppose, then, that Jesus Christ went into the Garden of Gethsemane and on the cross, and there he suffered so intensely that he paid the price for all those horrible things that Joshua Steed did in the past. Suppose that he suffered enough that Joshua's beating of his wife was paid for, not by Joshua, but by the Redeemer. Would Jessica be satisfied with such a payment? not from you, but from the Savior?"

"Jessica would," he finally said. "Others might not, but Jessica would."

"And Olivia? If she knew that the Savior of all mankind suffered all of the pain and all of the injustice that her father's foolishness brought upon her, would she say that justice had been paid?"

He dropped his head and ran his hands through his hair. "I don't know."

"Yes, you do," Nathan urged. "You *do* know, Joshua. You know that Olivia has already forgiven you and if you could see her right now, she would throw her arms around you and tell you how much she loves you. You know that, don't you?"

"Yes." It came out in a tortured whisper.

"That's how Christ makes things right, Joshua. Not by changing the past, but by making atonement for it. All the broken windows are paid for. All the injustice, all the terrible crimes. Why would he do such a thing, especially for someone who has turned his back on him and fought against the very idea of him? Why would he do that?"

"I don't know." He was feeling pummeled now.

"Yes, you do," Nathan said gently. "Why would you pay for the window?"

There was a choked sound, then, "Because I love Charles."

"Yes, because you love him enough to extend mercy to him, even though on the basis of his actions alone he doesn't deserve your mercy."

Nathan sat back. "Well, unless you have some questions, I think that's about enough for one day."

"Thank you. Thank you for taking my questions seriously and not making me feel like a fool for asking them."

"No," Nathan shot right back, "thank you, Joshua. Your questions have made me think more deeply about what I believe. I've learned some things in trying to answer them."

———••———

"Mama?"

Lydia turned from the wagon where she was checking to see if everything was lodged in tight and securely covered. It had rained during the night and was still continuing. "Yes, Elizabeth Mary?"

"Do you promise that we get to see Papa today?"

Lydia turned to her six-year-old and took her by the shoulders. There were so many things that could happen—the muddy roads would slow them down; there could be a broken axle or wagon tongue, someone in need of help, a difficult ford at a stream, a call for an early halt—but she didn't have the heart to dash the hope in those large blue eyes. "Yes, Elizabeth Mary, I promise."

She danced away, squealing out the news for Josiah and little Joseph. Rachel and Emily appeared at the front of the wagon. Emily had a bucket of water, which she poured into a barrel lashed onto the side of the wagon bed. Rachel had a wad of papers that she was carefully placing beneath the straw mattress. Lydia smiled. She knew that it was Rachel's journal, and that pleased her. Emily had started a journal at the same time as Rachel, but it had lasted only a week or so. Then Brigham had come to the fire that night and talked about the importance of keeping journals. She had kept at it as faithfully as Rachel ever since.

Rachel looked up and saw that Lydia was watching her and smiled. "That's everything, Aunt Lydia. I think we're ready."

"Good." She stepped back enough to see where Josh was fussing with the yoke of the wheel team. "Are you ready, Josh?"

His shoulders were dark with wetness, and rain dripped from his hat, but he smiled. "I am, Mama. Just waiting for the signal."

A few yards away, Derek had followed their conversation. "We're ready." He turned to the wagon just beyond him and called. "Ready, Caroline?"

She raised an arm. "Ready."

Beyond them, Mary Ann and Jenny were up in their wagon seat. They too raised a hand and waved. At the head of their team Rachel's brother Luke stood ready. He waved back as well.

Rachel came to stand beside her aunt. "Do you think we'll get to stay at Mount Pisgah for a time?"

"That would be nice, wouldn't it?"

"Then maybe Mama and Papa and the family could catch up with us."

Lydia gave her a spontaneous hug, feeling her loneliness. "I think there's a good chance of that, Rachel. They said they could come on once they got things established there."

"Let's roll 'em," someone up ahead cried out. There was a cry of "Giddap!" and the lead wagon began to move. Everyone up and down the line straightened in anticipation.

"You girls," Lydia said on sudden impulse to Emily and Rachel. "Why don't you go be with Grandma and Aunt Jenny this morning. Just to give them some company."

"Yes, Mama," Emily said brightly, and they turned and trotted away, their feet making squishing sounds in the wet grass. Lydia smiled. No sisters could ever have been closer than these two cousins, and no daughter could have been more loved than Rachel. She turned forward, then walked up to stand beside her son.

"You heard Elizabeth Mary, son. I promised we'd find her papa today."

"Yes, Mama. I'd like that too."

It was a simple lunch of bread and cheese and water. Nathan and Joshua still had a small slab of ham and enough cornmeal to make some johnnycake, but they decided they would wait and have a celebration supper if the family made it in today. With the permission of Heber Kimball, they left the rail-splitting assignment for a time and went to work on preparing a campsite for the family. By midmorning the rain stopped, and they made good progress. They decided that even though their camp was about a quarter of a mile away from the main encampment, it was still a good place for the family. They cleared out some bushes, leveled the ground, gathered a large stack of firewood, laid logs across the brook so the wagons could cross it easily, cut willows, and built four more lean-tos like their own. They had sufficient tents, but with the weather warming now, the temporary shelters would allow some of the children to sleep outside instead of everyone crowding into the tents.

Now at midday they lay on some willows that kept them off the grass, which was still wet. Their stomachs were full and their backs tired. Nathan had his hat pulled over his eyes. Joshua had one arm thrown across his face.

"Are you anxious to see them?" Nathan asked after a moment.

"Yeah, aren't you?"

"I am. It's only been thirteen days, but it seems like a month. I was thinking about Tricia a moment ago. At her age, thirteen days can make a real difference. I'm excited to hold her again."

"I'll bet Livvy has a hundred things to show me," Joshua chuckled softly. "She is so fascinated with everything around her."

"She is," Nathan agreed. "I don't know that I've ever seen a more inquisitive child." Then he laughed. "Unless it is Savannah."

"Ah, Savannah," Joshua sighed. "Now, there's one to turn a man's hair gray. I hope she finds a strong-minded man to marry."

"Savannah is a wonderful girl, Joshua. She has some unusual gifts."

"I know, I know. I love her dearly, but, oh my, can she be exasperating."

Nathan pushed the brim of his hat up with his thumb so he could look at Joshua. "Only because she is so much like you. You know what Mama says? She says sometimes when she watches Savannah she sees you as a little boy all over again."

"Poor Mama," he groaned.

They lapsed into silence again, both of them thinking of their families and savoring the reunion that would soon be theirs.

"They are the most important thing in life to you, aren't they?"

Joshua opened his eyes. "Of course."

"More important than barns and stables, businesses and warehouses."

Joshua shut his eyes again. "I learned that the hard way, but yes."

"A lot of Christians picture hell as a place of eternal burning. Want to know what my idea of hell is?"

"What?"

"Spending eternity without Lydia. Never seeing Josh and Emily and all of them again."

Joshua did not answer, and Nathan had a sudden worry that he had crossed the line and was pushing him a little. But so be it, he decided. This needed to be said.

"Do you think a loving God would make you live for eternity without Caroline? Without Savannah and Charles and Livvy? What kind of heaven would that be?"

"Actually," Joshua said after a long moment of consideration, "that is one of the things about the Church that is very attractive. I can't imagine being without them."

"Don't you see, Joshua, that that's why we were so obsessed with finishing the temple before we left Nauvoo? God has said that sealing families together is so sacred that it can only be done in his house. Oh, he may approve temporary places until we can build a temple to him, but it must be done in his way and by his authority. Families. That's what it's all about. God has made it possible for families to be sealed together, so husbands and wives can be married for eternity. When it's all said and done, that is the heart of the gospel—to bind families together in a way that time cannot undo and death cannot destroy."

He paused, then finished quietly. "As we lie here, longing to be reunited with those we love again, just think about that. Olivia. Papa. Our first little Nathan who died in his mother's arms. We can all be bound together again in a way that death cannot destroy and time can never undo."

After several seconds of silence, Joshua finally spoke. "It wouldn't be hard to sell me on that idea, little brother," he murmured.

———◆———

"I think that's them."

Nathan stopped in mid-swing and lowered the ax. He peered eastward, where the road appeared on bluffs that rimmed the Grand River. It was about four hundred yards away, but it was nearly four o'clock and the sun had the whole east bank bathed in its full glare. There were four wagons already over the crest, and as they watched, two more followed. It was more than just the Steeds, but that was to be expected. But in the slanting rays of the late afternoon sun, Nathan immediately recognized the lanky figure of his son beside the lead oxen of the third wagon. And just behind him was Derek's stocky figure, walking beside Rebecca.

"It *is* them!" He swung the ax and buried it in the log. "Let's go!"

Joshua dropped the beetle and started after him. As they reached the fence, Nathan stopped. "Joshua?"

"What?"

"Are you going to tell Caroline about any of this?"

There was a momentary hesitation, then a shrug. "I don't know yet."

"You need to. You know that, don't you? The rest of the family is your choice, but you need to tell Caroline."

"I'll think about it."

And with that, both men vaulted over the fence and started trotting up the hill toward the oncoming wagons.

———•———

Mary Ann sat back and watched the two families come together in joyous reunion. She smiled happily. To watch them, you would think it had been years since they had seen each other instead of just a couple of weeks. Nathan had baby Tricia tucked under one arm and at the same time had another arm around Elizabeth Mary. Joshua was surrounded by Caroline, Savannah, Charles, and little Livvy, with Livvy noisily catching him up on everything that had happened since he left, including the two caterpillars she had caught while at Garden Grove. But, she added with a grave face, Mama had made her let them go so they could turn into butterflies.

The only thing to lessen the joy was Jenny. She stood beside Mary Ann next to Matthew's wagon. Matthew, of course, was not part of this reunion, having already left Mount Pisgah to press on ahead to the Missouri River. So Jenny stood back with her two girls, rejoicing for the other wives and children, sorrowing for her own.

Finally, Nathan broke free and came over to where they sat. He reached up and took his mother's hands. "How are you, Mama?"

"I'm fine."

"Really?"

"Yes. It's not been a hard trip at all. Some rain, but the roads weren't that terrible."

He turned. "And how about you and the children, Jenny?"

"We're fine too," she said brightly. "Derek has been wonderful. He spends almost as much time watching over us as he does Rebecca and their children." She turned to where Luke Garrett stood beside the oxen. "And Luke here has taken over as well as any man ever could."

The stepson of Jessica and Solomon ducked his head and smiled shyly. "I didn't do much," he murmured.

"On the contrary," Mary Ann said, watching him proudly, "if your real father were here today Luke, he would be very proud."

"Thank you, Luke," Nathan said, feeling tremendous gratitude for the boy. "Joshua and I have worried a lot about how our families would come along with us gone. Now I know there was no need to worry." He turned back to Jenny. "We got to see Matthew several times before he left. He was doing fine and said to be sure to tell you that he thinks about you and the children every day."

She smiled, clearly cheered. "Did he really say that?"

"He did. And there is some more good news."

"What?"

"President Young has decided that there is no way that all of us can go on to the Rocky Mountains this season. So he wants some of us to push on to Council Bluffs and establish a winter settlement there. He's going to ask a lot of the people to stop either in Garden Grove or here in Mount Pisgah. But he asked Joshua and me to take our family on to the Missouri. Matthew will be waiting there for us."

Her face broke into a huge smile. The light sprinkling of freckles across her cheeks made her seem almost like a little girl. "Really? He won't go on ahead again?"

"No," he responded. "No one pushes on from Council Bluffs until the rest of us get there." For now he didn't say anything about the possibilities of the men then having to leave their families and go to the Rocky Mountains. That was still unsettled, and until it was settled, there was no sense in making her worry. "We'll stay here another three or four days, let the teams rest up a little, help the ones who are staying, finish the fencing and plowing, then we'll leave."

"Oh, thank you, Nathan. That is good news."

She turned and walked to where Betsy Jo was with her cousins to tell her the news. Mary Ann watched her for a moment, then turned back to Nathan. "And how have you and Joshua been?" Mary Ann asked.

"Wonderful!"

She gave him a strange look.

"Oh," he said quickly, looking around to make sure no one was listening, "yes, he told me about his reading the Book of Mormon, and he said you and Lydia are the only others who know."

Mary Ann nodded. "And did you two have a chance to discuss things?"

"Yes. He still has a hundred questions, Mama, but he's talking. He's asking questions."

"So you think there's a chance?"

His face fell. "Yes, but I can't be sure. Sometimes it's like he's hungry for it. He wants to know everything. We'll talk for an hour or more. Then the very next day it's like we have never talked at all, like he doesn't even want to think about it."

"But he's still reading?"

"Yes." He told her about Joshua's prayer about Olivia and the confirmation that came.

"That's wonderful, Nathan. I'm so glad for that. That will make a big difference."

He was less enthusiastic now. "Don't get your hopes too high, Mama. There's still a long way to go." And then, seeing Joshua coming toward them, he spoke more loudly. "How are Jessica and Solomon?"

"Sad to see us go," she replied, "as you would suppose, but you know those two. If that is what our leaders ask of them, that is what they will do and they will do it happily."

Joshua joined them, listened to her answer, then swept her up. "Hello, Mama."

"Hello, Joshua. It's so good to see you two again."

"We missed you." He set her down again. "So do you think Solomon and Jessica will stay there for very long?" He was thinking about Rachel, who looked a little lost now as the families came together. If they went on to the Missouri, she would be a long way from her parents.

"No," Mary Ann replied. "When Elder Taylor passed through, he asked Solomon to stay long enough to get the houses finished and then to come on."

"And how long will that be?"

"Another four or five days. Maybe a week."

"That's all?" he said, pleased with that unexpected news. "That's great."

Nathan turned back to look at the family, now so obviously rejoicing. "So tonight we will all be around the campfire again."

"Yes," said Mary Ann. "I have a letter from Melissa I'll read to you. I think you'll be pleasantly surprised." Then she felt a great peace come over her. "Together again around the fire. I have missed that in these last two weeks."

"And so have we," Joshua said with feeling. "So have we."

The deer—three does and the yearling—were in almost exactly the same place as they had been before, near the banks of the river, about a hundred yards from them. Joshua stopped just inside the willows, taking Caroline's hand. "Look," he whispered, pushing aside the screening branches. "There they are."

She stepped up beside him and leaned forward slightly. "Oh, Joshua," she breathed. "They're beautiful."

"Yes." He was deeply pleased. It was right that the deer should be here again, and somehow that would make it easier for him.

"It really is a lovely place. No wonder Elder Pratt felt inspired to call it Mount Pisgah."

Joshua nodded. "In a way, it's going to be hard to leave here. This wouldn't be a bad place to put down your roots."

"Thank you for bringing me here." She turned to him and went up on her toes and kissed him softly. "It's so good to be back together again."

He kissed her back, marveling at how totally fulfilled he felt to have her beside him. "I guess I'm getting old or something, but I don't like being away from you anymore."

"Anymore?" she teased. "You mean you once did?"

"You know what I mean. When I used to go out on the trail or down to St. Louis or Savannah, I always missed you, but it was nothing like this. I have lain awake every night, thinking about you and the children. I don't like being apart."

"Neither do I. I never sleep well when you're not there."

He took her hand. "Move slowly, and I think we won't spook them." He pushed carefully through the branches and stepped slowly out into the clearing. The four deer jerked up, ears forward, one leg lifted ready for flight. The biggest doe, and therefore probably the wisest, took a step or two toward the trees. "Easy now," he said in a low voice. He brought Caroline through very slowly; then they stood motionless.

The deer were like statues, brown stone in a meadow of green. Finally the lead doe flicked her tail. The ears moved back again as she relaxed. "Sit down real slow," Joshua whispered. They sank to the thick grass, and again stayed motionless. After another full minute the big doe turned back to the willows. There was no threat here. Taking their signal from her, the others returned to eating as well.

"This is so beautiful, Joshua," Caroline murmured.

He took a quick breath, not looking at her. "There's something I need to talk with you about, Caroline."

She looked at him closely. "Is that why Nathan insisted on keeping the children with them?"

There was a soft laugh. "I suppose." By suppertime Joshua had decided he needed to tell Caroline everything, but he said nothing to Nathan about his decision. When the meal was finished and the dishes washed and put away, he casually mentioned that he might take Caroline for a walk down by the river. Instantly the children clamored to accompany them, but Nathan stepped in and gently but firmly suggested that their children stay with his children and play. Did he sense that Joshua had made his decision or was it just plain hope? Joshua wasn't sure, but either way he was grateful. This was not a time for children.

"So," she said. "What is it?"

He had rehearsed it in his mind a dozen times while they walked, trying to choose the best opening, the most appropriate words. Now they all fled. "I've thought about telling you sooner, but I was afraid that you might make more of it than what it is."

She was mystified. "Make more of what, Joshua?"

And so he told her. At first he was hesitant, almost stumbling as he told her about the day he had taken Lydia's Book of Mormon. As she gaped at him in utter amazement, he rushed on, the words tumbling out. He told her about reading it from time to time, about telling Lydia on the morning of their departure, of swearing her to secrecy, especially when it came to telling Caroline.

Caroline was not looking at him now. The initial amazement and joy had turned to hurt. He reached out and took her hands. "I know not telling you was wrong, but can't you see why, Caroline? I know how much my being a member of the Church would mean to you. I was afraid that you would just be disappointed."

"Disappointed?" she cried, her eyes glistening now. "How could you ever think that?"

"Not disappointed in what I was doing. Disappointed when nothing came of it. Even now I can see it in your eyes. You're so amazed, so pleased that at last I'm doing something. But that's all I'm doing, Caroline. I'm reading. I'm asking questions. I'm not ready to join the Church. I have too many things that don't make sense to me. And if it comes out that I decide I don't want to be a Mormon, are you telling me you won't be terribly disappointed?"

She started a retort, but then stopped. It was a fair question. "Well, I . . . Of course I would be disappointed."

"I just thought it would be easier if you didn't know for a time. I'm not saying that it was right, but that was my feeling."

And then Caroline realized what she was doing. She was doing the very thing he had been afraid of. She squeezed his hands and smiled at him. "I understand. It's all right." She had to stop as tears instantly filled her eyes and her words choked off. "What matters is that you have decided to search, Joshua. I am so happy that you would do that. And if nothing comes of it . . ." She sniffed back the tears. "Well, I will always love you for being willing to ask."

Greatly relieved, he went on. He told her of shooting the deer, of the sudden strange feelings about life and death. When he told her how he had realized that he had been whistling Olivia's song to himself and the impact it had on him—enough to drive him to his knees—she looked at him strangely, tears welling up again to trickle down her cheeks.

"Did you know that Savannah sings that all the time now?" she asked.

"She does?"

"All the time I hear her humming it or singing it softly to herself."

"Well, it is a haunting melody. Once it starts with me, I can't get it out of my head. Anyway," he said, coming back to his experience, "it wasn't much, I suppose, when you think of all the questions I have, but after that prayer, at least I knew that Olivia wasn't gone. And I knew that Papa still lives."

"Yes," she whispered. "Oh, yes, Joshua. That's the most important thing." She moved closer to him and he put an arm around her. She snuggled against him, feeling as though she would burst with joy.

"I told Nathan on the way here." He laughed shortly. "He was as shocked as you. Since then we've talked a lot. He's been trying to answer my questions."

"Joshua, there's something you need to know."

406

"What?"

"Well, you know that Savannah prays every night and morning that you will join the Church."

He pulled her in a little more tightly to him. "I suspect she's not the only one in our family who does."

She flashed him a warm smile. "I think you would be surprised to know how many of us do."

He *was* surprised. "Who else besides you and Savannah? And Mother, of course."

"Keep going."

"Well, Lydia and Nathan probably."

"And Derek and Rebecca, and Jessica and Solomon, and Jenny and Matthew, and Rachel and Emily and Josh."

"Rachel?" he said, stopping her. "How do you know that?"

"Emily told me. She said she and Rachel and Josh made a promise to each other that they would pray for you every night."

Joshua suddenly felt a lump in his throat. He found that not only astounding but deeply moving.

"Anyway," Caroline went on, "Savannah never forgets. She is determined that you must become a member before we reach the Rocky Mountains. You know how determined she can be, even at nine years old."

He smiled, remembering the day she had hidden herself when he refused to let her be baptized. They had not found her until the whole family was in a panic. "Yes, I do know that."

"Are you going to say anything to her about all this?"

He shook his head immediately. "No, nor to anyone else. Not for now." He saw her look and went on quickly. "You know what it will be, Caroline. Everyone asking me every day how things are going, watching me like I was a bug on a rock. I don't want that. Not yet."

Before she could protest further, he straightened and looked around. The sun was fully down now and twilight was closing swiftly. The deer had gone sometime during their conversation and they had the river and meadow to themselves. He turned back to Caroline, who was watching him. Her eyes were soft and filled with love and joy. He bent down and kissed her again. She put her arms around his neck and kissed him back. It was a long, lingering kiss, and one that said much.

When she finally pulled back, she seemed a little breathless. She smiled. "Joshua?"

"Yes?"

"You know that your joining the Church would make me very happy."

He frowned. "Yes."

"But do you also know that you don't have to join to make me love you?"

He reached out with his finger, tracing a line down her nose and then onto her lips. His voice was filled with wonder. "I know. I find that hard to believe, but yes, I know."

"Good." She stood up and pulled him up to face her. "Then don't you do it for me. You do it only for yourself, because you don't have to do anything to prove your love for me."

Solomon and Jessica were working in the garden plot behind the log cabin in Garden Grove. The structure had actually been built for someone else and then assigned to them to live in for the few days before they started west again. They would never see the harvest, but then they had never thought they were planting for themselves.

For the moment they were alone. Rachel and Luke had gone on with Lydia's family to Mount Pisgah. Eleven-year-old Mark, much to his complete delight, had been asked by one of the brethren to accompany a small hunting party. It would be only for the day, but when Solomon let him take the rifle, it was as if he visibly grew a full foot right on the spot.

John, the only child born of Jessica's marriage to her second husband, John Griffith, was down with the cabin construction crews. He was only eight, but the building of the cabins fascinated him. He would fetch tools or hold plumb lines or clean up the piles of wood chips. Normally that was where Solomon would have been too, but by rotating assignment the men were asked to stay at home and plant gardens so that there would be fresh vegetables in the coming months. And today was his day. The men insisted that Solomon let young John come anyway. So Solomon and Jessica were left with only Miriam and little Solomon. Miriam was in the shade of the cabin, playing with the baby in his small rocking crib.

Solomon stopped for a moment and let his eyes sweep across the little village that was springing into existence virtually as they watched. It was something that filled him with satisfaction. Solomon, though a teacher by profession, had always been a man of the soil. He found a deep enjoyment in working with his hands and seeing something erected where nothing had been before, or seeing ripened crops waving gently in an afternoon breeze where before there had been only unbroken prairie.

It had been just over a month ago that Brigham Young determined to make Garden Grove the first of a series of semipermanent way stations along the way. Since that time, with the fifty or so men that Brigham had left, and the new ones coming in, they had cleared, plowed, and planted over five hundred acres. They had put in wheat and corn and rye and barley. They had acres of potatoes, squash, beans, and cucumbers. A hundred garden plots were already sprouting radishes, onions, peas, carrots, beets, and tomatoes. They had cut an estimated ten thousand rails for fencing—a staggering number when you thought about what work that entailed. They had enough logs cut for forty more houses in addition to the dozen or so that were already completed. His and Jessica's work here was nearly done, but when he left, it would be with a satisfied heart. There would be many people, especially those who were poor, who would reap the fruits of Solomon and Jessica's labors.

He looked back to where Jessica was bent over, dropping the kernels of sweet corn in small hills she had formed with the hoe.

Solomon was putting the entire upper northwest corner of the garden into hills of red potatoes. He had carefully cut up each potato so there were two "eyes" on each piece. From them would come the shoots that would grow into the deep green clusters that signaled a healthy potato hill.

About half a mile away a line of wagons came out of the trees and started toward them. It was a common sight, with dozens arriving almost every day now. But the sight of them always stirred him a little, and he stopped and leaned on his shovel, watching their slow progress. He wondered how many would stop here and how many would go on. He also wondered how long it would be before the presidency of the settlement said to him, "It is enough, Brother Solomon. You may continue on and join your family now." But such speculation was pointless. When it was time they would go. Until then they would try to do their part. With that, he straightened and went back to his digging.

It was five minutes later, as the wagons began passing them on the nearby road, that Jessica straightened and lifted a hand to shade her eyes. "Is that Mark?" she asked.

Solomon scanned the group of wagons, then nodded in surprise. About halfway back in the group there was Mark, rifle over his shoulder, striding along with some other men. Even as Solomon spotted him, he saw them and waved. He said something to the men, then broke off and trotted up and around the fence and then directly toward them.

When he reached them, Solomon spoke. "You're back early. No luck?"

Mark set the rifle down carefully against the rail fence and leaned against it. "They shot two deer. I shot at a squirrel"— there was a look of disgust—"but I missed him clean."

"Well, maybe some other—"

"Pa," he cut in, "there's news."

"Oh?"

"What?" Jessica said, coming over to join them now.

"We're at war with Mexico."

For a moment, that didn't register. "Who's at war with Mexico?" he asked.

"The United States. Those people just coming in said it's all over the papers back home. President Polk has declared war against Mexico. He's calling for troops to march to Texas and drive the Mexicans out."

Jessica turned to Solomon, her mouth twisting a little at the corners with anxiety. "Isn't where we are going supposed to be part of Mexico?" she asked.

Mark's eyes widened perceptibly. "Are we going to war, Papa?"

"No, no, nothing like that."

"So what *does* it mean, Solomon?" Jessica asked.

"Well, the United States drove us out," he said after a moment, still considering the implications of the news. "Maybe Mexico will be glad to take us in."

————— ◆ —————

Peter Ingalls stood beneath the huge oak tree, hat in hand, feeling the hot south wind pull at his hair and parch his face. No wonder the locals called it Kansas, he thought. Technically, this was somewhere between Indian Territory and that vast tract of land noted on the maps as "Unclaimed Territory." Indian Territory was that portion of land beyond the western borders of the United States that the U.S. government had designated for resettlement of the various eastern Indian tribes back in 1825. Over thirty tribes had eventually been brought here. It was a bewildering roll call of names—Chippewa, Omaha, Delaware, Fox, Iowa, Kickapoo, Ottawa, Shawnee, Sauk, Wyandot. They had all come to occupy the lands of the Kansa, or Kaw, tribe, who were native to the area. Someone in Independence had told Peter that the word *Kansa* meant "people of the south wind." After a week of moving across their territory, he believed it.

He turned his head, looking westward across the vast sea of sunflowers that bobbed in the wind like children playing "Mother, May I." He could see the faint line of trees that marked the winding Big Blue River and the circle of wagons waiting to cross the swollen stream. They had been stalled here for three days while they waited for the water to go down and the men constructed a ferry to take them across. They couldn't afford to delay much longer.

Peter felt momentary guilt. Was he more concerned about moving on than he was about old Mrs. Keyes? But then he shook it off. No. He was truly sorry to see Mrs. Reed's mother die. She had always been wonderful to him and Kathryn, and her passing would leave a void in the company. Patty, the Reeds' eight-year-old daughter, was especially devastated. She had been very close to her grandmother and had a deep fear that the Indians would dig up her body. But Peter also knew that the past few days had been one long agony for Mrs. Keyes, every jolt of the wagon adding to her growing pain and draining the last of her reserves. It was a blessing that she had finally succumbed early this morning.

He looked around. Mr. Reed had chosen the site for the burial of his mother-in-law well. They had dug the grave at the foot of a large upland burr oak tree near the bank of a small creek. This morning Baylis Williams, another of Mr. Reed's hired men, carved an inscription in its bark, and thus the tree also became the headboard. Once the services were over and the grave filled in again, they cut sod and laid over it. They also placed a stone at one end, which read simply, "Mrs. Sarah Keyes, Died May 29, 1846: Aged 70." The children gathered huge clusters of sunflowers to lay at their grandmother's last resting place. Kathryn, who due to her handicap rode in the wagon with Mrs. Keyes every day and who had grown quite close to her, had asked Peter to dig up some wildflowers and replant them around the tree. Reed had even found some young cedar trees somewhere and had them replanted nearby as well.

But now it was over. The company had returned to camp, about a mile away. Even the rest of their immediate party—the two Donner brothers and their wives, Baylis and his half sister, Eliza, some of the other hired help—had gone back, the men talking about needing to continue their work on the ferry. James Reed caught Peter's eye and nodded. He had seen Peter looking toward the river. He knew exactly what he was thinking and he agreed. This had been their first death and it cast a pall over the whole train. But everyone knew it wouldn't be the last. On the trail, death was part of life. On the trail, grief was expected and honored, but it was not waited on. There was work to do.

Reed turned to his wife. "Margret, we have to go."

She straightened slowly, her eyes red, her face haggard and drawn. When they had started from Springfield, Mrs. Reed had not been in wonderful health herself, but she had thrived on the regimen of the trek. Now the death of her mother had set her back visibly. She leaned heavily on his arm as they started back toward the wagon.

Peter turned to Kathryn. She sniffed, wiping at her eyes with the back of one hand, then bent down and laid a small bouquet of wildflowers on the mound. They were already withered and dying in the heat. "Good-bye, dear Mrs. Keyes," she whispered. "I shall miss you. And when we get to California, I shall plant flowers around the house for you as I promised."

She straightened and reached out for her crutches. Peter handed them to her. "She so wanted to see California," she mourned.

"I know, but now she can rest."

To his surprise, Kathryn let him take her arm as they started away, falling in behind the Reeds. When they reached the wagon, Peter saw Kathryn up safely inside, then went immediately to the oxen. They turned their heads at the sound of his voice. "Hello, Bully Boy," he said to the nearest of the wheel team, a brindled two-year-old that was his favorite. He scratched him behind the ear. "Did you think I'd forgotten you?" He reached across his back. "Hey, Dan, I know you're thirsty, old boy, but we'll be back to the river shortly. You'll have to be careful, though. You can't be drinking too fast in this heat."

From her seat in the wagon, Kathryn watched him move

alongside the four yoke. It amazed her to see the affection he had developed for them. To her they were but brute animals, valued because they kept the wagon moving, but all the same in temperament and looks. To him they were individual children, to be encouraged and praised, wheedled and coaxed, and occasionally scolded. Once, when old Bully, as he called him, had eaten something that left him lowing painfully throughout the night, Peter had sat beside him and stroked his neck until morning.

Mr. Reed appeared beside her. He gestured toward his wife, who was lying down nearby. "Margret is resting, Kathryn. I'm going to ride ahead and help the others. If there are any problems, have Peter fire one shot with the rifle and I'll come back."

"Yes, Mr. Reed."

He walked to the side entrance, hopped down, and walked to where his horse was tied. "All right, Peter. Let's move 'em out."

———•◆•———

The ferry was completed the following day, Saturday, and the company christened it the *Blue River Rover*. But they were able to get only eight or nine wagons across the river by the end of the day, and so they would have to spend all their time Sunday getting the rest over. The wagons belonging to the Donner and Reed families were among those that would have to be ferried across tomorrow.

When Peter came back from watering the oxen and then hobbling them for the night, the Reed family were all together in the wagon and the flaps were drawn. He could see their shadows on the canvas as they moved about and talked quietly. He stopped, seeing if he could distinguish a shadow with crutches, but he could not. About fifteen yards away, behind the Reeds' lead wagon, the two supply wagons were parked side by side. There was a blazing fire in front of them, and Peter could see Eliza Williams, the hired woman, sitting beside her half brother, Baylis. Eliza was very nearly deaf, and Baylis had his head close to hers and was talking loudly to her. But Kathryn was not there either.

Peter moved to the back of the family wagon and prepared to knock and ask Mr. Reed if Kathryn was inside, but as he came around the wagon, he saw her there before their own cook fire, which was now low and nearly gone, sitting on a log by herself.

He stopped for a moment, watching her and smiling to himself. She was staring into the embers, the profile of her face etched in the faint light of the glowing coals. As he had so many times before, he marveled that he, Peter Ingalls, bumbling, unlearned factory worker from Preston, England, had been lucky enough to have this winsome Irish lass agree to be his bride. Smiling more broadly, he stepped forward. "Hi."

She turned, her face instantly breaking into a joyous smile of her own. "Hello, Peter."

He moved over and sat down beside her.

"Are you finished?" she asked.

"Yep. They're settled for the night."

"And no guard duty?"

"Not tonight."

"Wonderful."

He put an arm around her. "What were you thinking about? You looked very contemplative."

She laughed. "Contemplative? You ought to be a writer, Peter. Maybe work for a newspaper or something."

Her comment struck a tender chord and his face sobered. "That would be nice again."

She snuggled against him. "It will come, Peter. You heard what Will and Alice said in their letter. The *Brooklyn* is carrying a printing press. They'll bring it to California and then on to wherever the Saints settle. That's how strongly President Young feels about having our own newspaper."

"Yes, I know. It seems like it will never happen, but someday we will find a home and then . . ." He sighed, then remembered his news. "Guess what."

"What?"

"You know that group that caught up with us this afternoon and joined us?"

"Yes."

"I told you about the two brothers-in-law—Pike and Foster—who are traveling with their mother-in-law, who is a widow."

She was puzzled now. "Yes?"

"Guess who the mother-in-law is."

She shook her head. "Someone we know?"

"Yes! Sister Murphy. Sister Levinah Murphy."

For a moment she was blank; then it hit her. "Sister Murphy from Tennessee, who was in Nauvoo for a time?"

"The very same. Can you believe it? Foster and Pike married her daughters. I thought their names sounded familiar when they introduced themselves today. I'm pretty sure she mentioned them to me in one of her letters. But it didn't all click in my mind until I had a chance to talk with them. The Pikes, along with Sister Murphy and her unmarried children, got an outfit together in Tennessee, then headed to Missouri and met the Fosters in St. Louis. When they all got to Independence they heard that Colonel Russell's big wagon train had already left and so they hurried along to join it, just like we did."

Now, there was a coincidence, Kathryn thought. It had been Sister Murphy who, in a letter, had first planted the thought in Peter's mind about going west with someone else so that he and Kathryn wouldn't have to try to outfit themselves.

"They took me to see her. It was her, all right. She was as flabbergasted as I was."

"So, are Pike and Foster members of the Church too?"

"I didn't dare ask. I don't think so. Sister Murphy didn't even mention the Church, and so I didn't either."

He sat back now. "It's not much to make a difference, but at least we won't be the only Latter-day Saints going west with this group."

Kathryn nodded. It was a strange coincidence. And she had

been a little worried about being in the same company as ex-Governor Boggs and other Jackson County mobocrats, who had joined up with the Russell train a few days before the Donners and Reeds had. Not that one widowed woman would make a lot of difference if the Missourians decided to make trouble.

So far, fortunately, she and Peter had had little to do with Lilburn W. Boggs and his group, and that was just fine with her. There had been a recent incident, however, that had left an impression on her mind. The other night, while many members of the company were sitting around a central campfire, one of the men mentioned hearing that groups of Mormons were heading west on the trail this season. Kathryn had glanced at Boggs at that moment, and she could see that he had become visibly nervous at the man's comment. It reminded her of what she once heard Joseph Smith say: "Those who have done wrong always have that wrong gnawing them." It was apparent to her that what Boggs had done to the Latter-day Saints back in Missouri gave him the face of a guilty man whenever he heard the word *Mormons*.

Peter seemed to sense the direction her thoughts were going. He leaned over and kissed her lightly. "Well, I see the Reeds have already started preparing for bed. Are you ready?"

She nodded. "I was just waiting for you."

"I'm glad." He stood up, holding out his hand.

She pushed it aside. "Watch, Peter. I want to show you something." Her crutches were propped on the log beside her. She picked them up, but only to toss them away from her. Then she straightened, bracing her hands on the log on which she was sitting.

To his amazement, after a moment she pushed herself up, her body straightening slowly. He could see that she trembled a little, but she was steady and there was no danger of her falling. In a moment she was fully erect and looking at him triumphantly.

"Bravo," he said softly and started toward her.

"No, no," she cried. "Stay there."

He stepped back again.

Biting her lip, concentrating fiercely, she lifted one foot and moved it ahead. Now he tensed, suddenly anxious that she might fall. But he willed himself to remain where he was. She shifted her body weight to that foot, steadied herself, then came forward five or six inches. Now her other foot was lifted slowly and placed ahead. Again there was the momentary steadying of herself, and then she stepped forward. Laughing quietly, she repeated it one more time. This time she started to wobble, and Peter took one step forward and let her fall into his arms. He was astonished. "You walked, Kathryn! Without your crutches!"

"Yes!" she exclaimed. "Can you believe it?"

He pressed her to him. "No, I can't. That's wonderful!"

"I know. Being out here is making me stronger, Peter. I can feel it."

He took her face in both of his hands and now saw the wetness on her cheeks. He kissed them both softly. "I love you, Kathryn McIntire," he whispered.

"No," she whispered back. "Kathryn Ingalls, Peter. And don't you ever forget it."

———◆———

Thirty-year-old Jesse C. Little, president of the Eastern States Mission, strode along the boardwalk of Pennsylvania Avenue, gazing across the broad lawns to the building that stood shimmering white in the noonday sun. It was as if it were lit from within and glowed of its own accord. Jesse had seen this building before, but its appearance was still impressive. After all, this was not just *a* white house; it was *the* White House.

Walking beside him was Amos Kendall, former postmaster general and current advisor to the president. During the past several days since Jesse's arrival in Washington, D.C., Kendall had proven to be very helpful, offering information and advice and acting as an intermediary between the Mormon leader and the president. Jesse had written a letter to President James K.

Polk two days ago, June first, earnestly appealing for the government's help in the Saints' westward migration. In response, the president had asked Kendall to bring Jesse to the White House today, June third, for a meeting at noon.

Realizing that his efforts were, it seemed, finally going to pay off, Jesse now found himself remembering the letter he had received some months before from Brigham Young. He had read it enough times by now that many parts of it were committed to memory. The letter had set forth Jesse's appointment as president of the Eastern States Mission of The Church of Jesus Christ of Latter-day Saints. In addition to noting his ecclesiastical duties, it instructed him to use "whatever means were at hand" to obtain from the government of the United States "those things which would be of mutual benefit" to Washington and to the Saints. It went on to say: "If our government shall offer any facilities for emigrating to the Western coast, embrace those facilities, if possible. As a wise and faithful man, take every honorable advantage of the times you can. Be thou a savior and a deliverer of that people, and let virtue, integrity and truth, be your motto—salvation and glory the prize for which you contend."

Wise and faithful man? Well, that was what he had tried his best to be. Jesse appreciated and was humbled by the confidence that Brigham Young placed in his abilities. Now he was going to meet with the president of the United States. Though Jesse was no wilting flower—when he set his mind to accomplish something, he pursued it with great energy and determination—and though he had already met President Polk during a reception at the White House a couple of weeks before, he could not help shuddering just a bit as he contemplated meeting privately with the chief executive of the United States.

"Nervous?"

He looked up in surprise. Amos Kendall was watching him with some amusement.

"No, not at all," Jesse answered. "I'm just trembling because of the cold."

Kendall laughed easily. It was almost noon on a summer day and both men were perspiring lightly beneath their coats. "Come on, now. The president is just a man like you and me." He motioned toward the gate. "He'll meet us in the Green Drawing Room."

When they got to the gate, a guard opened it for them and they stepped through. As they walked slowly up the long carriage drive, Kendall went on. "I think you'll like the Green Drawing Room. As you know, John and Abigail Adams were the first to move into the White House in 1800. Dolley Madison, that incomparable hostess, started a major and elegant redecoration when she moved in in 1809, but all that was lost when the British burned the house in 1814."

They had reached the steps now, and Kendall barely paused as he waved airily to the man posted there and walked straight in. "The Monroes were the first presidential couple to live in the White House after it was reconstructed. Mrs. Monroe decorated one small parlor room with green silks. It was very elegant. Then when John Quincy Adams was elected president, he began to use the room for small receptions or teas and called it the 'Green Drawing Room.' And through all the years since the Monroes were here, it's been kept decorated in green."

His voice dropped to a conspiratorial whisper. "But they say that the color Andrew Jackson later chose was roundly disapproved of by the women as being 'odious from the sallow look it imparts.'"

Jesse nodded, feeling a little sallow himself. If all of this historical patter was supposed to put him at ease, it wasn't working very well.

They moved up one flight of stairs, then down a long hallway. Kendall stopped at a door and knocked softly. There was a muffled "Come in," and he opened the door and motioned Jesse to go in.

The room was green, all right. And it was elegant beyond anything he had seen before. But there was no time to dwell on these impressions, for Jesse's attention was soon riveted on President James K. Polk, who rose from a chair as soon as the two men entered. Kendall quickly shut the door behind them. "Good afternoon, Mr. President. I believe you've met Mr. Jesse C. Little from New Hampshire."

For all Kendall's brave front, Jesse noted with satisfaction that during the brief interchange that followed, even Amos Kendall's demeanor changed when they were actually in the presence of the president of the United States. Not that Polk was a particularly imposing man. But the office that he held was imposing enough for any person. It was almost as though there were an aura surrounding it, and it affected Kendall too.

The president showed them to a sofa, and then sat down himself. Polk inquired briefly after Kendall's family, then turned the conversation for a minute or two to some items that were now before the Congress. Finally he turned to Jesse. "Mr. Little, I'm glad for this opportunity to speak with you. From your letter, which I have read with interest, I understand that you come as a representative of your people, the Mormons."

"Yes, Mr. President, I do."

"And I take it that you can speak for the leader of your people, Brigham Young?"

In his coat pocket Jesse was carrying the letter he had received from President Young. Now he withdrew it and extended it out. "I have a letter from him if you'd like to read it."

Polk waved a hand. "That won't be necessary. From the information I've received, I have full confidence in you. Let's move on to the matters you brought up in your communication. Please elaborate on what it is the Mormons want."

"Well, as I explained in my letter, a large body of our people is currently leaving the United States and heading for the Rocky Mountains."

"Yes, yes," the president said impatiently, "I've known of that for some time now." Jesse was a bit taken aback by the sudden exasperation in Polk's voice. "In January," the president continued,

"I received a letter from Governor Thomas Ford of Illinois saying that the Mormons were planning to emigrate westward. A shameful affair. Where was the governor in all of this? Why didn't he offer your people more protection?"

Jesse tried not to stare. So the president's irritation was not directed at him but at Governor Ford. That was like a cooling mist on a summer's day. It also confirmed what Kendall and others had told him about President Polk's relatively sympathetic attitude toward the Latter-day Saints.

"Senator Semple of Illinois has likewise briefed me on the situation," Polk went on. He looked at Kendall. "And, as I recall, Brigham Young offered to help when I made the proposal to Congress a few months back to build a series of stockade forts along the Oregon Trail, did he not?"

"That's correct, Mr. President. The Mormons offered to build *and* man them."

"Yes." He turned back to Jesse. "Now, from what you say in your letter, Mr. Little, you are here to seek assistance for your people, correct?"

"Sir, I am here to learn the policy of the federal government toward our people and especially toward our migration to Upper California."

The president rose from his chair and began to circle the room, studying the paintings on the walls as he spoke. "The Constitution of the United States of America requires that your people be treated as all other American citizens, without regard to the sect to which you belong or the beliefs which you may profess. What has happened in Missouri and Illinois is without excuse, in my eyes. But that can no longer be helped. I personally have no prejudices against your people that would induce any other form of treatment than that promised by the Constitution."

"Thank you, Mr. President," Jesse Little said with genuine relief. "That is an important thing for us to know. And you should know too, sir, that we are Americans in all our feelings and are friends of the United States."

Nodding in acknowledgment of Jesse's words, Polk came back around to face the two men. His hand came up and punctuated his speech as he talked. "As you know, our country is at war. We have seen American blood shed on American soil. The Mexican people have declared that they mean to stand in the way of our manifest destiny, which is to spread our country from the Atlantic to the Pacific. We cannot allow their actions to go unanswered. And while we are occupied with Mexico, I cannot be worrying about Britain or France stepping in to interfere or complicate matters."

"I understand that you are calling for fifty thousand volunteers to help win the war, Mr. President," Jesse volunteered, emboldened by Polk's firm declaration of impartiality toward the Mormons.

"Yes, I am. They will be formed up in three armies. Plans are already under way. We are at war, Mr. Little. Dithering and delay do not win wars."

"Yes, sir."

"And that is where you and your people come in. As I'm sure Mr. Kendall has already mentioned to you, I want to know if five hundred or more of the Mormons now on their way to Upper California would volunteer to enter the United States Army in that war and serve under the command of a United States officer."

Jesse straightened and leaned forward, feeling a sudden thrill at what he had just heard. Kendall had mentioned this possibility to him several days ago. Now the president himself was asking Jesse about it directly. This was far more than he had hoped for when he first arrived in Washington. Far more. "Yes, sir, Mr. President, I have no doubt that they will do as they are asked. And if the United States will receive them into service, I shall depart immediately to overtake our people and make the arrangements for them to do so."

The president had been intense and forceful. His demeanor now softened and he smiled broadly. "Good. That is what I wanted to hear. I have confidence in your people as American citizens. If I did not, I would not make such proposals." The president now stood. "I would like to discuss this subject further tomorrow with you and Mr. Kendall. I have matters I wish to go over with the secretary of the navy and others."

Jesse and Kendall now stood up as well. "We're happy to come back tomorrow," said Kendall.

Jesse nodded his assent. "Thank you, Mr. President," he said. "I am confident that President Young will respond positively to your request."

"I certainly hope so." Polk shook Jesse's hand briefly. Then, apparently as an afterthought, he said, "I understand that Colonel Thomas Kane is a mutual friend of ours."

Jesse smiled. "Yes. I met him only last month in Philadelphia, but he has become a very good friend and has offered me some sound advice."

"I don't doubt it. I've been in touch with him lately as well. I think your people have found a fine advocate in Thomas. His father and I are good friends." Polk then turned to the former postmaster general. "Amos, thank you for making the arrangements. You've been most helpful as always."

"It's my pleasure, Mr. President. But actually Mr. Little here deserves a lot of the credit. He can be very persuasive."

Jesse felt his face flush a little at that, and the president laughed as they moved toward the door. "I've learned that for myself now," Polk said. When they reached the door, he shook hands with Jesse one last time. "Again, Mr. Little, thank you for coming and for your response. I think we can take an action that will be mutually beneficial to the both of us."

"I think so too," Jesse said fervently. "Thank you again, Mr. President."

Chapter Notes

The Congress of the United States ratified President Polk's declaration of war against Mexico on 13 May 1846. It was not until 27 May that word of that declaration reached the settlement at Garden Grove. It would be even longer than that before Brigham Young would know. (See *CN*, 1 June 1996, p. 12.)

One of the reasons why James Reed had the unusual wagon, which Virginia Reed called the "pioneer palace car," constructed for his family was to provide comfort for Sarah Keyes, mother of his wife, Margret. But, reportedly suffering from consumption, Mrs. Keyes found the rigors of six weeks on the trail to be too much for her and she died on 29 May, somewhere near present-day Marysville, Kansas. This was the first recorded death in the Donner-Reed party. The details of her burial site were recorded by some of those who were present. (See Edwin Bryant, *What I Saw in California* [1848; reprint, Lincoln: University of Nebraska Press, 1985], pp. 63–64; diary of George McKinstry, in Dale Morgan, ed., *Overland in 1846: Diaries and Letters of the California-Oregon Trail* [1963; reprint, Lincoln: University of Nebraska Press, 1993], pp. 208–9. See also Kristin Johnson, ed., *"Unfortunate Emigrants": Narratives of the Donner Party* [Logan, Utah: Utah State University Press, 1996], pp. 18–19, 269 n. 11.)

The affection that the novel depicts Peter having for his oxen was common among the drovers along the trail. Joseph F. Smith, son of Hyrum and Mary Fielding Smith, drove his mother's teams across the trail in 1848. He later stated: "My team consisted of two pairs, or yokes, of oxen. My leaders' names were Thom and Joe—we raised them from calves, and they were both white. My wheel team were named Broad and Berry. Broad was light brindle with a few white spots on his body, and he had long, broad, pointed horns, from which he got his name. Berry was red and bony and short horned. Thom was trim built, active, young, and more intelligent than many a man. Many times while traveling sandy or rough roads, long, thirsty drives, my oxen, lowing with the heat and fatigue, I would put my arms around Thom's neck, and cry bitter tears! That was all I could do. Thom was my favorite and best and most willing and obedient servant and friend. He was choice!" (Cited in Joseph Fielding Smith, comp., *Life of Joseph F. Smith, Sixth President of The Church of Jesus Christ of Latter-day Saints* [Salt Lake City: Deseret Book Co., 1969], pp. 155–56.)

Levinah (sometimes spelled Lavinia or Lavina) Murphy was a member of the Church who, with her family, joined the Russell wagon train near the Big Blue River in present-day Kansas. This was about a week or so after the Donners and the Reeds had joined Russell's group. The records concerning Levinah Murphy's background are somewhat sparse and, in certain instances, apparently contradictory, but here is what can be generally said: Levinah was converted to the Church in 1836 while living in Tennessee, became a widow in 1839, and sometime after this moved to Nauvoo. After her two older daughters were married in late 1842, she and her unmarried children eventually moved back to Tennessee, where they were soon joined by Levinah's daughter Harriet and Harriet's husband, William Pike. It is thought that Levinah, now far from Nauvoo, may have heard about the Saints' plans to head to Upper California and perhaps saw her family's journey west as a way to join up with the Church. When the Donners and the Reeds split off from the large wagon train at the "parting of the ways" (near present-day Farson, Wyoming), the Murphy family chose to travel with the Donners and thus became part of the tragedy that later befell them. (See unpublished memoir of William G. Murphy, 1896, typescript; letter of Mary Murphy to her relatives, 25 May 1847, in Jack Steed, *The Donner Party Rescue Site: Johnson's Ranch on Bear River*, 3d ed. [Santa Ana, Calif.: Graphic, 1993], pp. 15–16; Joseph A. King, *Winter of Entrapment: A New Look at the Donner Party*, rev. ed. [Lafayette, Calif.: K&K Publications, 1994], p. 229; Eugene E. Campbell, "The Mormons and the Donner Party," *BYU Studies* 11 [Spring 1971]: 307–11.)

After declaring war on Mexico on 13 May 1846, the government of the United States, spurred on by the determination of President James K. Polk, a committed expansionist, immediately began to raise and equip an army. The need for men coincided exactly with the westward movement of the Latter-day Saints. Under date of 3 June 1846, President Polk's personal diary has a notation about the visit from "Mr. Amos Kendall & Mr. J[esse] C. Little of Petersborough, N. H. (a mormon)." The conversation recorded in this chapter is drawn from President Polk's diary and from Jesse C. Little's report to Brigham Young and the rest of the Twelve. (See *The Diary of James K. Polk During His Presidency, 1845 to 1849*, ed. Milo M. Quaife, 4 vols. [Chicago: A. C. McClurg and Co., 1910], 1:445–46; MHBY, pp. 211–21.)

Certain statements in Polk's diary have generated speculation as to when the president actually intended the Mormons to be enlisted in the army— before the Saints reached the West or after they did so. However, orders written by the secretary of war on 3 June 1846 and sent to the commander of the Army of the West, Colonel Stephen W. Kearny—orders that Polk undoubtedly had a hand in drawing up—seem to allow for the immediate enlistment of a Mormon battalion. Moreover, those orders granted Colonel Kearny plenty of latitude to do as he saw fit. So regardless of what Polk's intentions may or may not have been, there was obviously little doubt in Kearny's mind concerning what action to take: the Mormons were to be enlisted now. (See Richard E. Bennett, *Mormons at the Missouri, 1846–1852: "And Should We Die . . ."* [Norman: University of Oklahoma Press, 1987], pp. 52–56.)

By the first week of June, the determination of what to do and how to proceed had become firmly established in the mind of Brigham Young. The news brought by John Taylor that there were thousands of Saints strung across Iowa could not be ignored. They had two semi-permanent way stations now with over two thousand acres plowed and planted. Garden Grove and Mount Pisgah would provide critical places of shelter for the winter, which would come all too soon. But it wouldn't be enough. A third settlement established at Council Bluffs on the Missouri River would be needed, and it would be the largest of all. Once that was under way, a vanguard party, made up mostly of men with strong teams, good wagons, and ample provisions, would push on to the Rocky Mountains, arriving, it was hoped, in time to plant enough crops to see them through the winter. In the spring they would return to guide the rest of the Saints to their new home.

Both Joshua and Nathan believed strongly that some of the Steed men should become part of that vanguard company. But they didn't talk much about it. Their previous decision to hold a family council on the matter was postponed until they reached the Missouri River. There were too many unanswered questions, and there was not much point in stirring up anguish over something that was still so tentative. For now, they were content to enjoy having the family reunited.

Work on Mount Pisgah went forward at a breathtaking pace. With wagons pouring in every day, now there were three or four hundred men plowing, planting, building, hunting, fencing, grinding grain. The women were no less serviceable. They worked in the gardens, cut grass for the stock, cut and dried the meat the hunters brought in, mended clothing, aired out the bedding. For those who would be going on from Mount Pisgah, there were the additional tasks of preparing for departure. From first light until full dark the work rushed forward, with everyone except the smallest of children pressed into service.

The Steeds had a momentary scare on May thirty-first when, during the worship services, Brigham reminded the Saints that in spite of the fact that they were homeless wanderers in the wilderness, they could not forget their obligation to take the gospel to the world. Everyone in camp knew exactly what that meant. There were going to be missionaries called. With Wilford Woodruff back from England, that was the most likely place where help was needed. Since Derek was from England and Matthew had already served with him there, they were prime candidates. Nathan's successful mission to Canada put him in the running as well. Not that there was ever the slightest question about answering the call, but leaving now would be a particularly challenging sacrifice. They held their collective breath until later that afternoon when word went out that three missionaries had been called to serve—two to go to England and one to the Eastern States. The names were read, and a heartfelt sense of relief was experienced around the Steed camp. That feeling was dampened somewhat by their continued awareness that Matthew, gone ahead to help prepare the road, was absent from their family circle.

The first day of June, 1846, which was a Monday, dawned rainy and cold. It was not the heavy rains of March and April and May, but it was still discouraging. Never had they been so ready for summer. The rain continued off and on throughout the day, but Brigham was not deterred. With the warmer days here at last, usually some part of every day had clear skies and sunshine. The water drained quickly in the prairie sod, and the days of deep sloughs and endless mud bogs were mostly gone. Accordingly, at four that afternoon Brigham's first company of fifty crossed the river, though Brigham himself stayed at Mount Pisgah, needing to take care of some important Church business.

It was cold again the next morning, Tuesday, when more wagons began to line up at the narrow bridge that spanned the Grand River. Brigham was in the lead, his wagons rolling across shortly before ten a.m., and the rest soon followed. They moved only four miles up the river that day, catching up with the first company of fifty, who had arrived at this spot the evening before. That afternoon Brigham found it necessary to make a quick trip back to Mount Pisgah to finish up some business. He returned to the westward-bound camp later that night.

Then on Wednesday they left the Grand River for the last time and struck out in a northwesterly direction. They followed the faint trail left by George Miller's advance party. Happily, Bishop Miller was finally doing what Brigham had called him to do. When they came to a creek they found that the advance party had done one of three things—they had found a good fording place and marked it clearly, or they had cut down the banks so that the wagons could easily cross, or, if neither of the first two had been possible, they had built simple bridges.

The weather softened and cleared, and progress was steady. A succession of new names went into the journals—Twelve-

Mile Prairie Camp, Broomberry Hill Camp, Small Creek Prairie Camp. The company was helped greatly when on Friday they struck a well-traveled Indian trail which led westward to Council Bluffs on the Missouri River. This was viewed as a mixed blessing, since Indian trails meant Indian tribes. By Saturday, June sixth, they had come about sixty miles from Mount Pisgah. That afternoon, for the first time since leaving Nauvoo, Brigham ordered the wagons to form a large circle when they camped. To no one's surprise, this camp was quickly dubbed the "Ring Camp." It was a stirring sight. There were over seventy wagons, wheel to wheel, wagon tongues pointing inward. Even though all reports were that the Indians here, members of the Potawatomi tribe, were not hostile in any way, circling the wagons not only provided a good defensive perimeter in case there was trouble but also made a good "corral" for the stock. Even the friendly natives were notorious for stealing horses or cattle if given a chance.

About seventy or eighty miles from the Missouri River now, the company held worship services during the day on Sunday, and then that afternoon they headed out again and traveled seven more miles. They called the place where they camped that night Pleasant Valley.

———————————

They had the tent to themselves this Sabbath night. With the days pushing into the eighties now, the nights were pleasantly cool. The "sleep out" was Savannah's idea. Her proposal was simple. She and Charles and Livvy would transfer a few items from the wagon to the tent. Then they would move out to the wagon the two straw mattresses on which they slept, and there they would get to sleep out.

At first Caroline demurred. She, along with many of the other women, was a little skittish about the thoughts of being on Indian lands. But Joshua reassured her by noting first that there were guards posted for the night all around the camp and, second, that their tent would be only a few paces away from the wagon. The combination of three pairs of wide, pleading eyes and three sets of solemn promises for perfect behavior finally carried the day.

Now she and Joshua were alone in the tent. It was almost nine o'clock, time for lights out, but it pleased her that Joshua continued to read by the light of the lamp that stood on one of the trunks. She could see that he was nearly done with the Book of Mormon and guessed he was trying to finish it before the call came to put out the lights. She sat cross-legged, writing a letter that would go along with one from Mary Ann, Rebecca, and Lydia back to Nauvoo. She glanced up from time to time, watching him with quiet pleasure.

It was almost two weeks ago now since she and Joshua had been reunited at Mount Pisgah and he had shocked her with his revelation about having Lydia's Book of Mormon. They had talked on a few occasions since then, though not nearly as much as she had wished. The days were hectic, and at those rare times when there was a moment for reading, almost always there was someone else around. Joshua was still strongly opposed to letting the rest of the family know what he was doing, and she had honored that and never even hinted at the subject of religion around the children or other members of the family.

On the few occasions when they had managed to find time to talk about it, she ended up torn by conflicting emotions. One night they talked long after the children had gone to sleep. He told her about the questions he had put to Nathan and recounted in surprising detail Nathan's answers. He spoke easily of what he had learned and with seeming acceptance, and her heart soared with hope. Then at other times it was as if he had no interest at all. Then her expectations plummeted. At those times she had to remind herself that this was not the same old Joshua—skeptical, questioning, even caustic at times. But neither was he wildly embracing the Church and hounding anyone for baptism.

The bugle sounded and they both looked up. It was time to extinguish all lights and go to bed. She was surprised to see that the book was closed. She hadn't seen him do that. "Did you finish?"

He nodded without comment, as if it were something that happened every day, rolled over onto his back, and reached out to put the book on the trunk beside the lamp.

"I'm almost done." She wrote quickly, then lifted the paper and blew gently on the ink. After a moment she laid the paper aside, capped the ink bottle, and wiped the end of the quill with a small rag. Sure that the ink was now dry, she slipped the two pages into her leather stationery pouch, then nodded at him. "I'm ready."

Lifting the glass cover slightly, he blew on the wick and the tent was plunged into darkness. She started to remove her outer robe, then stopped. "Do you think we need to check on the children?"

"Nope. Do you want to ruin everything?"

She laughed at that. The last thing Savannah had said when they bid her good night was, "Now, Papa, you don't need to keep coming out here to see if we're all right. It will ruin everything."

"I suppose you're right," Caroline said. She removed the robe and set it aside, then crawled over and slid into bed beside him. He automatically extended his arm and she snuggled in against him, using his arm as a pillow. "So," she said after a moment.

"So what?"

She elbowed him sharply. "You finished; do you have nothing to say?"

"Actually, I've got a question."

"All right," she said, pleased and a little surprised.

"I've been thinking about it ever since Nathan and I talked, but something I just read reminded me of it."

"Well, I'm not nearly as incisive as Nathan in my understanding of the gospel, but I'll try to answer it."

"Okay." He thought for a moment. "So what's to keep a man from sidestepping the system?"

Caroline lifted her head to look at him, though her eyes were not yet adjusted to the darkness and she could see only the shape of his head. "I beg your pardon?"

"In the gospel, what's to stop a person from sidestepping the system?"

Caroline was totally confused. "I don't understand. What do you mean by sidestepping the system?"

"Well, Nathan told me that Christ died for the sins of people so that if they repent they won't have to suffer for them."

"Yes."

"So, let's say I believe that. What's to stop me from living as I want, then after I've had my fun, I repent a little, find God, maybe join the Church? All will be forgiven. Seems a whole lot easier than devoting your whole life to religion."

Caroline lay back, seeing it clearly now. For a moment, her mind wanted to agree with him. What was wrong with the philosophy? She had not ever thought of that possibility, but it did make a kind of perverse sense. But another part of her revolted at the very idea. The God she believed in would never have set up a plan with such an obvious flaw.

He read her silence as a sign of displeasure. "I'm sorry, Caroline, I don't mean to seem sacrilegious. I just—"

"No," she said hastily, "it's not that at all. I was just trying to gather my thoughts." Then as one answer popped into her head, she went on. "I see one problem with your reasoning."

"What?"

"Can I be honest?"

"Sure."

"Were you happy when you were gambling and drinking and beating up on Jessica?"

It was as though she had reached out and slapped him without provocation. There was a quick intake of breath, and she felt his body stiffen. She bit her lip, fighting back the temptation to withdraw the question and say how sorry she was.

"No," he said finally, his voice distant.

"How about that day in Independence when you helped tar and feather those two Mormons? Did that bring you joy? Did you go home that night just brimming with happiness?"

There was a long silence, then a quick shake of his head.

"I'm not trying to hurt you, Joshua, but I don't believe that living a life without God is 'fun,' as you put it. I'm sure you've known some rough men in your time—men who drink and cuss and gamble and are immoral. Would you say they are happy, really happy?"

"All right," he finally conceded, "I get the point. I was making light of something and I shouldn't have."

"No," she said in surprise. "I didn't mean to sound like I was being critical of you. I just don't believe that sin is fun. I know there are people who think that it is. They think God is a great stone around their necks, holding them back from all that makes life enjoyable, but the Savior said just the opposite. He said that he came so that we could have life and that we could have it more abundantly."

She could feel him relax against her, and she felt relieved that he had not gotten angry with her directness. Her mind was still working swiftly, wrestling with his question. "I also think there is another problem with your statement."

He chuckled softly. "And you think Nathan is more incisive than this?"

"Well," she chided him, "you asked. I'd like to try and answer."

"I'm listening."

"Who said you get to set the conditions?"

"What's that supposed to mean?"

"Well, you said that all you have to do is repent a little, find God, maybe join the Church. That means you're setting the conditions for having Christ's atonement applied in your behalf. That's not up to you, because you didn't pay the price."

"I'm still not sure I follow."

"Let's go back to the example Nathan used with you, about Charles and the broken window. If you pay the storekeeper to replace the window, is Charles off the hook completely? Or would you have him do something to help pay for his mistake?"

He thought a moment. "I'd likely make him do some chores around the house, something like that."

"Does Charles get to choose what he does for his punishment? Could he say, for example, 'I'll play five more games of stickball and then we'll be even'?"

"No. I'd set the conditions. All right, I see where you're coming from on this."

"Well, isn't it the same? You paid the price for the window, so you set the conditions. Christ paid the price for our sins, so he sets the conditions, and I don't see those conditions as being an easy way around what is required."

"So what are the conditions? Besides giving up wine, women, and song, I mean."

She smiled in the darkness. "I think you are allowed to keep the song."

He laughed, glad that she would play with him a little. Then he grew serious again. "So, what else?"

"They're simple, at least in concept. Faith in Jesus Christ. Repentance. Baptism into the Church. Receiving the gift of the Holy Ghost. Then enduring to the end in faith."

"Is that so tough?"

"It sure seems to be for you," she nearly quipped, but caught herself in time. "Not tough, but not an easy thing either. Faith is more than just believing. It is a commitment to Christ that changes what you are, how you think, what you feel. Repentance is much more than just saying you're sorry for doing something wrong. It's not enough to repent 'a little,' as you put it. It requires a deep sorrow for sin, for offending God. And those are just the first two conditions. If a person really does that, would you say he has beaten the system, or sidestepped it, as you call it?"

"No."

She waited for more than that, but nothing more came. Sometimes he could be so maddening, ducking behind that inner wall that allowed him to hide his thoughts from her. Had she answered his question to his satisfaction? Was he irritated? Contrite? Apathetic? There was no way to safely guess through that veil of inscrutability. So she decided to go one step further.

"Joshua, may I say something?"

"Of course."

"You're going to think I'm just getting pushy, but it really is another part of the answer to your question."

"I don't think you're pushy, Caroline," he said quietly.

Encouraged by that, she went on. For several days now she had been thinking about Joshua, where he was now, what he was thinking, his reservations about the Church. Before they had left Mount Pisgah, she too had finished reading the Book of Mormon—only for her it was the fourth time—and she decided to read the Doctrine and Covenants next. In the beginning sections of the "Covenants and Commandments" part of that wonderful book, several passages had leaped out at her as having direct application to Joshua and his inquiry.

She took her courage in her hands and plunged in. "I think you know enough now, Joshua."

"What?"

"One of the conditions of faith is to search for the truth. You have done that, and I am so pleased with what you've done and what you've learned. But I think you know enough now."

"What is that supposed to mean?" he asked cautiously.

"It means that learning the information is not enough. Another condition the Lord has set for us is to ask."

"Somehow I knew it would come to that," he said, almost under his breath, as if he were speaking only to himself.

"Remember," she gently reminded him, "*you* don't get to set the conditions." She paused, then went on. "In the Doctrine and

Covenants, in the very first section, it says that the voice of the Lord is unto all men. Tell me, Joshua, if the Lord spoke to you, how do you think it would come?"

"To a hardhead like me?" he scoffed. "Tree limb alongside the skull. Maybe a bolt of lightning to get my attention."

She smiled sadly and loved him the more deeply. She was walking on tender ground now, and his attempt at humor was simply another way of retreating. "No, really, I want you to think about it. If God wanted to speak to you, how would he do it?"

There was a long silence this time. Then, "I don't know."

"Well, God can speak to us in many ways, but in a revelation to Oliver Cowdery the Lord said that he speaks to us in our minds and in our hearts through the Holy Ghost."

She felt him nod in the darkness, so she went on. "If he were to speak to your mind, Joshua, how would you say it would come? What word would you use to describe it?"

"Thoughts, I guess."

"And if he spoke to your heart, how do you think it would come?"

"As feelings?"

"Yes, Joshua. That's how God speaks to us most often. He gives us thoughts and feelings. Often they are so subtle that if we are not careful, we won't recognize them as coming from God at all. This is why in another place his voice is described as being still and small and it whispers."

"Go on."

"Don't you see it, Joshua? You *have* had thoughts and feelings from the Lord."

"I have?"

"Yes," she exclaimed. "When you came back to Nauvoo to get us, you said that when you left camp, you were still determined that you were not going to take us back with you. Do you remember what changed your mind?"

"Well, I . . ." He let his mind go back to that night. "It was when I saw how filled with hate that one man was. I suddenly had the strongest . . ." He stopped and was very still.

"Go on, Joshua. Say it. You had the strongest what?"

There was no point in dodging it. She remembered clearly what he had told her. "I had a strong feeling that it wasn't safe to leave you and the children there," he finally said quietly.

"And that day you were out hunting, what was it that made you start thinking about Olivia and Father Steed and whether or not they were still alive somewhere?"

He shifted his weight a little, and she could feel his discomfort growing. But even this was astonishing to her. Even two months ago she would have been cut off sharply before she ever got this far.

"Shall I tell you what you said?" she offered. "You told me that as you were washing your knife in the river, suddenly the *thought* came into your mind, 'What is life?'"

"And you think that was from God?" he said dubiously.

"I do, Joshua," she said with deep fervency. "I don't think that was simply an accident. And look where it led you. You finally knelt down and asked God to help you understand."

Again he said nothing. Now she was to the point she wanted to make and she felt a clutch of anxiety. There was a line that she could not push past or it would set him back immeasurably, and she was not sure exactly where that line was. On the other hand, she might not get an opportunity like this again in many days.

She bit her lip, then began slowly. "There's something else the Lord said to Oliver Cowdery that reminds me of you. The revelation in which it is found was given when Oliver went to Harmony and met the Prophet Joseph for the first time. Do you know the story of how Oliver learned about Joseph Smith?"

"I don't think so."

"Well, Oliver came to Palmyra as a schoolteacher. The Smith family had some children in the school, and so they provided Oliver room and board to help pay the tuition. By now Joseph was married and down in Harmony, Pennsylvania, with Emma. Anyway, Oliver began hearing all those tales about Joseph Smith and gold plates and visions and angels."

"That probably set him back a little," Joshua said dryly.

"It did. But by then he knew the Smiths and believed them to be honest people, so he decided to ask God about it. Then, when he got his answer, he determined to go to Harmony and meet Joseph personally."

"Okay."

"Now, here is what I want you to hear, Joshua. When Oliver arrived in Harmony, Joseph received a revelation. In it the Lord said an interesting thing. It was the confirmation Oliver was looking for."

"What was it?"

"Oliver had not told Joseph anything about his prayers back in Palmyra, but in the revelation the Lord said something like this. 'As often as you asked of me, I have answered you. If that were not the case, you would not have come to this place. I tell you these things so that you may know that only God knows the thoughts and intents of your heart.'"

His head had turned and he was listening intently now.

"Then the Lord went on, 'If you desire a further witness of the truth, think back to that night when you cried unto me in your heart. Did I not speak peace to your mind? What greater witness can you have than from God?'"

Now she turned to him and pressed in against him. "Oh, Joshua, don't you see? That night when you dropped to your knees and asked God about Olivia, did he not speak to you then? You said you got an answer. You said you were at peace about Olivia. Don't you see that was from God?"

"I . . . Yes, I have to admit, it was very strange. At the time, it seemed like it came from God."

"But why then? Why did you get that answer right then?"

"Because I was thinking about life and death, I guess."

"That too, but what else?"

He shook his head. "I don't know what you mean, Caroline?"

"Because you *asked*," she said softly. "You just didn't think about it, Joshua. You asked."

He sighed, clearly troubled. "And that's what you think needs to happen now?"

"Yes," she cried. "You *know* enough, Joshua. Now you need to ask God if it isn't true."

"I've tried it, Caroline. I really have. I just can't make it work. I feel like such a fool."

"Then I will say to you what the Lord said to Oliver. 'If you desire a further witness of the truth, think back to that night when you cried unto me in your heart. Did I not speak peace to your mind? What greater witness can you have than from God?'"

He let her go and rolled away from her, lying on his back, staring up at the ceiling. Finally, she could bear it no longer. "Tell me what you're thinking, Joshua. Please."

He didn't turn his head. "It comes easy for you, doesn't it?" he murmured.

"What? Religion?"

"No, believing."

She thought about that, then slowly nodded. "Maybe it does. But there's something more important."

"What?"

"*Asking* came easy for me, Joshua. And that made all the difference."

Chapter Notes

The details for this portion of the trek across Iowa reflect the adaptation to his plans that Brigham Young made as the realities of the Saints' slow progress set in (see *CN*, 8 June 1996, p. 12; 15 June 1996, p. 5).

The two scriptures involving Oliver Cowdery's experiences which Caroline cites for Joshua are now Doctrine and Covenants 8:2–3 and Doctrine and Covenants 6:14–16, 22–23.

Brigham Young and his group moved out of Pleasant Valley Camp on the morning of June eighth, still following the westward track of the Indian trail that led to Council Bluffs and the Missouri River. They had been on the trail no more than a couple of hours when a cry went up near the head of the train. It came racing down the line, leaping from mouth to mouth. "Indians!" It had virtually the same effect as if someone had cried "Fire!" Men ran for their rifles. Women started screaming at their children to come back to the wagons. Instinctively the teamsters moved their wagons up closer to the one in front of them. The drovers watching the herd began pushing them into a tighter circle.

As the near panic swept up and down the line, Heber C. Kimball and Willard Richards came trotting back down the line on their horses. "It's all right!" Heber shouted. "Don't be alarmed!"

"What is it?" "Is it really Indians?" "How many?" "Are they armed?" The cries came at the two Apostles like a swarm of bees.

They reined up, just two wagons ahead of Nathan's. "Calm down, folks," Willard Richards said. "Listen." After a moment it was quiet enough for him to continue. "There's an Indian village ahead. They are evidently part of the Potawatomi tribe. There is no need for alarm. They are not hostile in any way."

Heber was looking around. "Put your rifles away. Keep your pistols in their holsters. There's not going to be any trouble. Just stay calm. We'll pass right by them, but we want them to know we mean them no trouble either."

"How many are there?" a woman called out.

"Two or three hundred," came the answer from Heber. "But that includes women and children. Just stay calm. They are not hostile in any way."

With that, they rode on to tell those farther down the line. "Do you really think it's safe?" Emily asked her father, anxiety clouding her face.

"Yes, Emily," Nathan answered easily. "President Young wouldn't march us into any danger. Let's just stay close together and be alert."

After three months of nothing but mud and prairie and an occasional settlement of white men, the sight that awaited the Saints was marvelous indeed. The Indian village was set back a hundred yards or more from the trail on the far side of the east fork of the Nishnabotna River. Its wigwams—made of stripped elm bark held together by a framework of saplings—looked like a giant scattering of half walnut shells turned upside down. Plumes of smoke came from holes in the top of each wigwam. If the Mormons were curious about the Indians, the Indians were equally fascinated by the great company that was passing by. Several of the warriors came racing toward them on horseback, only to turn away again. They had seen plenty of white men before, but not like this, not one great company with wagons and oxen and a large herd of cattle, sheep, and milk cows. The village emptied as everyone came to stand alongside the trail and solemnly watch as Brigham and the lead wagon approached. The only sound was the furious barking of two or three dozen dogs that raced out to meet them. There were several sharp, guttural commands from the Indian men, a few well-placed kicks, and the dogs slunk away, totally cowed.

As the lead wagon neared the first of the Indians, a man stepped out into the center of the trail and planted his feet. Brigham raised a hand and the wagons came to a halt. He swung down from his horse. The Steeds were back about halfway in the train and were craning their necks to see. Joshua went up in his stirrups, then turned to Nathan. "I'll go see what's going on," he said, and kicked his horse into a gentle canter.

As Brigham handed the reins of his horse to Heber Kimball, Heber frowned a little. "Careful, Brigham." He dismounted too, handed the reins of both horses to another man, then turned to watch his leader. He kept his hands to his sides, but they were not far from the pistol strapped in a holster on his belt. Behind them, Albert Rockwood and Willard Richards edged a little closer to the wagons where their rifles lay on top of their bedding.

"It's all right," Brigham said over his shoulder. He raised one hand in the universal symbol of greeting and walked forward.

The man was large, almost as tall as Joshua's six feet, and he was in superb physical shape. He wore a tanned skin shirt with no sleeves, and several necklaces of shells hung from his neck. He also wore two metal armbands and a wristband of some kind of animal hair, probably buffalo, fringed deerskin leggings, a leather breechclout, and soft-soled one-piece moccasins. Other men had their upper faces painted black with red around the eyes and looked terribly fierce, but his face was unmarked except for two diagonal red stripes on each cheekbone. His black hair was long and fell loose down his back. At the back of his head he wore a single eagle's feather. He stood motionless now, not even his eyes flickering as he waited for Brigham to reach him.

"Hello," Brigham said, stopping about ten yards short of the man.

There was a brief nod.

"Do you speak English? or any of your people?"

"I speak English."

"Good." He turned briefly, gesturing at what lay behind him. "We are Mormons, members of The Church of Jesus Christ of Latter-day Saints. We are your friends. We are your brothers."

The deep brown, nearly black eyes lifted slightly, taking in what Brigham had included in his wave. Then they came back to Brigham. "You cross our land."

"Yes," Brigham said, as calm as though he were speaking to one of the Twelve.

"You must pay."

"Your English is very good. Where did you learn it?"

"Missionaries. Traders." He dismissed that conversation with a shrug. "You must pay to pass through village. Your cattle eat our grass. You trample down the feed for our horses. You must pay."

Brigham nodded soberly. "I understand, but we cannot pay. We are very poor. We have no money. We have been driven from our homes by bad men, just as your people have been driven from their homes near the Great Lakes to the land of the Sioux."

He stopped but the Indian said nothing. He just waited, completely stoic.

"But we will not hurt your land. We will help it. We build bridges across the rivers and cut down the banks of the streams so they are crossed easily by your horses and their travois. This will help your people too as they travel. We ask permission to pass on your lands as brothers."

As Brigham finished, the man turned and walked to where a small group of men stood together in a tight circle. Their faces were as stone, just as the spokesman's was. One of the men was quite old. His hair, which hung past his waist, was streaked heavily with gray. Joshua suspected he was the chief of the village. The brave spoke quickly to the others in a soft, almost musical tongue. The men listened gravely, then turned to each other and consulted for a moment. Finally, the old man turned back and said a few words to the Indian brave. He nodded, and for the first time there was a softening in his features.

"What you say is good," he said loudly. "We have heard of Mormons and know you are brothers. You will not tear down the bridges after you have passed?"

Brigham shook his head emphatically. "More of our people come behind us. We leave the bridges for them and for your people. Where we dig wells, your people will have water. We shall plant crops. If you are hungry when the snows come, we shall give you food."

Again the brave turned back to his council and spoke rapidly. Now several, including the chief, nodded gravely. The old man spoke again, and the man inclined his head for a moment, then strode back to face Brigham. He raised his hand, then swept it outward in a smooth gesture of motion. "Pass through, my brother."

Brigham bowed slightly. "Thank you, my brother." He turned and walked back to where the others watched. "All right," he said to Heber. "Let's go on through, but tell the people to move slowly. Tell them to smile and be friendly. There is nothing to worry about here."

——————————

Savannah was absolutely enthralled. She walked slowly alongside the wagon, her green eyes like huge saucers as she stared at the sight before her. For the most part, no one spoke—not Indian, not white man—though the Saints forced strained smiles and nodded at frequent intervals. But the Indian children had no such reservations. They stood like little sentinels lining a parade route, their black eyes more enormous than marbles. They hid their whispered astonishment behind cupped hands, as if that might keep them unnoticed. Someone would point, there would be the chattering of squirrels, and then they would erupt with peals of laughter or uncontrollable giggling. The smallest wore nothing but what the Lord had blessed them with at birth and were totally unabashed by it. A few raised tentative hands and waved shyly.

Behind them stood the women. Their dresses consisted of two pieces of soft deerskin, fastened at the shoulder and belted at the waist. They also wore knee-length leggings, fastened at the knees with leather strips adorned with quillwork. Like the men, they wore moccasins, only more of theirs had decorative trim on them. Their hair, like the men's, was as black as a ball of pitch, and was worn in a single braid down the back. Pieces of ribbon and small beadwork were woven into the braids. The women were much more reserved than the children and would not look directly at the whites except for stealing surreptitious glances when they thought they were not observed.

In the rear were the braves, some on horseback, many standing behind their families. Unlike the one who confronted Brigham, many wore cotton shirts decorated with breastplates of beautiful and colorful beaded designs. Most were lean and hard, with flat stomachs and unreadable faces. The white slash of scars—evidence of some hunting accident or the wounds of war—could be seen here and there. There was interest in their eyes, but none of them spoke.

The dogs had come back to stand by their masters and watch, but only an occasional bark was heard as one of the dogs in the pioneer company rang out a challenge and they threw back their answer.

As Savannah started down the line of onlookers, the children went silent. Hands came up and their mouths formed into large O's. The women too would glance at her, then whip back around to gape at her. They pointed and whispered urgently to each other, reaching up to pull at their hair, showing signs of utter astonishment.

Joshua smiled down at his daughter. "I think your red hair is what's causing all the fuss."

Her hand came up and touched her hair as she realized he was right.

"I'll bet they've never seen red hair before," Emily called to Savannah. "They can't believe it."

They were coming abreast of the man who had spoken to Brigham. He stood with a heavyset woman and four children—two young boys about ten and twelve, a girl about Savannah's age, and another boy who wore nothing and was probably no more than two.

The girl watched Savannah approach, her jaw slack, her gaze fixed on Savannah. Then she turned and said something quickly to her mother. Her mother nodded, her eyes never leaving Savannah, then said something back to the girl. Savannah smiled broadly and waved at them gaily. The girl's copper cheeks colored and she dropped her eyes. When they came back up, Savannah waved again. This time one hand rose slightly and moved in a tiny return greeting.

When Joshua had come back to rejoin his family, he dismounted and tied his horse to the wagon. Now he and Caroline were walking alongside the oxen. To his surprise the Indian father stepped forward as they came abreast of the family. Caroline stopped, clutching at Joshua's shirtsleeve. Joshua whispered something to her, then spoke softly to the oxen, who stopped. Behind them, the rest of the family stopped too. Joshua came around the head of the oxen and raised his hand. "Hello."

The man's head bobbed once. Then he pointed to Savannah. "Daughter?"

"Yes, this is my daughter."

"My daughter say her hair like fire."

Joshua smiled. "And your daughter's hair is like the raven's feather. It is beautiful."

There was almost a smile and the head inclined briefly in acknowledgment of the compliment. Savannah came up and stuck out her hand. "Hi," she said brightly. "My name is Savannah."

Startled, the man took her hand, not sure what to do with it. He held it briefly, then dropped it again.

"What's your name?" she asked.

The man half turned. His wife looked frightened. The three boys were huddled with some other boys, whispering and pointing. The man turned back, looking down at Savannah now. He touched his chest. "I am No-taw-kah, the Rattlesnake."

"My name is Savannah."

"Sa-van-nah," he repeated.

"Yes." She was elated. She turned and pointed to his daughter. "What is her name?"

Just then a man cantered up on a horse and the Indian moved back a little, clearly nervous. It was Heber Kimball, come back to see why the train had stopped. Joshua turned. "It's all right," he said.

When Heber saw what was taking place, he reined up and said nothing more.

"What is your daughter's name?" Savannah asked again.

The father, seeing that Heber brought no threat, turned back to Savannah and uttered a guttural burst of sound that none of them understood. "It means Daughter of the Morning Mist."

"What a beautiful name!" Savannah said smoothly, not wanting to embarrass him by asking him to repeat it.

He bowed his head gravely. "You have beautiful name too."

"Thank you."

Heber called out softly. "Joshua, we need to get the train rolling."

"I know." He spoke to Savannah. "We have to go now, Savannah."

All a sudden her face, ever animated, came totally alive. She swung around to her mother. "Mama, can I give her my doll?"

Caroline was dumbfounded. "Your doll?"

"Yes. I want to give it to her." She didn't wait for an answer but ran around to the back of the wagon and started pawing through the packed bedding. In a moment she appeared again, holding up her doll in triumph. "Can I Mama, can I?"

"I . . . Savannah, are you sure? You already traded your big doll to Emma Smith back in Nauvoo, remember?"

"I know, Mama, but I want to."

Joshua was watching her in wonder too. Would she never stop surprising them? But when he saw her eyes, luminous with excitement, he turned back to the father. "My daughter wants to give your daughter a gift."

Rattlesnake, who had followed all of this with impassive eyes, searched Joshua's face for a moment, then nodded at Savannah. "Come!"

As he started back toward his family, Savannah trotting after him, Caroline gasped. "Joshua!"

"It's all right," he called, walking swiftly to catch up.

A great silence went up and down the line of Saints and Indians as the warrior led Savannah and Joshua to his family. Savannah walked boldly up to the girl, who shrank back behind her mother's dress. The woman smiled and gently pushed her forward again.

"This is for you," Savannah said, holding the doll out.

Her father spoke briefly. Finally, Daughter of the Morning Mist, blushing furiously, reached out and took the doll. All around, the other children edged closer, their mouths agape.

"Thank you," Rattlesnake said softly.

"Thank you for letting us cross your land," Joshua answered. He reached out and took Savannah's hand. "Come, Savannah. We have to go now."

They started back toward the wagon. The girl's mother stepped up beside her husband and whispered quickly in his ear. He nodded, then turned. "Sa-van-nah?"

They both stopped and turned back.

"My wife say we give Sa-van-nah Potawatomi name."

Now Caroline was smiling as she came forward to take Savannah's hand. "That would please us very much," she said.

He turned and eyed Savannah as though measuring her for a dress. After a moment, he nodded to himself, looking satisfied. "You shall be called Kee-wau-nay," he said.

"This Is for You"

"Kee-wau-nay," Savannah repeated.

"Yes. Good name for you."

"What does it mean?" Caroline asked.

He did not turn but continued to look into Savannah's eyes. "Kee-wau-nay means Prairie Chicken. You small. Very happy. Good heart. You Prairie Chicken."

It was late in the afternoon of the next day, June ninth, that Brigham's company reached the middle fork of the Nishnabotna River. It was deep and swift and had no natural fording place, but to Brigham's surprise Bishop Miller's advance party was camped on the east side of the river, preparing to construct a bridge across the stream. So Brigham called a halt for the day.

The Steed company of ten was only about a third of the way back in the line of wagons, but they had been stopped for almost ten minutes, waiting to swing out and find a place to camp.

Nathan stood beside his oxen, now almost to where a man was directing the wagons where to go. Lydia and the younger children had moved back with the rest of the family. Josh was at the head of the oxen for Matthew's wagon, his standard place since Matthew had left them. Joshua was next, and Derek brought up the rear of their four wagons. Only now could Nathan see clearly down near the river to where the wagons were gathering. He hadn't yet taken note of the fact that there were more wagons there than there should have been.

Suddenly he heard a whoop. He looked up, squinting. About a hundred yards away, a lanky figure had burst out from the circle of wagons and was waving his arms, running full tilt toward them. Nathan peered more closely, and then his face split into a big grin. He spun around. Jenny and Mary Ann were with the family. Jenny had Emmeline in her arms. Betsy Jo was off with the rest of the children.

"Jenny!"

She looked up.

"I think you have company."

She raised a hand to shade her eyes, but Nathan's wagon blocked her view. "Who is it?" she called.

He laughed aloud. "He looks quite familiar," he called. "Tall, big smile. Answers to the name of Matthew."

"Matthew!" she gasped. The whole family swung around now. "Is it really?" Mary Ann cried.

"It is, and coming like a greyhound after a rabbit."

Jenny shoved Emmeline into Rebecca's arms and sprinted forward. She reached up and ripped off her bonnet and sent it spinning, leaving her hair to stream out behind her. "Matthew! Matthew!" As she reached Nathan, she could see Matthew's running figure now and began waving.

He waved back and shouted something. As the two reached each other, he threw open his arms to catch Jenny as she hurled herself into them.

Mary Ann ran past Nathan and reached the couple just as Matthew finally set Jenny down. He opened his arms for his mother and swept her up now as well.

There was only one thing that could have made Jenny happier than seeing Matthew again, and that was his news. They were close enough now to the Missouri River that Brigham had declared that Matthew would no longer have to go ahead. He didn't have to leave Jenny again, at least not until they reached the Missouri River. It was a very happy family that gathered in around their son, brother, uncle, husband, and father who had rejoined them at last.

———————

Just before supper that same evening, Brigham sent word for the men of the company to come to a meeting. They gathered around his wagon as the women in the camp set to work preparing supper.

"Brethren," Brigham said, climbing up on a wagon tongue. "Could I have your attention, please."

The group quickly quieted.

"Thank you. Some of the Twelve and I have met in brief council. We are very pleased with our recent progress. At last we're making good time. Brother Clayton, who, as you know, has the responsibility of being our camp clerk, is still behind us but sends word that we are now making about fifteen miles per day. Striking the Indian trail was a great blessing to us. We are no longer knocking our wagons to pieces as we cross virgin prairie. The grass is good and our animals are healthy. We have been fortunate to catch up to Bishop Miller's party today, for, as you can see, we will have to construct another bridge. We'll use flood wood, and if we all pitch in together, we can finish it tomorrow and we won't have to swim our wagons across the river."

"Oh, I don't mind," someone called out. "It might drown the lice, bedbugs, and other creatures which seem to have taken residence with my family."

There was general laughter all around, Brigham included. Joshua smiled. Breaking out of the never-ending morass of mud had done wonders for their spirits. They were energetic, happy, and almost playful. He thought about that. They hadn't felt playful for a long time.

Brigham continued. "We now estimate that we are no more than thirty miles from the Missouri River. We hope to reach it by Saturday or Sunday. There we shall stop for a while so that we can establish another settlement for our people."

That brought nods of approval and a lot of excited comments. For many, the Missouri would be their stopping place until spring.

"And since we are making such good progress, the brethren and I feel to make another announcement. We don't have all of Brother Pitt's brass band with us—Brother Clayton being one of those not present—but Brother Heber assures me that we have enough to hold a concert and dance tonight."

The men erupted with applause and cries of approval.

Brigham nodded in satisfaction. This was exactly why it was needed. "We shall build a bonfire over in the meadow, and we shall commence festivities promptly at eight o'clock."

Caroline's cheeks were flushed with excitement. She reached out and grabbed Joshua's hand. "Come dance with me, Joshua."

He looked momentarily startled.

"Come on," she pleaded. "Please, Joshua."

He glanced at Nathan and Lydia with a forlorn look of surrender and allowed himself to be towed off. It wasn't much of a band, not considering what they had enjoyed during the first part of the journey, but no one cared. In William Clayton's absence, someone else played the violin. There were two clarinets, two flutes, three trumpets, a trombone, a drum, and someone had dragged out a set of sleigh bells to provide a different touch.

It was enough. The band played several marches and a rousing version of "The Upper California" to enthusiastic applause, then moved away from the center of the meadow so that there was room for dancing. It started with a grand cotillion, but from then on there were none of the more sedate dances—minuets or waltzes or stately quadrilles. This was a celebration of spirit, and the people were filled with exuberance. The violin became a fiddle, with the brass following along. They went through such dances as the Fox-Chase Inn, Gardens of Gray's Ferry, the Copenhagen Jig, and some French Fours.

As Caroline pulled Joshua forward, the band struck up the Virginia Reel. The people formed quickly into squares, with Joshua and Caroline joining Derek and Rebecca, Matthew and Jenny, and young Josh and his grandmother.

"I should make you take me in there too," Lydia said wistfully from the sidelines.

Nathan nodded, knowing that that wasn't a criticism of him but an admission of how tired she was. It was almost ten o'clock now, and they would have to return soon so she could feed Tricia. The past week they had pushed hard every day and it showed on her. Even though the baby was two months old now, Lydia was still not back to her full strength.

"Are you ready to start back?" he asked.

"Not yet." She was swaying to the music, and he saw her skirt moving where she was tapping her foot.

"This is a great thing for the camp," he observed.

"Yes. It does wonders for the spirit." Then she smiled. "Look at them, Nathan. Look at Joshua. You would think he was ten years younger to watch him right now."

"Yes. He certainly can surprise you, can't he?"

She turned to him. "Has he said anything more to you about what's going on in his mind?"

His mouth turned down. "Not a word."

"No more questions?"

"Not since we left Mount Pisgah. Not that we've had a lot of time to sit around and talk."

"Caroline told me he finished the Book of Mormon the other night."

"Really? Good for him. So does he talk with her about it?"

"Some, but not much," she replied, openly showing her discouragement. "Caroline is trying to convince him he needs to pray about it."

"I don't know why that is such a problem for him," Nathan mused. "It's almost like he's afraid he might actually get an answer and have to commit himself." He turned to watch the dancers, picking Joshua out quickly. He was fully into it now, any semblance of the reluctant partner completely gone. He spun Caroline around, then took her hand and ducked beneath it. He was thoroughly enjoying himself and Caroline was responding with great enthusiasm, laughing like a young girl. Was this the same man who had been dragged out to participate?

"Do you think he will make it, Nathan?"

Nathan turned to her. His face was solemn as he thought about that. Finally, he shrugged. "I don't know. There's something inside him that's like a big granite boulder standing in his way. On some days he goes after it with hammer and chisel. Then other times it's like he looks at the rock and says, 'Is it really worth what it's going to take to move that out of here?'"

Her head went up and down slowly as she watched him dancing.

"Out here is not the best place to try and think things through," he went on. "There are too many things to occupy your mind. Maybe once we get to the valley and things settle down to normal again, maybe then he'll finally make the choice."

She tipped her head back and closed her eyes. "Mmm, the valley. I like the sound of that. If it's as beautiful as Brigham says, it will be wonderful."

"Sometimes it seems like only a dream," he said, suddenly discouraged. It was still so far away, both in time and distance. If he left his family at the Missouri and went on with the vanguard company, that was going to be difficult. The whole thing just felt so overwhelming now.

Seeing his face, she came over to him and took his arm. "Come on, Mr. Steed. I think I have one more dance left in me. How about you?"

"I think I just might," he said, bringing up a smile. "Let's go show these youngsters of ours just what their mama and papa are capable of."

———◆———

The dancing didn't stop until just after eleven o'clock, when a laughing Brigham Young overrode the protests and reminded them that there was another day of work awaiting them on the morrow. He called for prayer and in a moment the camp was quiet. When it was done, the people began to disperse and return to their wagons and tents, talking happily.

"Thank you, Joshua," Caroline said, taking his arm and leaning against him as they walked. "That was wonderful."

"No, thank *you*, Caroline. That was enough to lift a man's soul tonight."

"Joshua!"

Joshua stopped at the sound of a man's voice and turned around.

Brigham Young was with Heber Kimball and Willard Richards. The senior Apostle waved his hand toward Joshua and Caroline. "Hold on a moment." He said a few more words to his brethren, then strode over to them. "Mind if I walk with you for a moment?"

"Of course not, President," Caroline said. "It's our pleasure."

"Glad for the company," Joshua agreed.

He fell into step beside them and walked slowly along. Joshua and Caroline had set a path back toward their encampment. Brigham's wagons were in a different direction, but that didn't seem to be on his mind at the moment. He looked up. Above them the sky was stunning. There was not a cloud and as yet no moon. It was as though they were under a thick canopy of branches, with every leaf a sparkling diamond of light.

"Isn't that something?" he breathed.

They both looked up. "It's beautiful," Caroline said in a half whisper. Joshua merely nodded.

"Hard to believe that that all happened by accident, isn't it?"

Joshua looked at him sharply. It was said as casually as if he were commenting on tomorrow's weather, but Joshua suspected the comment was aimed directly at him.

Caroline, also sensing that something had just happened, did not speak. She left it for Joshua. He had no choice but to answer. "It is enough to overwhelm a man," he said cautiously.

"Is it?" Brigham asked casually. "Are you overwhelmed, Joshua?"

Joshua's head came around. There was no mistaking the challenge. He was instantly on the defensive, but the glow of the evening was still on him and so he decided to let it pass.

Brigham laughed heartily and clapped him on the shoulder. "Sorry. My wife tells me I've got to learn to be a little more circumspect, not quite so brash and direct."

"I've never complained about directness," Joshua said, choosing his words carefully so as not to step off into an area where he didn't want to go.

"Good! So let me be direct. It's too late in the evening to chase each other around the gooseberry bush any longer."

Joshua stopped, now stiff and wary. Caroline, who was holding on to his arm, stopped with him. He could feel her grip on him tighten and he sensed her sudden tension.

Brigham went on a couple of steps before he too stopped and turned. "Are you still reading that Book of Mormon?" he asked suddenly.

Joshua's jaw dropped, then instantly tightened into a hard line. He looked down at Caroline, glaring.

Brigham leaned in, his own jawline looking a bit like a bulldog's. "Now, don't you be giving your wife a look like that. She hasn't said a word to me about this."

Caroline was as amazed as her husband. "I haven't, Joshua. I told you I wouldn't tell anyone unless you said I could."

He swung back on the Apostle. "Then how did you know? Was it Nathan?"

"So he knows too? I was wondering about that. That's good. He's probably been getting in a few good licks on you, hasn't he?"

"How did you know?" Joshua asked again, openly irritated now.

"I was passing by one day back in Mount Pisgah while you were splitting logs. Nathan was off in the trees somewhere. I saw that you were reading something. I couldn't tell for sure what it was, but it sure looked like a Book of Mormon to me." He grinned suddenly. "I was taking a shot in the dark just now by guessing that that was what you were doing, but as they say, 'Only the hit bird flutters.'"

"It's Lydia's book," Caroline said, realizing even as she said it that who owned the book was not very relevant at the moment.

Now Brigham stepped forward and thrust his face close to Joshua's. "I'm not going to be asking you any questions about what you believe and don't believe, Joshua. That's your affair. The fact that there's been no announcement about your impending baptism would tell me you're still not where you ought to be."

"I'm not where *you* think I ought to be," he said shortly.

Brigham ignored the correction. "So, here's what I've got to say. I'll say it, and if it offends you, then you can come duke it out with me in the morning. But it needs to be said."

Caroline gasped softly. This wasn't just directness. It was a full-scale frontal attack. She held her breath, expecting an explosion from Joshua any moment.

Joshua didn't flinch. "Say what you've got to say, Brother Brigham," he murmured.

Brigham's face softened now, and it was clear that what lay behind his directness was genuine concern. "I've just got one question for you, Joshua. Something I'd like you to think about. If I'm off the mark, then I'll apologize later."

"What is it?"

"It is simply this. Why is it, Joshua Steed, that you ask more of the Lord than you do of your business partners?"

Joshua looked at him blankly for a moment. "What?"

"You heard me. Why have you set a double standard here?"

"A double standard? I don't get your meaning."

"When you went into business with your various ventures, was there any risk involved?"

"Sure. There's risk with every venture."

"Of course there is. So why did you go ahead? Did you insist on having every possible question answered, every possible drawback resolved, before you were willing to commit yourself?"

Joshua felt as if he had just been shoved up against a stone wall. "Well, I—"

Brigham went on, quiet now, but very much in earnest. "Did you require a guarantee that every cotton crop would come in at full production? that no ship would ever be lost at sea? that the cotton market would always be strong when it was time to sell?"

Caroline had stepped away from Joshua a little, trying to see his face in the darkness. His head was still up, but she could tell he was being pummeled.

"Well, if none of that, then why are you being so confounded demanding of the Lord? No earthly partner would give you the kind of guarantees you're looking for here."

"I—" He stopped, then started again. "I don't see it quite that way, President. I—"

"I know you don't. But you think about it. You ask yourself if that's not your problem. Knowing you, I think you want every part of the 'deal' inked and guaranteed, every t crossed and every comma put in place. And what I'm saying is, that's asking more of the Lord than you would ask of a business partner."

He straightened, smiling now. "Well, that's about enough damage for one night," he said. He laid a hand on Joshua's shoulder. "The Lord wants you in the kingdom, Joshua Steed. Of that I have no doubt. So don't make it too difficult for him to bring you in, all right?"

He turned abruptly to Caroline. "Well, I told you. My Mary Ann says it's my greatest failing. Too brash. Too direct." He leaned over and kissed her cheek, startling her greatly. Then he looked at Joshua. "But I'm only that way with people who really matter to me."

Chapter Notes

Though specific details were supplied by the author, and though the encounter between Savannah and the Indian girl is part of the fictional structure of the book, the scene involving the Saints and the Indians is based on an actual experience. On the morning of 8 June 1846, the Latter-days Saints came upon a Potawatomi Indian village. It is recorded that one of the Indian braves demanded payment for the right to cross their lands, but Brigham convinced the Indians otherwise when he promised that the Saints' passing would leave the land better off than when they came. (See CN, 15 June 1996, p. 5.) Brigham Young always felt strongly that the Indians were to be viewed as brothers and sisters and treated with respect. Because of that, the reputation of the Mormons became widely known among the tribes, and the Saints experienced very little Indian trouble on the trek west.

When Caroline slipped out of the tent the next morning, it was full light, though the sun had not come up as yet. She stretched, looking around. In one or two places people were stirring. A few fires were already burning with pots hung over them. Men were looking to their wagons; sleepy-eyed boys stumbled around trying to look busy. But these were the exceptions. Because of the late night, the bugle had not sounded as usual and the camp was slow coming awake.

She found Joshua behind the wagons, sitting on a trunk, fixing some of the harnessing. He looked up as she came around to join him. "Good morning," he said.

"You didn't sleep much." She kept her voice light.

"No, not much. Are the children awake?"

"Not yet. I thought I'd let them sleep a little longer."

"Good."

She nodded, not asking what she was dying to know. "I'll start breakfast."

"Have you got a few minutes?" he asked casually.

She tried to keep her face impassive. "Of course."

He slid over and made room for her on the trunk. As she sat down, he looked away from her, down toward the river where they would begin working on the bridge this morning. "Do you agree with Brigham?" he finally asked.

She felt her heart twist a little. Now, there was a bear trap of a question if she had ever heard one. "Well, I'm not sure that I would agree with everything he said," she temporized, trying to collect her thoughts.

"Caroline." His look said it all.

She took a breath. "Joshua, first let me say this. We believe in miracles in the Church. I believe that Heavenly Father sent that terrible cold that froze the Mississippi River late in February so more of our people could leave Nauvoo in a hurry. I strongly believe that our finding those families stuck in the mud and making the trade with them for the wagons and all the goods we needed was not just a lucky accident. I believe that your life was spared when you were shot in the back in Missouri and that the priesthood blessing Nathan and your father gave you was directly responsible for that."

His hands were working the harnessing now, massaging the leather, even though he did not look down at it.

"But the greatest miracle of all, Joshua, is the changing of the human heart. And you have changed, Joshua. Surely you can see that."

"In some ways," he admitted.

"No, more than some. You have changed deeply, fundamentally. I can't even picture the person who was married to Jessica, who did all those horrible things you have told me about. I can barely even remember the man I married. You have changed a great deal even since then. I watch you with Savannah and Livvy now, with Charles, and I just thrill to see what you are becoming."

"So, does that mean you agree with Brigham or not?"

Her shoulders straightened and she looked directly at him. "I guess I am a little baffled. If it were the old Joshua fighting against the idea of accepting God, I could understand it. But why is this new person struggling so much? You've left your home. You're out here with your family following a prophet of God. You've read the Book of Mormon. What is it that is holding you back, Joshua? Is it fear of the risks that come with membership? On the surface, at least, it looks like what Brigham said, that you want the Lord to answer every single thing before you will commit."

He nodded. "Thank you for answering honestly." He pushed the harnessing away and it fell from his lap to the ground. She could feel he was starting to skitter away from her, like a wild thing that wanted what she held in her hand but was too fearful to come and get it.

"Tell me," she said, reaching out with her hand to hold him from standing up and moving away from her. "Just answer me this one question. Is there anything you *are* sure of?"

Her directness took him aback a little. "Well . . . ," he began. Then his body seemed to relax. "The other day, Nathan said something that struck me hard. He said that in the Church, families could be bound together in a way that time could not undo and death could not destroy."

"Yes." She wanted to cry out to him. *Oh, Joshua, can't you see? That's what I want.* But she just watched him, waiting for him to continue.

"I've thought a lot about that." Now he turned toward her and took her by the hand. "You know that you and the children are the most important thing in my life, don't you?"

"Yes, I do." There were no reservations of any kind in that answer.

"The burning of the stable, the loss of the money, Walter's selling me out so I lost all the businesses. I look back on those now and it's like, so what? I have Caroline. I have the kids. That's why I'm out here now, so that our family can be together with each other and with the rest of the Steeds."

"I understand."

"So the idea of being together forever is easy for me to accept. I want that very much, and if that were the only thing, I would be baptized this morning."

She tried not to stare. He had said it so casually. "So what else is there?" she asked softly.

He stood up now, pulling free of her grasp. "I don't know," he exclaimed. "It all just seems so unbelievable, so unreal, so . . . so impossible."

"When you say 'all,' Joshua, what do you mean?"

"This whole thing about Christ dying for us, giving his life so our sins can be taken away. I mean, I understand it better now. Nathan has helped me there. But it still seems like a fairy tale, like something that was made up so we could feel better about ourselves. How can I join the Church when something as fundamental as that is still bothering me?"

With a flash of insight that left her suddenly a little breathless, Caroline knew with perfect clarity that he was doing it again. Brigham was right. He wanted everything put in a box and sealed up tight. He wanted a guarantee up front. It was not that what he was telling her was a deception. She knew he really was troubled by certain aspects of the Atonement, but this was not the real thing holding him back.

And then, in wonder, she understood why. It was fear. He was afraid, and now she saw what it was that frightened him so terribly. He was afraid that he would surrender and give himself over to God, and that God would not accept him.

She stood slowly and faced him. She took his face in her hands. "Do you find it strange that I should love you so much?" she asked.

"I do," he whispered.

"Would you say that my love for you was unbelievable?"

He seemed puzzled by her persistence. "Yes."

"Unreal?" Her eyes searched his, and she saw that he understood now.

"Yes, unreal."

"A fairy tale?" she asked in a bare whisper.

He looked away. After a long moment, he nodded mutely.

"But it is true. Do you have any question about that?"

His voice cracked a little. "No. None."

"You just think about that. If our love for each other is something you can believe in, why can't you believe that our Heavenly Father would have that kind of love for us, only that his love would be perfect?" She smiled and put a finger over his lips before he could say more. "And now, I think we'd better wake the children and get them up and going. You're going to need a good breakfast if you spend all day working on the bridge."

Melissa burst into Carl's office at the brickyard, then pulled up short. There were three other men there. She knew none of them. "Oh. I beg your pardon."

Carl looked surprised. "Melissa? Is anything wrong?"

She hesitated; then, far too filled with anxiety to simply back out again, she nodded. "Stephen Markham has returned."

His brow furrowed slightly. "Stephen Markham?"

"Yes, Colonel Markham, one of the commanders in the Nauvoo Legion. He's just come back from Brigham Young."

He nodded. "I know. He has met with us already."

The other men looked at each other and something passed between them. One of them glanced at Carl and shook his head ever so slightly. Carl saw it, nodded back, then turned to Melissa. "Melissa, I don't think this is any concern of yours."

To her surprise, the anger inside her flared and her mouth went tight. She had just been dismissed, not even with a pat on the head. "Carl, may I speak with you for a moment?"

Carl stood up quickly. "Excuse me. I'll be right back."

She stalked outside, moving far enough away that they would not be heard.

"What is it, Melissa? We're working on this. We know about Colonel Markham."

"Carl!" She couldn't believe he was casual about it. "Brigham Young sent Colonel Markham back here to help."

"Melissa." There was a note of warning to his voice. "The new citizens committee is well aware of what is happening—"

"Do you know there is a mob of anti-Mormons camped just outside the city?"

To her surprise, he turned it around on her. "Did you know that nine of our committee have been out to meet with the group—not a mob—and have refused them entry as they have requested?"

"You have?"

"Did you know that Sheriff Backenstos has already called for reinforcements and that most of the antis have turned around and scooted for home?"

"No, I . . ." She peered at him more closely. "Are you sure, Carl?"

"Absolutely. You think our new citizens committee is a hollow shell. Well, you're wrong."

His eyes had narrowed and his mouth was tight, and she knew she was pushing him. There had already been too many words between them over the new citizens group. They were all non-Mormons, most of them newly arrived, who had banded together to protect the property they had purchased at ten cents on the dollar. Suddenly all this mob activity wasn't to their liking. Who would make sure that the angry men out there knew who was and who wasn't Mormon?

She reached out and laid a hand on his arm. "Carl, Colonel Markham has called a meeting. Just go and listen to what he has to say."

"We did listen, Melissa. It's under control. Now, go home and see to the children."

He had almost calmed her fears, leaving her feeling a little foolish, but his last comment, delivered with such a patronizing tone, infuriated her.

She whirled on him again. "Carl, if you don't want to leave Nauvoo, I can't say a word about that, because it was my stubbornness, my feelings that got us to this point. So I will just have to live with that."

"That's not entirely—"

"But my children—our children!—are in danger, and I will not stand by and do nothing. I will do anything it takes to help protect them."

He blew out his breath, thoroughly exasperated. "Melissa, you can't be going off and doing something foolish. You can't."

"You just wait and see what I can or can't do."

Shocked and bewildered, he finally saw that this was not some emotional cracking on her part. He took her hand. "Melissa. Listen. This is why we are meeting. I'm concerned too. We all are. Let me finish with the meeting and then we'll talk. I promise."

———— ❖ ————

"What happened, Carl?"

She was waiting for him and was on the porch before he was even through the gate. He walked up to her and kissed her lightly. "It's going to be all right, Melissa."

"What?"

"Between the new citizens and the forces Colonel Markham can muster, we've got seven to nine hundred men."

She looked at him closely, making sure he was not just telling her something to put her fears to rest. "Really? What are you going to do?"

"Circulate the word that we have seven hundred men and watch all those brave warriors melt away into the night."

"You think they will?"

"Yes. Like I said, some have already fled. Their leader is furious. They require three things to prop up their bravery—a bottle of liquor, a gun in the hand, and odds that favor them by four to one or more."

He spoke so confidently that she felt the fear ebb back a little.

He took her arm and turned her toward the door. They went inside. Sarah and Mary Melissa had been put to bed. The three boys were still up. They jumped to their feet as their parents entered. "How did it go, Pa?" twelve-year-old David asked quickly.

"It went fine. Everything's going to be fine." Then, before they could ask anything more, he spoke again. "It's past nine, boys. We've got a lot of work to do tomorrow. I think it's time you went to bed."

It was more their mother's face than their father's tone that cut off any further debate. Young Carl nodded. "Yes, Pa. Come on, Caleb and David. Let's go upstairs."

When they were finally gone, Melissa turned to her husband. "Thank you for sharing that with me, Carl."

"You're welcome. I didn't mean to make you angry today."

"I know. I was just so upset."

"I know. These are not easy times."

"So let's move, Carl."

He had started away from her toward the kitchen, wanting a drink. He stopped. "Melissa, let's not start that again."

"I'm not asking you to go west, Carl. I'll go to Kirtland if you want. Even if we go to Fort Madison or down to St. Louis for a time. I just don't want to be here right now."

He sighed wearily. "I've told you, Melissa. If we leave, even for a short time, there won't be anything for us to come back to."

"If we get ourselves killed, it won't matter if we have something to come back to or not."

"We're not going to get ourselves killed."

She looked away. "I'm terribly frightened, Carl. I know you're not. But I am. I don't want to stay."

"It's going to be all right," he said shortly, his tiredness showing through now. "You'll see. Word of our raising armed resistance will scatter those goons like baby chicks before the chicken hawk."

———•———

The pioneers finished the bridge over the middle fork of the Nishnabotna on Wednesday, June tenth, and began to move west again immediately. On the eleventh, they reached the west fork and bridged it easily. On they went, making good progress now. On Saturday afternoon they reached the banks of Mosquito Creek and halted again while the men set to work to build yet another bridge. There was a sense of excitement in the air now. In the distance they could see the line of trees that marked the Missouri River. Rumors were flying through the camp that this was the last creek to be crossed before they, at long last, reached their winter stopping place.

———•———

Matthew poked his head inside the wagon cover, where Jenny and Mary Ann were playing with the two girls. "Hi."

"Hi, Papa," Betsy Jo said happily.

"How's my girl?"

"Fine."

Jenny smiled at her husband. Her older daughter had missed Matthew terribly in those weeks when he had been out ahead of them. On more than one occasion she had cried herself quietly to sleep, wanting a good-night kiss or story from her daddy. But even though it had been only five days since they had been reunited, all the previous sorrow was forgotten. Matthew was gone most of the day, smoothing roads, preparing fords, cutting wood for bridges, and Jenny still had to manage the wagon with the help of Luke, but she could cope with that. He was back each night, and she and the children were happy.

"This is a nice surprise," she said. "Are you through with the bridge?"

"Yep, about half an hour ago. We'll start crossing in the morning."

"So we just wait here for our turn?" Mary Ann asked.

"Yep. We'll pack up in the morning," Matthew said, his eyes sparkling with delight now. "But I do have a surprise for you now."

"For me?" Betsy Jo cried, coming fully alert.

"For you and Mama and Grandma."

"What about Emmeline?" Betsy Jo demanded. She was always very protective of her baby sister.

"Oh, I don't think Emmeline would like this surprise very much."

Betsy Jo had inherited a generous share of her mother's looks, including the sprinkling of freckles across the cheeks, which seemed to be multiplying every day now that the summer had come. She jumped up, her brown hair bouncing lightly. "What is it, Papa? Tell me."

He had even piqued Jenny's curiosity now. "Yes, what is it, Matthew?"

"You have to close your eyes."

Betsy Jo did so, tightly enough that it put little crinkles around the corners of them.

"Come on, Mama and Grandma, you have to close your eyes too."

"Hurry, Mama," Betsy Jo cried. "Close your eyes."

"All right," Jenny laughed, "my eyes are closed."

Matthew withdrew his head, then a moment later came back with a small half-bushel basket. He reached inside the wagon and set it down. "All right."

They all opened their eyes, and for a moment they stared without comprehension at what he had brought. Betsy Jo came forward slowly. "What is it, Papa?"

Mary Ann, who was holding little Emmeline, leaned forward. "Strawberries?" she exclaimed in astonishment.

"Yes. Wild ones."

Jenny came over to the basket and dropped to one knee. "They *are* strawberries. Where ever did you get them?"

"Along Mosquito Creek. There are huge patches of them and they're just coming ripe."

Mary Ann reached across and took one and bit into it, then closed her eyes in sheer pleasure. "I can't believe it. This is wonderful."

"Can I have one, Papa? Can I?"

"Yes." He took one to show her. "You don't eat the green part on the top here. Just bite it off like this." He ate it and rubbed his stomach. "Oh, that's good."

She watched him, then carefully chose the biggest one she could see. Jenny followed suit, not waiting for her daughter. "Now, that is delicious," she murmured immediately.

Betsy Jo brought her strawberry up tentatively to her mouth, then delicately took a bite. Instantly her face screwed up into a fierce pucker. "Ooh," she exclaimed, "they're sour."

"Not sour, Betsy Jo," Jenny laughed. "The word is *tart*. That's what makes them so wonderful." She took another one and ate it. "Oh my, we'll have to be careful, or we'll all have a tummy ache."

"We can mash them and have them with bread and cream tonight," Mary Ann said, also sampling another one.

Betsy Jo finished hers, then immediately took another.

"Hey," Matthew said, pulling at her arm. "I thought you said they were sour."

"Not sour, Daddy, tart. And I like 'em."

"Good. So do I."

"Matthew, are you ready in there?"

It was Joshua's voice. Matthew withdrew his head. "Be right there." He looked back inside. "Come on. We've got another surprise, but we're going to have to take a bit of a walk for this one."

"Goody!" Betsy Jo cried. "What is it, Papa?"

Matthew climbed half in the wagon and reached out to his mother. "Let me take Emmeline. You get your bonnets and we'll go see."

It was a fair walk, two miles or more, but they were eager to take it. They walked across the simple bridge that George Miller's party, and others such as Matthew, had put up across the swift-flowing creek. The land had turned into rolling hills along here, and they moved along the top of one of them toward the southwest. The whole family was with them now, except for Josh, who stayed behind to watch their stock.

"Are you ready?" Joshua said to Caroline as they finally climbed a slight rise.

She could see that they were coming to the edge of the hill in what looked like a series of bluffs overlooking a low spot. She nodded, guessing what this might be and feeling a sudden stir of excitement. "I am."

Joshua trotted forward a few steps, then threw out his arm. "There it is."

"It" turned out to be a beautiful vista—a broad floodplain lined with cottonwood trees, huge stands of willows, and thick underbrush. Through it all, like a huge brown serpent, ran the broad, muddy river. There were gasps and aahs as the family stared down at the scene before them. This was not a river like the Des Moines River or the Chariton or the Grand or the Nishnabotna, all of which they had crossed since leaving Nauvoo. It was another Mississippi. It was not as broad—maybe only two-thirds the width—but this was a real river, with that majesty that brings a sharp intake of breath when first seen.

Emily finally turned to her father. "Is that the Missouri, Papa?"

"Yes, Emily. We are finally here."

"Three months and thirteen days, three hundred and twenty-seven miles," Derek said softly, "but yes, we are finally here."

"Is this where we're going to stay, Pa?" It came from Christopher, Derek's oldest, who had turned seven just three days before.

"That's what Brother Brigham says," his father answered. "Tomorrow we'll look for sites for our encampment, but yes, this will be our home until next spring, Christopher."

Rachel looked at her cousin. "We'll have to write this in our journals tonight, Emily."

"Oh, yes."

Lydia, who was holding baby Tricia, moved closer to Nathan. "Is it really over for now?" she murmured. "Are we really here?"

Nathan nodded. "It's hard to believe, isn't it?"

"It seems like we've lived our whole life in a wagon," Rebecca said. "I don't know if I can remember what it's like to have a real bed."

"Well," Joshua cautioned, "don't get your hopes too high. If you look carefully you'll see there's not a whole lot of timber down there. And we're only staying until spring. We won't be building two-story homes like we had back in Nauvoo."

"I know," Mary Ann said softly, "but until spring, this will be home. For now, that's enough."

They stood in silence for another few minutes, then turned to start back. As they did so, they saw Brigham Young striding toward them.

"Well, what do you think?" he boomed happily as he reached them. "Isn't it beautiful?"

"Yes," several of them said in unison.

"Do you know yet where we will actually set up the settlement?" Matthew asked his former employer and mentor.

"Not yet. Some of the Twelve plan to go scouting tomorrow to find a place where we can camp for now. Then we'll start exploring up and down the river and look for something more permanent."

"Where's the trading post?" Joshua asked. "I thought someone said there was an Indian trading post close by."

Brigham raised a hand and pointed downriver. "It's a little hard to see, but you can see a smudge of smoke, right there where the river takes the bend to the left."

"Oh, yes," Jenny cried. "I see it."

"I assume that's it."

The others looked more closely, then exclaimed aloud and

began pointing for the children. After a moment, Brigham turned and looked back to where they could see the wagons waiting on the far side of Mosquito Creek. "Well, we'd better get going. I wish we could get the wagons across tonight, but starting tomorrow should be acceptable."

With some reluctance they turned away from the vista below them to look where their leader was gazing. "Nathan," Brigham said, "could you and Matthew help supervise the crossing tomorrow?"

"Of course."

Some started back and the others fell in behind them. Brigham watched them for a moment, then casually spoke again. "Oh, Joshua. Could I see you for a minute? I want to show you something. You can come too, Caroline."

Surprised, and suddenly suspicious, Joshua turned. He looked at Brigham closely, but the face seemed innocent enough. They gave the two younger children into Savannah's charge, and then he and Caroline came back to where Brigham stood waiting for them.

Brigham was looking at the river below and seemed barely aware of their presence. He waited a full minute until the others were out of earshot before turning. There was a doleful smile when he finally turned to face them. "Thank you. I wasn't sure you were still speaking to me."

Joshua pulled a rueful face. "I've always said I'd rather deal with an honest tongue than a slippery one, but sometimes that's not without its pain."

Brigham nodded soberly. "I didn't mean to offend, Joshua, but I felt I had to say what I said."

"You didn't offend," he responded. "I'm all right." He glanced at Caroline quickly, then laughed and shook his head. "Unfortunately for me, my wife agrees with you."

"Good for her. That's a good woman you've got there, Joshua. You'd better be treating her right."

"He does, Brother Brigham," Caroline said quickly. "He really does."

"Good." Now his face grew more earnest. "I'm not going to preach to you anymore, Joshua, but I'd like to ask you a question. Will you give me an honest answer?"

Joshua was still clearly wary but he nodded. "Sure."

"Do you think I am an honest man?"

An eyebrow rose. "Of course."

"No, I want you to think about it. Do you think I would lie to you?"

Joshua thought about it. Then he grinned wryly. "No, I might question your tact sometimes, but I would not question your honesty. I have no reason to."

"Good. Thank you."

"Why do you ask?"

"Because there's something I want to tell you, and it's important that you believe me."

"What?" he asked slowly.

The blue-gray eyes were thoughtful now, lost in reflection. "Heber and I came out here a couple of hours ago," he finally said, "almost to this very spot, as a matter of fact. As I was looking down on the river and thinking about what it all meant—to finally be here, where to make the settlement, how to handle the thousands still coming behind us, about going on to the Rockies—I suddenly had a powerful thought strike me." Now he turned and looked squarely at Joshua.

Seeing the look in Brigham's eyes, Caroline held her breath.

"I thought," he went on slowly, "I thought to myself, 'Before we cross that river, before we go any farther west, Joshua Steed must be baptized.'"

The only change in Joshua's expression was a slight tightening along the jawline.

"At first," Brigham went on, "I thought it was just me, just my own strong hope that you would make that decision. But as

I thought about it, I realized it was much more than that. It was a very strong impression, Joshua. *Very* strong."

"So you think it was from the Lord," Joshua said. He hadn't meant to let it, but a touch of sarcasm edged into his voice.

"No," came the firm response. "I *know* it was from the Lord." One hand came up quickly to ward off further protest. "I know that doesn't prove anything to you, but hear me out. I told you the other day that the Lord wants you in the kingdom, Joshua. He has a work for you to do. An important work. I have felt that strongly for some time now, but today the Lord made it known that he feels the same way. It's important to me that you know that I wouldn't just cook up a story like this to convince you to join the Church."

Joshua sighed. Would this never go away? Would it never be resolved? "I believe you," he finally said. "I believe you had an experience of some kind."

"But you don't believe it's from the Lord." It was not a question; it was a statement of obvious fact.

Joshua rubbed at his eyes with the palms of his hands. "I don't know what I believe anymore, to be honest with you. I know it's easy to think the Lord's speaking to you when you want something badly."

"Yes, it is," Brigham agreed. "It's one of the most common mistakes good people make. So it comes down to just one question, doesn't it?"

"What question is that?"

"Was it the Lord or wasn't it?"

"And how do you propose we answer that?"

"What if I could?" Brigham came right back. "If I could convince you that it really was from the Lord, that it really was him saying, 'Joshua Steed, you just stop stalling and get yourself into the waters of baptism,' would you do it?"

Joshua turned and looked out across the river, out beyond where there was nothing but endless prairie and somewhere very far away the Rocky Mountains. Caroline watched him, her hands clenched, her body rigid with tension.

Finally, he turned back. "Yes. If I really knew that, then yes. I would be baptized."

Brigham visibly relaxed. He let out a long sigh of satisfaction. "Then all we've got to do is help you find out, isn't it? Have you been asking the Lord whether or not the Book of Mormon is true?"

Joshua's eyes couldn't meet his. "Yes," he finally said, "in my own way."

There was a kindly smile. "Maybe that's the problem. You're not the one setting the conditions here. You have to do it the Lord's way."

There was a quick, startled reaction. "What did you say?"

"I said that it's not up to you to set your own conditions. You have to—"

He saw that Joshua was staring at Caroline, who was suddenly smiling at him through tears. Brigham saw that something had just passed between them. "What?" he asked in surprise.

She half turned. "That's exactly what I told him the other day," she murmured, "that he can't set his own conditions."

That seemed to help Brigham make up his mind. "All right," he said to Joshua. "I have a request."

"You want me to be baptized," Joshua drawled sardonically.

"Of course," Brigham chuckled, "but that's a hope, not a request. Tell you what, I'll make you a promise. If you do what I ask, and it doesn't work like I hope it will, you'll not ever hear another word from me about you becoming a member. Fair enough?"

At that, Joshua laughed aloud. "Now, that's tempting."

"Okay, then it's a deal?" Brigham said with a triumphant smile.

"You haven't told me what the request is."

"It's simple. I'll walk Caroline back to camp. I want you to go off somewhere, maybe drop down off the bluffs to the river. Stay at least until dark. When you find a place where you are alone, you go down on your knees and you ask one simple question of the Lord. None of this just standing around thinking about things and assuming that constitutes a prayer. You get down on your knees and you close your eyes and you speak out loud and you ask the Lord this question: 'Was that you speaking to President Young, or was it just old Brother Brigham huffing and puffing as usual?'"

"And you'll think I'll get an answer?" he said skeptically.

"If you don't, then you won't be bothered by me again."

Joshua stood motionless, searching the older man's face. Caroline was frozen as well, hardly daring to hope.

"And that's it?" he finally asked. "No other conditions?"

"None."

There was a slow, thoughtful nod. "All right."

Caroline felt her whole body go weak with relief.

"Good," Brigham exclaimed, grabbing him by both shoulders and shaking him gently. "Good for you." He turned to Caroline. "Well, Sister Steed, I think it's time for us to leave this man for a time."

Joshua also turned to Caroline. He leaned over and kissed her lightly. "Don't wait supper," he said in a low voice. Then, without another word, he turned and walked away, dropping out of sight over the bluff as they both watched him go.

Chapter Notes

Conditions in Nauvoo continued to deteriorate as the enemies of the Church put more and more pressure on those who still remained in the city. The conditions described here—including the doings of anti-Mormons, the arrival of Stephen Markham, the actions of the new citizens committee (made up of non-Mormons living in Nauvoo), and the panicky exodus of the

Saints—are all accurately portrayed. (See *Iowa Trail*, pp. 65–66; *MHBY*, pp. 581–84.) When the anti-Mormons learned that an army of about seven hundred men—members and nonmembers of the Church—had been organized in defense of Nauvoo, they disbanded and returned to their homes. As time would prove, however, the anti-Mormons had not changed their minds, only their schedule.

As the Saints reached the western boundaries of Iowa Territory near the middle of June, several journals report their finding large quantities of wild strawberries, which provided a welcome change in their diet, even if it was only a temporary one (see *CN*, 15 June 1996, p. 5).

On Saturday, 13 June 1846, the company led by Brigham Young reached Mosquito Creek, and a bridge was built over it. From the hills near Mosquito Creek, the Missouri River was within sight. Fully two full months behind schedule, the pioneers greeted the sight of this important intermediate destination with great joy. The following day, which was Sunday, Brigham and a few others rode ahead about seven miles and found a good campsite in the river bottoms. Just before noon, the wagons began rolling over Mosquito Creek and down the bluffs. By five p.m. the wagons had formed a hollow square on the banks of the Missouri River. While they were far behind schedule, they were cheered by the fact that the last hundred miles, or about one-third of the total journey, had been covered in less than two weeks. This was an average of seven miles per day as compared to the less than two miles per day they had averaged the previous 116 days. (See *CN*, 15 June 1996, p. 5; 22 June 1996, p. 5.)

He didn't go far once he reached the bottom of the Missouri River's floodplain. There was a small grove of hickory trees, shaded enough by its canopy of leaves that it left the light within subdued and muted. Joshua looked all around once more, including a quick scan of the bluffs above him to see if anyone was observing him. Satisfied, he walked slowly into the stand of trees.

For almost a full five minutes he just stood there, gathering his thoughts, fighting back the sense of the ridiculous that seemed to assail him whenever he got to this point. If it hadn't been for Brigham's promise, he might even then have just gone for a walk. Keep moving so the feelings couldn't catch up to you. Stride out, concentrating on where your feet were landing, so that there was no room for other thoughts. But he had struck a bargain, and Joshua had always been a man of his word.

He found a log and sat down on it. Now he focused on what he might say, what words would be best. He had fumbled so awkwardly before, there as he knelt by the river a few steps from the deer he had slain. How did one properly address a God? What possible things could he say? If He was God, wouldn't He already know Joshua's thoughts? Wasn't that what Caroline had quoted him, that only God knows the thoughts and intents of your heart? So did He already know Joshua's heart? That was the rationalization that he had always turned to before. Just thinking about these things would be a prayer, in a way.

Then Brigham was there in his mind, pointing a finger and commanding him sternly. *I want you to kneel down and close your eyes and then speak aloud. Ask God your question.*

Slowly, reluctantly, he turned and went down to his knees, using the log as a resting place for his arms. The silence stretched on again. Joshua could hear the chirping of birds, the rustle of the wind in the leaves above him, a frog croaking happily down by the river. And then he bowed his head and began.

"O God." He stopped, then started again. "O Heavenly Father. I am here again to pray to you. I'm not very good at this. I don't know the right words. But I promised Brother Brigham I would come, so here I am."

He snorted in soft disgust at himself. That was a great way to begin, to tell God that you were only here because someone twisted your arm until you gave in. "I . . . That's not completely true. I want to know too. I want to know about you. I want to know if it was you who said that to Brigham Young this afternoon, about wanting me in the kingdom."

The sense of foolishness came sweeping in again, but he pushed it away. "Do you want me to be a member of your church? Is it *your* church?"

This time when he stopped, it was because his mind was mulling over the things that had been troubling him. "I know what I am, Heavenly Father. I know what I have been. A drunkard. A man of violence. Someone who treated people very badly, including my own wife and brother. When I think of those days of darkness and rage, I wonder why I was allowed to go on living. I was always the fool, always the hothead."

He took a deep breath, readjusting his position so that more of his weight shifted to the log. "Nathan says that you sent your Son to pay for things like that. That he came down here to make everything better. Frankly, God, I don't see how that is possible. No one made me do those things. I just lost control. I was—" He shook his head. "Why would your Son ever forgive something like that? The Book of Mormon talks about making a sacrifice of a broken heart and a contrite spirit. I think I'm way past those kinds of feelings. It would take so much more than that to bring me back."

Now it was almost as if he were half talking to himself. "Why would you forgive me, for that matter? Giving me Caroline and my family is more blessing than I could have hoped for. I have no right to ask for anything more. I don't know what ever could make me whole again."

There was a snap of a twig somewhere off to his left, and his head jerked up. He searched the gloom of his sanctuary, but saw nothing. A rabbit, or maybe a fox, he decided. He lowered his head again.

But he was out of words. Feeling ever more like the fool, he could think of nothing but Brigham's instructions. "I ask you again," he said lamely, "was that really you who spoke to Brigham? Do you really want me in your kingdom? Don't feel like you have to say yes. I understand perfectly if you don't. I'm not sure I would take me back."

And then the words just petered out. After a few moments he said, "Amen," and got slowly to his feet. He glanced up at the sky. It was probably no more than three o'clock. Five hours till dark, at least. He kicked at the leaves beneath his feet, searching inwardly to see if he felt anything different.

Thoughts and feelings. That's what Caroline had said. God spoke to people through thoughts and feelings. He sat down on the log again, waiting hopefully, "listening," if that was a word that fit here. But the primary thought that kept creeping in was that it was going to be a very long time until dark.

Darkness had closed in around them. They had waited supper half an hour later than usual, but finally started to eat. A
three-quarter moon was just rising in the eastern sky, bathing
the landscape in pale light. Caroline kept stealing glances in the
direction toward where she and Brigham had last seen Joshua,
barely able to concentrate on her eating. When she had
returned, the family had been curious, of course, but she simply
said that President Young had asked Joshua to go down to the
river and look around a little. That seemed to satisfy them,
though Nathan did give her a probing glance. How she had been
able to go about her work, outwardly calm, participating in the
conversation in a normal tone of voice, was beyond her. It was
as if her whole stomach had been twisted on a stick until it was
the size of a clenched fist.

"There's Papa," Charles said suddenly.

They swung around. He was just stepping out from between
two wagons, coming from a completely different direction than
she had expected. "Hi, big fella," he said, walking up to Charles
and ruffling his son's hair. Livvy nearly dropped her plate as she
got to her feet and ran over to greet him too. He swung her up
and into his arms, planting a kiss on her forehead. "Hello,
pumpkin."

"Supper's still hot," Mary Ann said, getting to her feet and
moving toward the fire. "Let me dish you up some."

"Thanks, Mama." His eyes met Caroline's for a moment,
then moved away, revealing nothing. He let Livvy slide to the
ground and shooed her back to finish her plate.

"So," Nathan said, "what did you find down there?"

It was as though a steel gate dropped behind his eyes. "Find?"
he asked slowly.

Caroline broke in quickly. "I told them Brigham had you go
down to the river to look around a little."

"Oh. Oh, that." The relief was obvious. He shook his head.
"There are lots of spots with good feed, but we'll have to look

some for a campsite. With the spring runoff there're still quite a few boggy places."

"Do you think we can ford the river, Uncle Joshua?" Emily asked.

"The Missouri?" He shook his head emphatically. "No. Too wide and too deep. And unless we're willing to spend a few weeks, there'll be no bridging it either. We'll have to ferry across."

That brought murmurs of disappointment from several. "Do you think the west side is going to be a better place to camp?" Matthew asked.

"Probably. We've got to cross it sooner or later either way." He snapped his fingers suddenly. "Oh, by the way, Caroline, I stopped at the wagon to look for my whetstone. I need to sharpen my knife. You haven't seen it, have you?"

"It was in the brown trunk."

"That's what I thought." He turned. "Let me look once more while Mama gets my supper ready."

Now Caroline understood. She set her plate aside and rose swiftly. "Let me help. I think I know right where it is."

They walked to the wagon and went around to the back. As soon as they were blocked from the family's view, Caroline reached out and took his elbow. Her eyes were wide and hopeful.

For a long moment, he gazed at her; then slowly he shook his head.

She visibly sagged.

He reached out and touched her face. "I'm sorry, Caroline," he said in a low voice. "I warned you that this might be how it turned out."

"What happened?"

"Nothing. Absolutely nothing. I may as well have been praying to the trees." He turned away from her, rummaging in the wagon. "Here it is!" he said loudly, holding up the stone. Then to her again, quietly, "I'm sorry. I really am sorry."

Somewhere within her she found the power to force a smile through the sick feeling that filled her body. "I told you, Joshua. I will love you no matter what happens."

"I know. I also know what this would have meant to you." Again he searched for the right words, but all that came out, and very lamely at that, was, "I'm sorry, Caroline."

She took a deep breath. "You go back. Tell them I'm looking for something else. I . . . Just give me a minute or two."

He couldn't bear the pain he saw in her eyes and turned away. "All right."

———◆———

Neither of them spoke of it again that night. Caroline managed to return to the family and put on a bright face while Joshua ate. After cleanup they sat around the fire and talked, and she contributed enough to allay any suspicions that something was wrong. Once they were in bed and the children were asleep, he acted as though he wanted to speak about it, but then changed his mind. They both lay awake for a long time, but didn't speak again.

This morning it was better. The disappointment was still as sharp as a tent peg driven into her side, but she was starting to accept it. He had been right about her getting her hopes too high. A lesson learned. But on the other hand, she wasn't ready to give up hope either. He had come so far. Perhaps it just needed more time.

Joshua watched her closely, guessing at her thoughts and feeling all the more depressed. Thankfully, although the family all ate dinner together, generally they did breakfast by individual wagons. Each family built a small fire if something needed cooking, or prepared their food cold. They were all close by each other—they always camped together—but not right on top of one another so everyone could see every expression, every flicker of emotion.

"Papa?"

He turned. Savannah was there beside him. Her eyes were downcast and her lower lip was pulled into half a pout.

"What, sweetheart?"

"I'll never get to see Daughter of the Morning Mist again, will I?"

"It's not likely," he said. "We're going west, many miles away from her village."

"I would like to be her friend."

He put an arm around her. "I know. And I'll bet she would have liked to be your friend too."

Charles put the last of the food back in the pantry box and came over to join them. "I want an Indian friend too, Papa."

Joshua chuckled. Savannah was now the envy of every young man and woman in the entire company. "I know. I think a lot of others would too."

Caroline had Livvy perched on the wagon tongue, brushing out her long brown hair with strong, even strokes. She looked at her son. "Maybe when we get to the Rocky Mountains, there will be Indians there, and you both can make friends with them."

"I would like that," Savannah said.

Joshua slapped her gently on the rump. "Okay, kids, we've got to get moving. It's almost nine o'clock already. We've got to be ready when it's our turn to cross the bridge." As they moved away he stood and stretched, breathing deeply. The air was clean and sweet and cool. "What a beautiful morning!" he said to no one in particular.

Matthew and Jenny's wagon was next to his. His mother was folding clothing they had washed the night before in the creek, her back partly to him.

He stopped to watch her. The sun was behind her, turning the gray in her hair to gold. She was singing a children's lullaby softly to herself as she worked. He was struck by the scene. It wasn't his mother he suddenly saw but young Mary Ann Morgan, who had been working on a New England turnpike when young Benjamin Steed rode up and saw her. No wonder his father had been smitten, he thought.

There was childish laughter and he turned. Charles and Savannah had grabbed the trunk with the food and were staggering toward the wagon. Then Charles tripped and nearly went down.

Savannah giggled. "It's a good thing our Indian friend Rattlesnake isn't here," she said with mock gravity. "He'd call you Old Stumbles and Falls." Charles, whose feelings for Savannah fell somewhere between total worship and complete adoration, only laughed merrily and labored gamely on. The lines around Joshua's mouth softened. There was a sweetness in that relationship that was like spun silver.

"Livvy. One more minute, then you can go. Please hold still."

He pivoted, turning back toward the wagon. Caroline was kneeling behind Livvy now, starting to braid her hair into two strands. It was no simple task. Livvy was already long past her limit for holding still, which was about ninety seconds. She tossed her head this way and that, trying to see every tiny movement around her. Caroline, eyes narrowed and lips pressed together in concentration, tried to follow the bobbing, bouncing head. He watched, smiling. What a little elf. And how he adored her. His eyes lifted to search Caroline's face. It was fully lit by sunlight now. He could see the first of the lines starting around her eyes—crow's feet, she called them—yet her skin, bronzed now by days in the sun, was still nearly flawless. It reminded him of that day when he had seen her coming across the grass near the docks in Savannah, looking for Will, who had been showing Joshua around the city. In that way, Joshua was like his father. One look had struck him down and he was never the same again.

This was what he needed, he thought. This was the perfect tonic for his gloom of the day before. It was a beautiful morning. He had his family—immediate and extended—around him and that made things seem right. So what if there had been no answer? That didn't change any of this. He wouldn't lose what mattered most to him because he wasn't capable of getting an answer. It was a crazy idea anyway to think that after a lifetime of folly you could go into the woods and come out with a miracle five hours later. He would keep searching, looking, questioning, and maybe someday it would come. But for now it would just have to wait.

Feeling much better about things, he reluctantly pulled himself out of his thoughts, called back by the duty that awaited him. Joshua guessed it would take another hour or so before it was their turn to go across the bridge, but there was plenty to do in the meantime. Nathan and Matthew were on duty helping the wagons over. Derek had been asked to help get the stock across the creek. Since the loose boards of the bridge made the cattle skittish, they had to be driven directly across the stream. It wasn't a difficult task, because the creek was neither very wide nor very deep, but it would still take some time to get the task done, so they had left right after breakfast. That left the supervision of the striking of the tents and packing up the camp his responsibility. He also had to round up the oxen and make sure they were watered before they were hitched to the wagons. He decided to do that first, so they would have some time after drinking before they had to pull.

"Caroline?"

She looked up, the exasperation clearly written on her face as Livvy jerked to look at her father and pulled the braid out of her mother's hand for the ninth or tenth time in half that many minutes.

"I'm going to water the oxen."

"All right."

"Can I come, Papa?" Livvy called.

"No, you need to help Mama get things put away, Livvy. I'll be back in about half an hour, then you can help me hitch the teams up."

His daughter sagged into a limp pile, disappointment clearly twisting her face. He laughed, waved, and started for the meadow where the hobbled oxen had been turned loose the night before.

———•———

He sat on the bank, idly watching as the several oxen drank deeply or munched the lush grass that lined the creek. His mind kept reverting back to his experience of the day before. There was a soft, self-deprecating laugh. He had actually gotten his hopes up. How was that for a joke? Joshua Steed actually thought he was going to get an answer to his prayers. He shook his head in disgust, examining again in memory what he had done. Or hadn't done? But that was what puzzled him. After Brigham's direct challenge, he had given it a sincere effort. He had not held back. Maybe it wasn't the right words. Maybe he was still too nervous about being seen—he had stopped his prayer several times at some imagined noise or other. And he had taken walks on three different occasions just because he didn't feel comfortable staying on his knees for five hours. Well, whatever he had or hadn't done, he had brought pain to Caroline's eyes.

He picked up a pebble and tossed it at a small fish he could see just below the surface. The fish flipped around and was gone in a flash of gray beneath the ripples. He barely noticed. Brigham said that if nothing happened he would leave him alone. Well, that wasn't a bad strategy for Joshua Steed either. Leave it alone. He was tired of seesawing back and forth, one moment determined that there might be some hope, the next feeling like an absolute fool. Maybe if he turned his back on it, the answers would come in time.

He turned his head as he heard a sound. Through the willows he could see that Savannah had stepped into view about two rods downstream from him. She had a bucket in one hand and in the other the kettle in which they had cooked their corn mush this morning. He watched, half smiling as she crouched down beside the water and submerged the kettle into it.

She had not seen him, probably could not because from that distance the willows would look like a solid screen to her. Glad for the diversion, he decided he would sneak around and give her a scare. That was one of their games, though they both had learned through sad experience that Caroline had little humor for it. They were constantly jumping out from behind doors, or tossing something as the other passed, or leaping out with a shriek when it was least expected.

He checked the oxen, saw that they were content where they were for the moment, and got to his feet. Moving like a cat, he went back around his hiding place and made a wide circle so he could come in directly behind her. The grass was thick and his boots made hardly a whisper as he moved carefully toward her. Then, about twenty feet away, he slowed even more. She was singing softly to herself as she scrubbed at the kettle with a rag. Over the gurgling sound of the water he caught just a wisp of the melody and stopped dead. It was Olivia's song. He was so struck by the scene before him that he totally forgot his purpose in coming in so quietly.

He leaned forward slightly, straining to hear. Her back was to him, so he couldn't pick it out clearly, but she was not just humming or singing wordlessly to herself. He heard words and phrases—"to your heart," "God," "Papa, don't you . . ." But it was just snatches, not enough to understand. Her voice was low and husky for a child of her age. Caroline said she would be a lovely contralto when she grew older, whatever that meant. Occasionally some of the other children teased her about sounding like a boy, which she flung back at them without the least bit of shame.

He took a step forward, wanting to hear what she was singing. He was not aware of any sound he made, but she gave a little cry and whirled around. For a moment he thought she was going to fall into the water as she tried to stand and teetered precariously.

"Papa! You scared me!"

He walked forward. "I'm sorry, Savannah. I didn't mean to."

She gave him a sharp look, obviously questioning his veracity. She knew the game as well as he did.

"Really. I was going to try and scare you and then—" He decided not to tell her everything. "What are you doing?"

"Washing the pot for Mama, and getting water for the wagon."

He nodded his approval. "Good."

Savannah had turned nine in March. But she had been at least ten years older than that since she was three. The red hair had darkened somewhat now, so that it wasn't such a fiery color. In facial features she didn't look much like either Joshua or Caroline, though she had Caroline's eyes. Mary Ann said that she looked a lot like her mother, Savannah's Great-grandmother Morgan. She had become a touch more serious as she grew, but Joshua suspected that that impish impudence would be something that would be part of her nature even into womanhood. He certainly hoped so, for he could not imagine her without it.

"Mama told me what a big help you were with Charles and Livvy while I was gone, Savannah. I'm proud of you."

She seemed surprised. "But Papa, I promised."

"You promised?"

"Yes. When you let me be baptized, remember? I promised I would always try to do what's right and to help Mama."

There was a sudden tightness in his throat. "Yes, you did, Savannah, and you've kept that promise." At the time it had been a compromise, a way to let two strong minds honorably back away from the impasse between them. He had accepted her promise, thinking it was just a child's willingness to say anything in order to get her way. He supposed it might last for a week or two or, knowing Savannah, maybe as long as a month. But he had been wrong. It had been over a year now, and she had not wavered even a trifle in her determination to be a better person. "I do remember, Savannah," he said softly, "and I am very pleased that you have kept that promise."

"Thank you, Papa."

He put an arm around her and squeezed her with deep affection. "I'm very pleased to have you as my daughter."

"Thank you, Papa. I thank Heavenly Father every night and morning that you are my father." It was said with such simplicity and such honesty. She had an astonishing ability to get to his heart.

"You do?"

"Yes, and Mama too, of course."

"Of course." He waited a moment. "Do you ever think of Grandpa, Savannah?"

Her head dropped and her hands came together. "All the time, Papa."

"Me too."

"Each day I try to remember that I wouldn't be here if it weren't for Grandpa."

"What he did was very brave."

"I know. I wish I could see him and thank him for it."

"You will someday."

She looked at him, a little surprised that he had said it. "I know," she said simply. "I just wish it were now."

He nodded, then decided the timing was good. "And what about Olivia? Do you think of her too?"

"Yes, Papa. Every day. I miss her so much."

"I do too, Savannah. A great deal."

She didn't answer. He heard the quiet buzz of a mosquito near his ear and brushed at it absently. "Do you know," he said, keeping his voice casual, "when I was out hunting the other day, I found myself humming Olivia's song? How's that for strange?"

"You did?" She peered up at him, trying to read his expression.

He decided he didn't want to be deceptive with her. "Wasn't that Olivia's song you were just singing?"

She blushed. "Yes."

"I love that song. I wish Olivia were here to play it for us."

"Oh, me too, Papa." And then, looking down, she said shyly, "Did you know I have made up some words for it?"

He chuckled. There was no sneaking up on this one. "I didn't know that, but I thought just now I heard you singing words."

She nodded. "I was."

"Will you sing them for me?"

She shook her head so quickly that the red hair danced briskly on her neck.

"Why not?"

"My voice sounds like a frog."

He laughed aloud, then sobered immediately. "You have a lovely voice, Savannah, and I can't think of any frog I would more like to have sing for me."

She was bright scarlet now. "I don't sing around people, Papa. I only sing to myself."

He nodded, disappointed but not wanting to push her against her will. He put an arm around her and pulled her in close. "Will you tell me what the words say, then?"

Her color only deepened. "I wrote the words for you, Papa."

"You did?" He certainly hadn't expected that. "What do they say?"

Again there was the wagging of her head. "I would feel funny telling you, Papa."

"Then just sing them to me."

"I only sing to myself," she said again, starting to feel cornered now.

He had an idea. "Then maybe someday you'll be singing to yourself, like now, and I'll sneak up and listen to you."

She giggled a little. "If I see you, I'll stop."

He rocked her back and forth, looking outraged. "You'd better not."

"Then don't let me see you," she suggested, with the impeccable logic of a child.

He laughed again. "Okay, I won't."

"Like now," she suggested in a tiny voice. "If I hadn't seen you coming, you could have heard me sing."

"Ah," he said slowly, understanding now. "All right. I've got to go, Savannah. I've got to go check on the oxen."

She smiled, her eyes showing her gladness that he understood. "All right," she called as he started away. "Good-bye, Papa."

"Good-bye, Savannah." He started back the way he had come, waving airily. When he reached the willows, he turned and started right back again, tiptoeing carefully.

She had her back to him, but not fully, and he saw that she had seen him out of the corner of her eye. She immediately turned her head away, bent down, and rinsed the kettle out one last time. By the time Joshua was only ten feet behind her, she had filled the bucket as well.

He stopped, standing perfectly motionless. She hesitated for a moment; then he saw her chest rise and fall as she took a breath. She began to hum the song. With the sweetness of the melody and the richness of her voice, it was all Joshua could do to stop from turning around and walking away. His eyes started to burn as the pain of Olivia's memory lanced through him with a sharpness that made him gasp.

She went all the way through the song, took another breath, half turned, careful not to look at him but moving around far enough that he could clearly hear her, and started to sing, only this time using the words.

> Listen to your heart,
> It will help you see
> That God is waiting now for you
> To turn to him.
> Papa, don't you know
> That I am praying for you?
> Oh, won't you turn to him
> So I can be with you?

The song was finished, but she didn't stop. Her eyes closed, and with even more feeling than the first time, she sang again the last few lines.

> Papa, don't you know
> That I am praying for you?
> Oh, won't you turn to him
> So I can be with you?

Only when she was finished and the last sounds of her voice had died away did she finally turn to face him. He had fully intended to play out the charade, throw up his hands in mock surprise, and say how he had just happened to stumble upon her singing and stopped to listen. But he couldn't. He couldn't speak. He couldn't move. His eyes were blurry and he could barely make out her form before him.

To his surprise, she walked up to him slowly, her eyes like great emerald pools. He dropped to one knee and held out his arms. She stepped into them willingly, then put her arms around him and held him tightly. "I love you, Papa," she whispered.

He put his arms around her and buried his face in her hair so she couldn't see his tears. "I love you too, Savannah, very much." He hesitated, then spoke. "You said you want to be with me, Savannah. I *am* with you. I'm not going to leave you. Don't you know that?"

She pulled back, surprised that he would misunderstand. "But I mean forever, Papa. I want you with me and Mama forever."

And that left him without an answer. After a moment, she touched his cheek once, then stepped away. "I'd better get back with the water. Mama will be wondering what happened to me."

Long after she was gone Joshua remained where he was, crouched down and staring at the stream in front of him. He was probably within sight of some of the camp, but he was not mindful of that. The smell of Savannah's hair lingered in his nostrils, and he could still feel the pressure of those thin little arms around his neck.

I love you, Papa.

The sweetness of the moment still lay upon him so powerfully that he could not have spoken if it had been required of him. It was the perfect cap to the things he had felt earlier, watching his mother in the morning sun, listening to Savannah and Charles as they worked, laughing at his elfish Livvy, who could not sit still for her mother's grooming. It was as though he had just awakened from a sleep and was seeing things clearly for the first time. Not physically. Mentally. *Spiritually!* He was at peace. There was no other word to describe it. It was the most sublime feeling of peace he had ever experienced.

It lasted for about a minute, and then slowly it began to subside. It didn't go away completely, just ebbed slowly until it was a wonderful glow somewhere down inside him.

And then, like a wave rushing in toward the shore, swelling and growing with every moment until it crested and crashed thunderously against the beach, it came to him. Was it thought or feeling? Even much later he would not be sure. Perhaps it was both. Whatever it was, it came in perfect simplicity and purity.

If I have given you all of this, how can you question my love for you?

He sat back fully in the grass, dazed by the power of the thought. Joy and happiness and peace welled up inside him, expanding so swiftly that it filled him with dizziness. He felt like he needed to dig his fingers into the earth so that he didn't simply float away. And then came the next thought, only this time it was an echo of Caroline quoting from the Doctrine and Covenants.

Did I not speak peace to your mind? What greater witness can you have than from God?

That was it, he thought, marveling. There was no other word which so perfectly described what he was experiencing. It was peace. A peace like gentle rain falling upon ground long parched and baked in the sun. From long ago, another scriptural phrase came tumbling back. Something about the "peace that passeth all understanding."

"Yes!" he exulted, closing his eyes. He was astonished by the crispness of his thoughts, the perfect clarity of all that was rushing through his mind. And then, as full realization of what had just happened to him sank in, an overwhelming feeling of gratitude took over. His head dropped. As naturally as if he had been on his knees since he was a child, the words came.

"Heavenly Father. Thank you! I have cried unto you in my anguish, and in your great mercy you have answered. I understand now how your love is possible. It is like I am on fire within me, O Father. Humbly I say thank you. You have given me my life again, and now I offer it back to you. I will enter your kingdom, though I am not worthy. Thank you, Father. You have made me whole again."

He walked slowly back to the camp, knowing that he needed to bring the oxen but also knowing they could wait for another few minutes. As he came back to the small circle of their wagons, he looked around, savoring every detail of what he saw. Lydia was by her collapsed tent, kneeling beside her son as they began to fold it up. Josh glanced up at him and smiled, then went back to helping his mother.

Mary Ann had been interrupted by three of the grandchildren. They stood before her, showing her something. As she explained whatever it was they wanted to know, they listened to her in rapt attention. Jenny and Betsy Jo were sitting on the wagon tongue trying to feed Emmeline, who kept turning her head away from the spoon. Betsy Jo wagged her finger at the baby, a miniature Jenny, telling her gravely what would happen if she didn't eat right. Rebecca was working with her children, putting things back in the wagon. Emily and Rachel were seated on the ground, their heads together as they whispered back and forth while they put silverware back in its box. Caroline was at the back of their wagon with Savannah and Charles, helping them organize what was going into the limited space. Livvy was down on her stomach in the grass beneath the wagon, peering at something with great fascination.

Again that sense of warmth and joy and peace came over him, and for a moment he stood there, just watching.

Caroline stepped out from behind the wagon and saw him. "Oh. Did you get the oxen watered?"

He shook his head. "They're still down at the creek. I'll go get them in a few minutes."

She seemed a little surprised by that, but it lasted only a moment as her mind came back to what had to go into the wagon next. He watched as Caroline bent down and started to sort through the pile.

"Caroline?"

Her head rose, but she didn't turn around. "Yes?"

"I'm ready."

She straightened and turned in surprise. There were still half a dozen things to be packed. Their tent was still up, the only one among those belonging to the Steeds that was not taken down as yet. The oxen were down at the creek. "What about all this?" she asked, then turned back to her work.

"Caroline," he said again. "I'm ready."

Something in his voice brought her head back around. She pushed back a loose tendril of hair, looking just a little exasperated with his persistence.

Laughing softly, he walked to her and took her hands. "It came, Caroline. Just now."

"What came?" And then her jaw went slack and her eyes snapped wide open. "What came?" she asked again, not daring to believe.

"Everything you've prayed for."

She just stared at him, as though his words had flown past her, over her head and not into her mind. Then her lower lip started to tremble. "Do you mean . . . ?" she started haltingly.

"Yes." He lifted a finger and touched her lips, smoothing the tremor, smiling down into her eyes.

She was still fumbling, dazed and bewildered. "Are you saying that—"

He cut her off exuberantly. "Yes!"

"That you're going to be—"

"Yes!" He laughed and picked her up in his arms. "Yes, Caroline! Yes! I have my answer. I know now. I want to be baptized."

With a sob of joy, she threw her arms around him and crushed him to her. Then it was too much for her. She pushed back, still in his arms. "Do you really mean it, Joshua? You're not just teasing me?"

"I wouldn't tease you about something this important," he said gravely.

Suddenly the tears came, welling up from some fountain deep within her and spilling in wet streaks down her cheeks. Her lips moved, but no words came out. She was gazing at him, her face filled with incredulity.

He bent down and kissed her gently, tasting the salt of her tears. "It's true, Caroline. I know now. I know for myself. Your prayers are answered."

"Oh, Joshua!" she whispered. "I can't believe it."

"Nor can I."

He saw past her now that they had attracted the attention of the family. Mary Ann had stopped what she was saying to the children and was staring at them. Lydia was motionless, her eyes wide. This was hardly the normal greeting a husband got after going down to the creek to water the oxen.

He laughed aloud at the expression on their faces. "Josh," he called to his nephew. "Would you go find Brother Brigham and ask him to come see us?"

He looked surprised. "Yes, Uncle Joshua."

"And get your father and Uncle Matthew and Uncle Derek. I know they're working, but tell them something urgent has come up. Tell them I need to talk to them."

"Papa?" Savannah had come around from the wagon now. She saw that her mother was crying and instantly rushed forward. "Papa, what's the matter?"

In two long steps he reached her and swept her up in his arms, crushing her against him. "Nothing is the matter, Savannah," he whispered into her hair. "Everything is going to be all right now."

The family was seated around him in a close circle. Every face was turned to him. Caroline sat in the midst of the women, most of whom were weeping joyfully with her. The men were still breathing hard from their run back to camp. When Josh had told Nathan that Aunt Caroline was crying and that his Uncle Joshua wanted them and President Young to come urgently, he had turned and sprinted for camp, his heart filled with dread. Now he looked as though he were still recovering from a stunning blow to his solar plexus.

"I think we are ready, Joshua," Mary Ann said. "I think we are all very ready to hear the full story now."

He smiled at her, feeling her love spanning the distance between them as tangibly as if it were one of Matthew's bridges. "I wish Papa were here." His eyes dropped. "And Olivia."

"They'll know," Mary Ann whispered. "They'll know."

"I guess I need to go back a ways," he started, "if you are going to understand how all this came about." And so he began. He started with Nathan's bullheaded insistence that they go back to Nauvoo and get Caroline, and his promise that if Joshua would just trust in God a way would be provided for that to happen. "When we found those families stuck in the mud and made the trade we did," he went on, "I was amazed. Something in me wanted to believe God had a hand in it, but I couldn't bring myself to accept that." He shook his head. "I can't believe what a hardheaded fool I've been."

"Hardheaded, yes," Nathan said with a warm smile, "but not a fool."

He nodded gratefully and continued. He told them about taking Lydia's Book of Mormon, about his questions, about Nathan's patience in answering those questions. He stopped, looking at his brother. "I'm still not sure I understand all you were trying to tell me, little brother," he said softly, "but as I think about it now, what mattered most to me was that my questions didn't shake you at all. I didn't know if what you were saying was true, but I knew that you knew, and that had a strangely reassuring effect on me."

"You asked some very important questions," Nathan answered.

Suddenly Joshua realized that there was someone standing behind him. He turned and there was Brigham Young, smiling in soft pleasure at him. "Go on," Brother Brigham urged. "I want to hear all of it."

He talked about his mother's gentle prodding, about the night he went hunting and got an answer about life and death, about Brigham's not-so-gentle call to repentance. He turned, smiling ruefully at the chief Apostle. "I nearly just walked away from it all that night," he confessed. "But I couldn't get what you said out of my mind, about me asking more from the Lord than I would from a business partner. That hit me pretty hard."

"I didn't sleep much that night," Brigham admitted. "I worried that I had been too strong with you."

"Us hardheads need a real pop on the jaw every now and then," he said. He rubbed his cheek as if he had been actually struck. "And you gave it to me."

He turned back to the family and told them about the day before on the bluffs, how Brigham had laid down the challenge, of his seemingly fruitless prayers and the great sadness he had as he came back and told Caroline that nothing had come of it all.

Brigham walked around now and stood behind Mary Ann. He laid a hand on her shoulder but still looked at Joshua. "When you didn't come see me last night, my heart just sank," he said. "I was so sure that you would get an answer."

"I did, just not when I expected it." Joshua took a breath. "So anyway, this morning I was kind of depressed, mostly for Caroline's sake." He had looked at her and that was his undoing. Her eyes were large and swimming with tears, but the absolute radiance on her face caused his voice to catch. He swallowed hard, fighting for control, then went on slowly. He described seeing his mother with the sunlight in her hair; he told of watching Savannah and Charles struggling with the food box and joking about it; he spoke of Caroline brushing out Livvy's hair.

"They were such simple things, but it brought me a great sense of peace. I decided that even if the Lord didn't want me yet, even though I wasn't ready to become a member, it would be all right, because I still had all this. Then—" He had to stop. He blinked rapidly, trying to stop the burning behind his eyes. "Then I went down to the creek to water the oxen. I saw Savannah and—"

He couldn't finish. The tears spilled out and his throat choked off. He dropped his head and stared down at the ground. The whole family was weeping now, watching this man whom for so long they had prayed for and hoped for, despaired for. To see him unable to speak, to see his face wet with tears, was enough to open up the floodgates in all of them.

Caroline got up and went to stand beside him, slipping an arm around his waist. She too was struggling to speak, but she did so, telling them what had transpired between father and daughter at the creek. She motioned for Savannah to come forward. "Savannah, I know you don't like to sing in front of people, but I'd like you to sing Olivia's song for the family. I think it will help them understand what happened to your father. Will you do that?"

Savannah looked up at her mother, obviously hesitant, then turned to Joshua.

"Please," he said softly. "It was what started it all for me, Savannah. Your song."

And then she smiled, thrilled to know that she had had a part in this. "Okay."

She stepped away from her parents and turned to the family. All went very quiet. And then, looking up at Joshua, she began to sing.

> Listen to your heart,
> It will help you see
> That God is waiting now for you
> To turn to him.
> Papa, don't you know
> That I am praying for you?
> Oh, won't you turn to him
> So I can be with you?
> Papa, don't you know
> That I am praying for you?
> Oh, won't you turn to him
> So I can be with you?

When she finished, Joshua dropped to his knees and took her in his arms. "Thank you," he whispered. "Thank you, my precious Savannah."

The sounds of sobbing and sniffling filled the air now. None of them had been able to resist the sight of her singing to her father. Mary Ann got to her feet and came up to Joshua and Savannah. Joshua stood slowly. Savannah and Caroline stepped back. Then, in a gesture that represented a thousand generations of mothers, she stepped forward and took her boy into her arms.

They gathered on the east banks of the wide and muddy river at about six o'clock that evening. They had moved from their camp at Mosquito Creek and come down the bluffs into the river bottoms. All told, they traveled about seven miles before the scouts showed them the spot they had chosen for the camp. By then everyone knew the news and the camp was electrified by it. Joshua Steed was to be baptized a member of The Church of Jesus Christ of Latter-day Saints as soon as their tents were pitched and the camp was set.

Joshua's back was sore from a hundred hands slapping him in congratulations. His right hand ached from the grip of iron-fisted men who felt as if the measure of their sincerity was the power by which they shook his hand. But in spite of the soreness, Joshua was deeply touched and welcomed each new person with a broad smile. It was a great, tremendous outpouring of affection, and it completely amazed him.

Now they were at the river's side. Brigham had picked a spot where the bank gently sloped into a quiet spot of the Missouri River. The water eddied and swirled but moved slowly by. There were five or six hundred people in all, lined up six and seven deep. Only a few of the older boys had been left behind to watch the stock. Every other member of the camp had come to see. Joy came hard on the trail; no one was about to miss its welcome visitation.

Had Benjamin still been alive, Joshua would have picked him. But with him gone, there was no question in his mind as to whom he wanted to baptize him. They both wore white shirts— Nathan had one in his possession; Heber Kimball had found another one for Joshua. But they wore only workaday trousers. The company was not carrying any special baptismal clothing. Neither wore shoes or socks.

As Joshua and Nathan walked gingerly toward the water, Elder Kimball nudged Josh. "Did you stop to think that this might be the first baptism in the Missouri River in over a thousand years?"

Josh turned in surprise. "A thousand years!"

"Yes. Perhaps the Nephites or the Jaredites got up this far and baptized people here, so you can't say for sure it is the first time ever. But I think it would be safe to say there hasn't been one since the time of the Nephites, not by proper authority anyway."

Josh was awed by that thought. "You think the Nephites once lived around here?"

"Don't know for sure, of course, but it's possible. The Book of Mormon says they spread across the whole face of the land."

"That's right," Josh said in wonder. He turned and whispered that thought to Rachel and Luke and Emily.

Lydia and Mary Ann had Caroline between them. Rebecca and the older girls were just behind them. As Nathan and Joshua reached the water's edge and stopped, Lydia slipped an arm around Caroline's waist. "Does this even seem real to you?" she asked.

Caroline shook her head. "I'm still in a daze."

"*You're* in a daze?" Rebecca exclaimed. "At least you had some signs that it might be coming. When Joshua told us he had taken Lydia's Book of Mormon and was reading it, I nearly fell off the log. I thought for a minute I was going to faint."

"Me too," Rachel exclaimed. "Oh, I wish Mama could be here to see it."

Caroline nodded sadly. "That is Joshua's one regret. Of all people, he would like Jessica to be here today."

Brigham raised his arms then, and immediately the crowd grew quiet. He waited for a moment, then spoke loudly. "Brothers and sisters, we welcome you here at the water's edge on this beautiful Sabbath evening. As you know, we are about to witness a momentous event." He looked at Joshua. "One of the great giants of the forest has fallen"—there was a sudden impish grin—"and I'm happy to say that he has fallen right into our hands."

The group laughed heartily at that. Joshua was smiling too and raised one hand in acknowledgment.

Then Brigham grew serious. "I'd like to say a few words before we proceed, if I may. As we all know now, life along the trail, though difficult and challenging, is still life. It contains the normal events that are part of any community—birth, death, sickness, celebration. We have even had a few courtships and one marriage that we know of since we left Nauvoo."

People were nodding, sobered now too as they thought back over the past four months of their lives.

"It has not been an easy journey to where we are today. With the incessant rain, hillocks became mountains, low spots became mile-long bogs, creeks became rivers, and rivers impassable torrents. When the rain stopped, it was replaced by prairie fires and rattlesnakes. We have had times of sorrow and we have had times of joy. We have wept and we have laughed, we have toiled and we have danced.

"As you know, most of us here left Nauvoo in February. The winds were cold; the river was frozen for a time. And we have come across Iowa in the worst spring in known memory. Why is that so? Why hasn't the Lord tempered the weather for us?"

He waited a moment. Every eye was on him. "Some of you have already heard. Those leaving Nauvoo now are covering the same distance in three weeks that it took us four months to cross. Some of you may be wondering, 'Why didn't Brother Brigham wait? Why didn't the Lord let us leave when the weather was warm and the grass was high?' Well, I'll tell you why, and it has a lot to do with Joshua Steed being baptized today.

"We underwent great preparations before leaving. We built wagons and filled them with provisions, we found the best teams, we searched out maps and compasses, and talked with those who had traveled the road before us. All of that was fine, and expected of the Lord. But the most important factor in preparing to go west is obedience. No amount of preparation, no amount of provisions, no wagonloads of tools and seed will take the place of our obedience. Only when we do what God requires of us, no matter how difficult or how trying, will we be blessed. God whispered to me, 'Brother Brigham, wait no longer. Cross the river and head west.' And so we did and we *have* been richly blessed.

508

"In an epistle written under the influence of the Spirit by our beloved brother Joseph, a question was asked of all of us. It has much to do with obedience. It has much to do with why we are here where we are today.

"Here is the question and the inspiring answer that follows: 'Brethren, shall we not go on in so great a cause? Go forward and not backward. Courage, brethren; and on, on to the victory!'"

Not a sound broke the silence of the moment. Then Brigham Young turned and looked at Joshua. "Here is a man who has gone on with us in so great a cause, even though he was not one of us. He has stayed with us—through the rain, through the mud, through the fires and snakes and floods. And now he will become one of us. Why? Because his family was obedient to the call of the Lord and did not hold back. Why? Because the Lord heard their cries in behalf of their husband and father, their brother and uncle and son. Why are we privileged to witness this event today? How is it that the Steeds have won this great victory? Because the Lord is pleased with Joshua's obedience and has softened his heart and given him answer to his prayers. It is a lesson for all of us. May we use this occasion, wherein we celebrate the obedience of Joshua Steed, to renew our own covenants with the Lord. Let us set in our hearts a greater determination to do his will so that he can surely call us his people."

Joshua was looking at the ground now, not out of embarrassment but because he was touched by Brigham's words.

"And so, my brothers and sisters, we come now to this glorious moment. We have seen life on the trail. We have seen babies born and people die. We have seen young people fall in love and be married. But as yet we have not had a baptism other than of our children who have reached the age of accountability. It is time to rectify that situation. Before we proceed, however, I would like Brother Steed to say a word to all of us. I want you to have a chance to see into his heart, as I have done." He motioned for Joshua to join him.

Surprised, Joshua moved away from Nathan and went to stand by Brigham's side. Brigham put his arm across his shoulder. "Joshua, tell us what is in your heart." Then he stepped back away from him.

Joshua stood there for a long moment, feeling the eyes of the crowd upon him, wondering what he could possibly say to people who had known for years what he had just found out for himself that morning.

Finally he looked up, letting his eyes move from face to face. "Well, for one thing, I want you to know that if it weren't for my family, this would never have happened. They have never lost hope when I myself found no reason to hope. They never lost faith, even when I ridiculed that faith. They never stopped praying for me, even though I could not pray for myself."

He looked at Caroline. Her eyes were shining, but she was not crying. "I love you," she mouthed to him.

"I love my wife," he said back, speaking to her now. "That was how I finally got my answer. God reminded me that if he had given me a family like this, that was proof enough that he loved me."

He took a breath, then another, fighting for composure. Finally, he went on slowly. "I do know that God loves me. I know that he is there. I know that he is more than my God. I better understand now why he is called our Heavenly Father."

Now he turned to look at Nathan. "I still can't comprehend why Jesus would die for me, or how he could actually pay for my sins. I have many. I did many terrible things when I was younger. But then I don't fully understand the love of my children either. But I know it's real and I am warmed by that reality. In that same way, I trust in God's love and in the love of his Son. It is like a great burden has been lifted from me and taken away."

Now he turned back to look at his wife. "You were right, Caroline. This is the greatest miracle of all. I have never felt such peace and joy."

He was overcome now and reached up to wipe at the tears with the back of his hand. He looked at Brigham. "It's been a long time in coming, Brother Brigham, but I'm here now. I want to be part of the kingdom. Just tell me what needs to be done."

Brigham nodded somberly. "You are about to take the first step, my dear brother. And I find it significant that it shall happen here in the Missouri River. Why? Because the Missouri River marks the beginning of the wilderness. Once we cross it, we shall be as Israel of old, wandering in the wilderness on our way to the promised land. Therefore, I think it is only fitting that you should be baptized in the Missouri River, symbolizing your willingness to become part of Israel and accompany us as we go to our new home."

He raised his head. "Nathan, are you ready to take this man into the water?"

"I am, President," Nathan called out.

"Then let us proceed."

Nathan moved the few feet to the water's edge. He gasped a little as the cold water hit his flesh, but he moved out until he was nearly up to his waist. Joshua followed behind him without hesitation. As Joshua reached him, Nathan couldn't help but smile. "You know how long I've been waiting for this day, big brother?" he said softly.

"Not nearly as long as I have, little brother," Joshua said with an answering grin. "I just didn't know that I was waiting, that's all."

Nathan nodded and took one elbow. His right hand came up to form a square. He bowed his head. Joshua did the same. All those on the banks of the river also bowed their heads. Amid the Steeds, several eyes closed on tears.

"Joshua Steed," Nathan said in a clear, ringing voice, "having been commissioned of Jesus Christ, I baptize you in the name of the Father, and of the Son, and of the Holy Ghost. Amen."

He grasped Joshua's arm firmly, put his other hand behind his back, then lowered him into the murky water.

When Nathan pulled him out, Joshua was gasping. Nathan let go and stepped back, giving him a moment to wipe away the water that streamed from his hair into his eyes. Then Nathan opened his arms and stepped forward. There in the Missouri River, some three hundred twenty-seven miles and one hundred and thirty days out of Nauvoo, two brothers embraced without a word, holding each other tightly for a very long time.

ABOUT THE AUTHOR

Gerald N. Lund received his B.A. and M.S. degrees in sociology from Brigham Young University. He also did extensive graduate work in New Testament studies at Pepperdine University in Los Angeles, California, and studied Hebrew at the University of Judaism in Hollywood, California.

During his thirty-five years in the Church Educational System, the author served as a seminary teacher, an institute teacher and director, a curriculum writer, director of college curriculum, and zone administrator. His Church callings have included those of bishop, stake missionary, and teacher.

Gerald Lund has written nineteen books, including such novels as *Fire of the Covenant, The Alliance, The Freedom Factor, Leverage Point, One in Thine Hand,* and *The Kingdom and the Crown, volume 1: Fishers of Men.* He has also written several books on gospel studies, including *The Coming of the Lord* and *Jesus Christ, Key to the Plan of Salvation.* He has twice won the Independent Booksellers "Book of the Year" Award and has received many other honors for his works.

He and his wife, Lynn, are the parents of seven children and live in Alpine, Utah.